Fodor's 96
New Orleans

"When it comes to information on regional history, what to see and do, and shopping, these guides are exhaustive."

—*USAir Magazine*

"Usable, sophisticated restaurant coverage, with an emphasis on good value."

—Andy Birsh, *Gourmet Magazine* columnist

"Valuable because of their comprehensiveness."

—*Minneapolis Star-Tribune*

"Fodor's always delivers high quality...thoughtfully presented...thorough."

—*Houston Post*

"An excellent choice for those who want everything under one cover."

—*Washington Post*

Fodor's Travel Publications, Inc.
New York • Toronto • London • Sydney • Auckland

Fodor's New Orleans

Editor: David Low

Editorial Contributors: Steven Amsterdam, Rob Andrews, Millie Ball, Jason Berry, Gene Bourg, Mary Gehman, Don Lee Keith, John Kemp, Lisa LeBlanc-Berry, Bevin McLaughlin, Honey Naylor, Tracy Patruno, Mary Ellen Schultz, M.T. Schwartzman, Dinah Spritzer, Michael Tisserand

Creative Director: Fabrizio La Rocca

Cartographer: David Lindroth

Cover Photograph: Peter Guttman

Text Design: Between the Covers

Copyright

Special Sales

CONTENTS

ON THE ROAD WITH FODOR'S

A GOOD TRAVEL GUIDE is like a wonderful traveling companion. It's charming, it's brimming with sound recommendations and solid ideas, it pulls no punches in describing lodging and dining establishments, and it's consistently full of fascinating facts that make you view what you've traveled to see in a rich new light. In the creation of *New Orleans '96*, we at Fodor's have gone to great lengths to provide you with the very best of all possible traveling companions—and to make your trip the best of all possible vacations.

About Our Writers

The information in these pages is a collaboration of a couple of extraordinary writers.

After nearly 10 years of restaurant reviewing in his native New Orleans, most recently for *The Times-Picayune,* **Gene Bourg,** who wrote the Dining chapter, still looks forward to discovering the next rising-star chef or restaurant in town. In the interim, when he's not taping his weekly "News You Can Eat" radio program, he's usually foraging for good restaurant food in Western Europe and Latin America.

A licensed tour guide, **Mary Gehman,** who has lived in New Orleans for 25 years, is always discovering novel things to do in the area—from festivals to museums, from restored homes to out-of-the-way nature preserves; she enjoys sharing them with visitors. The author of two history books, *Women and New Orleans* and *The Free People of Color of New Orleans,* she says that "history doesn't get any livelier than in this city, nor more accessible."

Honey Naylor, who wrote the Excursions chapter, delights in exploring the bayous and byways of South Louisiana, always with the hope of finding yet another zydeco dance hall in which to "pass a good time." From her home in the exotic French Quarter, she has uncovered many a canopied bed for the Lodging chapter, and discovered hundreds of treasures and trifles in Crescent City stores for the Shopping chapter.

Michael Tisserand, who updated the Nightlife and the Arts chapter, covers the music scene for *Gambit,* an alternative New Orleans weekly newspaper. He spends hours on end at local clubs and recommends that visitors check out the artistry of Snooks Eaglin (rhythm and blues), Kermit Ruffins (jazz), and Beau Jocque (zydeco), three popular Louisiana musicians who appear frequently in the area. Michael is currently working on a book devoted to zydeco music.

We'd also like to thank the staff at the New Orleans Metropolitan Convention and Visitors Bureau.

What's New

A New Design

If this is not the first Fodor's guide you've purchased, you'll immediately notice our new look. More readable and easier to use than ever? We think so—and we hope you do, too.

Let Us Do Your Booking

Our writers have scoured New Orleans to come up with an extensive and well-balanced list of the best B&Bs, inns, and hotels, both small and large, new and old. But you don't have to beat the bushes to come up with a reservation. Now we've teamed up with an established hotel-booking service to make it easy for you to secure a room at the property of your choice. It's fast, it's free, and confirmation is guaranteed. If your first choice is booked, the operators can line up your second right away. Just call 800/FODORS–1 or 800/363–6771 (0800/89–1030 when in Great Britain; 0014/800–12–8271 when in Australia; 1800/55–9109 when in Ireland).

Travel Updates

In addition, just before your trip, you may want to order a Fodor's Worldview Travel Update. From local publications all over New Orleans, the lively, cosmopolitan editors at Worldview gather information on concerts, plays, opera, dance performances, gallery and museum shows, sports competitions, and other special events that coincide with your visit. See the order blank in the back of this book, call 800/799–9609, or fax 800/799–9619.

And in New Orleans

Reconstruction has begun on Municipal Auditorium in Armstrong Park, with completion expected in 1995. The renovated auditorium will house Harrah's temporary casino. The $800 million **Harrah's Casino New Orleans,** to be erected on the site of the former Rivergate Exhibit Hall at the foot of Canal Street, plans to open in April 1996.

More and more **gambling boats,** all aslosh with roulette, craps tables, video poker, slot machines, and such, are operating these days on Crescent City waterways. The *Treasure Chest* (☎ 504/443–8000 or 800/298–0711) in Kenner, is docked on Lake Pontchartrain, across from Pontchartrain Center. American Enterprises' *Circus Circus* riverboat casino (☎ 504/278–5600) operates on the Mississippi River at Chalmette in St. Bernard Parish. And on the West Bank, the Harvey Canal's "riverboat" is the *Boomtown Belle* (4132 Peters Rd., Harvey, ☎ 504/366–7711 or 800/366–7711).

Two riverboat casinos, a joint venture of Grand Palais Riverboats Inc. and Capital Gaming Inc., are scheduled to open in late spring of 1995, upriver of the Crescent City area. The two boats will dock side by side at River City, and the casino development will include an entertainment complex with three new restaurants (*see below*). The larger *Flamingo* riverboat (☎ 504/587–7777 or 800/587–5825, outside New Orleans) has replaced the *Queen of New Orleans* at its berth at Riverwalk and the Hilton Hotel.

The expansion of the Ernest N. Morial Convention Center and the location of Harrah's Casino in Armstrong Park have spurred a whirlwind of hotel activity, mostly in the Central Business District. Properties that opened in renovated office buildings in late 1994 or early 1995 included the **Pelham,** a 60-room luxury hotel; the 186-room **Hampton Inn;** and the 100-unit **Comfort Suites,** all in the CBD. The **Chateau Sonesta,** a 241-room luxury property, opened in April 1995 in the landmark D.H. Holmes department store building on Canal Street. On the fringe of the French Quarter, plans have been announced for the $1.5 million **French Quarter Courtyard Hotel** near Armstrong Park. Most recently a nightclub called Monster's, the 1879 house has been a single-family dwelling, a steak house, a jazz club, and a 24-hour gay club. In the French Quarter, the French Quarter Maisonnettes were sold in 1994 after the death of long-time owner Mrs. Junius Underwood. The Maisonnettes had been a boon for budget travelers since the guest house opened in 1962. The property was purchased by Rodney and Frances Smith, who own and operate **Soniat House,** a luxury small hotel directly across the street from the Maisonnettes. Soniat House now incorporates several units of the former French Quarter Maisonnettes, which have been renovated into luxury Jacuzzi suites.

On the restaurant scene, the current hotspot is **Graham's,** just off Canal Street near the Mississippi River, where proprietor-chef Kevin Graham's nouvelle twists on international cuisines attract crowds. The New Orleans satellite of **Planet Hollywood,** a 15,000 square-foot restaurant, nightclub, and retail shop, opened in May 1995 in the Jackson Brewery complex along the French Quarter riverfront near Jackson Square. Also on the horizon are two new restaurants operated by Hollywood food guru Wolfgang Puck—one a pizza place, the other not—and a dining establishment from famed Cajun chef Paul Prudhomme, all of which are slated for the River City casino complex on the riverfront near the Ernest N. Morial Convention Center.

Restoration of **Laura Plantation** began in 1994 and will continue into the next century. The property, which includes the main house and six slave cabins, was named for Laura Locoul, the great-granddaughter of the Spanish commandant who built the plantation in 1805. Unlike other properties on the River Road, which focus on the antebellum period, Laura Plantation showcases early rural Creole plantation life. Based on historical records, including 100 pages of Laura's diary, the on-going restoration plans to allow visitors to observe the original brick-between-posts construction and find out Laura's story from costumed guides who represent some past residents. Future plans of project manager Norman Marmillion include bed-and-breakfast accommodations.

How to Use This Book

Organization

Up front is the **Gold Guide,** comprising two sections on gold paper that are chock-full of information about traveling within your destination and traveling in general. Both are in alphabetical order by topic. **Important Contacts A to Z** gives addresses and telephone numbers of organizations and companies that offer destination-related services and detailed information or publications. Here's where you'll find information about how to get to New Orleans from wherever you are. **Smart Travel Tips A to Z,** the Gold Guide's second section, gives specific tips on how to get the most out of your travels, as well as information on how to accomplish what you need to in New Orleans.

At the end of the book you'll find Portraits, wonderful essays about voodoo, Mardi Gras, jazz, dining, and historical events in New Orleans, followed by suggestions for pre-trip reading, both fiction and nonfiction. Here we also recommend movies you can rent on videotape to get you in the mood for your travels.

Stars

Stars in the margin are used to denote highly recommended sights, attractions, hotels, and restaurants.

Credit Cards

The following abbreviations are used: **AE,** American Express; **D,** Discover; **DC,** Diners Club; **MC,** MasterCard; and **V,** Visa.

Please Write to Us

Everyone who has contributed to *New Orleans '96* has worked hard to make the text accurate. All prices and opening times are based on information supplied to us at press time, and the publisher cannot accept responsibility for any errors that may have occurred. The passage of time will bring changes, so it's always a good idea to call ahead and confirm information when it matters—particularly if you're making a detour to visit specific sights or attractions. When making reservations at a hotel or inn, be sure to mention if you have a disability or are traveling with children, if you prefer a private bath or a certain type of bed, or if you have specific dietary needs or any other concerns.

Were the restaurants we recommended as described? Did our hotel picks exceed your expectations? Did you find a museum we recommended a waste of time? We would love your feedback, positive and negative. If you have complaints, we'll look into them and revise our entries when the facts warrant it. If you've happened upon a special place that we haven't included, we'll pass the information along to the writers so they can check it out. So please send us a letter or postcard (we're at 201 East 50th Street, New York, New York 10022). We'll look forward to hearing from you. And in the meantime, have a wonderful trip!

Karen Cure
Editorial Director

New Orleans

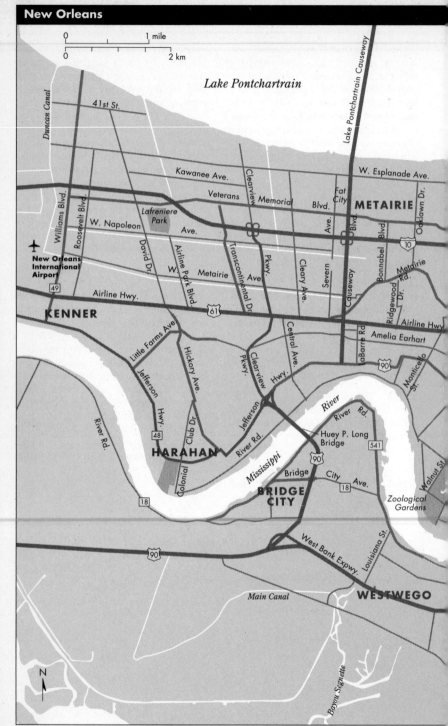

Lake Pontchartrain

0 1 mile
0 2 km

Duncan Canal

41st St.

Kawanee Ave.

W. Esplanade Ave.

Clearview

Veterans Memorial

Fat City

METAIRIE

Oaklawn Dr.

Lafreniere Park

Ave.

Blvd.

Williams Blvd.

Roosevelt Blvd.

W. Napoleon

David Dr.

Airline Park Blvd.

Metairie

Transcontinental Dr.

Ave.

Pkwy.

Cleary Ave.

Severn

Causeway

Bonnabel Blvd.

Ridgewood Rd.

Metairie Rd.

New Orleans International Airport

49

Airline Hwy.

61

10

KENNER

Airline Hwy.

Little Farms Ave.

Central Ave.

LaBarre Rd.

Amelia Earhart

Monticello St.

90

Jefferson Hwy.

Hickory Ave.

Club Dr.

Clearview Pkwy.

Jefferson Hwy.

River Rd.

Mississippi

River

River Rd.

Huey P. Long Bridge

48

541

HARAHAN

Colonial Dr.

Bridge

City Ave.

18

Walnut St.

18

BRIDGE CITY

90

Zoological Gardens

River Rd.

West Bank Expwy.

Louisiana St.

90

Main Canal

WESTWEGO

N

Bayou Segnette

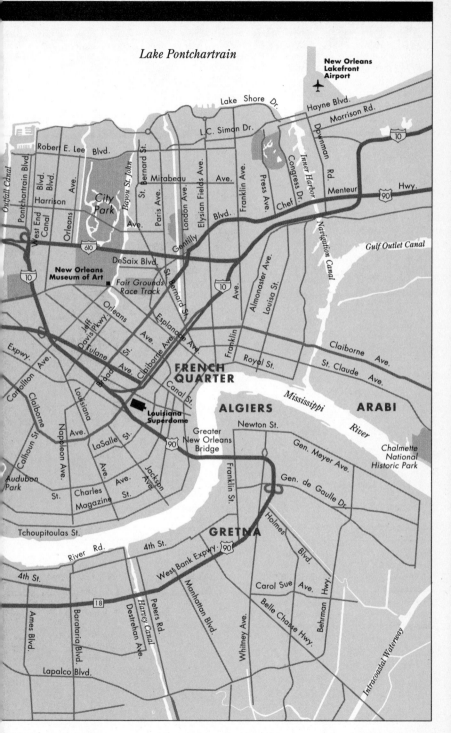

World Time Zones

Numbers below vertical bands relate each zone to Greenwich Mean Time (0 hrs.).
Local times frequently differ from these general indications,
as indicated by light-face numbers on map.

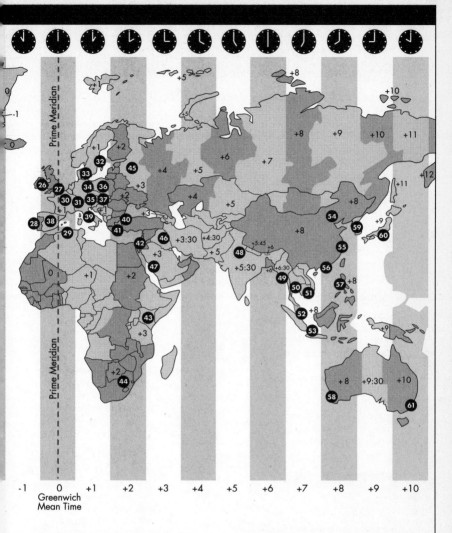

IMPORTANT CONTACTS A TO Z

An Alphabetical Listing of Publications, Organizations, and Companies That Will Help You Before, During, and After Your Trip

No single travel resource can give you every detail about every topic that might interest or concern you at the various stages of your journey—when you're planning your trip, while you're on the road, and after you get back home. The following organizations, books, and brochures will supplement the information in Fodor's *New Orleans '96*. For related information, including both basic tips on visiting New Orleans and background information on many of the topics below, study Smart Travel Tips A to Z, the section that follows Important Contacts A to Z.

A

AIR TRAVEL

The major gateway to New Orleans is **Moisant International Airport**, 15 miles west of the city in Kenner. Flying time is about 2½ hours from New York, 2¼ hours from Chicago, and 3½ hours from Los Angeles.

AIRPORT TRANSFERS

Shuttle bus service to and from the airport and downtown hotels is available through the **Airport Shuttle** (☎ 504/522–3500) or **New Orleans Tours** (☎ 504/592–1991). Buses leave regularly from the ground-floor level near the baggage claim. To return to the airport, call at least two hours in advance of flight time. One-way cost is $10 a person and the trip takes about 40 minutes.

Louisiana Transit (☎ 504/737–9611) also runs a bus between the airport and the Central Business District (CBD). The trip costs $1.10 in exact change and takes about 45 minutes. From the CBD, departures for the airport are every 10 to 20 minutes from Elks Place and Tulane Avenue across from the city library. The last bus leaves at 6:20 PM.

Taxis cut about 15 minutes from the trip but cost $21 for the first two people and $8 for each additional person.

By car, take the I–10 Expressway (from the CBD, go west to the Airport exit). Allow an hour for the drive during afternoon rush hour.

CARRIERS

Carriers serving New Orleans include **Aeromexico** (☎ 800/237–6639), **American** (☎ 800/433–7300), **Continental** (☎ 800/525–0280), **Delta** (☎ 800/221–1212), **Lacsa** (☎ 800/225–2272), **Northwest** (☎ 800/225–2525), **Southwest** (☎ 800/531–5601), **TWA** (☎ 800/221–2000), **United** (☎ 800/241–6522), **USAir** (☎ 800/428–4322), and **ValuJet** (☎ 800/825–8538).

For inexpensive, no-frills flights, contact **ValuJet** (☎ 404/994–8258 or 800/825-8538), based in Atlanta and serving New Orleans.

COMPLAINTS

To register complaints about charter and scheduled airlines, contact the U.S. Department of Transportation's **Office of Consumer Affairs** (400 7th St. NW, Washington, DC 20590, ☎ 202/366–2220 or 800/322–7873).

CONSOLIDATORS

Established consolidators selling to the public include **Euram Tours** (1522 K St. NW, Suite 430, Washington DC, 20005, ☎ 800/848–6789), and **TFI Tours International** (34 W. 32nd St., New York, NY 10001, ☎ 212/736–1140 or 800/745–8000).

PUBLICATIONS

For general information about charter carriers, ask for the Office of Consumer Affairs' brochure **"Plane Talk: Public Charter Flights."** The Department of Transportation also publishes a 58-page booklet, **"Fly Rights"**

($1.75; Consumer Information Center, Dept. 133-B, Pueblo, CO 81009).

For other tips and hints, consult the Consumers Union's monthly **"Consumer Reports Travel Letter"** ($39 a year; Box 53629, Boulder CO 80322, ☎ 800/234–1970) and the newsletter **"Travel Smart"** ($37 a year; 40 Beechdale Rd., Dobbs Ferry, NY 10522, ☎ 800/327–3633); **The Official Frequent Flyer Guidebook,** by Randy Petersen ($14.99 plus $3 shipping; 4715-C Town Center Dr., Colorado Springs, CO 80916, ☎ 719/597–8899 or 800/487–8893); **Airfare Secrets Exposed,** by Sharon Tyler and Matthew Wonder (Universal Information Publishing; $16.95 plus $3.75 shipping from Sandcastle Publishing, Box 3070-A, South Pasadena, CA 91031, ☎ 213/255–3616 or 800/655–0053); and **202 Tips Even the Best Business Travelers May Not Know,** by Christopher McGinnis ($10 plus $3.00 shipping; Irwin Professional Publishing, Box 52927, Atlanta, GA 30355, ☎ 708/789–4000 or 800/634–3966).

B
BETTER BUSINESS BUREAUS

Contact the New Orleans **Better Business Bureau** (1539 Jackson Ave., Suite 400, 70130–5843, ☎ 504/581–6222, 24 hours, or 504/528–9277). For other local contacts, consult

the **Council of Better Business Bureaus** (4200 Wilson Blvd., Arlington, VA 22203, ☎ 703/276–0100).

BUS TRAVEL

Greyhound Lines (1001 Loyola Ave., ☎ 504/525–6075 or 800/231–2222) has only one terminal in the city. It is located in the CBD in the Union Passenger Terminal. Ask about special travel passes. Check with your local Greyhound ticket office for prices and schedules.

WITHIN NEW ORLEANS

Call the **Regional Transit Authority** (RTA; ☎ 504/569–2700) for route information.

C
CAR RENTAL

Major car-rental companies represented in New Orleans include **Alamo** (☎ 800/327–9633, 0800/272–2000 in the U.K.), **Avis** (☎ 800/331–1212, 800/879–2847 in Canada), **Budget** (☎ 800/527–0700, 0800/181–181 in the U.K.), **Dollar** (known as EuroDollar outside North America, ☎ 800/800–4000 in the U.S. and Canada, 0181/952-6565 in the U.K.), **Hertz** (☎ 800/654–3131, 800/263–0600 in Canada, 0181/679–1799 in the U.K.), and **National** (☎ 800/227–7368, 0181/950–5050 in the U.K., where it is known as Europcar). Rates in New Orleans begin at $30 a day and $125 a week for an economy car with unlimited mileage.

CHILDREN AND TRAVEL
BABY-SITTING

The local **Accent on Arrangements** (☎ 504/524–1227) not only baby-sits but also plans activities and tours for individual children.

FLYING

Look into **"Flying With Baby"** ($5.95 plus $1 shipping; Third Street Press, Box 261250, Littleton, CO 80126, ☎ 303/595–5959), cowritten by a flight attendant. **"Kids and Teens in Flight,"** free from the U.S. Department of Transportation's Office of Consumer Affairs, offers tips for children flying alone. Every two years the February issue of **Family Travel Times** (see Know-How, below) details children's services on three dozen airlines.

KNOW-HOW

Family Travel Times, published 10 times a year by Travel With Your Children (TWYCH, 45 W. 18th St., New York, NY 10011, ☎ 212/206–0688; annual subscription $55), covers destinations, types of vacations, and modes of travel.

The **Family Travel Guides** catalogue ($1 postage; ☎ 510/527–5849) lists about 200 books and articles on family travel. Also check **Take Your Baby and Go! A Guide for Traveling with Babies, Toddlers and Young Children,** by Sheri

Andrews, Judy Bordeaux, and Vivian Vasquez ($5.95 plus $1.50 shipping; Bear Creek Publications, 2507 Minor Ave., Seattle, WA 98102, ☎ 206/322–7604 or 800/326–6566). **The 100 Best Family Resorts in North America** by Jane Wilford with Janet Tice ($12.95) and the two-volume **50 Great Family Vacations in North America** ($18.95 per volume) both from Globe Pequot Press, (add $3 for shipping; Box 833, 6 Business Park Rd., Old Saybrook, CT 06475, ☎ 203/395–0440 or 800/243–0495, 800/962–0973 in CT) help plan trips with children, from toddlers to teens.

LOCAL INFORMATION

New Orleans for Kids ($5 from the New Orleans Metropolitan Convention and Tourist Bureau, 1520 Sugar Bowl Dr., 70112, ☎ 504/566–5031) is an activity book and tour guide; it includes puzzles and pictures for coloring as well as a whole host of suggestions about where to take children in New Orleans.

For a riverboat trip that lasts longer than a day, contact the **Delta Queen Steamboat Company** (Robin Street Wharf, ☎ 504/586–0631 or 800/543–6789).

CANADIANS

Contact **Revenue Canada** (2265 St. Laurent Blvd. S, Ottawa, Ontario, K1G

4K3, ☎ 613/993–0534) for a copy of the free brochure **"I Declare/Je Déclare"** and for details on duties that exceed the standard duty-free limit.

U.K. CITIZENS

HM Customs and Excise (Dorset House, Stamford St., London SE1 9NG, ☎ 0171/202–4227) can answer questions about U.K. customs regulations and publishes **"A Guide for Travellers,"** detailing standard procedures and import rules.

D FOR TRAVELERS WITH DISABILITIES

BUS TRAVEL

Greyhound (☎ 800/752–4841) will carry a person with a disability and a companion for the price of a single fare.

COMPLAINTS

To register complaints under the provisions of the Americans With Disabilities Act, contact the U.S. Department of Justice's **Public Access Section** (Box 66738, Washington, DC 20035, ☎ 202/514–0301, TDD 202/514–0383, FAX 202/307–1198).

ORGANIZATIONS

FOR TRAVELERS WITH HEARING IMPAIRMENTS➤ Contact the **American Academy of Otolaryngology** (1 Prince St., Alexandria, VA 22314, ☎ 703/836–4444, FAX 703/683–5100, TTY 703/519–1585).

FOR TRAVELERS WITH MOBILITY PROBLEMS➤ Contact the **Information Center for Individuals**

with Disabilities (Fort Point Pl., 27–43 Wormwood St., Boston, MA 02210, ☎ 617/727–5540, 800/462–5015 in MA, TTY 617/345–9743); **Mobility International USA** (Box 10767, Eugene, OR 97440, ☎ and TTY 503/343–1284; FAX 503/343–6812), the U.S. branch of an international organization headquartered in Belgium (see below) that has affiliates in 30 countries; **MossRehab Hospital Travel Information Service** (1200 W. Tabor Rd., Philadelphia, PA 19141, ☎ 215/456–9603, TTY 215/456–9602); the **Society for the Advancement of Travel for the Handicapped** (347 5th Ave., Suite 610, New York, NY 10016, ☎ 212/447–7284, FAX 212/725–8253); the **Travel Industry and Disabled Exchange** (TIDE, 5435 Donna Ave., Tarzana, CA 91356, ☎ 818/344–3640, FAX 818/344–0078); and **Travelin' Talk** (Box 3534, Clarksville, TN 37043, ☎ 615/552–6670, FAX 615/552–1182).

FOR TRAVELERS WITH VISION IMPAIRMENTS➤ Contact the **American Council of the Blind** (1155 15th St. NW, Suite 720, Washington, DC 20005, ☎ 202/467–5081, FAX 202/467–5085) or the **American Foundation for the Blind** (15 W. 16th St., New York, NY 10011, ☎ 212/620–2000, TTY 212/620–2158).

IN THE U.K.

Contact the **Royal Association for Disabil-**

ity and Rehabilitation (RADAR, 12 City Forum, 250 City Rd., London EC1V 8AF, ☎ 0171/250–3222) or **Mobility International** (Rue de Manchester 25, B1070 Brussels, Belgium, ☎ 00–322–410–6297), an international clearinghouse of travel information for people with disabilities.

PUBLICATIONS

Several free publications are available from the U.S. Information Center (Box 100, Pueblo, CO 81009, ☎ 719/948–3334): **"New Horizons for the Air Traveler with a Disability"** (address to Dept. 355A), describing legally mandated changes; the pocket-size **"Fly Smart"** (Dept. 575B), good on flight safety; and the Airport Operators Council's worldwide **"Access Travel: Airports"** (Dept. 575A).

Fodor's **Great American Vacations for Travelers with Disabilities** ($18; available in bookstores, or call 800/533–6478) details accessible attractions, restaurants, and hotels in U.S. destinations. The 500-page **Travelin' Talk Directory** ($35; Box 3534, Clarksville, TN 37043, ☎ 615/552–6670) lists people and organizations who help travelers with disabilities. For specialist travel agents worldwide, consult the **Directory of Travel Agencies for the Disabled** ($19.95 plus $2 shipping; Twin Peaks Press, Box 129, Vancouver, WA 98666, ☎ 206/694–2462 or 800/637–2256).

Amtrak (☎ 800/872–7245) requests 24-hour notice to provide redcap service and special seats. All travelers with disabilities are entitled to a 15% discount on the lowest available fare.

TRAVEL AGENCIES, TOUR OPERATORS

The Americans with Disabilities Act requires that travel firms serve the needs of all travelers. However, some agencies and operators specialize in making group and individual arrangements for travelers with disabilities, among them **Access Adventures** (206 Chestnut Ridge Rd., Rochester, NY 14624, ☎ 716/889–9096), run by a former physical-rehab counselor. In addition, many general-interest operators and agencies (*see* Tour Operators, *below*) can also arrange vacations for travelers with disabilities.

FOR TRAVELERS WITH HEARING IMPAIRMENTS➣ One agency is **International Express** (7319-B Baltimore Ave., College Park, MD 20740, ☎ TDD 301/699–8836, FAX 301/699–8836), which arranges group and independent trips.

FOR TRAVELERS WITH MOBILITY IMPAIRMENTS➣ A number of operators specialize in working with travelers with mobility impairments: **Hinsdale Travel Service** (201 E. Ogden Ave., Suite 100, Hinsdale, IL 60521, ☎ 708/325–1335 or 800/303–

5521), a travel agency that will give you access to the services of wheelchair traveler Janice Perkins; and **Wheelchair Journeys** (16979 Redmond Way, Redmond, WA 98052, ☎ 206/885–2210), which can handle arrangements worldwide.

FOR TRAVELERS WITH DEVELOPMENTAL DISABILITIES➣ Contact the nonprofit **New Directions** (5276 Hollister Ave., Suite 207, Santa Barbara, CA 93111, ☎ 805/967–2841).

DISCOUNTS

Options include **Entertainment Travel Editions** (fee $28–$53, depending on destination; Box 1068, Trumbull, CT 06611, ☎ 800/445–4137), **Great American Traveler** ($49.95 annually; Box 27965, Salt Lake City, UT 84127, ☎ 800/548–2812), **Moment's Notice Discount Travel Club** ($25 annually, single or family; 163 Amsterdam Ave., Suite 137, New York, NY 10023, ☎ 212/486–0500), **Privilege Card** ($74.95 annually; 3391 Peachtree Rd. NE, Suite 110, Atlanta GA 30326, ☎ 404/262–0222 or 800/236–9732), **Travelers Advantage** ($49 annually, single or family; CUC Travel Service, 49 Music Sq. W, Nashville, TN 37203, ☎ 800/548–1116 or 800/648–4037), and **Worldwide Discount Travel Club** ($50 annually for family, $40 single; 1674 Meridian Ave., Miami Beach, FL 33139, ☎ 305/534–2082).

THE GOLD GUIDE / IMPORTANT CONTACTS

THE GOLD GUIDE / IMPORTANT CONTACTS

ORGANIZATIONS

The **International Gay Travel Association** (Box 4974, Key West, FL 33041, ☎ 800/448–8550), a consortium of 800 businesses, can supply names of travel agents and tour operators.

PUBLICATIONS

The premiere international travel magazine for gays and lesbians is **Our World** ($35 for 10 issues; 1104 N. Nova Rd., Suite 251, Daytona Beach, FL 32117, ☎ 904/441–5367). The 16-page monthly "Out & About" ($49 for 10 issues; ☎ 212/645–6922 or 800/929–2268), covers gay-friendly resorts, hotels, cruise lines, and airlines.

TOUR OPERATORS

For mixed gay and lesbian travel, contact **Toto Tours** (1326 W. Albion Suite 3W, Chicago, IL 60626, ☎ 312/274–8686 or 800/565–1241) sponsoring group tours worldwide.

TRAVEL AGENCIES

The largest agencies serving gay travelers are **Advance Travel** (10700 Northwest Freeway, Suite 160, Houston, TX 77092, ☎ 713/682–2002 or 800/695–0880), **Islanders/Kennedy Travel** (183 W. 10th St., New York, NY 10014, ☎ 212/242–3222 or 800/988–1181), **Now Voyager** (4406 18th St., San Francisco, CA 94114, ☎ 415/626–1169 or

800/255–6951), and **Yellowbrick Road** (1500 W. Balmoral Ave., Chicago, IL 60640, ☎ 312/561–1800 or 800/642–2488). **Skylink Women's Travel** (746 Ashland Ave., Santa Monica, CA 90405, ☎ 310/452–0506 or 800/225-5759) works with lesbians.

H

HEALTH ISSUES

Dial 911 for assistance. Emergency rooms closest to the CBD and the French Quarter are the **Medical Center of Louisiana** (1532 Tulane Ave., ☎ 504/568–2311) and the **Tulane University Medical Center** (220 Lasalle St., ☎ 504/566–5031). In Uptown go to **Touro Infirmary** (1401 Foucher St., ☎ 504/588–5263).

PHARMACIES

The only pharmacy in the French Quarter, **Royal Pharmacy** at 1101 Royal Street (☎ 504/523–7201), is open daily 9–6. Nearby is **Walgreens** at 900 Canal Street (☎ 504/523–7201), which is open Monday–Saturday 7 AM–9 PM, Sunday 9–7. The **Walgreens** at 3311 Canal St. (☎ 504/822–8070) is open 24 hours.

I

INSURANCE

Travel insurance covering baggage, health, and trip cancellation or interruptions is available from **Access America** (Box 90315, Richmond, VA 23286, ☎ 804/285–3300 or 800/284–8300), **Carefree Travel Insurance**

(Box 9366, 100 Garden City Plaza, Garden City, NY 11530, ☎ 516/294–0220 or 800/323–3149), **Near** (Box 1339, Calumet City, IL 60409, ☎ 708/868–6700 or 800/654–6700), **Tele-Trip** (Mutual of Omaha Plaza, Box 31716, Omaha, NE 68131, ☎ 800/228–9792), **Travel Insured International** (Box 280568, East Hartford, CT 06128-0568, ☎ 203/528–7663 or 800/243–3174), **Travel Guard International** (1145 Clark St., Stevens Point, WI 54481, ☎ 715/345–0505 or 800/826–1300), and **Wallach & Company** (107 W. Federal St., Box 480, Middleburg, VA 22117, ☎ 703/687–3166 or 800/237–6615).

IN THE U.K.

The **Association of British Insurers** (51 Gresham St., London EC2V 7HQ, ☎ 0171/600–3333; 30 Gordon St., Glasgow G1 3PU, ☎ 0141/226–3905; Scottish Provident Bldg., Donegall Sq. W, Belfast BT1 6JE, ☎ 01232/249176; and other locations) gives advice by phone and publishes the free **"Holiday Insurance,"** which sets out typical policy provisions and costs.

L

LODGING

APARTMENT AND VILLA RENTALS

Contact **Rent-a-Home International** (7200 34th Ave. NW, Seattle, WA 98117, ☎ 206/789–9377 or 800/488–7368).

HOME EXCHANGE

Principal clearinghouses include **Intervac International** ($65 annually; Box 590504, San Francisco, CA 94159, ☎ 415/435–3497), which has three annual directories; and **Loan-a-Home** ($35–$45 annually; 2 Park La., Apt. 6E, Mount Vernon, NY 10552-3443, ☎ 914/664–7640), which specializes in long-term exchanges.

M

MONEY MATTERS

ATMS

For specific **Cirrus** locations in the United States and Canada, call 800/424–7787. For U.S. **Plus** locations, call 800/843–7587 and enter the area code and first three digits of the number you're calling from (or of the calling area where you want an ATM).

WIRING FUNDS

Funds can be wired via **American Express MoneyGram** (☎ 800/926–9400 from the U.S. and Canada for locations and information) or **Western Union** (☎ 800/325–6000 for agent locations or to send using MasterCard or Visa, 800/321–2923 in Canada).

P

PASSPORTS
AND VISAS

U.K. CITIZENS

For fees, documentation requirements, and to get an emergency passport, call the **London passport office** (☎ 0171/271–3000). For visa infor-

mation, call the **U.S. Embassy Visa Information Line** (☎ 0891/200–290; calls cost 49p per minute or 39p per minute cheap rate) or write the **U.S. Embassy Visa Branch** (5 Upper Grosvenor St., London W1A 2JB). If you live in Northern Ireland, write the **U.S. Consulate General** (Queen's House, Queen St., Belfast BTI 6EQ).

PHOTO HELP

The **Kodak Information Center** (☎ 800/242–2424) answers consumer questions about film and photography.

R

RAIL TRAVEL

Amtrak arrives and departs at New Orleans's **Union Passenger Terminal** (1001 Loyola Ave., ☎ 504/528–1610 or 800/USA–RAIL), in the heart of the Central Business District.

S

SENIOR CITIZENS

EDUCATIONAL TRAVEL

The nonprofit **Elderhostel** (75 Federal St., 3rd Floor, Boston, MA 02110, ☎ 617/426–7788), for people 60 and older, has offered inexpensive study programs since 1975. The nearly 2,000 courses cover everything from marine science to Greek myths and cowboy poetry. Fees for programs in the United States and Canada, which usually last one week, run about $300, not including transportation.

ORGANIZATIONS

Contact the **American Association of Retired Persons** (AARP, 601 E St. NW, Washington, DC 20049, ☎ 202/434–2277; $8 per person or couple annually). Its Purchase Privilege Program gets members discounts on lodging, car rentals, and sightseeing, and the AARP Motoring Plan furnishes domestic trip-routing information and emergency road-service aid for an annual fee of $39.95 per person or couple ($59.95 for a premium version).

For other discounts on lodgings, car rentals, and other travel products, along with magazines and newsletters, contact the **National Council of Senior Citizens** (membership $12 annually; 1331 F St. NW, Washington, DC 20004, ☎ 202/347–8800) and **Mature Outlook** (subscription $9.95 annually; 6001 N. Clark St., Chicago, IL 60660, ☎ 312/465–6466 or 800/336–6330).

PUBLICATIONS

The 50+ Traveler's Guidebook: Where to Go, Where to Stay, What to Do, by Anita Williams and Merrimac Dillon ($12.95; St. Martin's Press, 175 5th Ave., New York, NY 10010, ☎ 212/674–5151 or 800/288–2131), offers many useful tips. **"The Mature Traveler"** ($29.95; Box 50400, Reno, NV 89513, ☎ 702/786–7419), a monthly newsletter, covers travel deals.

SIGHTSEEING

ORIENTATION TOURS

Several local tour companies offer three- to four-hour city tours by bus that include the French Quarter, the Garden District, Uptown New Orleans, and the lakefront. Prices range from $20 to $25 per person, with some lower rates for children; call **Gray Line** (☎ 504/587–0861), **New Orleans Tours** (☎ 504/592–1991), or **Tours by Isabelle** (☎ 504/391–3544).

Both Gray Line and New Orleans Tours offer a longer, seven-hour city tour by bus that includes a steamboat ride on the Mississippi River. Gray Line also operates a narrated loop tour by bus with 13 drop-off and pick-up points around the city.

RIVERBOAT CRUISES

Narrated riverboat cruises up and down the Mississippi and bayou cruises on authentic paddlewheelers are offered by the **New Orleans Steamboat Company** (☎ 504/586–8777 or 800/233–BOAT). Ticket sales and departures are at the Toulouse Street Wharf behind Jackson Brewery. **New Orleans Paddle Wheel** (☎ 504/524–0814) has a river plantation and battlefield cruise twice daily departing from the Riverwalk and also a river plantation harbor cruise and a Crown Point swamp tour. There is also an evening jazz dinner cruise from

8 to 10 (boarding at 7 PM); tickets are available for the dinner and cruise or just the cruise and live music. The ticket office is at the Poydras Street Wharf near the Riverwalk and at the Aquarium on Canal Street.

SELF-GUIDED TOURS

For visitors who wish to browse through the French Quarter at their own leisure, there are maps for self-guided walking tours available through the **New Orleans Metropolitan Convention and Visitors Bureau** (☎ 504/566–5031) at the **Tourist Information Center** at 529 St. Ann Street, on Jackson Square. Streetcar Tours (☎ 504/561–1001) rents cassettes to listen to while riding the St. Charles Avenue streetcar. The history of the route is interspersed with samples of New Orleans music. Cassettes are available at 17 Carondelet Street from Monday to Saturday 9–4.

SPECIAL-INTEREST TOURS

Exploring an exotic Louisiana swamp and traveling into Cajun country is an adventure not to be missed. Quality swamp tours are given by **American Acadian, Cypress Swamp Tours** (☎ 504/581–4501), **Gray Line, New Orleans Historic Voodoo Museum** (☎ 504/523–7685), **Tours by Isabelle,** and **Honey Island Swamp Tours** (☎ 504/242–5877). Tour companies pick up guests at downtown

hotels. Full-day tours often include visiting a plantation home.

To visit historic churches and shrines in the city, contact **Musicana Tours** (☎ 504/522–4311).

For highlights of African-American history and culture, **New Orleans Tours** (*see* Orientation Tours, *above*) conducts a half-day city tour by bus called "Roots of New Orleans," which includes lunch. A similar tour, the "Big Easy Deluxe," is offered by **Family Reunion Planning Services** (☎ 504/241–3985 or 800/891–3985). **Family Reunion and Le'Ob's Tours** (☎ 504/288–3478) also have city, plantation, swamp, Cajun, and VIP tours from the black perspective.

WALKING TOURS

Contact the **Jean Lafitte National Park** (☎ 504/589–2636), **Friends of the Cabildo** (☎ 504/523–3939), **Family Reunion Planning Services** (☎ 504/241–3985 weekdays), **Classic Tours** (☎ 504/899–1862), **Heritage Tours** (☎ 504/949–9805), **Hidden Treasures Tours** (☎ 504/529–4507), **Magic Walking Tours** (☎ 504/593–9693), **New Orleans Historic Voodoo Museum** (☎ 504/523–7685), and, for cemetery tours, **Save our Cemeteries** (☎ 504/588–9357).

OTHER TOURS

The **Superdome** (☎ 504/587–3810) offers guided tours from 10 to 4 daily.

Across the river in Algiers, visitors can tour **Blaine Kern's Mardi Gras World** (☎ 504/361–7821). *See* Tour 3 *in* Chapter 2.

For a view of the city from the air, **Southern Seaplane, Inc.** (☎ 504/394–5633) will fly you over the city and its surrounding areas.

Limousine services make arrangements for personal interests and private guides; rentals vary. Best known are **London Livery, Ltd.** (☎ 504/831–0700), **Carey Limousines** (☎ 504/523–5672), **A Touch of Class Limousine Service** (☎ 504/522–7565 or 800/821–6352), and **New Orleans Limousine Service** (☎ 504/529–5226).

STREETCARS

For information on schedules and visitor passes, check information centers at hotels and retail centers or call the **Regional Transit Authority** (☎ 504/569–2700).

STUDENTS

GROUPS

Contiki Holidays (300 Plaza Alicante, Suite 900, Garden Grove, CA 92640, ☎ 714/740–0808 or 800/466–0610) is a major tour operator.

HOSTELING

Contact **Hostelling International–American Youth Hostels** (733 15th St. NW, Suite 840, Washington, DC 20005, ☎ 202/783–6161) in the United States, **Hostelling International–Canada** (205 Catherine St., Suite 400,

Ottawa, Ontario K2P 1C3, ☎ 613/237–7884) in Canada, and the **Youth Hostel Association of England and Wales** (Trevelyan House, 8 St. Stephen's Hill, St. Albans, Hertfordshire AL1 2DY, ☎ 01727/855215 and 01727/845047) in the United Kingdom. Membership ($25 in the U.S., C$26.75 in Canada, and £9 in the U.K.) gets you access to 5,000 hostels worldwide that charge $7–$20 nightly per person.

I.D. CARDS

To get discounts on transportation and admissions, get the **International Student Identity Card** (ISIC) if you're a bona fide student or the **International Youth Card** (IYC) if you're under 26. In the United States, the ISIC and IYC cards cost $16 each and include basic travel accident and illness coverage, plus a toll-free travel hot line. Apply through the Council on International Educational Exchange (*see* Organizations, *below*). Cards are available for $15 each in Canada from Travel Cuts (187 College St., Toronto, Ontario M5T 1P7, ☎ 416/979–2406 or 800/667–2887) and in the United Kingdom for £5 each at student unions and student travel companies.

ORGANIZATIONS

A major contact is the **Council on International Educational Exchange** (CIEE, 205 E. 42nd St., 16th Floor, New York, NY 10017, ☎ 212/661–1450) with loca-

tions in Boston (729 Boylston St., Boston, MA 02116, ☎ 617/266–1926), Miami (9100 S. Dadeland Blvd., Miami, FL 33156, ☎ 305/670–9261), Los Angeles (1093 Broxton Ave., Los Angeles, CA 90024, ☎ 310/208–3551), 43 college towns nationwide, and the United Kingdom (28A Poland St., London W1V 3DB, ☎ 0171/437–7767). Twice a year, it publishes *Student Travels* magazine. The CIEE's Council Travel Service offers domestic air passes for bargain travel within the United States and is the exclusive U.S. agent for several student-discount cards.

Campus Connections (325 Chestnut St., Suite 1101, Philadelphia, PA 19106, ☎ 215/625–8585 or 800/428–3235) specializes in discounted accommodations and airfares for students. The **Educational Travel Centre** (438 N. Frances St., Madison, WI 53703, ☎ 608/256–5551) offers rail passes and low-cost airline tickets, mostly for flights departing from Chicago.

In Canada, also contact **Travel Cuts** (*see above*).

T

TAXIS

Call **Checker Yellow Cabs** (☎ 504/943–2411); **Liberty Bell Cabs** (☎ 504/822–5974), or **United Cabs** (☎ 504/522–9771).

TOUR OPERATORS

Among the companies selling tours and packages to New Orleans,

the following have a
proven reputation, are
nationally known, and
have plenty of options
to choose from.

GROUP TOURS

For a deluxe escorted
tour of New Orleans,
contact **Maupintour**
(Box 807, Lawrence KS
66044, ☎ 913/843–
1211 or 800/255-4266)
and **Tauck Tours** (11
Wilton Rd., Westport,
CT 06880, ☎ 203/
226–6911 or 800/468–
2825). Another opera-
tor falling between
deluxe and first-class is
Globus (5301 South
Federal Circle, Little-
ton, CO 80123, ☎ 303/
797–2800 or 800/
221–0090). For first-
class and tourist pro-
grams, try **Collette Tours**
(162 Middle St., Paw-
tucket, RI 02860, ☎
401/728–3805 or 800/
832–4656), **Domenico
Tours** (750 Broadway,
Bayonne, NJ 07002, ☎
201/823–8687 or 800/
554–8687) and **May-
flower Tours** (1225
Warren Ave., Downers
Grove, IL 60515, ☎
708/960–3430 or 800/
323–7604). For budget
and tourist class pro-
grams, look into **Cos-
mos** (*see* Globus,
above).

PACKAGES

Independent vacation
packages are available
from major carriers and
tour operators. Contact
**American Airlines Fly
AAway Vacations** (☎
800/321–2121), **Globe-
trotters** (139 Main St.,
Cambridge, MA 02142,
☎ 617/621–9911 or
800/999–9696) and its
subsidiary, **SuperCities**
(617/621–9988 or 800/
333–1234), **Continental**

**Airlines' Grand Destina-
tions** (☎ 800/634–
5555) **Delta Dream
Vacations** (☎ 800/872–
7786), **Certified Vaca-
tions** (Box 1525, Ft.
Lauderdale, FL 33302,
☎ 305/522–1414 or
800/233–7260), **United
Vacations** (☎ 800/328–
6877), **Kingdom Tours**
(300 Market St., Kings-
ton, PA 18704, ☎
717/283–4241 or 800/
872–8857), and **USAir
Vacations** (☎ 800/455–
0123). **Funjet Vacations**,
based in Milwaukee,
Wisconsin, and Gogo
Tours, based in Ramsey,
New Jersey, sell pack-
ages to New Orleans
only through travel
agents.

FROM THE U.K.➤ Con-
tact **British Airways
Holidays** (Astral Tow-
ers, Betts Way, London
Rd., Crawley, West
Sussex RH10 2XA,
☎ 01293/518–022),
Jetsave Travel Ltd.
(Sussex House, London
Rd., East Grinstead, W.
Sussex RH19 1LD, ☎
01342/312033), **Key to
America** (1–3 Station
Rd., Ashford, Middle-
sex TW15 2UW ☎
01784/248777), **Kuoni
Travel** (Kuoni House,
Dorking, Surrey RH5
4AZ, ☎ 01306/742–
222), and **Trailfinders**
(42–50 Earl's Court
Rd., London W8 6FT,
☎ 0171/937–5400; 58
Deansgate, Manchester
M3 2FF, ☎ 0161/839–
6969). Some programs
include New Orleans as
a stop on a multi-
destination tour.

THEME TRIPS

For jazz packages,
Mardi Gras trips, river-
boat cruises, Sugar
Bowl holidays, golf

itineraries, and other
theme vacations, con-
tact **Destination Man-
agement** (2 Canal St.,
Suite 1415, New Or-
leans, LA 70130, ☎
504/592–0500 or 800/
366–8882), **Tours By
Andrea** (2838 Touro
St., New Orleans, LA
70122, ☎ 504/944–
0253 or 800/535–
2732), and **Travel New
Orleans** (400 Magazine
St., Suite 201, New
Orleans, LA 70130,
☎ 504/561–8747 or
800/535–8747).

ORGANIZATIONS

The **National Tour
Association** (546 E.
Main St., Lexington,
KY 40508, ☎ 606/
226–4444 or 800/682–
8886) and **United States
Tour Operators Associa-
tion** (USTOA, 211 E.
51st St., Suite 12B, New
York, NY 10022, ☎
212/750–7371) can
provide lists of member
operators and informa-
tion on booking tours.

PUBLICATIONS

Consult the brochure
**"Worldwide Tour &
Vacation Package
Finder"** from the Na-
tional Tour Association
(*see above*) and the
Better Business Bureau's
**"Tips on Travel Pack-
ages"** (publication No.
24-195, $2; 4200
Wilson Blvd., Arling-
ton, VA 22203).

TRAVEL AGENCIES

For names of reputable
agencies in your area,
contact the **American
Society of Travel Agents**
(1101 King St., Suite
200, Alexandria, VA
22314, ☎ 703/739–
2782).

V

VISITOR INFORMATION

For free brochures and additional information, contact the **New Orleans Metropolitan Convention and Visitors Bureau** (1520 Sugar Bowl Dr., 70112, ☎ 504/566–5031), the **Greater New Orleans Black Tourism Network** (same address, ☎ 504/523–5652) which offers *Soul of New Orleans,* a black heritage directory, and the **Louisiana Department of Tourism** (1051 N. 3rd St., Baton Rouge, LA 70804, ☎ 800/33–GUMBO).

In the U.K., also contact the **United States Travel and Tourism Administration** (Box 1EN, London W1A 1EN, ☎ 0171/495–4466). For a free USA pack, write the USTTA at Box 170, Ashford, Kent TN24 0ZX). Enclose stamps worth £1.50.

W

WEATHER

For current conditions and forecasts, plus the local time and helpful travel tips, call the **Weather Channel Connection** (☎ 900/932–8437; 95¢ per minute) from a touch-tone phone.

THE GOLD GUIDE / IMPORTANT CONTACTS

SMART TRAVEL TIPS A TO Z

Basic Information on Traveling in New Orleans and Savvy Tips to Make Your Trip a Breeze

The more you travel, the more you know about how to make trips run like clockwork. To help make your travels hassle-free, Fodor's editors have rounded up dozens of tips from our contributors and travel experts all over the world, as well as basic information on visiting New Orleans. For names of organizations to contact and publications that can give you more information, *see* Important Contacts A to Z, *above*.

A

AIR TRAVEL

If time is an issue, **always look for nonstop flights,** which require no change of plane and make no stops. If possible, **avoid connecting flights,** which stop at least once and can involve a change of plane, although the flight number remains the same; if the first leg is late, the second waits.

CUTTING COSTS

For good information on deals, **consult the Sunday travel section your local newspaper.**

MAJOR AIRLINES➢ The least-expensive airfares from the major airlines are priced for round-trip travel and are subject to restrictions. You must usually **book in advance and buy the ticket within 24 hours** to get cheaper fares, and you may have to **stay over a Saturday night.** The lowest fare is subject to availability, and only a small percentage of the plane's total seats are sold at that price. It's good to **call a number of airlines—and when you are quoted a good price, book it on the spot**—the same fare on the same flight may not be available the next day. Airlines generally allow you to change your return date for a $25 to $50 fee, but most low-fare tickets are nonrefundable. However, if you don't use it, you can apply the cost toward the purchase price of a new ticket, again for a small charge.

CONSOLIDATORS➢ Consolidators, who buy tickets at reduced rates from scheduled airlines, sell them at prices below the lowest available from the airlines directly—usually without advance restrictions. Sometimes you can even get your money back if you need to return the ticket. Carefully **read the fine print** detailing penalties for changes and cancellations. If you doubt the reliability of a consolidator, **confirm your reservation with the airline.**

ALOFT

AIRLINE FOOD➢ If you hate airline food, **ask for special meals when booking.** These can be vegetarian, low cholesterol, or kosher, for example; commonly prepared to order in smaller quantities than standard catered fare, they can be tastier.

SMOKING➢ Smoking is banned on all flights within the U.S. of less than six hours' duration and on all Canadian flights; the ban also applies to domestic segments of international flights aboard U.S. and foreign carriers. Delta has banned smoking system-wide.

B

BUS TRAVEL

The Regional Transit Authority (RTA) operates a public bus transportation system with interconnecting lines throughout the city. The buses are generally clean and on time. Bus fare is $1 plus 10¢ for transfers. Visiting senior citizens 65 or over who have a valid Medicare ID card may ride public transit for only 50¢. Visitor passes apply to buses as well as streetcars and cost $4 for one day, $8 for three days.

C

CAMERAS, CAMCORDERS, AND COMPUTERS

LAPTOPS

Before you depart, **check your portable computer's battery,** because you may be asked at security to turn on the computer to prove that it is what it appears to be. At the airport, you may prefer to **request a manual inspection,** although security X-rays do not harm hard-disk or floppy-disk storage.

PHOTOGRAPHY

If your camera is new or if you haven't used it for a while, **shoot and develop a few rolls of film** before you leave. Always **store film in a cool, dry place**—never in the car's glove compartment or on the shelf under the rear window.

Every pass through an X-ray machine increases film's chance of clouding. To protect it, carry it in a clear plastic bag and **ask for hand inspection at security.** Such requests are virtually always honored at U.S. airports. Don't depend on a lead-lined bag to protect film in checked luggage—the airline may increase the radiation to see what's inside.

VIDEO

Before your trip, **test your camcorder, invest in a skylight filter to protect the lens, and charge the batteries.** (Airport security personnel may ask you to turn on the camcorder to prove that it's what it appears to be).

Videotape is not damaged by X-rays, but it may be harmed by the magnetic field of a walk-through metal detector, so **ask that videotapes be hand-checked.**

BABY-SITTING

For recommended local sitters, **check with your hotel desk.**

DRIVING

If you are renting a car, **arrange for a car seat when you reserve.** Sometimes they're free.

FLYING

On domestic flights, children under 2 not occupying a seat travel free, and older children currently travel on the "lowest applicable" adult fare.

BAGGAGE> In general, the adult baggage allowance applies for children paying half or more of the adult fare.

SAFETY SEATS> According to the FAA, it's a good idea to **use safety seats aloft.** Airline policy varies. U.S. carriers allow FAA-approved models, but airlines usually require that you buy a ticket, even if your child would otherwise ride free, because the seats must be strapped into regular passenger seats.

FACILITIES> When making your reservation, **ask for children's meals or a freestanding bassinets** if you need them; the latter are available only to those with seats at the bulkhead, where there's enough legroom. If you don't need the bassinet, **think twice before requesting bulkhead seats**—the only storage for in-flight necessities is in the inconveniently distant overhead bins.

LODGING

Most hotels allow children under a certain age to stay in their parents' room at no extra charge, while others charge them as extra adults; be sure to **ask about the cut-off age.**

CRUISES

The Delta Queen Steamboat Company offers three- to 12-day excursions up the Big Muddy and environs aboard the **Delta Queen,** a National Historic landmark built in the 1920s; the **Mississippi Queen,** built in 1976; or the **American Queen,** the largest paddlewheel boat ever built. Cruises up the Mississippi focus on the river's effect on history and historic on-shore sites such as antebellum plantation houses, Vicksburg, and Natchez. Founded in 1890, the company operates out of an enormous and efficient waterfront terminal complex adjacent to the Ernest M. Morial Convention Center.

To get the best deal on a cruise, **consult a cruise-only travel agency.**

CUSTOMS
AND DUTIES

IN NEW ORLEANS

Visitors aged 21 or over may import the following into the United States: 200 cigarettes or 50 cigars or 2 kilograms of tobacco; one U.S. liter of alcohol; gifts to the value of $100. Restricted items include meat products, seeds, plants, and fruits. Never carry illegal drugs.

BACK HOME

IN CANADA➤ Once per calendar year, when you've been out of Canada for at least seven days, you may bring in C$300 worth of goods duty-free. If you've been away less than seven days but more than 48 hours, the duty-free exemption drops to C$100 but can be claimed any number of times (as can a C$20 duty-free exemption for absences of 24 hours or more). You cannot combine the yearly and 48-hour exemptions, use the C$300 exemption only partially (to save the balance for a later trip), or pool exemptions with family members. Goods claimed under the C$300 exemption may follow you by mail; those claimed under the lesser exemptions must accompany you.

Alcohol and tobacco products may be included in the yearly and 48-hour exemptions but not in the 24-hour exemption. If you meet the age requirements of the province through which you reenter Canada, you may bring in, duty-free, 1.14 liters (40 imperial ounces) of wine or liquor or 24 12-ounce cans or bottles of beer or ale. If you are 16 or older, you may bring in, duty-free, 200 cigarettes, 50 cigars or cigarillos, and 400 tobacco sticks or 400 grams of manufactured tobacco. Alcohol and tobacco must accom-

pany you on your return.

An unlimited number of gifts valued up to C$60 each may be mailed to Canada duty-free. These do not count as part of your exemption. Label the package "Unsolicited Gift—Value under $60." Alcohol and tobacco are excluded.

IN THE U.K.➤ From countries outside the EU, including the United States, you may import duty-free 200 cigarettes, 100 cigarillos, 50 cigars or 250 grams of tobacco; 1 liter of spirits or 2 liters of fortified or sparkling wine; 2 liters of still table wine; 60 milliliters of perfume; 250 milliliters of toilet water; plus £136 worth of other goods, including gifts and souvenirs.

D

FOR TRAVELERS WITH DISABILITIES

When discussing accessibility with an operator or reservationist, **ask hard questions.** Are there any stairs, inside *or* out? Are there grab bars next to the toilet *and* in the shower/tub? How wide is the doorway to the room? To the bathroom? For the most extensive facilities, meeting the latest legal specifications, **opt for newer facilities,** which more often have been designed with access in mind. Older properties or ships must usually be retrofitted and may offer more limited facilities as a result. Be sure to **discuss your needs before booking.**

DISCOUNT CLUBS

Travel clubs offer members unsold space on airplanes, cruise ships, and package tours at as much as 50% below regular prices. Membership may include a regular bulletin or access to a toll-free hot line giving details of available trips departing from three or four days to several months in the future. Most also offer 50% discounts off hotel rack rates. Before booking with a club, **make sure the hotel or other supplier isn't offering a better deal.**

DRIVING

I–10 runs from Florida to California and passes directly through the city. To get to the CBD, exit at Poydras Street near the Louisiana Superdome. For the French Quarter, look for the Vieux Carré exit.

I

INSURANCE

Travel insurance can protect your investment, replace your luggage and its contents, or provide for medical coverage should you fall ill during your trip. Most tour operators, travel agents, and insurance agents sell specialized health-and-accident, flight, trip-cancellation, and luggage insurance as well as comprehensive policies with some or all of these features. Before you make any purchase, **review your existing health and homeowner policies** to find out whether they cover expenses incurred while traveling.

BAGGAGE

Airline liability for your baggage is limited to $1,250 per person on domestic flights. On international flights, the airlines' liability is $9.07 per pound or $20 per kilogram for checked baggage (roughly $640 per 70-pound bag) and $400 per passenger for unchecked baggage. However, this excludes a rather extensive list of items, shown on your airline ticket. Insurance for losses exceeding the terms of your airline ticket can be bought directly from the airline at check-in for about $10 per $1,000 of coverage, but first **see if your homeowner's policy covers lost luggage.**

FLIGHT

You should **think twice before buying flight insurance.** Often purchased as a last-minute impulse at the airport, it pays a lump sum when a plane crashes, either to a beneficiary if the insured dies or sometimes to a surviving passenger who loses eyesight or a limb. Supplementing the airlines' coverage described in the limits-of-liability paragraphs on your ticket, it's expensive and basically unnecessary. Charging an airline ticket to a major credit card often automatically entitles you to coverage and may also embrace travel by bus, train, and ship.

HEALTH

FOR U.K. TRAVELERS➤ According to the Association of British Insurers, a trade association representing 450 insurance companies, it's wise to **buy extra medical coverage when you visit the United States.** You can buy an annual travel-insurance policy valid for most vacations during the year in which it's purchased. If you go this route, make sure it covers you if you have a preexisting medical condition or are pregnant.

TRIP

Without insurance, you will lose all or most of your money if you must cancel your trip due to illness or any other reason. Especially if your airline ticket, cruise, or package tour is nonrefundable and cannot be changed, it's essential that you **buy trip-cancellation-and-interruption insurance.** When considering how much coverage you need, look for a policy that will cover the cost of your trip plus the nondiscounted price of a one-way airline ticket should you need to return home early. Read the fine print carefully, especially sections defining "family member" and "preexisting medical conditions." Also **consider default or bankruptcy insurance,** which protects you against a supplier's failure to deliver. However, such policies often do not cover default by a travel agency, tour operator, airline, or cruise line if you bought your tour and the coverage directly from the firm in question.

L
LODGING

APARTMENT AND VILLA RENTALS

If you want a home base that's roomy enough for a family and comes with cooking facilities, **consider a furnished rental.** It's generally cost-wise, too, although not always— some rentals are luxury properties (economical only when your party is large). Home-exchange directories do list rentals—often second homes owned by prospective house swappers—and some services search for a house or apartment for you (even a castle if that's your fancy) and handle the paperwork. Some send an illustrated catalogue and others send photographs of specific properties, sometimes at a charge; up-front registration fees may apply.

HOME EXCHANGE

If you would like to find a house, an apartment, or other vacation property to exchange for your own while on vacation, **become a member of a home-exchange organization,** which will send you its annual directories listing available exchanges and will include your own listing in at least one of them. Arrangements for the actual exchange are made by the two parties to it, not by the organization.

THE GOLD GUIDE / SMART TRAVEL TIPS

M

MONEY AND
EXPENSES

ATMS

Cirrus, Plus and many other networks connecting automated-teller machines operate internationally. Chances are that you can **use your bank card at ATMs** to withdraw money from an account and get cash advances on a credit-card account if your card has been programmed with a personal identification number, or PIN. Before leaving home, **check in on frequency limits** for withdrawals and cash advances.

On cash advances you are charged interest from the day you receive the money from ATMs as well as from tellers. Transaction fees for ATM withdrawals outside your home turf may be higher than for withdrawals at home.

TRAVELER'S CHECKS

Whether or not to buy traveler's checks depends on where you are headed; **take cash to rural areas and small towns, traveler's checks to cities.** The most widely recognized are American Express, Citicorp, Thomas Cook, and Visa, which are sold by major commercial banks for 1% to 3% of the checks' face value—it pays to **shop around.** Both American Express and Thomas Cook issue checks that can be counter-signed and used by you or your traveling companion.

WIRING MONEY

You don't have to be a cardholder to send or receive funds through MoneyGram^{SM} from American Express. Just go to a MoneyGram agent, located in retail and convenience stores and in American Express Travel Offices. Pay up to $1,000 with cash or a credit card, anything over that in cash. The money can be picked up within 10 minutes in cash or check at the nearest MoneyGram agent. There's no limit, and the recipient need only present photo identification. The cost, which includes a free long-distance phone call, runs from 3% to 10%, depending on the amount sent, the destination, and how you pay.

You can also send money using Western Union. Money sent from the United States or Canada will be available for pickup at agent locations in 100 countries within 15 minutes. Once the money is in the system, it can be picked up at any one of 25,000 locations. Fees range from 4% to 10%, depending on the amount you send.

P

PACKAGES
AND TOURS

A package or tour to New Orleans can make your vacation less expensive and more convenient. Firms that sell tours and packages purchase airline seats, hotel rooms, and rental cars in bulk and pass some of the savings on to you. In addition, the best operators have local representatives to help you out at your destination.

A GOOD DEAL?

The more your package or tour includes, the better you can predict the ultimate cost of your vacation. Make sure you know exactly what is included, and **beware of hidden costs.** Are taxes, tips, and service charges included? Transfers and baggage handling? Entertainment and excursions? These can add up.

Most packages and tours are rated deluxe, first-class superior, first class, tourist, and budget. The key difference is usually accommodations. If the package or tour you are considering is priced lower than in your wildest dreams, **be skeptical.** Also, **make sure your travel agent knows the hotels** and other services. Ask about location, room size, beds, and whether it has a pool, room service, or programs for children, if you care about these. Has your agent been there or sent others you can contact?

BUYER BEWARE

Each year consumers are stranded or lose their money when operators go out of business—even very large ones with excellent reputations. If you can't afford a loss, take the time to **check out the operator**—find out how long the company has been in business, and ask several agents about its reputation. Next, **don't book unless the firm has a consumer-protection program.** Members of the United States Tour Operators Association and the National Tour Association are required to set aside funds exclusively to cover your payments and travel arrangements in case of default. Nonmember operators may instead carry insurance; look for the details in the operator's brochure—and the name of an underwriter with a solid reputation. Note: When it comes to tour operators, **don't trust escrow accounts.** Although there are laws governing those of charter-flight operators, no governmental body prevents tour operators from raiding the till.

Next, **contact your local Better Business Bureau and the attorney general's office** in both your own state and the operator's; have any complaints been filed? Last, **pay with a major credit card.** Then you can cancel payment, provided that you can document your complaint. Always **consider trip-cancellation insurance** (see Insurance, above).

Big vs. Small➤ An operator that handles several hundred thousand travelers annually can use its purchasing power to give you a good price. Its high volume may also indicate financial stability. But some small companies provide more personalized service;

because they tend to specialize, they may also be experts on an area.

USING AN AGENT

Travel agents are an excellent resource. In fact, large operators accept bookings only through travel agents. But it's good to **collect brochures from several agencies,** because some agents' suggestions may be skewed by promotional relationships with tour and package firms that reward them for volume sales. If you have a special interest, **find an agent with expertise in that area;** the American Society of Travel Agents can give you leads in the United States. (Don't rely solely on your agent, though; agents may be unaware of small niche operators, and some special-interest travel companies only sell direct).

SINGLE TRAVELERS

Prices are usually quoted per person, based on two sharing a room. If traveling solo, you may be required to pay the full double occupancy rate. Some operators eliminate this surcharge if you agree to be matched up with a roommate of the same sex, even if one is not found by departure time.

PACKING FOR NEW ORLEANS

New Orleans is casual during the day, and casual to slightly dressy at night. Many restaurants in the French Quarter require men to wear a jacket and tie.

For sightseeing, **pack walking shorts, sundresses, cotton slacks or jeans, and T-shirts.** In winter, you'll want a coat or warm jacket, especially for evenings, which can be downright cold. In summer, pack for hot, sticky weather but be prepared for air-conditioning bordering on glacial, and bring an umbrella in case of sudden thunderstorms; leave the plastic raincoats behind (they're extremely uncomfortable in the high humidity). In addition, **pack a sun hat and sunscreen lotion,** even for strolls in the city, because the sun can be fierce. Insect repellent will also come in handy if you plan to be outdoors in the evenings or to dine alfresco, since mosquitoes come out in full force after sunset in the hot weather.

Bring an extra pair of eyeglasses or contact lenses in your carry-on luggage, and if you have a health problem, **pack enough medication** to last the trip. In case your bags go astray, **don't put prescription drugs or valuables in luggage to be checked.**

LUGGAGE

Free airline baggage allowances depend on the airline, the route, and the class of your ticket; ask in advance. In general, on domestic flights you are entitled to check two bags—neither exceeding 62 inches, or 158 centimeters (length + width + height), or weighing more than 70 pounds (32 kilograms). A third piece may be brought

THE GOLD GUIDE / SMART TRAVEL TIPS

aboard; its total dimensions are generally limited to less than 45 inches (114 centimeters), so it will fit easily under the seat in front of you or in the overhead compartment. In the United States, the Federal Aviation Administration gives airlines broad latitude to limit carry-on allowances and tailor them to different aircraft and operational conditions. Charges for excess, oversize, or overweight pieces vary.

SAFEGUARDING YOUR LUGGAGE➤ Before leaving home, **itemize your bags' contents** and their worth, and label them with your name, address, and phone number. (If you use your home address, cover it so that potential thieves can't see it.) Inside your bag, **pack a copy of your itinerary.** At check-in, **make sure that your bag is correctly tagged** with the airport's three-letter destination code. If your bags arrive damaged or not at all, file a written report with the airline before leaving the airport.

PASSPORTS AND VISAS

CANADIANS

No passport is necessary to enter the United States.

U.K. CITIZENS

British citizens need a valid passport. If you are staying fewer than 90 days and traveling on a vacation, with a return or onward ticket, you will probably not need a visa. However,

you will need to fill out the Visa Waiver Form, 1-94W, supplied by the airline.

While traveling, **keep one photocopy of your passport's data page** separate from your wallet and leave another copy with someone at home. If you lose your passport, promptly call the nearest embassy or consulate, and the local police; having the data page can speed replacement.

R

RADIO STATIONS

AM

WWL 870, news, talk, country music late at night; WYLD 940, gospel; WQUE 1280, sports; WSMB 1350, talk.

FM

WWNO 89.9, classical, National Public Radio, late-night jazz; WWOZ 90.7, regional music, jazz; WTUL 91.5, Tulane student–operated: rock and new music; WKCW 92, rock; WQUE 93.3, contemporary; WNOE 101, country; WLMG 102, easy listening.

RAIL TRAVEL

Three major Amtrak lines arrive at and depart from New Orleans's Union Passenger Terminal. The *Crescent* makes daily runs from New York to New Orleans by way of Washington, DC. The *City of New Orleans* runs daily between New Orleans and Chicago. The *Sunset Limited* makes the two-day trip between New Orleans and Los Angeles. It

departs New Orleans on Monday, Wednesday, and Saturday, and leaves Los Angeles on Sunday, Wednesday, and Friday. The same line makes the 24-hour trip to Miami three times a week, but days and departure times vary. Some routes may also change with cutbacks in Amtrack funding.

RENTING A CAR

Having a car in New Orleans is no problem—except when you're likeliest to be there, at Mardi Gras. Then the whole French Quarter is closed to traffic, and cars parked on parade routes get whisked away. For excursions to surrounding areas, cars are advisable.

CUTTING COSTS

To get the best deal, **book through a travel agent and shop around.** When pricing cars, **ask where the rental lot is located.** Some off-airport locations offer lower rates—even though their lots are only minutes away from the terminal via complimentary shuttle. You may also want to **price local car-rental companies,** whose rates may be lower still, although service and maintenance standards may not be up to those of a national firm. Also **ask your travel agent about a company's customer-service record.** How has it responded to late plane arrivals and vehicle mishaps? Are there often lines at the rental counter, and, if you're traveling during a holiday period, does a confirmed reservation guarantee you a car?

INSURANCE

When you drive a rented car, you are generally responsible for any damage or personal injury that you cause as well as damage to the vehicle. Before you rent, **see what coverage you already have** by means of your personal auto-insurance policy and credit cards. For about $14 a day, rental companies sell insurance, known as a collision damage waiver (CDW), that eliminates your liability for damage to the car; it's always optional and should never be automatically added to your bill.

SURCHARGES

Before picking up the car in one city and leaving it in another, **ask about drop-off charges or one-way service fees,** which can be substantial. Note, too, that some rental agencies charge extra if you return the car before the time specified on your contract. To avoid a hefty refueling fee, **fill the tank just before you turn in the car.**

FOR U.K. CITIZENS

In the United States you must be 21 to rent a car; rates may be higher for those under 25. Extra costs cover child seats, compulsory for children under 5 (about $3 per day), and additional drivers (about $1.50 per day). To pick up your reserved car you will need the reservation voucher, a passport, a U.K. driver's license, and a travel policy covering each driver.

S

SENIOR-CITIZEN DISCOUNTS

To qualify for age-related discounts, **mention your senior-citizen status up front** when booking hotel reservations, not when checking out, and before you're seated in restaurants, not when paying your bill. Note that discounts may be limited to certain menus, days, or hours. When renting a car, **ask about promotional car-rental discounts**—they can net lower costs than your senior-citizen discount.

SIGHTSEEING

SPECIAL-INTEREST TOURS

Full-day plantation tours by bus from New Orleans, which include guided tours through two antebellum plantation homes along the Mississippi River and a stop for lunch in a Cajun-Creole restaurant outside the city, are offered by Gray Line and New Orleans Tours. Tours by Isabelle includes lunch in its full-day plantation package that traces the history of the Cajun people. Also available is the Grand Tour: A full-day minibus tour that includes a visit to one plantation, lunch in a Cajun restaurant, and a 1½-hour boat tour in the swamps with a Cajun trapper. American-Acadian has a six-hour tour that includes the city's Garden District plus two plantations upriver.

Nightlife tours that visit popular jazz clubs and Bourbon Street nightclubs are given by New Orleans Tours. The evening concludes at Cafe du Monde. The Pete Fountain tour includes drinks at the Top of the Mart lounge and at the Hilton Hotel, where the famous Fountain performs.

A visit to either the Audubon Zoo or the Aquarium of the Americas or both can be combined with an exciting ride on the river on the *John James Audubon,* a ship operated by the New Orleans Steamboat Company that can accommodate 600 passengers. The 7-mile (11-kilometer) ride takes 30 minutes. Tickets for such package tours are available in kiosks at both the zoo and the aquarium. Prices vary depending on whether you choose only the cruise or combine it with zoo and aquarium admissions.

WALKING TOURS

Free 1½-hour general history tours of the French Quarter are given daily at 10:30 AM by rangers of the Jean Lafitte National Park. Occasionally at 11:30 AM, a daily "tour du jour" is given, which focuses on a particular historical or cultural aspect of the Quarter. Each visitor may procure tickets for either tour at the Park Service office in the French Market after 9 AM on the morning of the tour. Tickets are limited; call for details. Three-hour general history tours are given daily at 10 and 1:30 by Friends of the

Cabildo. The tour price includes admission to two state museums of your choice. Family Reunion Planning Services conducts black heritage walking tours of the French Quarter.

Several specialized walking tours conducted by knowledgeable guides on specific aspects of the French Quarter are also available. Because some of these tours accommodate as few as two people, be sure to **make advance reservations.** Classic Tours is operated by a native Orleanian who loves to share her city on casual insider tours that cover art, antiques, architecture, and local lore. Heritage Tours offers a general literary tour and others focusing on either William Faulkner or Tennessee Williams. The New Orleans Historic Voodoo Museum and Magic Walking Tours offer two daily esoteric walking tours, a voodoo tour at 1 PM, and a ghost tour at night. A Garden District walking tour, called "Faubourg Promenade," is given daily at 2:30 PM by Jean Lafitte National Park rangers. Mile-long walks last for 90 minutes. Reservations are required. Classic Tours also conduct tours in this historic section of New Orleans, as does Hidden Treasures Tours, which takes walkers into the interior of a home.

The cemeteries of New Orleans provide a universal fascination with their unique above-ground tombs. The most famous, St. Louis Cemetery #1, is just outside the French Quarter and Magic Walking Tours, Hidden Treasures Tours, Save our Cemeteries, and the New Orleans Historic Voodoo Museum offer guided walking tours. Reservations are generally required.

STREETCARS

The city's Regional Transit Authority (RTA) operates the historic St. Charles Avenue streetcar, established in 1835, that makes the 5-mile (8-kilometer) trek from the CBD to Carrollton along picturesque St. Charles Avenue. The fare is $1 plus 10¢ for transfers.

The Riverfront streetcar covers a 1.9-mile route along the Mississippi River, connecting major sights from the end of the French Quarter (Esplanade Ave.) to the New Orleans Convention Center (Julia St.). Eight stops en route include the French Market, Jackson Brewery, Canal Place, the World Trade Center, the Riverwalk, and the Hilton Hotel. The streetcar operates weekdays 6 AM until midnight and weekends 8 AM until midnight passing each stop every 15 minutes. One of the cars is specially equipped for elderly passengers and those with mobility impairments. The fare is $1.50 a ride. One-day and three-day visitor passes are available at $4 and $8, respectively, for unlimited rides on both the St. Charles Avenue and Riverfront streetcar lines. Visitor passes apply to buses as well as streetcars.

STUDENTS ON THE ROAD

To save money, **look into deals available through student-oriented travel agencies.** To qualify, you'll need to have a bona fide student I.D. card. Members of international student groups also are eligible. *See* Students *in* Important Contacts A to Z, *above.*

T
TAXIS

Cabs are metered at $1.70 minimum plus 50¢ for each additional passenger and $1 per mile. You can either hail cabs in some of the busier areas, or call one.

TELEPHONES

LONG-DISTANCE

The long-distance services of AT&T, MCI, and Sprint make calling home relatively convenient and let you avoid hotel surcharges; typically, you dial an 800 number.

W
WHEN TO GO

CLIMATE

In New Orleans, as in most of the South, May through October is hot and humid. Just mustering the energy to raise a mint julep to your lips may cause malaise. During these infamous long, hot summers, the sun shines for as long as 11 hours each day, which may explain why things are less hurried down here—there's lots of time and it's so hard to stay cool! If you must visit during these sticky months, you'll find that all hotels and restaurants are air-conditioned.

June through November are the months to watch for torrential rains, twisters, and even hurricanes. These conditions occur mainly with quick changes in temperature that accompany cold fronts.

Heavy fogs can plague October to March. Although winters are mild compared to those in northern climes, the high humidity can really put a chill in the air. Don't be surprised to see women wearing fur coats in many of the city's finer establishments.

Perhaps the best time to visit the city is early spring. Days are pleasant, except for seasonal cloudbursts, and nights are cool. The azaleas are in full bloom while the city bustles from one outdoor festival to the next.

The following are average daily maximum and minimum temperatures for New Orleans.

Climate in New Orleans

Jan.	62F	17C	May	83F	28C	Sept.	86F	30C
	47	8		68	20		73	23
Feb.	65F	18C	June	88F	31C	Oct.	79F	26C
	50	10		74	23		64	18
Mar.	71F	22C	July	90F	32C	Nov.	70F	21C
	55	13		76	24		55	13
Apr.	77F	25C	Aug.	90F	32C	Dec.	64F	18C
	61	16		76	24		48	9

THE GOLD GUIDE / SMART TRAVEL TIPS

1 Destination: New Orleans

DREAMING IN THE BIG EASY

WHEN THE SUN rises over New Orleans's French Quarter, it sends the waterfront rats scurrying for wharf cover. Next, it shakes awake the vagabonds whose eyes and memories have failed in the night; before long, that lost society must also retreat to some other darkness.

But day is never the real victor in the capricious 108 square blocks that cling to the crescent banks of the Mississippi. Even at noon the French Quarter is seldom fully awake. In its dreams are still splendid riverboats, passionate romance, and pistol duels beneath moss-draped oaks, undisturbed by the more modern sounds of delivery trucks and commercial barges. For more than two and a half centuries New Orleans has dreamed those dreams, and perhaps through them has managed to survive the ravages of plagues and fires and storms that would have laid waste far less vulnerable cities.

By mid-morning the Vieux Carré (or Old Square) is forced by business schedules to yawn a bit here, stretch a bit there. Up go the umbrellas of the artists near the Place d'Armes, with its narcotic view of St. Louis Cathedral. Early tourists wander along the cracked and uneven sidewalks, pausing occasionally to examine the lacy, foreign-looking ferns that sprout from crevices. Canvas awnings on little shop fronts are unfurled. Stuffed "mammies" appear outside candy stores. And bag after bag of ice crunches its way from truck beds to the shoulders of deliverymen and finally into a saloon where it will be served in rum-based drinks called Hurricanes.

By lunchtime, a perfume boutique can be sensed a half block off, its flowery scents mingling with the aromas of rich coffee and red beans and rice from small restaurants.

As afternoon progresses, jazz tunes float from the open doors of musty buildings. A leftover hippie on the steps of a T-shirt emporium gets surprisingly few frowns as he methodically and peacefully plaits strips of leather. In the French Quarter he has found his niche, and shares a sense of freedom with others whose lifestyles demand a degree of tolerance not afforded in other sections of the city.

In most cases, it is difficult to conceive of native Orleanians "belonging" elsewhere. The giveaway is the very identifiable quality of their speech, which puts a homemade label on inflections. It's also what they say, not just how they say it: The median strip that divides a wide street is a "neutral ground"; when a grocer or shop owner includes a little something extra in a customer's order, it's "lagniappe"; a sidewalk is a "banquette."

When you ask for directions, you're not likely to hear the words north or south, east or west. Rather, it'll be Riverside, Lakeside, Uptown, Downtown. That's New Orleans talking, and talking is something its people do a lot of. Only the tones differ with the neighborhoods.

For instance, Uptown (anything on the other side of Canal Street from the French Quarter) is where the tone of New Orleans is generally thought to be somewhat gentler. And indeed, Uptown—with its fabled St. Charles Avenue, having rounded Lee Circle and set its course toward meeting the river some 75 blocks away—often thinks of itself as *being* gentler.

Such a claim would have been hastily challenged in the early 1800s, when the Louisiana Purchase paved the way for Americans to settle Uptown. Creoles, the original settlers whose roots were very much Downtown, considered the interloping Americans to be vulgar, barbaric, and thoroughly unsavory. By 1820, however, the Americans outnumbered the Creoles three to one, and the newer Orleanians would soon be far less concerned about what Creoles thought than about their own neoclassical existence in their Uptown utopia. That residential area was to be known eventually as the Garden District, and even now, it is a neighborhood that inspires awe.

Many of the gigantic antebellum mansions, with their vast lawns, look exactly as they looked more than a century ago;

a few are still in the same families. There is less activity on these streets than in Downtown neighborhoods, fewer people on the sidewalks. A sort of imposed quiet prevails. Perhaps it was that aspect of the Garden District that prompted writer Oliver Evans to propose that the area is like "an elegant corpse."

ON THE RIVERSIDE end of the Garden District, and extending several blocks closer to Canal Street, is the Irish Channel, a blue-collar neighborhood that is considerably nearer in feeling to Downtown. Here attitudes seem more relaxed, less formal, and pleasures are simpler.

Uptown from the Garden District, the University Section spreads toward the lake. A turn of streetcar tracks signals the end of St. Charles Avenue and the beginning of Carrollton Avenue. Soon, Carrollton Avenue will lead through portions of Mid-City, along the periphery of City Park, and eventually to the lakefront. Any traveler who has reached that final point has crossed over into the realm of *déjà vu* realty. The expensive surroundings and manicured lawns of green are mute reminders that seldom, if ever, has New Orleans's peculiar potion of charm employed predictability as a vital ingredient.

The components of that charm remain a mystery that ranks with the location of the buried loot of the pirate Jean Lafitte.

Several years ago, a group of urban anthropologists, armed with the sacrosanct premise that New Orleans's distinctive appeal merely reflects the distinctive nature of its people, set out to define that nature and to determine what made it distinctive. Questions were posed and answers were recorded, and once the city had been sampled as randomly as credibility required, a computer spat out the survey's findings.

Among the revelations were certain disclosures about one deeply Downtown neighborhood that lies immediately below the French Quarter. The survey indicated that a higher percentage of residents in that section do 10 specific things that just might be considered heavy with the flavor of New Orleans:

- More residents there go to early mass on Ash Wednesday, the day following Mardi Gras;

- More people won't drink coffee unless it's brewed with chicory;

- More people can name at least one hit record by New Orleans native Fats Domino;

- More have actually seen mirlitons (vegetables grown locally and usually stuffed like bell peppers) growing on the vine;

- More live in a house that has a Zulu coconut somewhere on the premises (these coconuts are handed to crowds during the black Zulu parade on Mardi Gras);

- More are related to (or know someone who is related to) a girl named Darlene;

- More shop at Schwegmann's, a locally owned supermarket chain, at least once a week;

- More know what number is worn by the Saints' star quarterback;

- More consider a po-boy (an overstuffed sandwich on French bread said to have originated in New Orleans) to be the ideal lunch for a working day; and

- More say "N'Awlins."

A good many residents of that neighborhood, like those of several other sections, admitted in the questionnaire that a favorite time of day is late afternoon, when they sit on the stoops in front of their houses, chatting with neighbors and "unwinding."

Dusk is when the muscle of the French Quarter begins to flex. Softly lit by glowing gas lanterns, the Vieux Carré wears darkness well. Imperfections seem less distracting, almost appealing; no wonder the sun shines shyly—in New Orleans, night is brighter. A background fugue seems to play as an aura of the past hovers, its magic empowered by the proximity of the buildings and the close, narrow streets.

In the beginning those streets were little more than open gutters, and early residents lived with the dangers of malaria, floods, and snakes. Ownership of the colony kept switching—French, then Spanish, then French again, and finally American. Still, the changing of flags did not affect its settlers' allegiance in establishing themselves as individuals in a city that was already individual itself.

Somewhere along the early way, the city had also developed a peculiar pride that would turn treacherously malignant. It would distort the city's values during the suffocating occupation by the Union's Yankee soldiers, turn the city's back on the politically frenzied Reconstruction, and fuel an attitude of aloofness during the strangling Depression. New Orleans somehow figured that to dismiss the enemy was to disarm the enemy; the result of this refusal to recognize reality was a crippling scar on the city's progress. Only within the last dozen or so years has New Orleans begun to live because of itself rather than despite itself.

Ironically, the French Quarter—by tradition the most decadent area of the city—has emerged as particularly progressive. Significant buildings are constantly being carefully restored and pedestrian malls have been designated for parts of Bourbon and Royal streets. The riverfront adjacent to the square is at its liveliest since antebellum days. The historic French Market, where Native Americans once swapped their goods, has been modernized for increased public use. And young professionals, many of them native to the city, are moving into the Vieux Carré and finding their way into the life of the section.

Residents of the French Quarter are primarily concerned with, and fiercely protective of, their right to live as they please. Up-and-coming yuppies live alongside the likes of the leftover hippie, clear evidence of the more eccentric nature of this neighborhood. New Orleans's nickname, the Big Easy, seems perfectly apropos in the Vieux Carré, a neighborhood that perfectly reflects the flavor of New Orleans.

—*Don Lee Keith*

WHAT'S WHERE

New Orleans covers approximately 365 squares miles of flat, swamp-drained land that extends between the Mississippi River and Lake Pontchartrain. The city has a small-time atmosphere, and its neighborhoods, populated by families who have lived within the same blocks for decades, tend to flow into each another.

The French Quarter

Most visitors to New Orleans spend much of their time in the French Quarter, or Vieux Carré, a 6-by-12-block rectangle along the Mississippi River, where the city was first established by the French in 1718. The only neighborhood in the city laid out in a grid pattern, this area is both a residential and business district, with streets lined with historic landmarks, beautifully restored residences, shops, restaurants, and offices. Except for Bourbon Street, a world-famous entertainment strip, the French Quarter has no neon signs, and its buildings conform to the architectural style of the late 18th- to mid-19th centuries. The center of Vieux Carré is Jackson Square, an exquisite landscaped park where artists, musicians, and street performers gravitate.

Central Business District

Upriver from the French Quarter, this neighborhood, often called CBD, encompasses several impressive office buildings, hotels, shopping malls, and the Louisiana Superdome, home to the New Orleans Saints football team. CBD also takes in the foot of Canal Street, one of the city's fastest growing areas, and only a 10-minute walk from the French Quarter and downtown hotels. Here you'll find the spectacular Aquarium of the Americas, the ferry across the river to Algiers Point, the award-winning Piazza d'Italia, and Riverwalk, a half-mile marketplace of more than 200 shops, galleries, and restaurants. Near Riverwalk is the Warehouse District—Julia Street between St. Charles Avenue and the river—which is a center for many of the city's top art galleries.

The Garden District

West of the Central Business District, the Garden District, which traditionally begins where St. Charles Avenue crosses Jackson Avenue, was settled by Americans who built their fortunes in New Orleans after the 1803 Louisiana Purchase. This wealthy neighborhood is renowned for its sumptuous antebellum homes (several in the Greek Revival style with lovely iron-work) surrounded by beautifully land-scaped gardens. The Garden District is bordered on the south by the Magazine Street shop-ping area and claims one of New Orleans grandest contemporary Creole restau-rants, Commander's Palace.

Uptown

Southwest of the French Quarter and the Central Business District, this area stretches from the Garden District past the Tulane and Loyola university neighborhoods, all the way to the end of the St. Charles streetcar line, which stops at Carrollton and Claiborne avenues. Uptown has his-torical mansions, several good music venues for everything from jazz to zy-deco, and the Riverbend shopping area, with stores in turn-of-the-century cot-tages. South of the universities is Audubon Park, a former plantation that now includes a world-class zoo, a golf course, and miles of winding lagoons and hiking trails.

Mid-City

This working-class neighborhood north of the French Quarter and south of Lake Pontchartrain is mostly residential, but it also contains two sights of interest to vis-itors: the Fair Grounds, the third-oldest racetrack in the country, and City Park, once a sugar plantation belonging to Louis Allard in the late 1700s. The park in-cludes the New Orleans Museum of Art, the enchanting Botanical Garden, Story-land amusement park, a turn-of-the-cen-tury carousel, and plenty of picnic and hiking areas.

Lakefront

If you have a car, it's worth heading to Lakeshore Drive on the northern edge of the city for views of Lake Pontchartrain, especially around sunset. Lakeshore Drive is a favorite spot for boating, fishing, picnicking, and walking. Within the lake-front area are Lakeview, a residential neighborhood with modern ranch-style homes; a public and private marina; and West End Park, with several casual seafood joints.

PLEASURES & PASTIMES

Dining

New Orleans–style cooking reflects a blend of ethnic culinary influences, with contributions from Africans, Spaniards, Frenchmen, Choctaw Native Americans, and Acadians. Creole, the traditional New Orleans cuisine, blends French, Spanish, Caribbean, and African cooking styles. Cajun is a kind of cooking de-rived from Acadiana, a Southwestern Louisianan region of coastal prairie, bay-ous, and marshlands. Cajun dishes tend to be more heavily spiced and more rus-tic in presentation than Creole entrées, with less attention paid to cream and buttered sauces. Besides these two cuisines, which are sometimes blended together at some newer establishments, visitors have many other international restaurants from which to choose, including French, Italian, Chi-nese, Mexican, Greek, Spanish, and even Lebanese eateries. Beyond the first-class restaurants, casual diners, bistros, and seafood houses, food lovers can also cel-ebrate at cafés, coffeehouses, and pastry shops, where they can stuff themselves with beignets and pralines, as well as at sand-wich shops serving hearty po'boys and muffulettas. Servings at many places are often generous, so don't come to New Or-leans if you're planning to diet!

Excursions

Two areas within driving distance of New Orleans are worth investigating if you have the time. East and west of the Mis-sissippi, the Great River Road extends between New Orleans and Baton Rouge and contains beautifully restored ante-bellum plantation homes furnished with period antiques. The area is also called LA 44 and 75 on the east bank, and LA 18 on the left bank. Standouts among the plan-tations are Oak Alley, named for the 28 gnarled oak trees on the grounds; the Greek Revival mansions Houmas House and Madewood; and Nottoway, the South's largest plantation home, a white Greek Re-vival–Italianate castle with 64 rooms that was refurbished in 1993. Another region to explore is Cajun Country. Cajun cul-ture came to Louisiana when Acadians (French settlers in Nova Scotia and New Brunswick) relocated to the southwestern part of the state after being expelled from Canada by the British in the early 18th century. The best way to become acquainted with Cajun life and lore is to visit the city of Lafayette (128 miles west of New Orleans on I–10), where you can visit a recreation of an early 19th-century bayou settlement with examples of Acadian architecture, furnishings, and tools. From Lafayette, you can head for a number of nearby tiny towns and villages with old buildings and antique shops. Visitors to Cajun country will want to sample the region's rich, spicy cuisine and celebratory foot-stomping music.

Mardi Gras

The day before Lent, in February or early March, is New Orleans's world-famous Mardi Gras. During the week and weekend before Fat Tuesday (Mardi Gras day), certain streets are filled with long winding parades of magnificent floats, marching bands, and entertainers. Schedules for parades are printed in the daily newspaper. Revelers riding two- and three-story floats toss plastic bead necklaces, silver-dollar size doubloons, and a variety of plastic toys and cups. Those lining the parade route push, shove, and holler "Throw me something, Mister!" as they try to catch a small memento. If you miss the real thing, there are several museums in the city that give you a sample of what Mardi Gras is like: The Mardi Gras Museum, the Mardi Gras Museum of Jefferson Parish, the Germaine Wells Mardi Gras Museum, and Blaine Kern's Mardi Gras World in Algiers Point.

Music

Many visitors come to New Orleans just to hear music. The city has long been famous for fostering jazz artists—Louis Armstrong, Jelly Roll Morton, and more recently, Wynton Marsalis—but it has embraced many other kinds of music as well. Almost every night of the week you can find a place to hear jazz, rhythm and blues, gospel, salsa and Latin rhythms, Cajun music and zydeco, rock-and-roll, and more. The largest number of music clubs are concentrated in the French Quarter, with many of them clustered on Bourbon, Toulouse, and Decatur streets. Preservation Hall on St. Peter Street is world-renowned for its traditional jazz per-

formers. More music clubs and bars with music are scattered throughout the Central Business District, the Warehouse District, and Uptown, which has several clubs featuring rhythm and blues and Cajun music. Many hotels have their own popular piano bars; the one in the Royal Orleans, for instance, is quite elegant. During late April, the New Orleans Jazz and Heritage festival of more than 4,000 musicians attracts huge crowds to the Fair Grounds.

Walking

New Orleans has several delightful areas for those who like to walk. The French Quarter, with its carefully restored 18th- and 19th-century buildings is a good place to start. Free 90-minute walking tours of the neighborhood are offered daily by park rangers of Jean Lafitte National Park, who also provide daily tours of the wealthy Garden District. Moon Walk is a well-landscaped promenade facing the river in front of Jackson Square; there are benches where you can sit and enjoy the activities of ships, tugboats, and cruise paddlewheelers on the water. Another good river view can be savored at Woldenberg Riverfront Park, a 16-acre attractively landscaped stretch between Jackson Brewery and the Aquarium of the Americas. Walkers will also enjoy a stroll along Lake Pontchartrain, with miles of seawall for relaxation. New Orleans has two excellent parks with hiking trails, City Park and Audubon Park.

FODOR'S CHOICE

No two people will agree on what makes a perfect vacation, but it's fun and helpful to know what others think. We hope you'll have a chance to experience some of Fodor's Choices yourself while visiting New Orleans. For detailed information about each entry, refer to the appropriate chapters within this guidebook.

Favorite Sights

★ **Audubon Zoo.** One of the best natural-habitat animal parks in the country provides hours of amusement, with sea lions, a white tiger, a flamingo pond, a tropical bird house, and the Louisiana Swamp, featuring large alligators.

★ **Beauregard-Keyes House.** This stately 19th-century mansion on Chartres Street—restored in the 1940s by novelist Frances Parkinson Keyes—has a beautiful walled garden, landscaped in a sun pattern, which is in bloom year-round.

★ **City Park.** Encompassing 1,500 acres, this enchanting park has the New Orleans Museum of Art specializing in pre-Columbian, African, and local creations; the lovely Botanical Garden; and man-made lagoons.

★ **French Market.** This bustling complex of renovated centuries-old buildings, extending several blocks along Decatur and North Peters streets, encompasses specialty shops, restaurants, cafés, and a flea market.

★ **Napoleon House.** A longtime favorite haunt for local writers and artists, this bar and café in an 1814 house with murmuring ceiling fans and a lovely patio is perfect for late afternoon people watching.

Special Moments

★ **Canal Street Ferry Ride.** The most romantic view of the city and its skyline can be seen from the deck of the ferry that crosses the Mississippi River to Algiers Point every 20 minutes from the Canal Street terminal.

★ **City Park Carousel.** Adults and children alike love riding the exquisitely refurbished 1906 Last Carousel, replete with authentic wooden flying horses, giraffes, zebras, and other exotic creatures.

★ **New Orleans Streetcar.** The most fun way to explore the Central Business District, the Garden District, and Uptown is to take a morning or afternoon ride on one of the historic city streetcars which run along the riverfront and St. Charles Avenue.

★ **Sunset at Lake Pontchartrain.** This is the perfect time to visit the enormous lake, which has miles of seawall where you can relax and stroll along the cool waterfront.

After Hours

★ **Café du Monde.** No trip to New Orleans would be complete without a cup of chicory-laced café au lait and a few sugar-dusted beignets at this venerable Creole institution with views of Jackson Square and Decatur Street.

★ **Frenchmen Street.** This bohemian thoroughfare in Faubourg Marigny, the neighborhood just outside the French Quarter, has three of the city's hottest music clubs (jazz, salsa, reggae) and venues for poetry readings.

★ **Mid-City Bowling Lanes.** At this combination bowling alley/music club near Uptown, joyful dancers edge into the lanes when a favorite zydeco band takes the stage.

★ **Palm Court Café.** The best of traditional jazz is presented in a classy setting, with tile floors, a handsome mahogany bar, and a fine Creole-International kitchen.

★ **Preservation Hall.** Although it's grungy and uncomfortable with crude wooden benches and a cramped standing room, this cultural French Quarter landmark showcases some of the best traditional jazz musicians in the world.

Hotels

★ **The Pontchartrain Hotel.** Since 1927, honeymooners have flocked to St. Charles Avenue in the Garden District to stay at this quiet European-style hotel in the grand tradition, where accommodations range from lavish sun-filled suites to small pension rooms. $$$$

★ **Windsor Court Hotel.** One of the top places to stay in New Orleans, this exquisite, eminently civilized lodging has remarkably large rooms with plush carpeting, canopy and four-poster beds, marble vanities, and oversize mirrors. Don't miss the scrumptious daily afternoon tea at Le Salon. $$$$

★ **Hotel Maison de Ville.** This small, antique-furnished gem with a romantic 19th-century ambience allows guests to escape the contemporary bustle of the French Quarter. Hideaway seekers can stay in the privately enclosed Audubon Cottages. $$$–$$$$

★ **Josephine Guest House.** The graceful pleasures of an old New Orleans home are found at this beautifully restored 19th-century Italianate mansion, complete with European antiques, Oriental rugs on gleaming hardwood floors, and a complimentary Creole breakfast. $$–$$$

★ **Le Richelieu in the French Quarter.** Guests appreciate the friendly, personal atmosphere of this intimate, reasonably priced hotel with luxe accents such as up-scale toiletry packages; it's near the old Ursuline Convent and the French Market. $$

Restaurants

★ **Commander's Palace.** New Orleans's gastronomic heritage and celebratory spirit are perfectly captured in the creatively prepared Creole dishes served in a stately Garden District mansion. $$$$

★ **The Grill Room.** British furnishings and paintings spanning several centuries fill the dazzling dining spaces of this grandly formal Windsor Court Hotel restaurant, where entrées on the changing menu combine exotic and sumptuous ingredients, often flown in from Europe and the Orient. $$$$

★ **Graham's.** A dining room with flat white walls, bare arched windows, and uncovered dark-green granite tables serves as the stark setting for some of the most innovative and celebrated dishes in town, prepared by English-born chef Kevin Graham. $$$

★ **Dooky Chase's.** In a friendly yet elegant dining room decorated with works by local black artists, you can sample definitive versions of classic Creole dishes, including crab soup, sausage jambalaya, buttery panéed veal, and stewed okra. $$

★ **Galatoire's.** At this old-style French–Creole bistro, you can savor time-tested winners (bouillabaisse, spring lamb chops in béarnaise sauce, seafood-stuffed eggplant) in a perfect setting—a single, narrow dining room lit with glittering brass chandeliers and swathed in white-framed mirrored panels. $$

★ **The Praline Connection.** Down-home cooking in the Southern–Creole style is the forte in this laid-back, likeable eatery near the French Quarter. $

★ **Progress Grocery and Central Grocery.** These two old-fashioned French Quarter Italian grocery stores produce irresistible, authentic muffulettas—sandwiches made with soft round loaves of seeded bread and ham, salami, mozzarella, and a green olive salad. $

FESTIVALS AND SEASONAL EVENTS

Top seasonal events in New Orleans include the Sugar Bowl on New Year's Day, Mardi Gras celebrations, the Spring Fiesta and the Jazz and Heritage Festival in April, and a New Orleans Christmas throughout the month of December.

WINTER

JAN.➤ The **Sugar Bowl Classic** (1500 Sugar Bowl Dr., 70112, ☎ 504/525–8573), the city's oldest annual sporting event, includes not only one of the biggest college football games of the year, but also tennis, basketball, sailing, running, and flag football championship events.

JAN.➤ The **N.O. Film and Video Festival** (☎ 504/523–3818) brings a week of the best foreign and domestic films with visits from directors and writers.

SPRING

LATE FEB. OR EARLY MAR.➤ **Mardi Gras** is rollicking, raucous, and ritualistic. It's street celebrations, parades, and formal masked balls (*see* Carnival *in* Chapter 9, Portraits of New Orleans).

EARLY MAR.➤ The **Black Heritage Festival**

(Audubon Zoo, Box 4327, 70178, ☎ 504/861–2537) includes gospel and jazz performances, art exhibits, and soul food.

MID-MAR.➤ The **St. Patrick's Day Parade** begins at Molly's at the Market Pub (1107 Decatur St., 70116, ☎ 504/525–5169) and covers the French Quarter.

LATE MAR.➤ The **Tennessee Williams–New Orleans Literary Festival and Writer's Conference** (☎ 504/286–6680), features performances of the author's plays and tours of his favorite French Quarter haunts.

LATE MAR.➤ **Earth Fest** (c/o the Audubon Zoo; *see* Tour 4 *in* Chapter 2) is a fun-filled educational celebration with exhibits, shows, and nationally known entertainers, all with an eye on the environment.

LATE MAR. OR EARLY APR.➤ The **Crescent City Classic** (8200 Hampson St., Suite 217, 70118, ☎ 504/861–8686) is a very popular 10-km foot race culminating in a huge party in Audubon Park.

APR.➤ The **French Quarter Festival** (1008 N. Peters St., 70130, ☎ 504/522–5730) is a weekend of free music and entertainment for all ages throughout the Quarter. It includes fireworks as well as the world's largest jazz brunch.

EARLY TO MID-APR.➤ The **Spring Fiesta** (☎ 504/581–1367) spotlights

the French Quarter's historic homes and includes a parade and the coronation of a queen.

LATE APR.➤ The **New Orleans Jazz and Heritage Festival** (1205 N. Rampart St., 70116, ☎ 504/522–4786) at the Fair Grounds involves more than 4,000 musicians.

LATE MAY➤ The **Greek Festival** (☎ 504/282–0259) fills the Hellenic Cultural Center with Greek music, food, and crafts. Ouzo and baklava are plentiful.

SUMMER

JUNE➤ The **Great French Market Tomato Festival** (☎ 504/522–2621) includes cooking demonstrations and tastings at the French Market.

LATE JUNE➤ **Carnaval Latino** (☎ 504/522–9927) brings the Latin beat downtown for four glorious days. You'll find national and international entertainment, a golf tournament, a foot race, and lots of food and music.

JULY 4➤ The Fourth of July is celebrated in grand style in **Go Forth on the River** (☎ 504/522–5730), a day-long series of music, food and entertainment events along the riverfront and in Woldenberg Park. A spectacular fireworks completes the day.

AUTUMN

FIRST WEEKEND IN SEPT.➤ The **African Heritage Festival International** (☎ 504/949–5610) brings drummers, dancers, craftspeople, and lecturers from across the country to perform in and around Armstrong Park.

EARLY OCT.➤ The **Swamp Festival** means hands-on contact with live Louisiana swamp animals, Cajun food, music, and crafts at Audubon Zoo (*see* Tour 4 *in* Chapter 2).

OCT.➤ **Jazz Awareness Month** is celebrated by daily concerts throughout the city. Check the local daily newspaper for listings of musicians and lecturers.

LATE NOV.–DEC.➤ From Thanksgiving through December, thousands of tree lights surround Storyland and the Carousel Gardens for the evening **Celebration in the Oaks** at City Park (1 Dreyfous Ave., 70119, ☎ 504/483–9415).

DEC.➤ **A New Orleans Christmas** (French Quarter Festival, 1008 N. Peters St., 70116, ☎ 504/522–5730) includes tree lighting, teas, caroling, parades, and open houses all month long. Also included are Réveillon celebrations at various restaurants, including Alex Patout's, Arnaud's, Begue's, and the Rib Room, which feature special fixed price menus for the occasion. Special hotel rates are available Dec. 5–25.

DEC. 24➤ **Christmas Eve Bonfires** are lighted on the Mississippi levees in St. James Parish. The bonfires, legend says, originally were lit by the early settlers to help Papa Noel (the Cajun Santa Claus) find his way to their new homes. The natives begin gathering wood for these huge pyres on Thanksgiving. *New Orleans Paddlewheels* (☎ 504/529–4567) and *New Orleans Steamboat* (☎ 504/586–8777) run boats up the muddy Mississippi for this blazing festival.

DEC. 31➤ **Countdown** is a huge, televised New Year's Eve celebration in Jackson Square, similar to the one in New York's Times Square.

2 Exploring New Orleans

By Mary
Gehman

DO YOU KNOW what it means to miss New Orleans?" The old jazz song, so popular in this city, aptly suggests that there is much to experience while one is here and much to miss when one is away. Despite its sprawling size, to its residents New Orleans is intimate and small-town, made up of dozens of neighborhoods where families have lived within the same blocks for generations. Red beans and rice are served throughout the city on Mondays, people visit the tombs of their departed on All Saints Day, and from the smartest office to the most down-home local bar, folks are ready to celebrate anything at the drop of a hat. As they say in New Orleans, *laissez les bons temps rouler*—let the good times roll!

To experience this fun-filled city, you can begin with the usual tourist attractions, but you must go beyond them to linger in a corner grocery store, sip a cold drink in a local joint, or chat with a stoop-sitter. Orleanians love their city—most of them wouldn't live anywhere else. They treasure custom and tradition, take in stride the heat and humidity of a semitropical climate, and look at life with a laid-back attitude that makes New Orleans a close cousin to her Caribbean neighbors.

The city radiates out from an 8-mile stretch between the Mississippi River and Lake Pontchartrain, covering roughly 365 square miles of flat, swamp-drained land. The heart of the city, Downtown, includes the famous old French area called the *Vieux Carré* (Old Square) or the French Quarter, the Central Business District or the CBD, and the riverfront. Across the river from Downtown is an extension of New Orleans known as the West Bank, which includes the areas of Algiers and Gretna.

The city of New Orleans is composed of four sections that spread out from Downtown: Uptown to the southwest, Mid-City to the north, and Faubourg Marigny and Gentilly to the east. Large suburban areas such as Metairie and Kenner to the west and New Orleans East to the east have developed in the past 30 years and today make up what is called Greater New Orleans.

Receiving directions in a city that bases its compass on the curve of the river can be hopelessly confusing. Canal Street, a long avenue that runs from the river to the lake, divides the city roughly into uptown and downtown sections. Streets to the north of Canal are named North and run downtown, while those to the south of Canal are named South and run uptown. Only the French Quarter is laid out in a grid pattern. Ask an Orleanian for directions and you are likely to hear about so many blocks downriver or upriver on the lake or river side. The best advice is to keep a map handy at all times.

New Orleans's housing patterns are very mixed. It is not uncommon to find mansions on one block and run-down tenements on the next, or nearby. Visitors should be alert to conditions around them, taking precautions not to wander alone on deserted streets or in questionable areas. A high crime rate, as in other cities, is a problem in New Orleans. If in doubt about the safety of sites to visit, ask hotel personnel for advice, tour areas in groups when possible, and take a cab at night. (Areas requiring special precautions are noted in the tours that follow.)

The tours described here introduce various areas of New Orleans and suggest things to see and do in each. The Downtown and Algiers sections are best explored on foot because sites are near each other and should be experienced at a slow pace. For the other areas, biking or driving is recommended owing to the long distances covered. For further ideas, check the Off the Beaten Track and What to See and Do with Children sections before starting out on a given tour. Finding the unexpected is what makes New Orleans fun; the tours that follow are designed with that sense of adventure in mind.

The heart of New Orleans is the French Quarter or Vieux Carré, a 6-by-12-block rectangle along the Mississippi River where the city originally was settled by the French in 1718. Here the Creoles (children born in the colony to French and Spanish settlers) built their stately town houses, cathedral, marketplace, opera houses, and theaters. Here, served by African slaves, they developed one of the most sophisticated styles of living in North America.

Much of this Old World influence began to fade when, in 1803, the Louisiana Purchase was signed and the Americans, predominantly Anglo-Saxon, moved into power. Eventually, the Civil War in the 1860s put an end to the Golden Age of antebellum New Orleans, and the French Quarter went through years of decline and neglect. Only in the past 50 years have the buildings been restored and the French Quarter regained its place as a rare and fascinating center of the city.

Unlike historic downtown areas of many other American cities, the French Quarter is a residential district, sharing streets with shops, restaurants, and offices. It is alive with the sights, sounds, and odors of a major port city and entertainment hub. Yet, behind the wrought-iron gates of its buildings are tranquil, intimate courtyards hidden from view. This intertwining of the public and private in the Quarter gives it a charm rarely matched in other U.S. cities. The Vieux Carré Commission, formed in 1936 to preserve the historic integrity of the Quarter, controls all renovation and rebuilding with strict codes. Notice that, with the exception of Bourbon Street, there are no neon signs or garish flashing lights, and that buildings throughout the Quarter conform to the architectural style of the late 1700s to mid-1800s.

Seeing and doing everything in the French Quarter can take days. The area is best savored on several different occasions, allowing for leisure time to browse in shops, tour museums, snack at cafés, and listen to a street musician or watch a portrait artist at work.

The Quarter is conventionally divided into Upper and Lower, with Jackson Square at the midpoint, but for the following tours we have designated Inner and Outer sectors. The Inner French Quarter includes Jackson Square, the riverfront, and several immediate blocks containing the most frequented and photographed sites. For adventurers with more time and stamina for walking, we recommend the Outer French Quarter, which encompasses some exciting fringe places not as well known but still well worth the effort. You may wish to combine aspects of both tours into one, depending on your interests and the amount of time you have.

Tour 1: Inner French Quarter

Numbers in the margins correspond to points of interest on the Tours 1–3: The French Quarter, Central Business District, and Algiers Point map.

★ ❶ Tours conventionally begin in **Jackson Square.** It is the heart of the French Quarter, much as almost every French town has a square around which are built the church, the seat of government, and major

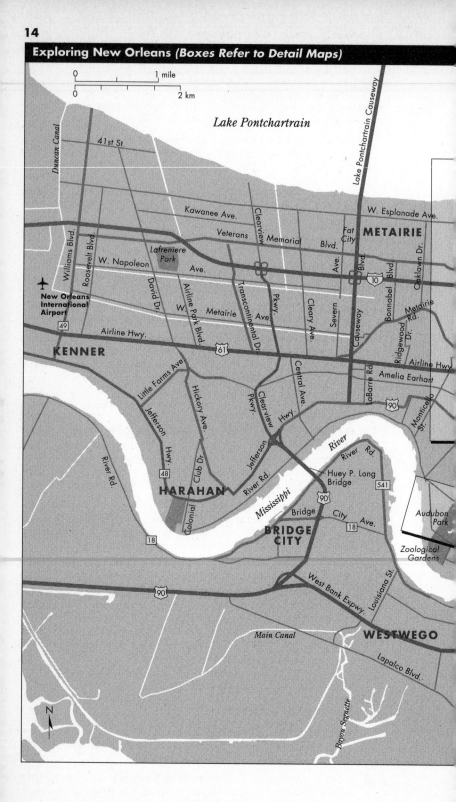

0   1 mile

0   2 km

Lake Pontchartrain

Duncan Canal

41st St.

Kawanee Ave.

W. Esplanade Ave.

Veterans

Clearview

Memorial

Blvd.

Fat
City

METAIRIE

Lake Pontchartrain Causeway

Lafreniere
Park

W. Napoleon

Ave.

Williams Blvd.

Roosevelt Blvd.

David Dr.

Airline Park Blvd.

W.

Transcontinental Dr.

Pkwy.

Ave.

Cleary Ave.

Severn

Ave.

Causeway

Blvd.

Bonnabel Blvd.

Ridgewood

Dr.

Metairie

Rd.

Oaklawn Dr.

**New Orleans
International
Airport**

Metairie

I-10

49

Airline Hwy.

61

KENNER

Airline Hwy

Amelia Earhart

LaBarre Rd.

90

Monticello

St.

Little Farms Ave.

Hickory Ave.

Central Ave.

Clearview

Pkwy.

Jefferson

Hwy.

River

Rd.

River

Road

River Rd.

Huey P. Long
Bridge

541

Jefferson
Hwy.

Club Dr.

48

HARAHAN

River Rd.

Colonial

Mississippi

**Audubon
Park**

Bridge

City

Ave.

18

**BRIDGE
CITY**

18

*Zoological
Gardens*

18

West Bank Expwy.

Louisiana St.

WESTWEGO

90

Main Canal

Lapalco Blvd.

N

Bayou Segnette

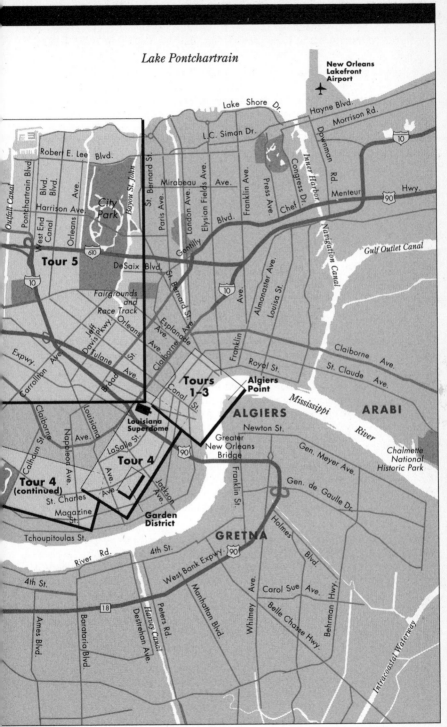

shops. Until the 1850s, the square was called the Place d'Armes, a military marching ground. It was also the site of public executions carried out in various styles, including burning at the stake, beheading, breaking on the wheel, and hanging.

Today Jackson Square is a beautifully landscaped park. A statue of Andrew Jackson, victorious leader of the Battle of New Orleans in the War of 1812, commands the center of the square. The words carved in the base on the cathedral side of the statue—"The Union must and shall be preserved"—are a lasting reminder of the Federal troops who occupied New Orleans during the Civil War and who inscribed those words.

The park is landscaped in a sun pattern, with walkways set like rays streaming out from the center, a popular garden design in the royal court of King Louis XIV, the Sun King. Beware of feeding the pigeons in the park; signs warn of fines imposed on bird feeders. This law is necessary to control the pigeon population. Park gates are open from 8 AM to 6 PM except for special events. In the daytime, dozens of artists hang their paintings on the park fence and set up outdoor studios where they work on canvases or offer to draw portraits of passersby. These artists are easy to engage in conversation and are knowledgeable about many aspects of the Quarter and New Orleans.

Surrounding the park is a flagstone pedestrian mall, which is closed to traffic. All sorts of first-rate street performers entertain here: musicians, break dancers, tap dancers, jugglers, acrobats, mimes, and clowns. Performers are licensed by the city and depend on donations from their audiences to make a living.

❷ St. Louis Cathedral, named for the French king who led two crusades, is the oldest active cathedral in the United States. The current building, which replaced two former structures destroyed by fire, dates from 1794, although it was remodeled and enlarged in 1851. In 1964 the cathedral was elevated to the status of minor basilica, one of only 15 such churches in the United States. Pope John Paul II held a prayer service for clergy here during his New Orleans visit in 1987; to honor the occasion, the pedestrian mall in front of the cathedral was renamed Place Jean Paul Deux. The cathedral is open to the public. Worshipers are always welcome; tours of the building are given daily, 9–5, free of charge.

St. Anthony's Garden, which extends behind the rectory to Royal Street, is dominated by the statue of the Sacred Heart of Jesus at its center. From Royal Street can be seen a monument to 30 members of a French ship who died in a yellow fever epidemic in 1857. In the right-hand alley beside the garden, at **624 Pirate's Alley,** is a house where William Faulkner lived and wrote in the 1920s; today it is a shop, Faulkner House Books. Sherwood Anderson, who resided in the nearby Pontalba Apartments (*see below*), persuaded Faulkner to go back to his home town in Mississippi and write about the people and places he knew best.

Return to the front of the cathedral. The Spanish colonial-style buildings that flank the cathedral were the seat of government for New Orleans during the colonial period; today they are part of the Louisiana State Museum Complex, housing some permanent and ❸ some changing exhibits. The **Presbytere** was originally designed to house the priests of the cathedral; instead, it served as a courthouse under the Spanish and later under the Americans. The *Pioneer,* the first submarine used by the Confederate Navy in the Civil War, is the

★ ❹ curious metal object on display in front of the Presbytere. To the left of the cathedral is the **Cabildo,** named for the Spanish council—or cabildo—that met there. (In 1988 the Cabildo suffered terrible damage from a four-alarm fire. Most of the historic pieces inside the building were saved, but the top floor and roof were destroyed.) The transfer of Louisiana to the United States was made in 1803 in the front room on the second floor overlooking the square. After 1803, the Cabildo served as the city hall and later the supreme court. There are three floors of multicultural exhibits recounting Louisiana history—from the Colonial period through Reconstruction—with countless artifacts, including the death mask of Napoleon Bonaparte. The Cabildo is the older of the two buildings, dating from 1799; the Presbytere was under construction from 1795 to 1847. *Jackson Sq.,* ☎ *504/568–6968.* ☛ *$4 adults, $3 senior citizens and students, children under 12 free.* ☉ *Tues.–Sun. 10–5.*

❺ The **Pontalba Apartments,** two sets of buildings, one on each side of Jackson Square, were built in the late 1840s by the Baroness Micaela Pontalba. The daughter of a wealthy Spaniard, Don Almonester y Rojas, she inherited the prime real estate around the square and had these apartment buildings constructed to leave a permanent European imprint on the heart of the old city. She also helped to fund the landscaping of the square and the erection of Jackson's statue in its center. The strong-willed baroness married her cousin Baron Celestin de Pontalba in France. She caused a scandal on both sides of the Atlantic when she had a near-fatal fight with her father-in-law, left her husband, and returned to Louisiana in the 1840s to build the apartments on the square. She later returned to Paris and is buried there.

❻ The Pontalba Apartments are publicly owned, the side to the right of the cathedral by the state and the other side by the city. In the state side is the **1850s House,** a model of one of the apartments as it looked in 1850 for the first residents. Notice the lovely ironwork on the balconies of the apartments. The baroness introduced cast (or molded) iron with these buildings, and it eventually replaced much of the old handwrought ironwork in the French Quarter. The initials for her families, A and P—Almonester and Pontalba—are worked into the design. A gift shop and bookstore run by Friends of the Cabildo is downstairs. *523 St. Ann St.,* ☎ *504/568–6968.* ☛ *$4 adults, $3 senior citizens and students, children under 12 free.* ☉ *Tues.–Sun. 10–5.*

❼ The **Louisiana Office of Tourism** is a few doors away and a good place to pick up brochures and information about the Quarter, the city, and Louisiana in general. *529 St. Ann St.,* ☎ *504/568–5031.* ☉ *Daily 9–5.*

As you walk up St. Ann Street away from the cathedral you'll notice the carriage stand in front of Jackson Square on Decatur Street, where mule-drawn carriages await passengers from early morning till midnight. These carriages, integral to the Quarter, take half-hour tours around the narrow streets while drivers recite a mixture of folklore and fact about the old city. Mules have replaced horses because mules are more tolerant of high temperatures and can go longer without water.

❽ Cross Decatur Street (beware of the heavy traffic here) and walk up a flight of steps leading to an **overview** of the square on one side and of the Mississippi River on the other. This is a great spot for photographing both attractions.

18

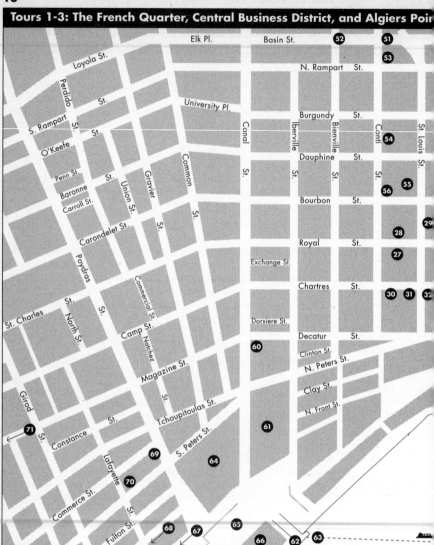

Louis Armstrong Park

N. Rampart St.

Burgundy St.

Toulouse St.   St. Peter St.   Orleans St.   St. Ann St.   Dumaine St.   St. Philip St.   Ursulines St.   Gov. Nicholls St.   Barracks St.   Esplanade Ave.

Dauphine St.

Bourbon St.

Pére Antoine Alley

Pirate's Alley

Royal St.

Wilk Row

Madison St.

Chartres St.

Jackson Square

Decatur St.

Moon Walk

French Market Pl.

N. Peters St.

Mississippi River

Algiers Point

| 0 | 440 yds |
| 0 | 400 m |

Mardi Gras
Museum, **39**

Maspero's
Exchange, **31**

Miltenberger
Houses, **19**

Mint's old walls, **41**

Moon Walk, **11**

Musée Conti Wax
Museum, **54**

Napoleon House, **32**

New Orleans Historic
Voodoo Museum, **47**

New Orleans Jazz
Collection, **40**

New Orleans
Pharmacy Museum, **33**

New Orleans School
of Cooking, **10**

Old Farmer's
Market, **36**

Old Mint, **38**

Old Ursuline
Convent, **16**

Our Lady of
Guadalupe Chapel, **53**

Overview, **8**

Pat O'Brien's Bar, **58**

Piazza d'Italia, **69**

Pontalba
Apartments, **5**

Presbytere, **3**

Preservation Hall, **59**

Quadroon
Ballroom, **23**

Riverwalk, **67**

St. Louis Cathedral, **2**

St. Louis
Cemetery #1, **51**

Spanish Plaza, **66**

Spring Fiesta historic
town house, **48**

Storyville (former
site), **52**

Woldenberg
Riverfront Park, **12**

World Trade
Center, **65**

9 Across the square, to your left on Decatur Street, will be **Jackson Brewery,** also called Jax Brewery, a former brewery now remodeled to house a three-section shopping and entertainment complex. Outside are multilevel terraces facing the river, and inside is a collection of shops, galleries, restaurants, and theme bars. Live music often sounds from various areas. A branch of the **Planet Hollywood** restaurant chain is on the first two floors of the brewery. The **Hard Rock Cafe** in the third section of Jax is another popular attraction (*see* Bars and Lounges *in* Chapter 7, Nightlife and the Arts).

10 For those interested in Creole and Cajun cooking, the **New Orleans School of Cooking** in the first section of the brewery features television cooking personality and local chef Joe Cahn. Reservations for classes and demonstrations are a must. ☎ *504/525–2665.* ☛ *$20 (includes meal).* ◷ *Mon.–Sat. 10–1.*

In front of the overview, beyond the railroad tracks, is a promenade **11 12** along the levee called **Moon Walk** that connects with **Woldenberg Riverfront Park.** This landscaped arcade is named for Moon Landrieu, who was mayor of the city in the 1970s when the walk was built. Here is a breathtaking view of the mighty Mississippi as it curves around New Orleans, giving the city the name of the Crescent City. When facing the river, you see to the right the Greater New Orleans Bridge, a twin span connecting New Orleans to the West Bank, and a ferryboat that crosses the river every 20 minutes as an alternative to the bridge. The river flows to the left downstream for another 100 miles until it meets with the Gulf of Mexico. Directly across the river is the ferry landing and a ship-repair dry dock. A bit farther to the left is a ramshackle multilayer building that is actually a good restaurant and popular nightspot, the Pointe at Algiers Landing. The river is always active with steamboats carrying tour groups, tugboats pushing enormous barges, and ocean-going ships plying its waters. Sometimes a dredge boat is visible, dredging the river's bottom of silt to keep the channel open for large ships. If you are lucky, the steamboat *Natchez* will be readying to leave its dock upriver to the right, and the burst of steam from the engines, followed by the playing of the calliope, will give you the age-old sound of life on the river.

After a stroll along the levee, go back to the overview and walk down **13** to your right to a canopied landmark, **Café du Monde.** For generations locals and visitors have come here for around-the-clock café au lait (equal parts of strong chicory-laced coffee and hot milk) and beignets (pronounced ben-yays), square French doughnuts heaped with powdered sugar. If you step around to the large window behind the café, you can watch the beignets being rolled, cut, and flipped into vats of deep fat for frying. This is especially fun for children.

14 Café du Monde marks the beginning of the **French Market,** a complex of renovated buildings that extends several blocks along Decatur and North Peters streets. Originally an Indian trading post, later a bustling open-air market under the French and Spanish, the French Market has always figured strongly in the life of the city. The buildings, some of them now glass-enclosed, contain shops, offices, and eating places. You'll enjoy exploring them not only from the street but also from the flagstone areas alongside and behind the buildings. On weekends there are usually street performers and musicians enlivening the outdoor areas of the market.

15 Check with the **Folklife and Visitor Center** of the Jean Lafitte National Historical Park for free exhibits on the life and customs of various ethnic groups in Louisiana, as well as for free daily history tours of the French Quarter and Garden District. This office also supervises and provides information on the Jean Lafitte National Park, located across the river from New Orleans, and the Chalmette Battlefield, where the Battle of New Orleans was fought in the War of 1812. *916–918 N. Peters St., in the French Market,* ☎ *504/589–2636.* ☉ *Daily 9–5.*

A few doors down from the visitors center on North Peters Street is the **French Market Information and Visitors Center,** with emphasis on the history, architecture, food, shopping, and entertainment of the French Market itself. *1008 N. Peters St.* ☎ *504/522–2621.* ☉ *Daily 9–6.*

TIME OUT If you are ready for a little relaxation, the **Mediterranean Café,** at the intersection of North Peters and Decatur streets, and the **Gazebo,** a short walk back behind the Mediterranean Café, offer live jazz and cool drinks outdoors in graceful settings. Across Decatur Street is the **Central Grocery** (923 Decatur St.), known for its imported foods and its *muffuletta* sandwich (a round loaf of Italian bread filled with ham and other cold cuts, cheese, and an olive salad), a local favorite.

When you leave the vibrant French Market, walk down Decatur Street to Ursulines Street, named for the nearby convent and grounds of the Ursuline nuns. The Ursulines were the first of many orders of religious women who came to New Orleans and founded schools, orphanages, and asylums, and ministered to the needs of the poor. **16** The **Old Ursuline Convent** stands to the right at the next corner, Chartres Street. Built in 1734, the convent is the oldest French colonial building in the Mississippi valley. Our Lady of Victory Church, adjoining the convent, was added in 1845. The original tract of convent land covered several French Quarter blocks, and the sisters were attended by slaves who occupied a small narrow building still visible from the side facing Ursulines Street. Now an archive for the archdiocese, the convent was used by the Ursulines for 90 years. The Ursuline Academy, the convent's girls' school founded in 1727, is now uptown on State Street, where the newer convent and chapel were built. The academy is the oldest girls' school in the country. The formal gardens, church, and first floor of the old convent are open for guided tours. *1100 Chartres St.,* ☎ *504/529–3040.* ☛ *$4 adults, $2 senior citizens and students, children under 8 free.* ☉ *Tours Tues.–Fri. at 10, 11, 1, 2, and 3; weekends at 11:15, 1, and 2.*

17 Across Chartres Street from the convent is the **Beauregard-Keyes House.** This stately 19th-century mansion was the temporary home of Confederate General P.G.T. Beauregard. The house and grounds had severely deteriorated in the 1940s when the well-known novelist Frances Parkinson Keyes moved in and helped restore it to its former glory. Her studio at the back of the large courtyard remains intact. Keyes wrote 40 novels in this studio, all in longhand, among them the local favorite, *Dinner at Antoine's.* If you do not have time to tour the house, be sure to take a peek through the gates at the beautiful walled garden at the corner of Chartres and Ursulines streets. Landscaped in the same sun pattern as Jackson Square, the garden is in bloom throughout the year. Both garden and courtyard have been a popular romantic setting for several movies filmed in New Orleans. *1113 Chartres St.,* ☎ *504/523–7257.* ☛ *$4 adults, $3 senior citizens, $1.50 children under 12.* ☉ *Mon.–Sat. 10–3; tours on the hr.*

TIME OUT Continuing down Ursulines Street, you'll notice a café on the right, **Croissant d'Or/Patisserie,** where French pastries are baked on the premises. This used to be an Italian ice-cream parlor, Brocato's, and the interior is still adorned with ornate Italian decorations. *617 Ursulines St.,* ☎ *504/524–4663.* ⏲ *Daily 7–5.*

At the next corner turn right on Royal Street and walk a few doors
18 down to **Gallier House** on the right. Gallier House is a restored 1857 town house, originally built by local architect James Gallier as his residence. Besides tours of the house, servants' quarters, and grounds, there are also short films on architectural crafts, changing exhibits on 19th-century life in the city, and a gift shop. Take a moment to look through the carriageway; it is the only one in the city with a carriage parked in it. You can almost hear the horses in the stable shaking their harnesses in anticipation of a trip. *1132 Royal St.,* ☎ *504/523–6722.* ☛ *$5 adults, $4 senior citizens, $2.50 children 6–12.* ⏲ *Mon.–Sat. 10–4:30, Sun. 12:30–4:30.*

Turn and stroll down Royal Street, back past Ursulines Street, and note why this is called the street of balconies. Royal Street boasts some of the most celebrated and beautiful balconies in the country. During the Civil War, while New Orleans was occupied by Federal troops, women in the Quarter used the protection of their balconies to hurl household objects at passing troops and shout out insults. The situation between the ladies and the unwelcome soldiers became so tense that General Benjamin Butler issued the Woman Order in 1862, threatening to arrest offenders and treat them as women of the street "plying their avocation"—a challenge that was met by some local women and that shocked and outraged men of the North and South alike.

Two blocks down Royal Street, at the corner of Dumaine Street, is a complex of three town houses built in 1838 by the widow Marie Mil-
19 tenberger, the **Miltenberger Houses** (900–906 Royal St.). Besides their beautiful iron balconies, the houses also are known for being the birthplace of Alice Heine, the first American princess of Monaco at the turn of the century, preceding Grace Kelly by many years. Princess Alice divorced the prince, however, before any children were born.

At this corner, turn left on Dumaine Street and walk a few doors up
20 to **Madame John's Legacy** (632 Dumaine St.) across the street on the right. Notice the West Indian architecture, with the first floor built high off the ground and a porch (called "gallery" in New Orleans) running around the front and side of the house. The original building dates back to 1726, but the building you see here is an exact replica that was built in the late 1700s, when the 1726 structure was destroyed by fire. The house has undergone some renovation through the years and has had a colorful past. The first owner, Jean Pascal, a French sea captain, was killed by Natchez Indians. Today the historic building is owned and operated by the State Museum Complex and is currently closed to the public. The name "Madame John's Legacy" was adapted in the late 1800s from a short story by New Orleans writer George W. Cable. The popular tale was about Madame John, a "free woman of color" (a localism for free African Americans), who, like many women of her race, became the mistress of a Frenchman. Having never married, her master, John (Jean), bequeathed his house and estate to her on his deathbed.

Turn back to Royal Street and walk to the left a few doors down to
21 one of the Quarter's most unusual shops, **Hové Parfumeur.** This perfume shop was founded in 1931 by Mrs. Alvin Hovey-King, whose

family continues to run the business. Hové perfumes, colognes, and soaps are known internationally, mainly through mail order. Local fragrances created here (such as magnolia and vetiver) are much in demand. New Orleans once had many such shops, but only this one remains. *824 Royal St., ☎ 504/525–7827. ⊘ Mon.–Sat. 10–5.*

A few doors down from the parfumeur, stop and examine the building to the left, an art gallery, and the one across the street and a door down. Both houses are of a modern, 1930s style, in sharp contrast to the balconied buildings on either side of them. The contrast gives you an idea of the buildings of the Quarter that were lost before 1936 when the Vieux Carré Commission was formed to restrict the rapid destruction of the old Quarter.

㉒ Around the corner, left on St. Ann Street, is the **Elizebeth Werlein House** (630 St. Ann St.), the residence of Elizebeth Werlein, who was instrumental in saving many of these old abandoned buildings in the 1930s and 1940s. She died in 1946, but her preservationist efforts continue to this day.

Go back to Royal Street, turn left, and pass the park behind the cathedral. Pause at Orleans Street, which begins there, and look down **㉓** Orleans on the right. The former **Quadroon Ballroom** (717 Orleans St.) is the white wooden balcony on the second floor where, it is believed, free women of color met their French suitors (as Madame John of the house on Dumaine Street is said to have done). The quadroons (people whose ethnic makeup is one-quarter African American) who met here were young, unmarried women. The girls' mothers traditionally accompanied them to the balls to make sure that any man who took a serious interest in their daughters had the means to support both a mistress and the several children who would be born to the relationship. If the Frenchman married a woman of his own race and had a legitimate second family, he often continued to support his first family. If you read the plaque on the building at 717 Orleans Street, you'll learn that the ballroom later became part of a convent and school for the Sisters of the Holy Family, a religious order founded in New Orleans in 1842 by the daughter of a quadroon. The nuns moved in 1964 to a suburb in eastern New Orleans, and the building is now the elegant Bourbon Orleans Hotel.

Royal Street at Orleans Street is closed to traffic for several blocks from 11 AM to 5:30 PM to allow pedestrian access to the lovely shops, art galleries, antiques stores, and restaurants on both sides of the street. At the corner of the next block, at St. Peter Street, on the left is **㉔** **Labranche House** (700 Royal St.), which has some of the finest examples of ironwork in New Orleans on its balconies. Notice the intricate design of oak leaves and acorns. The building and ironwork date back to the 1830s. This corner is one of the most photographed spots in the city, and it is easy to see why. The **A&P Supermarket** across the street is the only such store in the French Quarter. Small and antiquated by today's standards, it nevertheless does a good business with locals.

㉕ Continue down Royal Street and on the right is the **Court of Two Sisters Restaurant** (613 Royal St.), which is housed in a building that dates from 1832 and has one of the most beautiful courtyards in the Quarter. It is named for two sisters, long since gone, who ran a dry-goods shop there. You might want to step down the carriageway and take a look at the courtyard (or court) with permission of the maître d'.

Among the shops on the next block is a local research treasure, the
(26) Historic New Orleans Collection. This private archive, with thousands of historic photos, documents, and books, is one of the finest
research centers in the South. Housed in the 19th-century town house
of General Kemper Williams and the 1792 Merrieult House, the collection offers changing exhibits on local history and tours of the
houses, grounds, and archives. *533 Royal St.,* ☎ *504/523–4662.*
☛ *Tours $2; gallery exhibit and use of research library free. No chil-
dren under 12.* ☉ *Tues.–Sat. 10–5.*

The imposing Victorian building that takes up the whole next block
between St. Louis and Conti streets is the Old New Orleans Court
erected in 1908 to replace a former court facility. After years of
vacancy and neglect, this magnificent edifice has been recently
(27) restored as the elegant new home of the **Louisiana Supreme Court.**
Part of the movie *JFK* was shot here in 1991. Several old and famous
(28) New Orleans restaurants are in this area, including **Brennan's
Restaurant** (417 Royal St.), across the street from the court building,
(29) and **Antoine's Restaurant** (713 St. Louis St.), just around the corner
on the right. Both establishments are located in historic houses and
are known for their traditional Creole cuisine.

Walk around the court building to Chartres Street and take a left. On
(30) the right-hand side in the middle of that block is **K-Paul's Louisiana
Kitchen** (416 Chartres St.), named for the Cajun chef Paul Prudhomme. In recent years Prudhomme has been creating and serving the
Cajun specialties here that have become the rage in other parts of the
country. At the corner on the right is another well-known local eatery,
(31) Maspero's Exchange (440 Chartres St.), which once was a slave
auction house, and for many years thereafter the Exchange Coffee
House, where the city's notable Creoles gathered. An interesting feature of the building is that it seems from the outside to have only two
floors, whereas inside there is a middle floor, called an entresol, in the
section above the window arch at the top of what appears to be the
first floor. This narrow middle floor was used for storage. Only a few
buildings in the Quarter have an entresol.

On the corner across from Maspero's is another landmark, the
(32) Napoleon House (500 Chartres St.). A longtime favorite haunt for
local writers and artists, the house was built in 1814 and reportedly
offered to Napoleon when he was exiled on St. Helena in 1821, but
Napoleon died before arrangements for his rescue could be completed. Now a bar and café, it's a good place to soak up local color
and atmosphere.

(33) Just up Chartres Street is the **New Orleans Pharmacy Museum.** It
bills itself as "the finest historical pharmacy museum in the U.S." This
building was the apothecary shop and residence of America's first
licensed pharmacist, Louis J. Dufilho, in the 1820s. His botanical and
herbal gardens are still cultivated in the courtyard. To tour the
museum is to step back into 19th-century medicine. Even the window
display, with its enormous leech jar and other antiquated parapherna-
lia, is fascinating. *514 Chartres St.,* ☎ *504/565–8027.* ☛ *$2 adults, $1
students, children under 12 free.* ☉ *Tues.–Sun. 10–5.*

La Marquise, across the street at 625 Chartres Street, is a fine French
pastry shop. A half block to the right, on Chartres Street, is Wilkin-
son Row, a shop-lined alley that is closed to traffic during the day to
provide a mall effect. On the next corner at the square and on the left
(34) is **Le Petit Théâtre,** with its entrance around the building on St. Peter

Street. Founded in 1916, this is the oldest community theater in continuous operation in the United States. The building was erected in 1789 and underwent considerable reconstruction in 1960. The patio itself is a Quarter landmark. Seven plays are produced here each season, plus several children's plays. *616 St. Peter St., ☎ 504/522–9958. Admission is by ticket during the theater season, Sept.–June.*

35 Next to the theater is **Le Petit Salon** (620 St. Peter St.), a typical Creole home, which has housed a women's salon or literary group since 1924. Founded by local author and historian Grace King, the salon originally entertained the casts and staff of productions at Le Petit Théâtre. Notice that each of the three balcony railings is unique, so designed by the builder's three daughters, and that the building leans a bit to one side, evidence of age and of the soft soil on which the city of New Orleans rests.

A few doors down, at 636 St. Peter Street, is the house where Tennessee Williams wrote *A Streetcar Named Desire*. An annual spring Williams festival features performances and tours (*see* Festivals and Seasonal Events *in* Chapter 1, Destination: New Orleans).

A turn right and up Pirates Alley brings you into Jackson Square and the spot at which you began.

TIME OUT For the taste of French New Orleans, try the croissants and French breads baked in a brick oven at **La Madeleine** on Jackson Square, corner of Chartres and St. Ann streets. A cup of café au lait adds the crowning touch. *547 St. Ann St., ☎ 504/568–9950. ⊙ Daily 7 AM–9 PM. No credit cards.*

Tour 2: Outer French Quarter

The Outer French Quarter tour requires more walking than the Inner French Quarter tour. The effort will be worth it, as you will get to explore the fringe elements of the Quarter and dabble in voodoo.

36 Begin at the end of the French Market at the covered fruit and vegetable area called the **Old Farmer's Market.** You will see farmers hauling their produce into the city from outlying areas and salespeople hawking garlands of onions, boxes of mirlitons, and other Louisiana **37** produce. Toward the end of this building is the **Community Flea Market,** a child of the 1960s, where dozens of merchants rent tables to sell a variety of goods. The sharp-eyed shopper can find bargains here, especially among the collectibles and local memorabilia, jewelry, ceramics, old magazines, and records. ☛ *Free. ⊙ Daily 7–7.*

38 Walk across Barracks Street, at the end of the market, into the entryway of the **Old Mint,** an imposing building between Decatur, Barracks, and Esplanade streets. Built in 1835, it was the place where the Confederacy minted its money during the Civil War; later Confederate soldiers were imprisoned in the thick-walled mint while Union troops occupied New Orleans. After the war, legal tender again was printed in this building until 1909. Thereafter the mint served a number of needs, among them as an office for the U.S. Coast Guard.

In the late 1970s the state undertook a complete restoration of the mint, turning it into the landmark **Louisiana State Museum.** Housed **39 40** here are the **Mardi Gras Museum** and the **New Orleans Jazz Collection.** The Mardi Gras exhibit includes extravagant costumes, gowns, and Carnival floats. A visit here is not the same thing as a trip to New Orleans during Mardi Gras, but the museum conveys the feeling that stirs the city on Fat Tuesday (Mardi Gras Day). The Jazz Collection is filled with memorabilia of this native music form; a highlight is Louis Armstrong's first trumpet. Also housed in the Old Mint is the **Louisiana Historical Center,** which includes French and Spanish Louisiana archives, open free to researchers by appointment. ☎ *504/568–6968.* ☛ *Either museum: $4 adults, $3 senior citizens, children under 13 free.* ⊙ *Tues.–Sun. 10–5.*

At the Barracks Street entrance of the Mint notice the one remaining ❹❶ sample of the **Mint's old walls**—it'll give you an idea of the building's deterioration before its restoration.

Walk out the gate, turn right to Decatur Street, and go one block up to Esplanade Avenue, the once-grand promenade for Creoles of the French Quarter. You can imagine the sound of horses' hooves and the sight of bonneted women in long dresses carrying their dainty parasols, or of gentlemen in top hats toting walking canes.

❹❷ Make a left on Esplanade Avenue to reach the **Lamothe Guest House** across the avenue (621 Esplanade Ave.), a typical example of the 19th-century mansions that once lined both sides of this tree-covered avenue.

Continue along Esplanade and at Royal Street (the next corner) turn left toward the French Quarter, walk one block to Barracks Street, ❹❸ and make a right. The **first studio of John James Audubon** (706 Barracks St.), the naturalist painter, was a few doors around the corner of the next block. In 1821, Audubon rented a small room in this unassuming house for several months before going to rural Louisiana to work on his bird drawings. His association with New Orleans is memorialized in the name of Audubon Park and the acclaimed Audubon Zoo.

One block down Royal at the corner of Governor Nicholls Street is a ❹❹ **haunted house** (1140 Royal St.). Within this splendid mansion, in the 1830s, Delphine Lalaurie, wealthy mistress of the house, reportedly tortured her slaves; when a fire broke out in the attic in 1834, firefighters found slaves shackled to the walls and in horrible condition. An outraged community is said to have run Madame Lalaurie from the house and demolished what was left of it after the fire. Although much of this story was later put in doubt, rumors persist to this day that the house is haunted by the groans and screams of the unfortunate slaves.

Turn right on Governor Nicholls Street, away from the haunted ❹❺ house, to the **Latrobe House** (721 Governor Nicholls St.), which dates back to 1814. Built by the young New Orleans architect Henry Latrobe, this house, with its modest porticoes, started a passion for Greek Revival architecture in Louisiana, evidenced later in many plantation houses upriver, as well as in a significant number of buildings in New Orleans.

Continuing down Governor Nicholls Street, you come to Bourbon Street. The raucous nightclub-filled area that makes Bourbon Street synonymous with New Orleans doesn't begin for another few blocks. At upper Bourbon you get a sense of the quiet, residential street it was until the 1940s, when lower Bourbon developed its current reputation as "the playground of the South." This area of upper Bourbon has its own reputation as the center of the gay community. In the surrounding blocks is a cluster of lesbian and gay bars (*see* Chapter 7, Nightlife and the Arts); gay men perform as female impersonators in a few clubs farther down on Bourbon Street. This community also stages the outrageous male beauty queen contests at Mardi Gras.

On the next corner, at St. Philip Street, is an ancient, weathered build-
46 ing, **Lafitte's Blacksmith Shop** (941 Bourbon St.). The striking anvil no longer sounds here, only the clinking of glasses—this has long been a favorite local bar for patrons from all walks of life. Legend has it that the pirate Jean Lafitte and his cronies operated a blacksmith shop here as a front for their vast, illicit trade in contraband, though no historic records have been found to support this legend. The building, dating from 1772, is interesting as one of the few surviving exam-
ples of soft bricks reinforced with timbers, a construction form used by early settlers.

This area of Bourbon Street was once known as the home of voodoo queens and doctors. There are no more public voodoo rituals in the city, but some followers still believe in aspects of the religion brought to New Orleans by their ancestors from Haiti and Sainte Domingue.
47 The **New Orleans Historic Voodoo Museum,** to the right on Dumaine Street, is the only such museum in the world and has a large collection of artifacts and information on voodoo. The gift shop sells gris-gris potions and voodoo dolls; readings, lectures, and voodoo and cemetery tours are also available through the museum. *724 Dumaine St.,* ☎ *504/523–7685.* ☞ *$5 adults, $4 senior citizens, $3 children (under 5 free).* ☉ *Daily 10 AM–dusk.*

The famous voodoo queen Marie Laveau lived nearby, but before visiting her stomping grounds, return to Bourbon Street and walk one
48 block to the **Spring Fiesta historic town house.** This lovely 19th-
century home has been restored to its former splendor by the same people who sponsor the annual Spring Fiesta, a celebration of the Quarter's beautiful homes and genteel lifestyle of days gone by. *826 St. Ann St.,* ☎ *504/581–1367. Open to group tours by appointment only.*

Make a left on St. Ann Street and continue another two blocks; in the 1000 block, on the edge of the Quarter, was the home of Marie Laveau, the greatly feared and respected voodoo queen of antebellum New Orleans. Little is known of her historically, although dozens of stories, folktales, and rumors persist today. With her power to cast spells and heal physical ailments as well as heartaches, she became quite influential, counting among her clients some of the wealthiest people in the city. It is not certain which of the small houses on the left side of this block was hers, or even if the original house has survived. Important, though, was the proximity of her house to the park across the next cross street, where the slaves and "free persons of color" congregated in her day in Congo Square, spoke in their native African tongues, danced to their music, and joined Marie Laveau in solemn voodoo rituals.

As you reach the next block, North Rampart Street, the large park
49 that runs for several blocks in front of you is **Louis Armstrong Park,** named for the native son and world-famous musician whose statue is near the brightly lit entrance. It is ironic that Armstrong was not welcome to play the better clubs of his home city during his illustrious career. To the left inside the park is a stone-inlaid circle of ground
50 with a fountain at its center, **Congo Square.** In the distant back-
ground is the **Mahalia Jackson Theater of the Performing Arts,** and to the left, behind Congo Square, is a large gray building, the **Morris F.X. Jeff Municipal Auditorium,** temporary home of **Harrah's Casino** while a permanent casino is being constructed at the foot of Canal Street. A complex of smaller buildings near the center

*of the park houses the new **Black Music Hall of Fame and Museum,** with exhibits and live performances of music from the African diaspora, and of musical styles from around the world. (WWOZ, an FM radio station that broadcasts only New Orleans music, is part of the museum complex.)* ☎ *504/565–6104.* ☛ *$4.* ◷ *Daily 9–5; check local schedules for nighttime activities. Armstrong Park is patrolled by a security detail, but be very careful when wandering through less populated areas of the park.*

The name North Rampart Street indicates that a wall once stood here, at the back of the French Quarter; it was built to protect early settlers against Indian attacks. Walking down North Rampart to the left you will pass **Covenant House,** an architectural award-winning complex constructed in 1988 to house teenage runaways. Another block down, turn right on St. Louis Street, which intersects at the next corner with Basin Street, for which the "Basin Street Blues" was named.

Looking down Basin Street you can see the future site of the **New Orleans Jazz National Historical Park.** Congress approved funding for this project in 1994 to honor the birthplace and creators of jazz. Operated by the Jean Lafitte National Historical Park of which the French Quarter is a part, it will be a linear park with markers at many spots significant to the development of the music.

51 Ahead on Basin Street is **St. Louis Cemetery #1,** the oldest cemetery in the city and typical of the unique, aboveground burial practices of the French and Spanish. Due to the high water level, it was difficult to bury bodies underground without having the coffin float to the surface after the first hard rain. Modern-day burial methods permit underground interment, but many people prefer these ornate family tombs and vaults, which have figured in several movies, among them *Easy Rider.*

Buried here are such notables as Etienne Boré, father of the sugar industry; Homer Plessy of the *Plessy* v. *Ferguson* 1892 U.S. Supreme Court decision establishing the separate-but-equal Jim Crow laws for African Americans and whites in the South; and most notably, Marie Laveau, voodoo queen. Her tomb is marked with Xs freshly chalked by those who still believe in her supernatural powers.

A second Marie Laveau, believed to be her daughter, is buried in **St. Louis Cemetery #2,** four blocks beyond this cemetery, on Claiborne Avenue. A third St. Louis Cemetery is located at the end of Esplanade Avenue, a good drive from here. *Although these cemeteries are open to the public daily from 9 AM to 3 PM, it is dangerous to enter them alone because of frequent muggings inside. See Sightseeing in The Gold Guide's Smart Travel Tips for group tours of cemeteries, or call 504/588–9357.*

Continue down Basin Street one block to Conti Street. In the next blocks of Basin Street to the right is a government housing project, **52** the **Iberville project,** which stands on the former site of **Storyville.** A legitimatized red-light district that lasted from 1897 to 1917, Storyville spawned splendid Victorian homes that served as brothels, and brought uptown and downtown jazz players together for the first time to create what became known as New Orleans jazz. This area has been the subject of many novels, songs, and films; the Louis Malle film *Pretty Baby,* starring a teenage Brooke Shields, was inspired by the Storyville photographer E.J. Bellocq. Always controversial, the district was shut down in 1917 and the buildings razed almost overnight; the housing project was built in the 1930s. Only a historical marker on the "neutral ground" (median) of Basin Street remains to mark alderman Sidney Story's notorious experiment attempting to legalize prostitution and vice.

53 Going from vice to virtue, take a left on Conti Street and follow it to North Rampart Street, where **Our Lady of Guadalupe Chapel** (411 N. Rampart St.) dominates the corner on the left. Known for its large St. Jude shrine, this church was built in 1826 at the edge of the Quarter and found much use as a burying chapel during the waves of yellow fever that later hit the city.

54 Follow Conti Street for another two blocks to the **Musée Conti Wax Museum.** Over 100 wax figures of past and present Louisiana celebrities are arranged in tableaus with written and audio explanations; the gift shop stocks a variety of local memorabilia. *917 Conti St.,* ☎ *504/525–2605.* ☛ *$5.75 adults, $3.50 children 4–17 (amounts include tax).* ✆ *Daily 10–5.*

55 Make a left on Conti to Dauphine Street, and left again on Dauphine to St. Louis Street, where you will find the **Hermann-Grima House** in the middle of the block. This is one of the largest and best preserved examples of American architecture in the Quarter. It has the only restored private stable and the only working 1830s Creole kitchen in the Quarter. Cooking demonstrations on the open hearth are held here all day Thursday from May through October. You'll want to check the gift shop, which contains many local crafts and books. *820 St. Louis St.,* ☎ *504/525–5661.* ☛ *$4 adults, $3 senior citizens, $2 children 8–18.* ✆ *Mon.–Sat. 10–4. Last tour at 3:30.*

56 Continue on St. Louis Street a half block to **Bourbon Street,** the busy, world-famous entertainment strip. On the right is Jelly Roll's, a slick music club featuring Al Hirt and his trumpet (*see* Chapter 7, Nightlife and the Arts). There is probably a **Lucky Dog vendor** nearby, with a vending cart shaped like a hot dog—John Kennedy Toole immortalized these in his Pulitzer Prize–winning novel about New Orleans, *A Confederacy of Dunces.* **Chris Owens Club** (502 Bourbon St.) is the last of a tradition of one-woman shows on the strip. For several decades Owens has been a favorite local cabaret dancer and performer. Go left to the next corner at Toulouse Street, where an **57** engraved marker points out the former location of the **French Opera House,** which burned down in 1919 and was never rebuilt. Probably no other building in the South saw more celebrities and musical hits in its day; the elegant elliptical auditorium, with its four tiers of seats, accommodated 1,800 guests. While on rowdy Bourbon Street, keep in mind that until the end of World War II, this was a quiet residential area, with small shops and an occasional cabaret or theater.

58 At the corner of the next block (St. Peter St.), music blares from several clubs. To your right is the party animal's landmark, **Pat O'Brien's Bar** (718 St. Peter St.). Many visitors don't consider their stay in New Orleans complete without a Pat O'Brien's Hurricane, a sweet, highly intoxicating mixed drink served in a tall lantern-shaped glass (which you may keep). You can toast to your future in a beautiful courtyard to the sounds of a rousing piano tune.

★ **59** Our tour concludes on a slightly less boisterous musical note at **Preservation Hall.** Although a neighbor to Pat O'Brien's, this music club offers strictly old-time New Orleans jazz, and it is one of the best places in town to catch native singers and musicians. The admission allows you to stay for as many sets as you wish. No food or drink is served on the premises. The room is neither heated nor air-conditioned, and the plain wooden benches are hard; this is serious, no-frills music. *726 St. Peter St.,* ☎ *504/522–2841.* ☛ *$3.* ☾ *Daily 8 PM–midnight.*

Tour 3: Foot of Canal Street and Algiers Point

One of the fastest-growing and most exciting areas of New Orleans is where Canal Street meets the river. Referred to by locals as the foot of Canal Street, it is within walking distance of the French Quarter (about 10 minutes) and most downtown hotels. The riverfront has been dramatically developed in recent years, and the former riverfront site of the 1984 World's Fair has been incorporated into the commercial CBD. The RTA (Regional Transit Authority) has a streetcar that rolls through the bustling riverfront area. You may want to catch it to some of the sites covered in the following tour (*see* Streetcars *in* The Gold Guide).

Begin a few blocks from the river on Canal Street at Decatur, where 200 years ago the river met the land; look down the four blocks to the left that lead to the Mississippi River and note how much alluvial soil has been deposited by the river over the years—land that today is some of the most valuable in the city.

A word about the wide median strip in Canal Street, called neutral ground by locals: In the early 1800s, after the Louisiana Purchase, the French Creoles residing in the French Quarter were strictly segregated from the Americans who settled on the upriver side of Canal Street. The two communities had separate governments and police systems, what is now Canal Street was neutral ground between them. Today animosities between these two groups are amusing history, but the term neutral ground has survived as the name for all medians throughout the city.

60 On the corner of Decatur and Canal streets is an enormous building, the old **Custom House,** which occupies the whole block. Built in 1849, it replaced what had been Fort St. Louis, which guarded the old French city. The building has identical entrances on all four sides, because at the time it was completed no decision had been made as to which side would be the main entrance. The Custom House has been home to many, including General Butler, commanding officer of the Union troops during the Civil War occupation of New Orleans; today it houses government offices.

61 Down Canal Street to the left is **Canal Place,** a fashionable shopping complex with such tony stores as Saks Fifth Avenue, Brooks Brothers, and Ralph Lauren Polo. **Canal Place Cinema** on the third floor is the only place in this area that screens first-run movies. The four comfortable screening rooms and concession stand feature artwork based on local novelist Walker Percy's *The Moviegoer.* The Westin Canal Place Hotel tops the complex; its dining rooms and lobby have a fantastic view of the river.

62 At the end of Canal Street on the left is the **Aquarium of the Americas,**
★ with **Woldenberg Riverfront Park** (*see* Tour 1, *above*) around and behind it, forming a major educational and entertainment attraction. In

the aquarium, more than 7,000 different aquatic creatures swim in 60 separate displays ranging from 500 to 500,000 gallons of water. There are four major exhibit areas: the *Amazon River Basin,* the *Caribbean Reef,* the *Mississippi River,* and the *Gulf Coast,* each featuring fish and animals native to that environment. The spectacular design allows viewers to feel part of the watery world by offering close-up encounters with the inhabitants. A gift shop and café are on the premises. The beautifully landscaped 16-acre park surrounding the aquarium is a tranquil spot with an excellent view of the ever active Mississippi. *Foot of Canal St.,* ☎ *504/861–2538.* ☞ *Aquarium: $9.75 adults, $7.50 senior citizens, $5 children 3–12.* ☼ *Aquarium: Sun.–Wed. 9:30–5, Thurs. 9:30–8, Fri.–Sat. 9:30–6, closed Dec. 25; Woldenberg Riverfront Park: weekdays 6 AM–10 PM, weekends 6 AM–midnight. Package tickets for the aquarium and a river cruise are available outside the aquarium. You can also combine the aquarium, river cruise, and the Audubon Zoo in a package or you can take the river cruise by itself. Call 504/586–8777 for cruise and combination prices.*

The **Liberty Monument,** a controversial reminder of the 1874 battle of whites to regain power over a black and white Reconstruction regime, is secluded on a small plot behind the aquarium and facing the parking lot of Canal Place. The monument was removed from its prominent original location on Canal Street in 1989 and re-erected by court order at the current site three years later. It continues to draw occasional rallies and protests around racial issues.

63 Directly ahead on Canal Street is the terminal for the **Canal Street Ferry,** offering a ride across the river to a part of New Orleans called Algiers. Pedestrians climb the stairs and board the ferry from above, while bicycles and cars board from below on the left of the terminal. The trip takes about 20 minutes; ferries run from 6:30 AM to about 9:30 PM, sometimes until midnight during special events. Be sure to check with the attendants if you are crossing in the evening—it is no fun to be stranded on the other side. Keep in mind, too, that there are no rest-room facilities in the terminals or on the ferry itself, and no food or drink concessions. Special arrangements for people with disabilities must be made with an attendant. The ferry ride is an experience in itself, offering great views of the river and the New Orleans skyline, and the heady feeling of being on one of the largest and most powerful rivers in the world. ☎ *504/364–8100.* ☞ *$1 round-trip per car, free for pedestrians.*

If you ride the ferry, you can explore the historic district of Old Algiers and tour the warehouses in **Blaine Kern's Mardi Gras World,** where the parade floats are made. This could be a morning or afternoon excursion by itself (*see* Algiers Point Side Trip, *below*).

By the time you read this, the area up Canal Street on the left may be undergoing major changes (and a good deal of disruption) as
64 Louisiana's first land-based casino, **Harrah's,** (*see* Chapter 7, Nightlife and the Arts) is constructed on the site of the former Rivergate Exhibition Center. Traffic may be rerouted to open the area around the casino to pedestrians.

65 Across from the casino site stands the **World Trade Center** (2 Canal St.), home to dozens of foreign consulates and many international trade offices. There is an observation deck near the top of this 33-floor building. ☎ *504/581–4888.* ☞ *$2 adults, $1 children.* ☼ *Daily 9–5.*

For adult visitors to the Trade Center there is a revolving bar on the top floor called **Top of the Mart.** A live dance band makes this a most romantic spot. ☉ *Weekdays mid-morning–midnight, weekends mid-morning–1 AM.*

The World Trade Center is surrounded by statues and plazas from three countries. Joan of Arc straddles her horse in a gold-plated statue in **Place de France** out front. Winston Churchill is memorialized in a bronze statue in **British Park Place,** to the right. A bronze equestrian statue of Bernardo de Galvez, Spanish governor of Louisiana in the 1780s, guards the entrance of **Spanish Plaza** to the left. These statues represent the countries that contributed to the settlement and success of New Orleans—France, Spain, and England. Because Harrah's Casino is under construction across the way, some of this area may be inaccessible; there are even plans to relocate the statue of Joan of Arc.

Behind the World Trade Center toward the river are a loading area and ticket offices for riverboats and a large plateau with beautiful inlaid
66 tiles and a magnificent 50-foot fountain. This **Spanish Plaza** was a gift from Spain in the mid-1970s; a platform near the fountain often hosts local bands. To the right, down several steps, is the entrance into
67 **Riverwalk,** an old warehouse district that has been transformed into a half-mile marketplace holding more than 200 shops, cafés, and restaurants. There are three tiers, connected by a promenade that stretches along the river's edge. Plaques along the walkway relate bits of the Mississippi River's history and folklore. At the Poydras Street streetcar stop is a grand splash of color, a 200-foot-long Mexican mural on the flood wall. The tropical motifs are creations of Julio Quintanilla, and the mural is a gift to New Orleans from Merida, Mexico, the artist's native city.

If you exit from the third level of the Riverwalk, you can see how the marketplace complex conveniently ties the Hilton Hotel and Spanish Plaza at its lower end to the New Orleans Convention Center at its upper end. This stretch of land held the 1984 Louisiana World Exposition (World's Fair).

68 The **Ernest N. Morial Convention Center** (900 Convention Center Blvd.) is another outgrowth of the World's Fair. One of the largest convention facilities in the country, it was completed in 1985 and has since undergone two expansions to accommodate even larger bookings. The center has 1.1 million square feet of space and is named for the mayor who oversaw the construction of the center's first phase.

Take Convention Center Boulevard back to Poydras Street and walk
69 left on Poydras for three short blocks to **Piazza d'Italia.** This modern, award-winning plaza has been featured in several movies, most prominently in the opening scene of *The Big Easy.* There has been considerable controversy over the current construction of a hotel complex that includes the Piazza in its design. *The areas around the Convention Center and the Piazza tend to be deserted at times and can be unsafe; use caution when displaying cameras and travel bags.*

70 To the left of the piazza is the **American-Italian Museum,** where Italian-Orleanian customs are explained. The research library includes records of local Italian immigrants. *537 S. Peters St., ☎ 504/522–7294. ☛ Free. ☉ Wed.–Fri. 10–4; call ahead.*

71 The **Louisiana Children's Museum,** which has undergone a major expansion, is a few blocks behind the piazza. The museum, with its hands-on activities, miniature hospital, grocery store, and so forth, is a special treat for children up to age 12. *428 Julia St., ☎ 504/523–*

1357. ☛ *$4 adults, children under 1 free.* ☉ *Tues.–Sat. 9:30–5:30, Sun. noon–5:30. Hrs may vary by season.*

TIME OUT **L'Economie Restaurant,** a block behind Piazza d'Italia, is an intimate sidewalk French bistro owned by chef Hubert Sandot of France. The menu consists of nouvelle cuisine at reasonable prices ($7–$10 entrées). Be sure to try Abita Beer, a local brew from across the lake in Abita Springs. Sandot has lovingly restored this 75-year-old restaurant, which retains its working-class warehouse-district look. *325 Girod St.,* ☏ *504/524–7405.* ☉ *Mon.–Sat. 11 AM–2 PM and 6–9:30 PM. MC, V.*

Algiers Point Side Trip

Directly across the Mississippi River from the French Quarter and Canal Street is the neighborhood of Algiers. Extending out into the curve of the river is the area known as **Algiers Point.** This 25-block area is accessible by a ferry ride across the river that departs from Canal Street (*see above*).

Settled at the turn of the century, this extension of New Orleans is a world apart from the city. Its quiet, tree-lined streets, quaint shops, and renovated Victorian houses are aspects of a community that has managed to remain somewhat isolated. In the early days of New Orleans, Algiers was a holding area for the African slaves from the many ships that made their way into the port. The slaves were ferried across the river to the French Quarter, where they were auctioned. It is speculated that Algiers is named for the North African slave port.

The best way to appreciate the beauty of the houses and their varied architecture is on foot. As you disembark the ferry, walk down to the right where Delaronde Street curves around to the left and follow it several blocks past the finest homes in **Algiers Point's historic renovation district.** On the left is a large sand-colored building owned by Louisiana Power & Light Co.; notice how the initials LP&L are worked into a decorative pattern within the blocks used to make the building.

There is a one-man Algiers welcoming and information committee, Russell Templet, in the Hair and Style Shop across from the LP&L building. Feel free to drop in at Templet's shop to say hello. Dry Dock Café, to the right of the barbershop, is a friendly restaurant and bar with moderate prices.

Follow Delaronde Street for three more blocks to Verret Street. Note the various sizes and styles of houses, from ornate mansions to modest shotgun houses (in which all the doors open one behind another in a straight line, so you could fire a gun from the front step to a backyard wall without hitting a wall in between), a popular working-class architecture in New Orleans. Since these homes were all built around the early 1900s, they reflect the Victorian influence in vogue at that time. In the last 30 years, many of these old homes have been restored to their original elegance.

Turn right at Verret Street. In the next block down Verret Street, in a scene reminiscent of provincial French towns, is a triangular park surrounded by small houses and shops with a large Catholic church, **The Holy Name of Mary Church,** a fine example of 1920s Gothic, dominating the left side.

Follow Verret another two blocks to **Opelousas Street,** heart of Old Algiers, and turn right. This wide tree-canopied avenue looks much like those of Uptown New Orleans. The playground to the right has six great magnolia trees. Across Opelousas Street are shops and churches like those in any small-town center.

The operational **firehouse** on the next corner looks as if it's straight out of the 1930s. Turn-of-the-century houses with typical New Orleans gingerbread lend a nostalgic atmosphere to this tranquil area.

Opelousas Street ends after the next block, and predictably curves left to follow the river on Brooklyn Avenue. Straight ahead is a cluster of newly renovated cottages purchased and moved here to use as offices for the Compass Barge Company. Surprisingly, these offices create a harmonious, almost rural setting.

To the left, three blocks down Brooklyn Avenue, is the real attraction on this side of the river, **Blaine Kern's Mardi Gras World,** the largest float-building firm in the world. A tour here takes you through the warehouses, or dens, where the spectacular floats for over 40 Mardi Gras parades are constructed. Visitors can watch the artists and builders at work, view a film about Mardi Gras, and buy Carnival memorabilia in the gift shop. A photo of yourself with one of the giant figures used on the floats makes a terrific souvenir. Blaine Kern has for many years been the best-known artist and creator of Mardi Gras floats; he often personally conducts tours through this one-of-a-kind facility. A free shuttle van meets the ferry to take visitors to Mardi Gras World (and it's a good idea to use it; the blocks before you get there are often deserted). *233 Newton St.,* ☎ *504/361–7821.* ☛ *Guided tours: $5.50 adults, $4.50 senior citizens, $3.25 children 3–12.* ⊙ *Daily 9:30–4:30, except 2 wks before Mardi Gras.*

To conclude the Algiers Point tour and return to the ferry, follow Powder Street, right from the end of Opelousas Street, back along the river. **Algiers Iron Works and Dry Dock Company** is on the left, as evidenced by the huge steel equipment used to repair river-going vessels. Where Powder Street curves into Pelican Street, take the footpath to the left leading up onto the **levee** and follow this for two blocks back to the ferry landing. This is a great spot for picture taking, with a view of the river and the New Orleans skyline.

The Pointe at Algiers Landing, a deceptively ramshackle multilevel building visible from the bend of the river past the ferry entrance, is a fine restaurant with a magnificent view.

Tour 4: St. Charles Avenue Streetcar Tour

Numbers in the margin correspond to points of interest on the Tour 4: St. Charles Avenue Streetcar Tour maps.

★ The best way to explore the CBD, the Garden District, and Uptown New Orleans is a ride on the historic **New Orleans Streetcar,** the hallmark of the city. In the early 1900s streetcars were the most prominent mode of public transit and ran on many streets, but today they run along the riverfront and up and down St. Charles Avenue; the streetcars are well maintained by the RTA, which also operates the city buses. ☛ *$1 one-way (exact change).* ⊙ *24 hrs daily, about every 10 min 7 AM–8 PM, every ½ hr 8 PM–midnight, every hr midnight–7 AM.*

You can also rent a cassette at 127 Carondolet (☎ 504/561–1001; ⊙ Mon.–Sat. 9–4) near the start of the line to narrate the ride along St. Charles Avenue and introduce you to lively New Orleans music.

People living and working along its route depend heavily on the streetcar; plan your trip to avoid rush hours—7 to 9 AM and 3 to 6

PM—or you may have to stand much of the way and will not be able to enjoy the scenery or sites.

A number of sightseeing points in the area are not visible from the streetcar route and require walking several blocks. These side trips can be condensed into three main points of diversion, each taking from one to two hours. You may want to skip one or two of them this time and plan a return trip later. The streetcar route also has been shortened here to end at Riverbend, where St. Charles Avenue becomes Carrollton Avenue. If you have more time and want to take the streetcar to its end at Claiborne Avenue, stay on for about another 10 minutes and enjoy the ride through what was once the separate town of Carrollton.

Whether you exit the streetcar at Riverbend or Claiborne Avenue, you can return to Canal Street and the French Quarter either by streetcar or bus. Remember to exit the streetcar from the front; the signs may say to exit in the rear, but no one does—only the tourist!

❶ To begin the tour, board the streetcar at the **St. Charles/Common Street carstop,** off Canal Street (in the French Quarter, Royal St. changes its name to St. Charles Ave. upon crossing Canal St.). The stop is at Common Street, marked by a small yellow sign. If you miss one streetcar, duck into the **Pearl Restaurant's** oyster bar, two doors down on St. Charles, and have some fresh, salty, raw oysters while awaiting the next streetcar.

The first 4 blocks up St. Charles are not remarkable; they include office buildings and banks typical of any central business district. At the third stop, Poydras Street, the skyscrapers on either side are among the most impressive in the city—the 27-story **Pan American Life Insurance building** on the left and the 50-story **One Shell Square** on the right. Exit at Poydras Street for the Civic Center and Superdome side trip.

Superdome and Civic Center Side Trip

A good walk—about 8 blocks—down Poydras to the right off St. Charles Avenue brings you to the Louisiana Superdome and the nearby Civic Center. Along the way you will pass several impressive office buildings, the newest and most innovative being the **Louisiana Land and Exploration Building** (901 Poydras St.) fronted by two lovely bronze sculptures by Enrique Alferez, and the **Energy Centre** (1100 Poydras St.), with its towering fountain sculpture in front. Don't be intimidated by the policeman poised near the fountain; he is made of bronze and is one of several lifelike bronzes scattered around the city.

Across Loyola Avenue, on the left, is a complex of interconnected buildings that include the **Hyatt Regency Hotel,** the **Texaco Build-**
❷ **ing,** and **Poydras Plaza** (facing Loyola Ave.). The **New Orleans Centre,** farther down on the left, is the city's newest and poshest shopping mall, positioned opportunely between the Superdome and the Hyatt Regency. The center services the many conventions and
★ ❸ events held in the **Louisiana Superdome,** site of many Sugar Bowls and Super Bowls and home to the New Orleans Saints football team. The dome seats up to 100,000 people and can be partitioned into smaller areas for special events. The parking garage accommodates 5,000 cars and 250 buses. With a 166,000-square-foot playing field and a roof that covers almost 8 acres at a height of 27 stories, this is one of the largest buildings of its kind in the world. It was built in 1975 for more than $180 million.

Tour 4: St. Charles Avenue Streetcar Tour

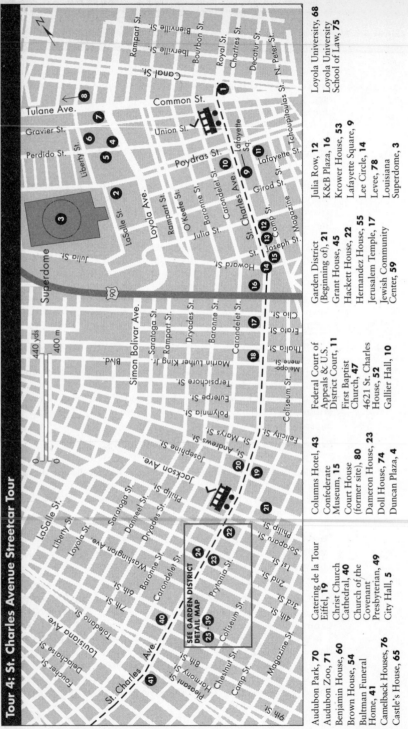

Audubon Park, **70**
Audubon Zoo, **71**
Benjamin House, **60**
Brown House, **54**
Bultman Funeral Home, **41**
Camelback Houses, **76**
Castle's House, **65**

Catering de la Tour Eiffel, **19**
Christ Church Cathedral, **40**
Church of the Covenant Presbyterian, **49**
City Hall, **5**

Columns Hotel, **43**
Confederate Museum, **15**
Court House (former site), **80**
Dameron House, **23**
Doll House, **74**
Duncan Plaza, **4**

Federal Court of Appeals & U.S. District Court, **11**
First Baptist Church, **47**
4621 St. Charles House, **52**
Gallier Hall, **10**

Garden District (Beginning of), **21**
Grant House, **45**
Hackett House, **22**
Hernandez House, **55**
Jerusalem Temple, **17**
Jewish Community Center, **59**

Julia Row, **12**
K&B Plaza, **16**
Krower House, **53**
Lafayette Square, **9**
Lee Circle, **14**
Levee, **78**
Louisiana Superdome, **3**

Loyola University, **68**
Loyola University School of Law, **75**

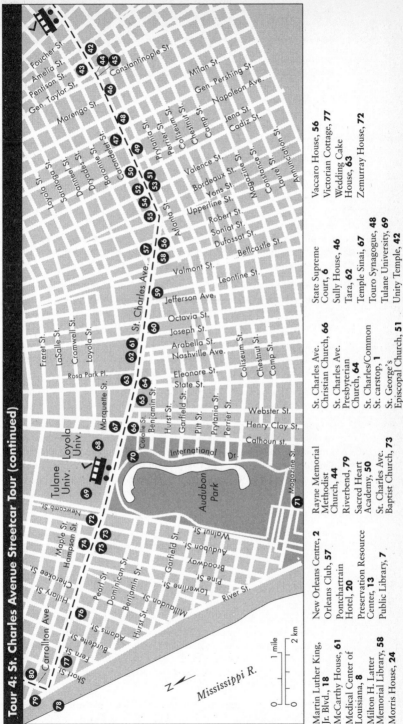

Tour 4: St. Charles Avenue Streetcar Tour (continued)

The Arena, a 20,000-seat multipurpose sports arena, is under construction behind the Superdome. It will be home court for Tulane basketball and is designed to attract an NBA franchise in the future.

In addition to sports, the Superdome has a full schedule of conventions, Mardi Gras balls, and such events as the circus and ice-skating shows. The National Republican Convention was held here in 1988. *One Sugar Bowl Dr.,* ☎ *504/587–3810.* ☛ *Tour: $6 adults, $5 senior citizens, $4 children 5–10.* ☯ *Tours daily at 10, noon, and 2, except during some Superdome events.*

Across from the Superdome on Poydras is a large abstract sculpture called **The Krewe of Poydras,** by Ida Kohlmeyer, designed to evoke the frivolity and zany spirit of Mardi Gras. It has had many other interpretations. Walk back one block to Loyola Avenue and take a left at the Juvenile Court Building at the corner. Beyond the courthouse on

❹ the left is a wide open area, **Duncan Plaza,** landscaped with grassy knolls and a large, open, African-style pavilion in the center. Around the plaza are the buildings that make up the **Civic Center: City Hall** on

❺ the left, the **State Office Building** straight ahead, and (until it moves

❻ to the French Quarter) the **State Supreme Court** to its right.

❼ To the right, across Gravier Street, is the **public library,** and a block

❽ behind it towers the **Medical Center of Louisiana** (formerly Charity Hospital). The massive public hospital system includes two nearby medical schools—Louisiana State University and Tulane University.

The streets around the Superdome and Civic Center are usually busy during business hours, but at night and on weekends this area generally is deserted and should not be explored alone after dark.

To see more of the CBD, return to the St. Charles Avenue streetcar by way of Gravier Street, at the lower end of Duncan Plaza.

The next three stops along St. Charles Avenue pass through the seat of the American government during New Orleans's antebellum years.

❾ **Lafayette Square** is on the left at the first stop (Lafayette St.), and

❿ **Gallier Hall,** the former city hall, is on the right. (The French Creoles controlled the French Quarter and had their own city government on Jackson Square.) The statue in Lafayette Square on the white granite pedestal facing St. Charles Avenue is of John McDonogh, benefactor of public education in New Orleans and the man for whom many public schools are named. The bronze statue in the center of the square is of Henry Clay, the Kentucky statesman who was a frequent visitor to the city in the mid-1800s.

Gallier Hall is considered the finest example of Greek Revival architecture in New Orleans, with Grecian Ionic touches and a portico of white marble. Built in 1850, it was designed by local architect James Gallier, whose name it bears. This was the seat of Reconstructionist rule after the Civil War, and the building saw many political demonstrations during its days as city hall. In the 1950s a new city hall was built in the Civic Center, six blocks to the right on Loyola Avenue. Gallier Hall has since been used for city offices and as a reception facility and theater.

⓫ On the far side of Lafayette Square is the **Federal Court of Appeals,** and barely visible to its left is the **U.S. District Court,** site of the two lengthy federal trials of Louisiana Governor Edwin Edwards in 1986 and 1987. The Cajun governor, nicknamed the Silver Fox, was acquitted of racketeering in both trials but lost his bid for another term as governor to Buddy Roemer in 1987. He came back to defeat Roemer in 1991.

⑫ Just past the next stop is Julia Street; the block on the left, **Julia Row,** has 13 row houses lining the entire right side of the block. These homes were occupied by prominent Americans in the 1840s, but the whole area deteriorated badly during this century. Ambitious and extensive renovations in the early 1980s have brought the original row houses back to some of their former finery.

⑬ In Julia Row is the **Preservation Resource Center,** with materials and displays on local historic architecture. The center also offers architectural tours through various neighborhoods to groups by special arrangement; check for details. *604 Julia St.,* ☎ *504/581–7032.* ☉ *Weekdays 9–5.*

The 400 and 500 blocks of Julia Street, between St. Charles Avenue and the river—the **Warehouse District**—is now the hub of the city's art community (*see* Galleries *in* Chapter 7, Nightlife and the Arts).

The most notable establishment in the next block of St. Charles is the **Hummingbird Grill** (804 St. Charles Ave.), an aging greasy spoon fictionalized by New Orleans novelists and dear to many Orleanians of all social strata. Coming up at the intersection of Howard Avenue is **⑭** **Lee Circle,** a neatly trimmed mound with a pyramid-like base that supports a 60-foot white marble column topped with a bronze statue of Confederate General Robert E. Lee. He stands facing due north as he has since 1884. Several historic buildings on Lee Circle are being renovated and will eventually join the **Contemporary Arts Center**— a block to the left—in forming a major arts complex of the South. The center, developed by the University of New Orleans with developer and art collector Roger Ogden and oilman Patrick Taylor, will eventually include an art museum, and conference, studio, and retail art facilities.

⑮ To the left of the circle, barely visible from the streetcar, is an ivy-covered stone building, the **Confederate Museum,** the oldest museum in Louisiana. Built in 1891, the museum contains an extensive collection of artifacts and records from the Civil War. *929 Camp St.,* ☎ *504/523–4522.* ☛ *$4 adults, $2 children under 16.* ☉ *Mon.–Sat. 10–4.*

⑯ To the right, as the streetcar turns at Lee Circle, is the **K&B Plaza** (1055 St. Charles Ave.), a tall office building with a wonderful collection of outdoor sculptures. The eye-catching abstract piece facing Lee Circle, titled "The Mississippi," is by Isamu Noguchi. Other sculptures include those by Henry Moore, Duane Hanson, and George Segal. The plaza, erected in 1973, won an award from the American Institute of Architects. A collection of works by local and international artists (including Renoir, Boccioni, and Calder) is displayed throughout the building. ☎ *504/586–1234.* ☉ *Plaza: 24 hrs daily; Building lobby: Weekdays 8–5.*

On the next corner, where the I–10 expressway enters St. Charles **⑰** Avenue, is the **Jerusalem Temple** (1137 St. Charles Ave.), home to the city's large Shriner community. Built in 1916, the temple features intricate mosaic tile scenes on its facade. Two stops after Lee Circle is the **⑱** intersection of **Martin Luther King, Jr. Blvd.** on the right, which is called Melpomene Street on the left. The stretch was renamed in the early 1970s to honor the martyred civil rights leader; his bust is displayed on Claiborne Avenue near the intersection of Martin Luther

King, Jr. Blvd. King helped found the Southern Christian Leadership Conference (SCLC) in New Orleans in the **New Zion Baptist Church** (2319 Third St.) in this area.

(19) After three more stops comes a wildly different building on the left, the home of **Catering de la Tour Eiffel** (2040 St. Charles Ave.). Adding a modern French touch to New Orleans, this structure was salvaged from the original restaurant inside the Eiffel Tower in Paris. Each piece was shipped here and carefully reassembled in 1986, to become one of the more novel restaurants in the city. On the right approaching the **(20)** next stop is the **Pontchartrain Hotel** (2031 St. Charles Ave.), a venerable, old-style grand hotel (*see* Chapter 6, Lodging).

(21) The wide intersection at the next stop is Jackson Avenue, traditionally considered the beginning of the **Garden District.** Stately mansions on either side of the avenue attest to the taste and wealth of the American settlers who swarmed to New Orleans and built their fortunes after the Louisiana Purchase in 1803. St. Charles Avenue cuts through the edge of the fashionable Garden District; most of the district is located in the next five blocks on the left. To get a closer look at these homes, exit the streetcar three stops up at Washington Avenue and take the Garden District side tour (*see below*).

(22) On the left before the next stop, First Street, is the **Hackett House** (2336 St. Charles Ave.), dating back to the 1850s. The Greek Revival style (a simple, columned design) of the Hackett House is typical of the early days of the Garden District. Other houses of note are the **(23)** **Dameron House** (2524 St. Charles Ave.), on the left at the Third **(24)** Street stop, and the **Morris House** (2525 St. Charles Ave.), across on the right. Washington Avenue, intersecting at the next stop, is in the heart of the Garden District. Exit here for the Garden District side trip.

Garden District Side Tour

The Garden District lives up to its name in its beautifully landscaped gardens surrounding elegant antebellum homes. None of the private homes is open to the public on a regular basis, but their occupants do not mind visitors enjoying the sights from outside the wrought-iron fences that surround these magnificent estates.

Group tours of this area are available (*see* Tour Operators *in* The Gold Guide). The helpful book *The Great Days of the Garden District,* by Ray Samuel, can be bought at the first stop on the Garden District tour, The Rink.

Numbers in the margin correspond to points of interest on the Garden District Side Tour map.

(25) Begin one block from the streetcar at the intersection of Washington Avenue and Prytania Street. On the left corner is **The Rink** (2727 Prytania St.), a roller-skating rink—the South's first—in the 1880s; now it houses a collection of specialty shops. At the Rink, **PJ's Coffee Shop** is a good place to relax and read something from the **Garden District Bookstore,** which has a good selection of regional, rare, and old books. Sometimes the novelist Anne Rice does autographings of her vampire books here. You can ask about her proposed doll museum in the former girls' orphanage, St. Elizabeth's, nearby on Napoleon Avenue where Rice now lives.

(26) Across Washington Avenue is the facade of the **Behrman Gym** (1500 Washington Ave.), which dates from the turn of the century, when it was the Southern Athletic Club. This gym contained the first indoor pool in the South, and is also famed for being the training site of John

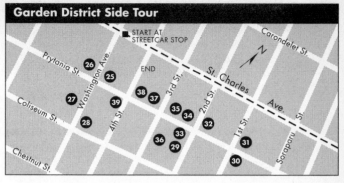

Garden District Side Tour

L. Sullivan when he fought "Gentleman Jim" Corbett. Today only the impressive facade on Washington Avenue remains.

Continuing down Washington Avenue toward Coliseum Street, notice that the 1600 block, on the right, is taken up by the white-walled **Lafayette Cemetery.** This area used to be the city of Jefferson in the early 1800s; the Americans settled here when the French Creoles would not welcome them into the older part of the city.

From the gates of the cemetery you can see the lavish aboveground vaults and tombs of the families who built the surrounding mansions. Although the gates are generally open during working hours, it is not advisable to wander among the unguarded tombs. The cemetery and environs figure in Anne Rice's popular trilogy, *The Vampire Chronicles*. A guided tour of this cemetery is offered by Save our Cemeteries (*see* Tour Operators *in* The Gold Guide).

One of the grandest restaurants in New Orleans is **Commander's Palace** (1403 Washington Ave.), across from the cemetery. Owned by the Brennan family, it specializes in Creole cuisine (*see* Chapter 5, Dining).

Turn left at the corner onto Coliseum Street and walk three blocks to Second Street. This stroll will give you a general overview of the area.

What cannot be appreciated from the outside of these mansions is the sumptuous, carefully preserved interiors: ceilings as high as 22 feet; crystal chandeliers, hand-painted murals, Italianate marble mantels and fireplaces, pine floors, spiraling staircases, mahogany window and door frames, handmade windowpanes, and beautiful carved moldings. The histories of only a few of the more unusual houses in the district are known; those few houses in this four-block area are highlighted below.

Turn left on Second Street and walk to the **Schlesinger House** (1427 Second St.). This home is a classic example of the Greek Revival style popular in the 1850s when this mansion was built. The lovely iron-work on the front gallery was added in the 1930s.

Continue down Second Street and turn right onto Prytania Street, and walk one block down to the **Toby–Westfeldt House** (2340 Prytania St.). This unpretentious raised cottage dates back to the 1830s and sits amid a large, plantationlike garden, surrounded by a copy of the original white picket fence. Thomas Toby, a Philadelphia business-man, moved to New Orleans and had this house built well above the ground to protect it from flooding. The simple Greek Revival archi-tecture lacks the embellishments that later became popular on homes of that style. This house is thought to be the oldest in this part of the Garden District.

③ Across Prytania Street, on the opposite corner, is the **Louise S. McGehee School for Girls** (2343 Prytania St.), built in 1872, 40 years after the Toby house. Originally a private residence, it has been home to a private girls' school since 1929. The Renaissance Revival building combines fluted Corinthian columns, classic window design, and a sweeping spiral staircase inside.

③ Walk back up Prytania Street and stop at the **Adams House** (2423 Prytania St.) to admire the unusual curved gallery on its left. Here again the Greek Revival style is evident in the columns and the windows; this house is believed to have been built around 1860.

③ In the next block, the **Women's Guild of the New Orleans Opera Association House** (2504 Prytania St., ☎ 504/899–1945) is one of the few houses in the area open to the public, but only for groups of 20 or more with advance reservations. This Greek Revival house, built in 1858, has a distinctive octagonal turret, which was added in the late 19th century. The last private owner, Nettie Seebold, willed the estate to the Women's Guild of the New Orleans Opera upon her death in 1955. It is now used for receptions and private parties.

③ Across Prytania Street is the **Brennan House** (2507 Prytania St.), built in 1852, also in Greek Revival style. Notice the Ionic and Corinthian columns that support the broad galleries; inside is a magnificent gold ballroom decorated by a Viennese artist for the original owners.

③ A few doors down is **Our Mother of Perpetual Help Chapel** (2521 Prytania St.), built as a private residence in 1856. Its marble entrance hall is distinctive; also notice the detail in the extravagant cast ironwork on the galleries. The house is now a chapel maintained by the Redemptorist Fathers.

③ Cross Prytania at Third Street and walk up Third Street to the **Robinson House** (1415 Third St.), on the left. Built in the late-1850s, this home is one of the largest and most elegant in the district, styled after an Italian villa with rounded galleries supported by Doric and Corinthian columns. This is believed to be the first house in New Orleans with "waterworks," as indoor plumbing was called then.

③ Return to Prytania Street and cross to the other side to the **Briggs–Staub House** (2605 Prytania St.), one of the few Gothic Revival houses in the city. It was built around 1849 and contrasts sharply with its neighbors. Farther down this block, on the same side of the street,
③ is the **Villere–Carr House** (2621 Prytania St.), interesting for its Greek Revival features, which include a squared Greek-key doorway and squared window frames. This eclectic mansion was built around 1870.

Cross Prytania at the corner of Fourth Street to more closely observe
③ the cast-iron cornstalk fence around **Colonel Short's Villa** (1448 Fourth St.). In addition to the prevalent Greek Revival style and the unusually abundant ironwork of the gallery, the house is known for its iron fence, with its pattern of morning glories intertwining cornstalks. Legend has it that Colonel Short purchased the fence for his wife, who was homesick for Kentucky. Another cornstalk fence very much like this one appears in the French Quarter at 915 Royal Street.

To conclude the Garden District side trip, walk down Fourth Street to St. Charles Avenue, board the streetcar, and continue up the avenue.

There are many more mansions along the route of the same style and magnitude as those of the Garden District, though most gardens along St. Charles Avenue are not as large.

Numbers in the margin correspond to points of interest on the Tour 4: St. Charles Avenue Streetcar Tour maps.

40 Continuing on the streetcar, past the next stop on the right is a beautiful Gothic Revival Episcopalian Church, **Christ Church Cathedral** (2919 St. Charles Ave.), completed in 1887. Note its arched windows and steeply pitched gables, architectural features that were precursors to the New Orleans Victorian style. This is the seat of the Episcopalian Church of the South.

41 Look to the left at the intersection of Louisiana Avenue for a huge white mansion, the **Bultman Funeral Home** (3338 St. Charles Ave.), built in 1852. This is considered by many Orleanians to be the most prestigious funeral home in the city.

Several hospitals are located in the few blocks directly past Louisiana Avenue. **St. Charles General Hospital** is on the avenue to the left, and 2 blocks behind it (but not visible from the streetcar) are **Touro Hospital** and a related medical complex.

42 At the next stop on the left is a circular church building called **Unity Temple** (3722 St. Charles Ave.). Designed by a student of Frank Lloyd Wright, it was built in 1960. The harmonious and simple design reflects Wright's influence.

43 Coming up on the right in the next block is the **Columns Hotel** (3811 St. Charles Ave.), which was built in 1884 as a family home but in recent years has been renovated and operated as a hotel. The interior was used to film the Louis Malle movie *Pretty Baby*. The hotel has a popular upscale bar and a grand veranda for sipping cocktails alfresco on the avenue (*see* Chapter 6, Lodging).

44 In the next block on the left is **Rayne Memorial Methodist Church** (3900 St. Charles Ave.), built in 1875 and notable for its Gothic-style gables and arched windows. A few houses down from the church on **45** the same side is **Grant House** (3932 St. Charles Ave.), a good example of the Queen Anne style, with a highly decorative porch and balcony balustrades; it dates back to 1887. Popular architect Thomas Sully built the Grant House and the house in the middle of the next **46** block, **Sully House** (4010 St. Charles Ave.), his family home. The gables, towers, and gingerbread look of the Sully House were prized in that era and appear on many other homes in the vicinity.

47 Approaching the major intersection of Napoleon Avenue, you can see on the right the **First Baptist Church** (4301 St. Charles Ave.), built in 1954, though its congregation dates back to the early 1800s. On the **48** left is the **Touro Synagogue** (4238 St. Charles Ave.), built in 1908 and named for one of the city's great philanthropists, Judah Touro.

The large avenue intersecting at the next stop is **Napoleon Avenue,** the starting point for the many Mardi Gras parades that wind their way down St. Charles Avenue to Canal Street. **Copeland's Restaurant,** on the corner to the left, is named for its proprietor, Al Copeland, the former owner of Popeye's Famous Fried Chicken. He is a New Orleans native whose spicy Cajun cooking has become **49** nationally popular. Dominating the opposite corner is the **Church of the Covenant Presbyterian** (4422 St. Charles Ave.). The church, built in the early 1900s, reflects a Colonial Revival style, favoring English houses of two centuries before.

50 On the right in the next block is the even more spectacular **Sacred Heart Academy** (4521 St. Charles Ave.), one of the most beautiful sites on the avenue. Built in 1899 by the Sisters of the Sacred Heart, it has housed their private girls' school since then. Unique aspects of this building include wide, wraparound balconies (or galleries) and colonnades that face a large garden.

51 **St. George's Episcopal Church** (4600 St. Charles Ave.) is another fine building, from 1900; it reflects a Romanesque style with its softly **52** curved arches. The oldest house on St. Charles Avenue is the **4621 St. Charles House** on the right in this same block. Its history is not certain, but it is believed to date back to the 1850s. Renovations have since added details that are obviously not part of the original building.

53 The **Krower House** (4630 St. Charles Ave.), on the left, is unique for its partially underground basement, a rare feature in New Orleans. The basement was probably used to house servants rather than quartering them in a wing of the house or in separate quarters. Coming up on the right is the largest mansion on St. Charles Avenue and obvi-**54** ously among the most expensive, the **Brown House** (4717 St. Charles Ave.). Completed in 1902, it took five years and cost a quarter of a million dollars to build. The structure is a choice example of Romanesque Revival with its solid, monumental look, Syrian arches, **55** and steep gables. The **Hernandez House** (4803 St. Charles Ave.), in the next block to the right, illustrates the Second Empire style, characterized by the mansard roof, relatively rare in New Orleans. This house, originally located back a half block, had become sadly neglected until the early 1980s, when it was moved to face the avenue and was miraculously restored to the showcase home it is today.

Several houses in the next block are turn-of-the-century buildings, **56** though they artfully re-create an antebellum style. The **Vaccaro House** (5010 St. Charles Ave.), after the streetcar stop on the left, dates to the 1910s. The Tudor style, with its steep gables, Gothic arches, and half timbering, was popular when banana magnate Joseph Vaccaro built the home for his family.

57 In the next block, on the right, is the **Orleans** (pronounced Or-lay-ahn) **Club** (5005 St. Charles Ave.). It was built as a residence in 1868 but in 1925 became the home of one of the city's oldest women's organizations, the Orleans Club, which remains active today. On the left in the **58** next block is the **Milton H. Latter Memorial Library** (5120 St. Charles Ave.). Occupying a complete city block, this mansion was built in 1907 and was donated to the city in 1948; silent-film star Marguerite Clark married the former owner and lived there in the 1940s. Today it serves as the most elegant public library in New Orleans. Its spacious Beaux Arts architecture and lovely lawns make it a prized site on the avenue (*see* Off the Beaten Track, *below*).

De la Salle High School, a co-ed Catholic facility, is ahead on the left. The historic marker at the corner in front of the school notes that this site (5318 St. Charles Ave.) was the location of Gilbert Academy and New Orleans University, black educational institutions under the auspices of the Methodist Church from 1873 to 1949. They later became part of the current Dillard University located in the eastern part of the **59** city. At the streetcar stop is the **Jewish Community Center** (5342 St. Charles Ave.), one of the most modern buildings in the area, built in **60** 1963 where the Jewish Home for Children once stood. **Benjamin**

House (5331 St. Charles Ave.), on the right at the next stop, is a stunning building from around 1916 that is made of limestone, an expensive and unusual building material for New Orleans.

61 **62** In the next block is **McCarthy House** (5603 St. Charles Ave.), a typical Greek Revival home, with ornate columns and flat-topped doors and windows. Watch for **Tara** (5705 St. Charles Ave.), coming up on the same side of the avenue in the next block. Tara, the plantation home used in the film *Gone with the Wind,* was a set, but this house in New Orleans is a replica built from the plans of the movie set.

63 Look carefully or you'll miss the Georgian Colonial Revival **Wedding Cake House** (5809 St. Charles Ave.), in the next block on the right. Outshining Tara with its portico and decorative balconies, its key beauty is the beveled lead glass on its front door, one of the most beautiful entryways in the city.

64 **65** **66** **67** As you enter the university district, dominating the next block on the left is the Gothic **St. Charles Avenue Presbyterian Church.** On the same side in the next block is **Castle's House** (6000 St. Charles Ave.), another Georgian Colonial Revival similar to the Wedding Cake House. The **St. Charles Avenue Christian Church** (6200 St. Charles Ave.), two blocks farther on the left, is 1923 Colonial Revival. On the right is **Temple Sinai** (6227 St. Charles Ave.), the first Reform Jewish congregation in New Orleans. This building dates back to 1928; the annex on the corner was built in 1970.

68 **Loyola University** (6363 St. Charles Ave.), on the right, takes up the next block. The modernistic Gothic-style building on the corner is the **Louis J. Roussel Building,** which houses Loyola's renowned communications department. Lining the horseshoe curve farther down is **Marquette Hall,** directly ahead, with **Thomas Hall** to the right and the **Church of the Holy Name of Jesus** on the left. The Jesuits built this complex in 1914 for their university, which today extends for two blocks behind the masterfully constructed Gothic and Tudor edifice.

69 Directly beside Loyola is **Tulane University** (6823 St. Charles Ave.), which was founded in 1884. The central building facing St. Charles Avenue is **Gibson Hall,** built in 1894, with the additions of **Tilton Hall** (1901) on the left and **Dinwiddie Hall** (1936) on the right. The Romanesque style, with its massive stone look and arched windows and doors, is repeated in the campus buildings behind these. Modern campus buildings extend another three blocks to the rear. Tulane is known for its medical school, law school, and fine library. The **Sophie H. Newcomb College for Women** shares part of the Tulane campus, but has a separate dean and faculty.

★ **70** The streetcar makes three stops in this stretch, but there is so much to see that you must watch carefully. On the left, across the avenue from the two universities, is **Audubon Park,** formerly the plantation of Etienne de Boré, the father of the granulated-sugar industry in Louisiana. It is one of the largest and most acclaimed metropolitan parks in the United States and includes a world-class zoo, picnic and play areas, golf course, swimming pool, miniature train, riding stables, tennis court, and a river view. There are miles of winding lagoons and trails for biking, hiking, and jogging. The park is closed to all vehicles but bicycles. It was named for the famous naturalist and painter John James Audubon, who spent many years working in and around New Orleans. The zoo is also named for him, and his statue stands in the park. Exit here for the Audubon Park and Zoo side trip.

Audubon Park and Zoo Side Trip

Audubon Park encompasses 340 acres. None of the original buildings from its former plantation days remain standing; in fact, none of the buildings that housed the 1884–85 World's Industrial and Cotton Centennial Exposition, which was held on these acres and brought New Orleans its first international publicity since the Civil War, have survived. The park, however, began its development with the exposition a century ago. (New Orleans hosted another World Exposition a century later in 1984, but on a site nearer the business district.) In 1914 the Audubon Park Commission was formed, and it governs the area to this day. Landscape architect Frederick Law Olmsted (who also laid out New York's Central Park) designed the current layout of the park.

★ ⑦   The **Audubon Zoo** did not receive much attention until the late 1970s, when a major fund-raising effort brought about a new and greatly enlarged zoo, using the natural-habitat concept of displaying and breeding animals. Since the 1980s the zoo has taken its place as one of the most outstanding in the country.

As you exit the streetcar at Walnut Street and pass through the dramatic columned entrance to Audubon Park, the Audubon Zoo lies directly ahead, about 12 city blocks in the distance. You can walk there by taking the macadam path to the right across the park (approximately a 25-minute walk), or you can walk to your left along a lagoon for a more picturesque stroll and then return to the St. Charles Avenue entrance to catch the free shuttle van to the zoo, which operates every 15 minutes daily 9:30–5.

Walkers can also continue along the route to the left, across the park to the zoo; although scenic, this is a considerably longer walk. The aforementioned, shorter route to the right takes you through the golf course and down Oak Alley, a stretch of aged moss-hung oak trees that form a canopy over the path, one of the most enchanting settings in New Orleans. Emerging from Oak Alley you will cross Magazine Street, a busy thoroughfare; from there signs will direct you to the zoo entrance, another two blocks ahead.

Once inside the zoo you may wish to wander for several hours. Of special interest are the seasonal exhibits, the Louisiana Swamp, the Tropical Bird House, the flamingo pond, the sea lions, and the white tiger. Directions are clearly marked; there are concession stands and an unusual gift shop. *6500 Magazine St.,* ☎ *504/861–2537.* ☛ *$7.75 adults, $3.75 senior citizens and children under 12.* ☉ *Daily 9:30–4:30 in winter, 9:30–6 during daylight-saving months.*

To return to the streetcar on St. Charles Avenue, board the free shuttle van outside the zoo. To go directly back downtown, the Magazine Street bus passes the zoo entrance regularly and goes to Canal Street. You can also take a boat to Canal Street, as explained below.

Audubon Park includes a long stretch of land behind the zoo, on the levee overlooking the Mississippi River. If time permits, you may want to take the road to the left as you exit the zoo, cross the railroad tracks, and stroll along **Riverview Drive.** The river lookout includes **Audubon Landing,** where the *John James Audubon* cruise boat docks. ☎ *504/ 586–8777.* ☛ *You can combine admission to the Aquarium of the Americas downriver with the cruise. Combination prices vary.* ☉ *Cruises leave daily 11:30, 2:30, and 5 for the 7-mi river ride to the French Quarter and Canal St.*

Back along St. Charles Avenue again, the heavy stone archway on the right just after Tulane University is the entrance to **Audubon Place,** referred to locally as Millionaire's Row. A security guard checks people entering the two-block-long private drive that boasts some of the most

72 elegant mansions in the city. **Zemurray House** (2 Audubon Pl.), the columned white mansion facing the archway, is the stately home of the president of Tulane University. It was built in 1907 by Sam Zemurray, president of the United Fruit Company. If you glance quickly to the left of the avenue here, you will catch the splendid beveled lead-glass door and transom of the **Park View Guest House** (7004 St. Charles Ave.), built as a hotel for the World Exposition in 1884.

73 On that same side at the next stop is the **St. Charles Avenue Baptist Church** (7100 St. Charles Ave.). It was constructed in 1926, but the establishment of the congregation dates back to the late 1800s. The intersection at the next stop is Broadway, with a row of fraternity houses a few blocks down on the right. Notice the miniature house in

74 the corner yard on the right. The **Doll House** (7209 St. Charles Ave.), designed in the same Tudor style as the main house beside it for the daughter of a former owner, is the smallest house in New Orleans to have its own postal address.

75 To the left is the **Loyola University School of Law** (7214 St. Charles Ave.). This Italianate building was the main house of the Dominican Sisters, who operated the Dominican School for Girls from around 1864. It became St. Mary's Dominican College for Women in 1910, but was forced to close in the 1980s and now is home to the Broadway campus of Loyola University, which includes Loyola's Law School. The Dominican Sisters still maintain several buildings on the campus.

St. Charles Avenue continues for two more stops until it turns, just short of the levee. Some of the houses in this stretch, originally part of the small town of Carrollton, are more modest structures. Especially

76 interesting are two houses on the left, called the **Camelback Houses** (7628–30 and 7632–34 St. Charles Ave.) and built in the late 1800s. A house in those days was taxed by the width and height of its facade; working-class homes were usually narrow and long. Sometimes a second floor was added to the back half of the house, giving it the architectural designation of "camelback." The camelback and the gingerbread-type decoration on porches were very popular features in the 1800s; another house in much the same style (but minus a camel-

77 back) is the **Victorian Cottage** (7922 St. Charles Ave.), on the left another three blocks up. This style is also known as a "shotgun" house (*see* the Algiers Point Side Trip *in* Tour 3, *above*).

As the streetcar makes the bend in the following block, St. Charles turns into Carrollton Avenue. To the left in the distance is the grassy

78 knoll of the **levee,** a man-made earthen wall built for flood protection and to keep the Mississippi River flowing in its original course. Around the turn is an area filled with shops and restaurants, called

79 **Riverbend.** The tour ends at the next stop, so prepare to leave the streetcar, unless you wish to stay aboard another 10 minutes to ride to the end of the line.

As you exit, the large, white-columned building on the right is the former city hall of what was once the town of Carrollton. Later it served

80 as the Jefferson Parish **Court House.** The building is now used as an elementary school.

TIME OUT
One of the city's first and favorite counter-food establishments is the **Camellia Grill,** a columned building a block back toward St. Charles Avenue. The service here is renowned and the food highly recommended. *626 S. Carrollton Ave.,* ☎ *504/866-9573.* ⊙ *Mon.–Thurs. 9 AM–1 AM, Fri. 9 AM–3 AM, Sat. 8 AM–3 AM, Sun. 8 AM–1 AM. No credit cards.*

Tour 5: Bayou St. John–Lakefront Car Route

Numbers in the margins correspond to points of interest on the Tour 5: Bayou St. John–Lakefront Car Route map.

The following car route will occupy at least half a day. Begin on **①** **Canal Street,** the main avenue of downtown New Orleans, which connects the Mississippi River with Lake Pontchartrain. Take a right at South Jefferson Davis Parkway, approximately 3 miles from where Canal Street begins at the river. Follow Jefferson Davis 4 blocks and over the railroad tracks. Directly ahead on the left begins an inlet of **②** water called **Bayou St. John,** which leads into Lake Pontchartrain about 5 miles out. This is the only remaining bayou in New Orleans.

Take a left immediately after the railroad tracks and just before the end of the bayou; turn right after half a block to follow the bayou to Moss Street. Pass the traffic light at the Orleans Avenue Bridge and continue for one more long block to the Dumaine Street Bridge; take a right, cross over the bridge, and turn left at the end onto Moss Street. Bayou St. John will now be on your left.

③ The first stop is the **Pitot House** (1440 Moss St.). This is one of the few surviving houses that lined the bayou in the late 1700s. It was bought by James Pitot in 1810 and used as a country home for his family. Pitot built one of the first cotton presses in New Orleans and served as the city's mayor from 1804 to 1805, and later as parish court judge. The Pitot House was restored and moved to its current location in the 1960s to mark the 1708 site of the first French settlement in the New Orleans area. The house is noteworthy for its stucco-covered brick-between-post construction. The galleries across the front and right side are typical of the West Indies style brought to Louisiana by early planters. Inside, the house is furnished with American antiques of the early 1800s. *1440 Moss St.,* ☎ *504/482–0312.* ☞ *$3 adults, $2 senior citizens and students, $1 children under 13.* ⊙ *Wed.–Sat. 10–3; last tour at 2:15.*

Leaving Pitot House, follow Moss Street for another few blocks as it curves with the bayou until it intersects with Esplanade Avenue. Turn left and cross the Esplanade Avenue Bridge; **City Park** lies directly ahead. Go halfway around the **statue of General P.G.T. Beauregard,** the Civil War hero, mounted on his horse, and enter City Park, once the sugar plantation of Louis Allard in the late 1700s. The 1,500 acres make City Park one of the largest in the country; they include an art museum, winding lagoons, a golf course, tennis courts, a children's entertainment park, a botanical garden, two sports stadiums, and lots of picturesque picnic and hiking areas. The man-made lagoons are home to a variety of wild geese, ducks, and swans; among the ancient moss-draped oaks is a proliferation of native flowers and fauna.

 ④ As you enter the park, the **New Orleans Museum of Art** comes into view directly ahead on Lelong Avenue. This nationally recognized museum has a large permanent collection that specializes in pre-Columbian, African, and local art, with representation from the

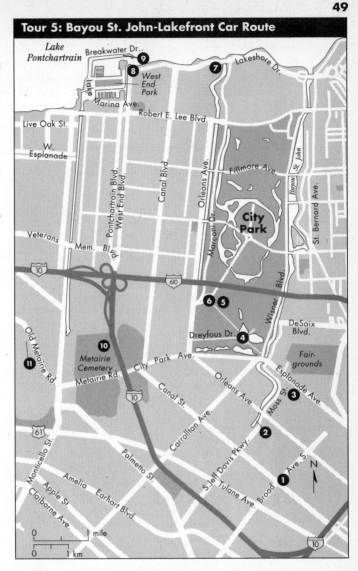

Tour 5: Bayou St. John-Lakefront Car Route

European and American masters as well. The Courtyard Café in the museum looks out on a lovely sculpture garden. *City Park,* ☎ *504/ 488–2631.* ☛ *$6 adults, $3 senior citizens and children 3–17; free Thurs. 10–noon to Louisiana residents.* ☉ *Tues.–Sun. 10–5.*

❺ After touring the museum, drive around the half circle behind the museum to the right and over the bridge. Directly after the bridge turn left onto Victory Avenue; the **Botanical Garden** is on the right, with a tropical conservatory, a water-lily pond, a formal rose garden, azalea and camelia gardens, and horticultural gardens, all decorated with fountains and sculptures by world-renowned local artist Enrique Alferez. The Pavilion of the Two Sisters is a European-style orangery, which houses an educational center, a horticultural library, and a gift shop. The Botanical Garden is a must-see for anyone interested in flora and fauna of the South. *City Park,* ☎ *504/483–9386.* ☛ *$3* *adults, children under 12 free.* ⊙ *Tues.–Sun. 10–4:30. Hrs may vary by season.*

❻ Past the gardens is **Storyland,** a whimsical and entertaining theme park for children featuring fairy-tale characters. Right next door is the exquisitely refurbished **Last Carousel,** replete with authentic wooden horses, giraffes, zebras, and other exotic creatures. The spectacular carousel and grounds cost $1.5 million to renovate (each horse was shipped to Connecticut for expert restoration). The surrounding Amusement Park includes various rides for children. *City Park,* ☏ *504/483–9382.* ✒ *$1.50 Storyland, $1 Amusement Park, $1.75 Carousel, $6 unlimited ride ticket; children under 2 free. Hrs may vary by season.*

As you drive away from Storyland, on the left are tennis courts. Make a left at the end of the courts, and left again onto Dreyfous Drive. The peristyle on the right, with its tall columns and cement lions over-looking the lagoon, is a favorite spot for picnics and parties. Farther along this avenue is the **Casino,** a concession stand with rest-room facilities and a large playground for small children. In the lagoon beyond, paddleboats and canoes ply the water; they can be rented for $10 and $7 per hour at the Casino. ☏ *504/483–9371.* ⊙ *Daily 8 AM–4 PM. Hrs may vary by season.*

Cross the narrow bridge, keeping to the left; the two large gnarled oaks on the left in the curve are known as the **Dueling Oaks** because of the frequent duels held under them in the late-1700s to early 1800s. Follow the road to the right, past the museum, and back to the front of the park where you entered. Notice the Art Deco lines of the benches along the avenue as you leave; these same lines are prevalent in the cement work throughout City Park, a remnant of the 1930s refurbishment during the Works Progress Administration. There are many illustrations of this style in the fountains, bridges, ironwork, and statues of the park.

Take a left halfway around the Beauregard statue onto Wisner Boule-vard, along Bayou St. John (now to your right). To the left is the City Park golf course, and farther out, Pan-American Stadium, where soc-cer games are played on weekends. Continue on Wisner Boulevard for another 3½ miles to the lakefront. City Park will be on the left most of the way. At Harrison Avenue look to the right for **Park Island,** with its beautiful modern homes and gardens facing the bayou. Farther up on the left is the driving range for the City Park golf club, then John F. Kennedy High School, and the U.S. Department of Agriculture South-ern Regional Research Laboratory. Cross Robert E. Lee Boulevard, go straight a few blocks until the road bears to the right and around to the right again. The lake—not yet visible from behind the levee—is on the right. Keep right on **Lakeshore Drive,** along **Lake Pontchartrain,** for about 2 miles. You can't follow this route Friday through Sunday, when Lakeshore Drive becomes one-way, west to east; for an alterna-tive route, *see* bullet 8, *below.*

The sight of the lake is impressive; it measures 24 miles across and stretches as far as the eye can see. The **University of New Orleans Lakefront Arena,** a new sports and entertainment facility, and **Lake-front Airport** (for small aircraft) are to the right, but not visible from here. To the left, farther out, is the marina, and beyond that the sub-urb of Metairie.

The seawall (the cement steps bordering the lake) is a 5½-mile levee and seawall protection system, built in the 1940s by the U.S. Army Corps of Engineers. Occupied by Army and Navy installations during and after World War II, the land was turned into private residential districts in the 1950s; the large modern homes in the subdivisions behind the levee were built around that time. Lakefront real estate is among the most expensive in the city.

Along Lakeshore Drive you can see many park and picnic areas that are generally filled on warm weekends and holidays. This is also a popular spot for fishing and boating. Swimming is not advisable—the lake is heavily polluted. There are many parking bays along Lakeshore Drive; you may want to stop here for a walk along the lake. Open to the public from 8 AM to 10 PM daily, the lakefront recreational area is relatively safe because of frequent police patrol.

Along Lakeshore Drive you will notice several shelters with rest-room facilities and telephones. Soon after passing Marconi Drive, on the
❼ left are the **Mardi Gras Fountains.** These circular, 60-foot fountains rise and fall in varying heights with changing Mardi Gras colors— gold, purple, and green. Worth the walk from the parking area to the fountains is a series of ceramic tiles bearing the names, symbols, and colors of the different Mardi Gras krewes (clubs). The fountains and plaques were installed in 1962. A major face-lift for the fountains and displays is underway; access may be limited.

Lakeshore Drive has two-way traffic along its entire length from Monday through Thursday; on weekends, it becomes one-way (west to east) at Paris Avenue. If you are traveling this route on a weekday, follow Lakeshore Drive past the end of the lake until it turns left into
❽ West End Boulevard. The first street on the right leads to the **Orleans Marina.** On weekends, turn right on Lakeshore Drive, cross the bridge, and immediately turn right onto St. Bernard Avenue. Continue to Robert E. Lee Boulevard; take a right, and follow Robert E. Lee for a mile to the intersection with West End Boulevard. Turn right and then turn left one block later onto Lake Marina Avenue. This becomes Breakwater Drive and the Orleans Marina will be on the right.

Take the very first right and make a long, horseshoe curve around **West End Park,** which is actually a very wide median. Enter the Orleans Marina parking lot to the right, almost at the end of the horseshoe curve. When you walk down the pier of the marina, the **Southern Yacht Club** will be to the right. This is one of the most refreshing scenes in New Orleans, far from downtown, with soft breezes blowing, gulls calling, and the rhythmic patter of sailboat
❾ cables slapping the masts. The **lighthouse** that marks the harbor is visible across the channel on the right.

As you leave the marina, take a right to the end of the curve, then turn left back onto Breakwater Drive; a collection of restaurants and night spots surrounds the parking lot to the right. These seafood restaurants cater not only to the marina, but to Orleanians from all areas of the city.

To return downtown, continue on Breakwater Drive to West End Boulevard, at the traffic light take a right, and at the next traffic light turn right again, then circle to the left onto Pontchartrain Boulevard. A large civil defense air-raid shelter is on the left, partially underground. Just past the shelter stands a large Celtic cross on a landscaped mound, which commemorates the thousands of Irish immigrants who built a canal through this area in the 1830s. The canal has long since been covered over. The boulevard eventually becomes Pontchartrain Expressway, part of I–10.

About a mile down the expressway, prepare to take the first exit at the METAIRIE ROAD–CITY PARK sign. Metairie Road runs along the expressway; on the right is **Metairie Cemetery,** which you can drive through to observe a variety of lavish aboveground tombs and vaults. To reach the cemetery, continue to Metairie Road at the traffic light, turn left under the overpass, and left again to drive along the other side of the expressway. A sign will indicate where you should turn to enter the cemetery. If you are interested in a particular tomb or aspect of the cemetery, personnel in the office, in the back to the right, will be glad to assist.

Leaving Metairie Cemetery, return on the feeder road beside the expressway, turning right at the traffic light onto Metairie Road. On the left is the **New Orleans Country Club.** Turn left farther on at the sign for **Longue Vue House and Gardens** on Bamboo Road. This city estate, fashioned after the great country houses of England, is surrounded by 8 acres of beautiful gardens embellished with fountains. The Greek Revival mansion is decorated with its original furnishings of English and American antiques, priceless tapestries, modern art, porcelain, and pottery. The gardens have various themes, and the formal Spanish court is modeled after a 14th-century Spanish garden. Longue Vue was once the private residence of Edith and Edgar Stern, two great New Orleans philanthropists. Since their deaths the house and gardens have been open to the public for guided tours. *7 Bamboo Rd.,* ☎ *504/488–5488.* ☛ *$7 adults, $6 senior citizens, $3 students and children.* ☉ *Mon.–Sat. 10–4:30, Sun. 1–5. Last tour at 4* PM.

After the tour of Longue Vue, return to Metairie Road, turn right, and go under the expressway overpass. At the next traffic light, turn right onto Canal Street, which will take you downtown and to the French Quarter.

Historic Buildings and Sites

New Orleans's major sites and attractions have already been described in the preceding tours. If you have more time to explore, here are some other interesting stops.

Chalmette National Cemetery is the final resting place for hundreds of Louisiana soldiers from various wars since 1864. Visitors are free to drive through and view the war monument. *Rte. 42, 6 mi from downtown New Orleans,* ☎ *504/589–4428.* ☛ *Free.* ☉ *Daily 8:30–5.*

Chalmette National Historic Park includes the site of the Battle of New Orleans, fought in 1815 by the United States under Andrew Jackson against the British under Gen. Sir Edward Packenham. The **Beauregard Plantation House,** constructed in 1840, serves as a visitor's center, with historical exhibits, a diorama, and films about the battle. *Rte. 42, 6 mi from downtown New Orleans,* ☎ *504/589–4428.* ☛ *Free.* ☉ *Daily 8:30–5.*

Both the Chalmette National Cemetery and the Chalmette National Historic Park are operated by the Jean Lafitte National Park of the National Park Service. Park headquarters are in the Chalmette National Cemetery.

The **Doullout Steamboat Houses** (at the end of Egania St. off St. Claude Ave.) are two identical houses built in 1904 and 1909 by the husband and wife river pilots, the Doullouts. One house was for them, the other for their son. The houses look like steamboats, with authentic wooden decorations, and are situated to allow a view of boats passing beyond the levee. You can walk up on the levee for a great view of the Industrial Canal. The houses are privately owned, but one is open for tours by appointment only. The neighborhood around them is not considered safe, and precaution should be taken. *400 Egania St.,* ☎ *504/949–1422.*

Margaret statue (at the intersection of Camp and Prytania Sts.) depicts Margaret Gaffney Haughery, who gave bread and milk from her dairy and bakery to feed the destitute of the city, during the mid-1800s. Erected in 1884, hers was the first statue of a woman erected in the United States. The statue was refurbished in 1988, and efforts are underway to relandscape Margaret Park to its turn-of-the-century condition.

The **Martin Luther King, Jr. statue** (on the median of Claiborne Ave., at the intersection of Martin Luther King, Jr. Blvd.) stands at the boulevard named for the famous civil rights leader, who often visited New Orleans. The bust of King rests on a pillar engraved with excerpts from his "I have a dream" speech; it is also the site of an annual rally and wreath-laying ceremony on the Martin Luther King, Jr. national holiday.

The **Molly Marine statue** (Canal St. and Elks Pl. Park) is the only statue to honor women in the U.S. military. It was sculpted by Enrique Alferez and was installed in 1943.

Rivertown, USA (located at the end of Williams Blvd.) is the historic district of Kenner, a town that has become part of the greater New Orleans area because of its proximity to the New Orleans (Moisant) International Airport. Turn-of-the-century buildings have been refurbished to house quaint antiques shops, offices, and a Victorian tearoom. Along the main stretch are museums commemorating the state's railways, wildlife, fisheries, the Saints football team, and Kenner history. There's a beautiful overview of the Mississippi at Lasalle's Landing.

What follows is a list of historic sites that have already been described. For further information see the specific tours in this chapter, noted below in parentheses.

French Market (Tour 1: Inner French Quarter)
Gallier Hall (Tour 4: St. Charles Avenue Streetcar Tour)
Jackson Square (Tour 1: Inner French Quarter)
Julia Row (Tour 4: St. Charles Avenue Streetcar Tour)
Lafitte's Blacksmith Shop (Tour 2: Outer French Quarter)
Latrobe House (Tour 2: Outer French Quarter)
Le Petit Théâtre (Tour 1: Inner French Quarter)
Madame John's Legacy (Tour 1: Inner French Quarter)
Miltenberger Houses (Tour 1: Inner French Quarter)
Napoleon House (Tour 1: Inner French Quarter)
New Zion Baptist Church (Tour 4: St. Charles Avenue Streetcar Tour)
Old Ursuline Convent (Tour 1: Inner French Quarter)
Piazza d'Italia (Tour 3: Foot of Canal Street)
Pontalba Apartments (Tour 1: Inner French Quarter)
Preservation Hall (Tour 2: Outer French Quarter)
Quadroon Ballroom (Tour 1: Inner French Quarter)
St. Charles Streetcar (Tour 4: St. Charles Avenue Streetcar Tour)

Museums, Galleries, and Collections

New Orleans is a city rich in tradition. A number of historic houses have been restored with their original furnishings and are open to the public; there are also many museums and collections that cater to browsing visitors and professional researchers. (A number of the city's major museums, galleries, and collections have already been described in the preceding tours.)

Amistad Research Center is an important archive of primary source materials on the history of America's ethnic minorities, race relations, and the civil rights movement. It is the only such archive in the Deep South and the largest collection of primary documents on African-Americans in the United States. *Housed at Tulane University, Tilton Hall,* ☎ *504/865–5535.* ☛ *Free.* ⊙ *Mon.–Sat. 8:30–5.*

Contemporary Arts Center features works by local artists and traveling special exhibits. The center also hosts concerts, films, theatrical and dance performances, and art-related workshops and seminars. *900 Camp St.,* ☎ *504/523–1216.* ☛ *Admission varies with event.* ⊙ *Mon.–Sat. 10–5, Sun. 11–5. Sometimes closed when preparing new exhibits.*

Elms House is a St. Charles Avenue mansion open for tours and receptions. The house, built around 1869, features marble fireplaces, stained-glass windows, and original tapestries. *3029 St. Charles Ave.,* ☎ *504/895–5493. Group tours only.*

Freeport–McMoRan Daily Living Science Center/Planetarium has a wonderful variety of hands-on activities to teach science, health, and environmental issues. An observatory with a high-powered telescope, and a planetarium with three shows daily are also part of the center in the suburb of Kenner. *409 Williams Blvd.,* ☎ *504/468–7229.* ☛ *$3 adults, $2 senior citizens and children under 12. $1 separate admission to either observatory or planetarium.* ⊙ *Tues.–Sat. 9–5.*

The **Germaine Wells Mardi Gras Museum,** a private family collection owned by Germaine Wells and her parents, exhibits mannequins dressed in the many gowns and costumes worn by Wells and her family as kings and queens of various Mardi Gras krewes from about 1910 to 1960. *On 2nd floor of Arnaud's Restaurant, 813 Bienville St. (enter through restaurant),* ☎ *504/523–5433.* ☛ *Free.* ⊙ *Sun.–Fri. 11:30–10, Sat. 6–10.*

House of Broel's Victorian Mansion and Doll House Museum is a three-story restored 1847 home filled with antique furnishings. The dollhouse collection of owner Bonnie Broel includes beautiful miniatures of Victorian, Tudor, and Plantation-style houses. The St. Charles Avenue streetcar stops at the door. *1508 St. Charles Ave.,* ☎ *504/522–2220 for mansion, 504/525–1000 for dollhouse museum.* ☛ *Mansion and museum: $5.* ⊙ *Mon.–Sat. 10–4.*

The **Irish Louisiana Museum** is a recent addition to O'Flaherty's Irish Channel, a Celtic-style pub and cultural center in the French Quarter. Housed above the pub, the museum collects letters, photos, artifacts, and family memorabilia of the thousands of Irish immigrants who came to Louisiana as laborers in the 1800s. A gift shop sells authentic Irish music and literature. *508 Toulouse St., ☎ 504/ 529–1317. ⊘ Daily noon–late evening.*

Kenner Historical Museum is part of the Rivertown development in a New Orleans suburb near the International Airport. The museum includes photos and local artifacts of Kenner history and a Black History Room. *1922 Third St., Kenner, ☎ 504/468–7258. ☛ $3 adults, $2 senior citizens and children under 12. ⊘ By appointment only. Multimuseum tickets available ($10 adults, $5 senior citizens and children under 12) for the Louisiana Toy Train Museum, the Louisiana Wildlife and Fisheries Museum, the Saints Hall of Fame, the Mardi Gras Museum of Jefferson Parish, and the Freeport– McMoRan Daily Living Science Center, all within walking distance of one another.*

The **Louisiana National Guard Museum** is an outdoor display of aircraft and tanks used by Louisiana's Air National Guard and Army National Guard. *Jackson Barracks, St. Claude Ave. at the Orleans Parish line, ☎ 504/271–6262. ☛ Free. ⊘ Weekdays 7:30–4.*

The **Louisiana Nature and Science Center** is an 86-acre wilderness park dedicated to preserving what is left of the natural environs that once surrounded the city. The center's main building contains exhibitions on south Louisiana flora and wildlife, a media center, lecture hall, and gift shop. The center offers guided nature walks through woodland trails, bird-watching classes, canoe trips through swamplands, crafts workshops, and field trips. A planetarium offers shows at 2, 3, and 4 PM weekends. *11000 Lake Forest Blvd., in New Orleans East, ☎ 504/246–5672. ☛ $4 adults, $3 senior citizens, $2 children under 12, $10 family (2 adults and up to 4 children). Planetarium shows: $1 per person. ⊘ Tues.–Fri. 9–5, Sat. 10–5, Sun. noon–5.*

The **Louisiana Toy Train Museum** depicts railroad history through a display of photos, model trains, films, and slide shows. It also features 4-4-0 10″-gauge steam locomotives. Children love the hands-on displays. *Rivertown, 519 Williams Blvd., Kenner, ☎ 504/468–7223. ☛ $3 adults, $2 senior citizens and children under 12. ⊘ Tues.–Sat. 9–5.*

The **Louisiana Wildlife and Fisheries Museum** is part of the Rivertown complex in the suburb of Kenner. The exhibit displays 700 species of animals, some in their natural habitat, and has a 2,500- gallon aquarium. *Rivertown, 303 Williams Blvd., Kenner, ☎ 504/ 468–7232. ☛ $3 adults, $2 senior citizens and children under 12. ⊘ Tues.–Sat. 9–5.*

The **Middle American Research Institute** has exhibits of pre-Columbian and Central and South American culture. Established in 1924, the institute has an extensive collection of pre-Columbian Maya artifacts and the largest collection of Guatemalan textiles in the nation, as well as a large library on Central America. *Tulane University, 4th Floor, Dinwiddie Hall, ☎ 504/865–5110. ☛ Free. ⊘ Weekdays 8:30–4.*

Saints Hall of Fame Museum displays memorabilia of the popular home pro football team. Highlights of all past seasons are shown on video. The museum also houses a playing-field room. *Rivertown, 409 Williams Blvd., Kenner, ☎ 504/468–6617. ☛ $3 adults, $2 senior citizens and children under 12. ⊘ Tues.–Sat. 9–5, Sun. 9–1, except during football season.*

The **Treasure Chest Mardi Gras Museum** is a participatory experience with live music, moving floats, and revelers tossing throws. There are also a king cake display and tasting and a theater showing footage of Mardi Gras parades and celebrations. *Rivertown, 407 Williams Blvd., Kenner,* ☎ *504/468–7258.* ☛ *$3 adults, $2 senior citizens and children under 12.* ⊙ *Tues.–Sat. 9–5.*

The **Ursuline Museum** is a collection of memorabilia and documents tracing the history of the Ursuline nuns from France to New Orleans in 1727. *2635 State St.,* ☎ *504/866–1472.* ☛ *Free, by appointment only.*

What follows are museums, galleries, and collections that have already been described. For further information, see specific tours in this chapter, noted in parentheses.

American-Italian Museum and Library (Tour 3: Foot of Canal Street)
Beauregard-Keyes House (Tour 1: Inner French Quarter)
Black Music Hall of Fame and Museum (Tour 2: Outer French Quarter)
Blaine Kern's Mardi Gras World (Algiers Point Side Trip)
Confederate Museum (Tour 4: St. Charles Avenue Streetcar Tour)
Folklife and Visitor Center (Tour 1: Inner French Quarter)
Gallier House (Tour 1: Inner French Quarter)
Hermann-Grima House (Tour 2: Outer French Quarter)
Historic New Orleans Collection (Tour 1: Inner French Quarter)
K&B Plaza of Sculpture (Tour 4: St. Charles Avenue Streetcar Tour)
Longue Vue House and Gardens (Tour 5: Bayou St. John–Lakefront Car Route)
Louisiana Children's Museum (Tour 3: Foot of Canal Street)
Louisiana State Museum Complex: Cabildo (Tour 1: Inner French Quarter); Presbytere (Tour 1: Inner French Quarter); 1850s House (Tour 1: Inner French Quarter); Old Mint (Tour 2: Outer French Quarter)
Mardi Gras Museum (Tour 2: Outer French Quarter)
Musée Conti Wax Museum (Tour 2: Outer French Quarter)
New Orleans Historic Voodoo Museum (Tour 2: Outer French Quarter)
New Orleans Jazz Collection (Tour 2: Outer French Quarter)
New Orleans Museum of Art (Tour 5: Bayou St. John Car Route)
New Orleans Pharmacy Museum (Tour 1: Inner French Quarter)
Pitot House (Tour 5: Bayou St. John–Lakefront Car Route)
Preservation Resource Center (Tour 4: St. Charles Avenue Streetcar Tour)
Women's Guild of the New Orleans Opera Association House (Tour 4: St. Charles Avenue Streetcar Tour)

Parks, Zoos, and Gardens

New Orleans is fortunate to have a warm climate and lots of green, open spaces for outdoor activities. There are two large public parks within the city, a nationally acclaimed zoo, and a national park, plus several state parks surrounding the city. Some of these have appeared in the tours described earlier in this chapter.

American Aquatic Gardens, a short hike from the French Quarter, is a wonderfully relaxing place in which to wander and observe the variety of grasses, reeds, and water lilies that grace local gardens. Dozens of artistic fountains add pleasant water sounds. Although this is a commercial nursery and garden supplier, guests are welcome to browse uninterrupted. *621 Elysian Fields,* ☎ *504/944–0410.* ⊙ *Daily 9–5.*

Jean Lafitte National Historical Park is one of the newer parks in the national park system and celebrates the diversity of the Delta region. The park has three major units: the **French Quarter, Chalmette,** and **Barataria.** The French Quarter unit, headquartered at the Old French Market, introduces visitors to New Orleans and the cultural traditions of the region through a Folklife and Visitor Center and a variety of free guided tours of the area. The Chalmette unit preserves the battlefield where, in 1815, the American forces turned back the British advance on New Orleans. The Barataria unit preserves an area of rich and beautiful coastal wetlands. The park is also a study center, researching the history of the region and documenting the culture of the many ethnic groups that have contributed to the special flavor of the Delta. *National Park Service, U.S. Dept. of the Interior, Superintendent's Office, 423 Canal St.,* ☎ *504/589–3882.* ☛ *Free (all functions of the park).*

Louisiana State Parks is a system of 40 state parks and state commemorative areas throughout Louisiana. Those within quick driving distance from New Orleans are the **St. Bernard State Park** in Violet, 18 miles southeast of New Orleans; **Bayou Segnette State Park** in Westwego, across the Huey P. Long Bridge; and **Fontainebleau State Park** southeast of Mandeville across Lake Pontchartrain on U.S. 190. All three parks feature camping and picnic areas as well as nature trails, fishing, and general sightseeing. Bayou Segnette Park has a large, popular wade pool, too. Some also offer cabins and meeting facilities. *Dept. of Culture, Recreation and Tourism, Box 94291, Baton Rouge, LA 70804,* ☎ *504/568–5661 or 800/33–GUMBO.*

What follows are parks, zoos, and gardens that have already been described. For further information, see specific tours in this chapter, noted below in parentheses.

Aquarium of the Americas (Tour 3: Foot of Canal Street)
Armstrong Park (Tour 2: Outer French Quarter)
Audubon Park (Tour 4: St. Charles Avenue Streetcar Tour)
Audubon Zoo (Tour 4: St. Charles Avenue Streetcar Tour)
City Park (Tour 5: Bayou St. John–Lakefront Car Route)
Longue Vue House and Gardens (Tour 5: Bayou St. John–Lakefront Car Route)
New Orleans Lakefront (Tour 5: Bayou St. John–Lakefront Car Route)
Riverwalk (Tour 3: Foot of Canal Street)
Woldenberg Riverfront Park (Tour 3: Foot of Canal Street)

What to See and Do with Children

Don't be reluctant to bring the children to New Orleans. Daytime activities are plentiful, and for those evenings when parents want to be out on the town, most of the city's major hotels offer baby-sitting services. The pleasures of New Orleans generally appeal to adults and children alike; however, there are a number of things to see and do that are especially recommended for children. The New Orleans Metropolitan Convention and Visitors Bureau publishes an entertaining 128-page children's guide to the city, *New Orleans for Kids* ($5; GNOTCC, 1520 Sugar Bowl Dr., 70112, ☎ 504/566–5028).

Accent on Arrangements (☎ 504/524–1227) specializes in activities—including adventuresome full- and half-day trips and tours—for children.

Bicycle Michael's, one block across Esplanade Avenue from the French Quarter, rents three-speed and 10-speed bicycles and mountain bikes.

Locks are provided. *618 Frenchman St.,* ☎ *504/945–9505.* ☛ *$3.50 per hr, $12.50 per day.* ۞ *Mon.–Sat. 10–7, Sun. 10–5.*

Endangered Species, a French Quarter shop, is owner William Doak's private museum of art and curios collected from his travels around the world. Children of all ages thrill to the exotic range of exhibits here. *619 Royal St.,* ☎ *504/568–9855.* ۞ *Usually Wed.–Mon. 10–5:30. Closed Tues. and occasionally Wed.; call ahead.*

Past Finders is a workbook of things for children to do in the French Quarter. Each page asks the child to look for some special point of interest, describe it, draw it, or answer questions about it. Children who complete the approximately 30 activities are given instructions on how to contact the authors and receive a certificate stating that they are certified "past finders." *Write to Myrna Bergeron, 4748 St. Roch St., 70122.*

Streetcar Tours is a cassette you can rent and listen to while riding the St. Charles Streetcar. The narration is lively and interspersed with samples of New Orleans music. Stops along the streetcar route provide opportunities to get off and explore (*see* Tour 4, *above*). A picnic in Audubon Park near the end of the tour is a great way to give children a break before riding the streetcar back to Canal Street. *127 Carondolet St.,* ☎ *504/561–1001.* ۞ *Mon.–Sat. 9–4.*

The following children's activities are discussed in the tours described above:

Aquarium of the Americas (Tour 3: Foot of Canal Street)
Audubon Park (Tour 4: St. Charles Avenue Streetcar Tour)
Audubon Zoo (Tour 4: St. Charles Avenue Streetcar Tour)
Black Music Hall of Fame and Museum (*see* Museums, Galleries, and Collections, *above*)
Blaine Kern's Mardi Gras World (Algiers Point Side Trip)
Café du Monde (Tour 1: Inner French Quarter)
Canal Street Ferry (Tour 3: Foot of Canal Street)
City Park (Tour 5: Bayou St. John–Lakefront Car Route)
Germaine Wells Mardi Gras Museum (*see* Museums, Galleries, and Collections, *above*)
House of Broel Victorian Mansion and Doll House Museum (*see* Museums, Galleries, and Collections, *above*)
Louisiana Children's Museum (Tour 3: Foot of Canal Street)
Louisiana Nature and Science Center (*see* Museums, Galleries, and Collections, *above*)
Mardi Gras Museum (Tour 2: Outer French Quarter)
Mardi Gras Museum of Jefferson Parish (*see* Museums, Galleries, and Collections, *above*)
Moon Walk (Tour 1: Inner French Quarter)
Musée Conti Wax Museum (Tour 2: Outer French Quarter)
Steamboat Ride (*see* Theme Trips *in* The Gold Guide)
Storyland (Tour 5: Bayou St. John–Lakefront Car Route)

Off the Beaten Track

Bird-watchers' Delight. Nature offers birding enthusiasts an exciting way to catch the sunset. Every evening at dusk from April through August, massive flocks of purple martin swallows gather near the Causeway bridge that spans Lake Pontchartrain. For 20 to 25 minutes the sky around the entrance to the Causeway in Metairie (a 15-minute drive from downtown New Orleans) blackens with fluttering wings and resounds with swallow calls. Gradually the swirling clouds of birds swoop under the bridge and find roosts for the night. In recent years a viewing area has been set up for the many locals who are enchanted with this natural phenomenon, and there are also plans to build a large bird sanctuary near the bridge. On either side of the causeway is a hiking path (*see* Linear Parkway, *below*).

Freeport McMoRan Audubon Species Survival Center. This breeding and research center preserves endangered animals, mostly from the southern United States, Central America, and Indonesia. It includes a public wilderness park with nature trails and shelters. The center is unique because it lies within the limits of a metropolitan area, 10 miles from downtown New Orleans. *14001 Patterson Rd.,* ☏ *504/398–2025. Call for directions and hrs.*

High Tea New Orleans Style. The English custom of high tea has taken hold in French New Orleans. It is royally served daily in the British-owned Windsor Court Hotel downtown (300 Gravier, ☏ 504/523–6000), and every day but Sunday at Le Jardin, a restaurant with a breathtaking view atop the Westin Hotel (Canal Place, 100 Iberville St., ☏ 504/553–5083).

Linear Parkway. Along the south shore of Lake Pontchartrain is a 7½-mile path for biking and hiking. This is a great place to see and hear local birds, watch the sunset over the lake, or chat with other walkers. You can plan a picnic for one of the informal rest stops along the way, but be well prepared because there are no rest rooms, water fountains, or concession stands anywhere nearby. Free parking is provided at both ends of the trail: in Bucktown and at the Williams Boulevard Boat Launch. Depending on the season, you can combine walking here with the Bird-watchers' Delight, *above.*

Milton H. Latter Memorial Library. Ornamenting its own beautifully landscaped block, this mansion was once the home of silent-screen star Marguerite Clark. It was later purchased by the Latter family and given to the city as a library in memory of their son, who was killed in World War II. Here you can sit a spell and leaf through a copy of Walker Percy's *The Moviegoer* or Anne Rice's *The Vampire Lestat* (two popular novels set in New Orleans), or just relax in a white wicker chair on the library's glass-enclosed porch; this is one of the few mansions on St. Charles Avenue that is open to the public. *5120 St. Charles Ave.,* ☏ *504/596–2625.* ☉ *Mon. 10–8, Tues.–Thurs. 10–6, Sat. 10–5, Sun. 12:30–4:30. Hrs may vary with city budget restraints, so call ahead if you wish to tour.*

Neighborhood Gallery. This lively uptown center for African-American arts provides exposure for local artists, poets, writers, actors, and musicians. It also mounts exhibitions and conducts cultural tours. *2131 Soniat St.,* ☏ *504/891–5573.* ☉ *Tues.–Sun. 3–7.*

Next door to the gallery is **Borsodi's Coffeehouse,** an institution in the city's alternative culture. It doesn't even need a sign or telephone because all the regulars know where it is and its erratic open hours. The clutter and laid-back atmosphere create a cozy meeting place for poets, artists, students, and social activists, and the crowded bulletin board here is the most esoteric in the city.

The Passing Parade. Often the best musical performers are found not in bars and clubs in New Orleans but out on the streets in the age-old traditions of colorful jazz funeral processions and neighborhood second-line jazz parades. Both of these are word-of-mouth events. Jazz funerals are usually mentioned in the daily *Times-Picayune* a day or two in advance. Onlookers are welcome as long as respect is paid the deceased and his or her family. The neighborhood second-line parades are spontaneous; almost any Sunday finds the best jazz bands accompanying high-stepping dancers twirling beribboned umbrellas. Anyone who turns out is welcome to join in the fun. Try the **Zulu Lounge** (☎ 504/822–9850) for information on what's happening on a particular Sunday.

St. Alphonsus Church and **St. Mary's Assumption Church.** Not as well known as St. Louis Cathedral, these two Baroque churches in the 2000 block of Constance Street date back to the mid-1800s. Located in the Irish Channel section of New Orleans, St. Alphonsus originally served the English-speaking Irish immigrants, while St. Mary's Assumption served the German-speaking immigrants of the neighborhood. Today St. Alphonsus has been restored to highlight its beautiful frescoes and stained glass dating to the 1850s. It no longer serves as a church but as a reception area and art history facility. *2001 Constance St., ☎ 504/482–0008. ☛ $5 donation. Tours by appointment.*

St. Mary's Assumption across the street continues to function as a local parish church. The church, built in the Baroque architecture that was popular among Germans of that day, is well restored and contains some of the largest stained-glass windows in the city. The exterior brickwork is noteworthy and the elaborate works you can see inside the church were crafted in Germany. For a tour, contact the rectory. Exercise extreme caution when traveling through this less touristed neighborhood; we recommend you go with a group. *St. Mary's Assumption Church, 2030 Constance St., ☎ 504/522–6748. ☉ Daily 8:30–4:30 to public, tours by appointment.*

Westgate. In a gothic city like New Orleans, which inspired Anne Rice's vampire trilogy, it is not surprising to find a purple-painted 19th-century house uptown devoted to the Angel of Death. Artist and author Leila Wendell welcomes visitors to her gallery of necromantic art and literature and pleasantly explains the macabre nature of the work displayed there by herself and local artists. *5219 Magazine St., ☎ 504/899–3077. ☉ Tues.–Sat. 12:30–5:30 and by appointment.*

Your Daily Bread. The streetcar stops a block away from this bakery/deli in the Uptown area. The bread here is absolute heaven, especially the round spinach cheese bread; they also pack breakfast baskets and picnic lunches to enjoy in Audubon Park, just four blocks away. *7457 St. Charles Ave., ☎ 504/861–GOOD. ☉ Mon.–Sat. 7 AM–8 PM, Sun. 7 AM–6 PM. No credit cards.*

Zulu Social Aid and Pleasure Club. Few other institutions embody local African-American heritage as well as this venerable club, home to the Mardi Gras krewe of the Zulus. Activities here usually are open only to members, but the lounge has an exuberant clientele that welcomes visitors, and the souvenir shop is open to anyone wishing to take home a bit of authentic New Orleans black history. The club is located in Mid-City, away from the area frequented by tourists; we recommend you take a taxi there. *Lounge: 732 N. Broad St., ☎ 504/822–9850, ☉ Daily 1 PM–1 AM. Souvenir shop: 722 N. Broad St., ☎ 504/822–1559, ☉ Mon.–Sat. 11–6. Hrs of both places may vary during Mardi Gras.*

3 Shopping

THE FUN OF SHOPPING in New Orleans is in the many regional items available throughout the city, in the smallest shops or the biggest department stores. You can take home some of the flavor of the city: its pralines (pecan candies), seafood (packaged to go), Louisiana red beans and rice, coffee (pure or with chicory), Creole and Cajun spices (cayenne pepper, chili, and garlic), and packaged mixes of such local dishes as jambalaya, gumbo, beignets, and the sweet red local cocktail called the Hurricane. A variety of cookbooks also share the secrets of preparing distinctive New Orleans dishes.

Updated by
Honey Naylor

Beautiful posters celebrating Mardi Gras, the Jazz and Heritage Festival, and the Crescent City Classic all are issued each year and quickly become collector's items. Ceramic or feather masks serve both for Mardi Gras and as attractive wall hangings during the rest of the year. Mardi Gras costumes, beads, and doubloons make wonderful gifts, too. Posters, photographs, and paintings on canvas and slate capture scenes in New Orleans. Jewelry, antiques, ceramics, carved wooden toys, kites, jazz umbrellas, and wreaths of dried flowers are often handmade and make lovely gifts and souvenirs.

The sounds of New Orleans are available on tapes and albums in music stores throughout the city. There is a wide spectrum, including old Dixieland jazz, contemporary jazz, swinging Cajun and zydeco, and the hot, sweet wail of rhythm and blues.

All major bookstores carry books about the city; local history and photography books are especially popular. Good bets are cookbooks, guides to special-interest sightseeing, and books that specialize in local ethnic history. There are a number of small, independently operated bookshops where perseverance can yield some real finds in local literature and lore. Stock in these shops often combines old photographs, posters, and postcards.

There are many clothing shops that offer fabric designs popular in the semitropical heat: Panama hats, lacy lingerie, and the ubiquitous T-shirt and sports clothes. Designer clothes have become more available in recent years with the opening of national stores such as Macy's, Saks Fifth Avenue, and Brooks Brothers. Department stores that have become traditions on Canal Street are the family-owned Krauss Co. and the now nationally owned Maison Blanche.

Shopping guides and suggestions can be found in most of the tourist magazines available in hotel rooms and lobbies. The New Orleans Tourist and Convention Commission office on Jackson Square (St. Ann St. side) also offers pamphlets on shopping.

Shopping Areas

The main shopping areas in the city are the French Quarter, with its narrow streets lined with specialty, gift, and antiques shops and art galleries; the Central Business District (CBD), including Canal Street, which features department stores and clothing and jewelry shops; Magazine Street, known for its antiques shops and galleries; and Uptown, with its neighborhood and specialty shops in several fashionable shopping areas.

Store Hours

Store hours are generally from 10 to 5:30 or 6, with shorter hours—from noon to 5—on Sunday. In areas with active nightlife, such as the

French Quarter and the shopping malls, many stores stay open until 9 PM. Sunday is a good shopping day in heavily trafficked areas, though some of the smaller shops and boutiques may not be open.

Tax-Free Shopping

Louisiana is the first and only state to grant a sales-tax rebate to shoppers from other countries. Look for shops, restaurants, and hotels that display the distinctive tax-free sign and ask for a voucher for the 9% sales tax tacked onto the price of many products and services. Present the vouchers with your plane ticket at the tax rebate office at the New Orleans International Airport, and receive up to $100 in cash back. If the amount redeemable is more than $100, a check for the difference will be mailed to your home address.

The Central Business District

Canal Street is the anchor for a thriving shopping business located in the heart of Downtown. **Maison Blanche** department store (901 Canal St., ☎ 504/566–1000) is in the CBD, with branches in the suburban shopping centers. It carries designer labels as well as full lines of appliances and home furnishings.

In addition to Maison Blanche, there is the fashionable **Canal Place,** with Saks Fifth Avenue, Gucci, Polo/Ralph Lauren, and Brooks Brothers, (1 Canal Pl., ☎ 504/587–0739). The **New Orleans Centre** (1400 Poydras St., ☎ 504/568–0000), a shopping complex between the Superdome and the Hyatt Regency Hotel, houses Macy's and Lord & Taylor. **Riverwalk** (1 Poydras St., ☎ 504/522–1555), a Rouse development along the riverfront (*see* Tour 3 *in* Chapter 2, Exploring New Orleans), features a half-mile-long marketplace with more than 200 nationally known shops, restaurants, and cafés.

Books

Deville Books and Prints (Riverwalk, ☎ 504/595–8916; 344 Carondelet St., ☎ 504/525–1846), a locally owned bookstore specializing in New Orleans books and collectibles, is the place for local literary memorabilia.

Clothing

Abercrombie & Fitch (Riverwalk, ☎ 504/522–7156) has fine sportswear and casual clothes.

Banana Republic (Riverwalk, ☎ 504/523–6843), whose safari clothes and catalogues are famous, is a good place to buy casual and travel clothes and sportswear.

Brooks Brothers (Canal Pl., ☎ 504/522–4200) is internationally known for classic, tailored menswear.

Esprit Outlet (901 St. Charles Ave., ☎ 504/561–5050) has chic sportswear and casual wear, significantly discounted, in a chrome-and-glass showplace. The staff is helpful and upbeat.

The Gap (Riverwalk, ☎ 504/529–4962) and **Kids Gap** and **Baby Gap** (Riverwalk, ☎ 504/522–5828) are great places to shop for comfortable fashions for infants, children, and young adults.

G. H. Bass (Riverwalk, ☎ 504/522–3918) carries classic styles in footwear for men and women.

Lord & Taylor (New Orleans Centre, ☎ 504/581–5673) features fine designer clothes for men and women.

Macy's (New Orleans Centre, ☎ 504/592–5985) is a New York-based department store with fashions for all ages.

Meyer the Hatter (120 St. Charles Ave., ☎ 504/525–1048 or 800/882–4287), which celebrated its 100th birthday in 1994, has a large selection of Stetsons, Dobbs, Biltmore hats, and baseball caps.

Polo/Ralph Lauren (Canal Pl., ☎ 504/561–8299) stocks fashions for men by the popular designer.

Rubenstein Brothers (102 St. Charles Ave., ☎ 504/581–6666), a local, family-owned men's clothier, carries Yves St. Laurent, Pierre Cardin, and others.

Yvonne LaFleur Editions (Riverwalk, ☎ 504/522–8222) is unsurpassed in its selection of custom millinery, silk dresses, and the finest lingerie.

Food
Riverwalk (1 Poydras St., ☎ 504/522–1555), a several-block-long marketplace along the river, features many local restaurants and food retailers. Among the best for local products are **Evans Creole Candies** and **Creole Delicacies.**

Gifts
Rapp's Luggage and Gifts (604 Canal St., ☎ 504/568–1953; New Orleans Centre, ☎ 504/566–0700; 1628 St. Charles Ave., ☎ 504/524–5400) is a locally owned variety store, specializing in fine leather goods and unusual gift items.

Rhino (Canal Pl., ☎ 504/523–7945) has locally made handicrafts, including Mardi Gras masks.

Riverwalk (1 Poydras St., ☎ 504/522–1555) has dozens of specialty shops that feature a dazzling display of toys, crafts, cards, curios, and gift ideas. Look for **The Body Shop, Masks and Make Believe, The Kite Loft, The Partridge, The Nature Company, The Local Cat House, Warner Bros. Studio Store,** and **The Disney Store.**

Jewelry
Adler & Sons (722 Canal St., ☎ 504/523–5292) is a family-owned local store with top-of-the-line jewelry, watches, and silver.

Ricarde Fine Jewelry (Canal Pl., ☎ 504/522–8080), owned by the local Sutton family, has fine jewelry and accessories.

Music
Odyssey Records (1012 Canal St., ☎ 504/523–3506), one of the city's largest record and tape stores, specializes in Dixieland, historical jazz, and rhythm and blues.

The French Quarter

The charm of this area and its fascinating merchandise should be enjoyed at a leisurely pace. Remember, there's always a bistro or café nearby for a rest stop. With the advent of the casino, rents in the Quarter have risen sharply and some small shops have been squeezed out, making it hard to predict what the shopping scene will be like in 1996. In addition, in early 1995 Planet Hollywood announced plans to open its 15,000-square-foot facility in the Jackson Brewery Brewhouse. As a result, many of the small Brewhouse shops have had to relocate.

Antiques

The French Quarter is well known for its fine antiques shops, located mainly on Royal and Chartres streets. The **Royal Street Guild** (☎ 504/949–2222), a merchants' association, has informative brochures in shops and hotels. In addition, local antiques shopping consultant **Macon Riddle** (☎ 504/899–3027) conducts half- and full-day shopping expeditions by appointment, advising on the best shops and imparting information on styles, values, and prices.

French Antique Shop (225 Royal St., ☎ 504/524–9861) has a large selection of European chandeliers and furniture; some Creole and local designs are also available.

Lucullus (610 Chartres St., ☎ 504/528–9620) carries Continental and English 17th- to 19th-century furniture, art, and cookware.

Manheim Galleries (403–409 Royal St., ☎ 504/568–1901) offers the city's largest collection of antique English, Continental, and Asian furnishings, porcelains, paintings, silver, and jade. This is the agent for Boehm Birds.

Miscenich Antiques (834 Chartres St., ☎ 504/523–4718) has a complete selection of Baroque and Renaissance art.

Moss Antiques (411 Royal St., ☎ 504/522–3981) features a large selection of antique and estate jewels, as well as fine French and English furnishings, paintings, and bric-a-brac.

M.S. Rau, Inc. (630 Royal St., ☎ 504/523–5660 or 800/544–9440) stocks American, French, English, Oriental furniture, china, glass, silver, ornamental iron, and American cut glass.

Patout Antiques (920 Royal St., ☎ 504/522–0582) is the best place in town for antiques from Louisiana plantation houses.

Rothschild's Antiques (2 locations: 241 Royal St., and 321 Royal St., ☎ 504/523–5816) carries a large collection of furniture, silver, jewelry, mantels, and clocks from 18th to 20th century.

Royal Antiques (307–309 Royal St., ☎ 504/524–7033) specializes in French and English 18th-century furnishings.

Waldhorn Company (343 Royal St., ☎ 504/581–6379), the oldest antique store in New Orleans, was established in 1881. It sells English furniture, Victorian and Early American jewelry, and antique English porcelain and silver.

Whisnant Galleries (222 Chartres St., ☎ 504/524–9766) has delightfully eclectic antique jewelry, African sculptures, clocks, and unusual pieces.

Art

Bergen Galleries (730 Royal St., ☎ 504/523–7882) showcases a large selection of collectibles and the city's largest display of posters by local artists.

The Black Art Collection (309 Chartres St., ☎ 504/529–3080) focuses on the works of major local and national black artists, including posters, jazz images, and antique African artifacts.

Circle Gallery (316 Royal St., ☎ 504/523–1350) features paintings, sculptures, and graphics by internationally known artists including Vaskely, Lebadang, and Peter Max, as well as jewelry by Erté and drawings by Walt Disney.

66

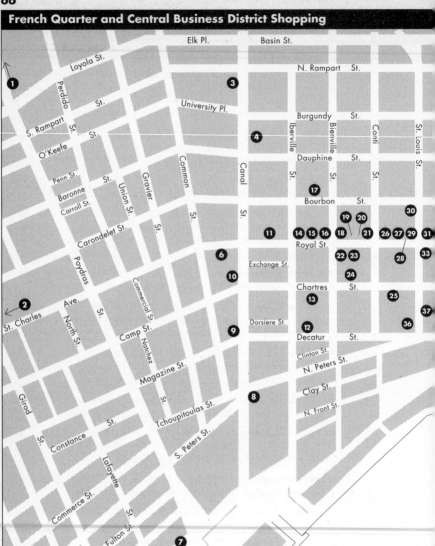

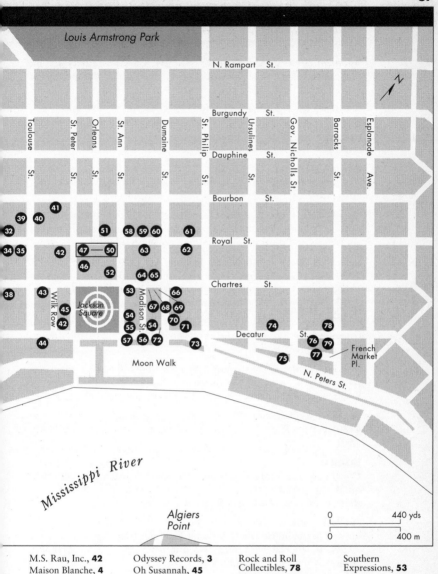

M.S. Rau, Inc., **42**

Maison Blanche, **4**

Manheim Galleries, **26**

Mardi Gras Center, **65**

Merrill B. Domas American Indian Art, **67**

Miscenich Antiques, **68**

Moss Antiques, **27**

Nahan Galleries, **35**

New Orleans Centre, **1**

Odyssey Records, **3**

Oh Susannah, **45**

Old Children's Books, **50**

Patout Antiques, **62**

The Quarter Smith, **37**

Rapp's, **9**

Ray Cole Collection, **31**

Record Ron's, **74**

Rhino, **8**

Ricarde Fine Jewelry, **8**

Riverwalk, **7**

Rock and Roll Collectibles, **78**

Rodrigue Gallery, **49**

Rothschild's Antiques, **16, 20**

Royal Antiques, **18**

Rubenstein Brothers, **5**

Rumors, **32**

Rumors Too, **19**

Serendipitous Masks, **72**

Sigle's Historic New Orleans Metal Craft, **61**

Southern Expressions, **53**

Victoria's Shoes, **38**

Vieux Carré Wine and Spirits, **25**

Waldhorn Company, **21**

Wehmeier's Belt Shop, **40**

Werlein's for Music, **12**

Whisnant Galleries, **13**

Yesteryear's, **41**

The Crabnet (925 Decatur St., ☎ 504/522–3478) has a large collection of wood ducks and decoys, mostly by Louisiana carvers and wildlife artists.

Dyansen Gallery (433 Royal St., ☎ 504/523–2902) offers a comprehensive collection of Erté's sculpture, lithographs, and serigraphs, as well as art by Paul Wegner, Martinique, and Sasonne.

A Gallery for Fine Photography (322 Royal St., ☎ 504/568–1313), bastion of local fine art photographer Joseph Pailet, exhibits leading American and European photographers, past and present, as well as rare 19th-century photographs and books.

Hanson Galleries (229 Royal St., ☎ 504/566–0816) concentrates on contemporary master graphics and originals by internationally known artists (Miró, Calder, Tamayo) as well as some locals.

Kurt E. Schon, Ltd. (510 St. Louis St., ☎ 504/524–5462) stocks art from the 17th to the 20th centuries and has a stunning collection of landscapes and portraits. The staff is very knowledgeable.

Merrill B. Domas American Indian Art (824 Chartres St., ☎ 504/586–0479) displays antique and contemporary North American Indian baskets, weavings, sculpture, jewelry, and beadwork.

Nahan Galleries (540 Royal St., ☎ 504/524–8696), a long-established, locally owned gallery, exhibits and publishes works of contemporary Europeans such as Theo Tobiasse, Max Pappart, and James Coignard.

Rodrigue Gallery (721 Royal St., ☎ 504/581–4244 or 800/899–4244) showcases the work of internationally known Cajun artist George Rodrigue. His "blue dog" paintings are especially popular.

Southern Expressions (521 St. Ann St., on Jackson Sq., ☎ 504/525–4530) carries regional paintings, prints, and watercolors by local artists.

Books

Cookbooks and local history books are available in gift shops throughout the Quarter. Fun for any collector are the various musty used-book shops that proliferate in this area.

Faulkner House Books (624 Pirate's Alley, ☎ 504/524–2940), located in the house where William Faulkner lived and wrote in the 1920s, is stocked with rare and out-of-print books by Southern authors. A find for bibliophiles.

Librairie Book Shop (823 Chartres St., ☎ 504/525–4837) has the Quarter's largest selection of local lore in books, old posters, and postcards.

Old Children's Books (734 Royal St., ☎ 504/525–3655) stocks lots of antiquarian and out-of-print children's literature; there is an original Oz series for collectors.

Clothing

Fleur de Paris (712 Royal St., ☎ 504/525–1899), an innovative and elegant women's apparel shop, features designer dresses, custom hats, and silk lingerie.

Kruz (432 Barracks St., ☎ 504/524–7370), billed as an ethnic boutique, has unique items from around the world at reasonable prices.

New Orleans Hat Attack (Jackson Brewery Millhouse, ☎ 504/523–5770), a fun place to visit, is New Orleans's last word in headgear for men and women.

Ray Cole Collection (503 Royal St., ☎ 504/588–1194) showcases the award-winning designer's paintings of local scenes on silk dresses and scarves. Look for his voodoo doll motifs.

Victoria's Designer Discount Shoes (532 Chartres St., ☎ 504/568–9990) carries famous-name shoes at substantial discounts.

Wehmeier's Belt Shop (719 Toulouse St., ☎ 504/525–2758) has a large selection of finely crafted alligator and exotic leather goods, including belts, wallets, handbags, boots, and shoes.

Foods and Gift Packages

Café du Monde Shop (800 Decatur St., ☎ 504/525–4544), a French Quarter landmark, sells its delicious Creole coffee in 15-ounce cans. Also available is the mix for beignets, the French doughnuts that accompany the coffee. The shop will ship anywhere in the country.

Coffee, Tea, or . . . (630 St. Ann St., ☎ 504/522–0830) stocks teas, spices of the world, and gift ideas, too.

Farmer's Market (N. Peters St., ☎ 504/522–2621) is an open-air emporium where Louisiana's farmers sell their produce in town. The variety of local fruits and vegetables in season includes pecans, sugarcane, mirlitons, Creole tomatoes, and okra. Garlic wreaths hang from the rafters of the building where the great chefs of New Orleans shop for their kitchens.

Gumbo Ya-Ya (219 Bourbon St., ☎ 504/522–7484) carries pralines, spices, cookbooks, and gift packages.

Laura's Original Fudge and Praline Shoppe (115 Royal St., ☎ 504/525–3886) has pralines (made fresh daily), hand-dipped chocolates, Creole spices, and other local favorites.

Louisiana Products (507 St. Ann St., on Jackson Sq., ☎ 504/524–7331) sells Cajun and Creole foods, Mardi Gras beads, local crafts, and novelties. Gift boxes filled with your choice of food items can be shipped anywhere.

Vieux Carré Wine and Spirits (422 Chartres St., ☎ 504/568–WINE) serves wine by the glass, with frequent wine tastings. The store has a large selection of imported and domestic beers, wines, spirits, and cheeses. Gift baskets are available.

Jewelry

The Acorn (736 Royal St., ☎ 504/525–7110) features estate, contemporary, and elephant-hair jewelry, with a good selection of gift items.

Barrister's Gallery (526 Royal St., ☎ 504/525–2767) features exotic tribal jewelry from around the world and the largest range of international primitive art in the Deep South.

Cynthia Sutton (429 Royal St., ☎ 504/523–3377) specializes in estate jewelry.

Joan Good Antiques (809 Royal St., ☎ 504/525–1705) has beautiful garnets, cameos, blue topaz, and marcasite pieces, as well as some antique Japanese pieces.

The Quarter Smith (535 St. Louis St., ☎ 504/524–9731) carries a selection of estate jewelry; you can also have Ken Bowers create a piece from your own design.

Masks

The masks worn at Mardi Gras are popular as gifts, souvenirs, and decorative pieces. Be careful of cheap imitations; the better hand-crafted, locally made masks bear the artist's insignia and are more expensive than the mass-produced ones. A good ceramic or feather mask starts at around $10 and can run as high as $1,000, depending on the materials, workmanship, and size of the mask.

Little Shop of Fantasy (523 Dumaine St., ☎ 504/529–4243) show-cases the handmade leather-and-feather masks of Mike Stark.

Mardi Gras Center (831 Chartres St., ☎ 504/524–4384) is where locals serious about Carnival go for custom-made masks, costumes, and accessories. Hundreds of masks, including animal masks, make this a great place to browse.

Rumors (513 Royal St., ☎ 504/525–0292) and **Rumors Too** (319 Royal St., ☎ 504/523–0011) both have large selections of top-of-the-line ceramic and feather masks.

Serendipitous Masks (831 Decatur St., ☎ 504/522–9158) has an excellent selection of feather masks made by artists on the premises. The shop carries an extensive array of ornate Mardi Gras headdresses, and masks can be made to order.

Yesteryear's (626 Bourbon St., ☎ 504/523–6603) is a welcome alter-native to the T-shirts and poster shops on Bourbon Street. Owner Teresa makes her own elaborate feather masks. Voodoo dolls and folklore items are also available.

Music

GHB Jazz Foundation (1204 Decatur St., ☎ 504/525–0200) operates eight record labels and publishes the quarterly *Jazzbeat*. Listening facility and catalogues are available at a unique jazz information cen-ter in the Palm Court Jazz Café, which houses the foundation and pro-vides a place where music lovers can meet, eat, and enjoy live music.

Record Ron's (1129 Decatur St. and 407 Decatur St., ☎ 504/524–9444) stocks a large selection of new releases, oldies, and local music. If it's pressed in plastic, this shop has it or can locate it for you.

Rock and Roll Collectibles (1214 Decatur St., ☎ 504/561–5683) buys, sells, and trades an array of records, tapes, CDs, and videos. The shop specializes in rock and roll, including local artists.

Werlein's for Music (229 Decatur St., ☎ 504/883–5080), a historic store, has a complete selection of records and tapes, as well as musical instruments. Salespeople are in the know about the local music scene.

Novelties and Gifts

Angel Wings (710 St. Louis St., ☎ 504/524–6880), a whimsical, Vic-torian shop, features handcrafted and unique items, including wear-able ceramics, art gifts, crystals, and hair sticks. After closing, a sign in the door reads, "The angels are gathering stars."

Coghlan Gallery (710 Toulouse St., ☎ 504/525–8550), housed in the historic Lion's Court, has a peaceful courtyard with displays of locally crafted fountains, statuary, and other garden accessories.

Community Flea Market is an open-air market with dozens of tables displaying everything imaginable: jewelry, antiques, clothing, leather goods, and local crafts. *The French Market at Gov. Nicholls St., ☎ 504/596–3420. ⊙ Daily 7 AM–8 PM, though hrs vary with weather and season.*

Crafty Louisianians (813 Royal St., ☎ 504/528–3094), which resembles a local crafts fair, has New Orleans and Louisiana wares such as carved ducks and birds, cypress knees, Mississippi mud dolls, and designs on slate.

Flag & Banner Co. (543 Dumaine St., ☎ 504/522–2204 or 800/774–FLAG) has flags and banners of almost any imaginable size, country, or color. The shop rents, sells, and custom-designs its wares.

The Idea Factory (838 Chartres St., ☎ 504/524–5195) stocks one-of-a-kind gifts, such as miniature steamboats, streetcars, and antique cars, as well as jewelry and dolls; most items are handmade by owners Peg Bacon, Kenny Ford, and Roberta Sklar.

Sigle's Historic New Orleans Metal Craft (935 Royal St., ☎ 504/522–7647) sells original cast-iron wall planters, handcrafted since 1938; these are often seen on Quarter balconies and patios.

Perfumes
Bourbon French Parfums (525 St. Ann St., ☎ 504/522–4480) has been custom blending fragrances since 1843. It carries an established line of more than 30 women's and men's fragrances.

Hové Parfumeur, Ltd. (824 Royal St., ☎ 504/525–7827) creates and manufactures fine fragrances for men and women. Oils, soaps, sachets, and potpourri made to order on the premises. Local family-run business since 1932.

La Belle Epoque (820 Decatur St., ☎ 504/271–3577), creators of Can-Can, Creole Rose, and other New Orleans fragrances, can be found in the All That Jazz Shop.

Toys
Hello Dolly (815 Royal St., ☎ 504/522–9948) has one of the largest collections of regional dolls. The locally made Gambina doll is a specialty here.

Le Petit Soldier Shop (528 Royal St., ☎ 504/523–7741) stocks whole armies of hand-painted toy soldiers, beautifully crafted to become heirlooms.

The Little Toy Shoppe (900 Decatur St., ☎ 504/522–6588) carries the largest Downtown selection of children's toys, books, and posters. The store features beautiful, locally produced Gambina dolls and Madame Alexander dolls. Many regional items for children of all ages are also for sale.

Oh Susannah (518 St. Peter St., ☎ 504/586–8701) showcases pricey collector's dolls from the likes of Annette Hinestedt and Hildegard Gunzel. Dolls of all types are ubiquitous in the French Quarter, but this shop has the edge.

Magazine Street

Magazine Street is one of the oldest and most diverse shopping districts in New Orleans. Named for the French word for shop—*magasin*—this street runs parallel to St. Charles Avenue, but several blocks closer to the river, and passes through old, established neighborhoods.

Along its 5 miles, Magazine Street sports dozens of antiques shops, bric-a-brac vendors, used clothing and furniture stores, art galleries, and specialists in furniture restoration, interior decorating, and landscaping. Name it and it will probably be somewhere on Magazine Street.

The main stretch of shops begins at the intersection of Melpomene and Magazine streets. The Magazine Street bus runs there from Canal Street, and the St. Charles streetcar stops within blocks of this shopping district. The best and safest way to shop on Magazine Street is by taxi, as shops are in clusters, and areas between can be somewhat dangerous.

Macon Riddle (☎ 504/899–3027), a local antiques expert and consultant, offers guided shopping expeditions of Magazine and Royal streets. This is a super way to see the best antiques shops in the area and to judge selection, quality, and price. The tours are especially good for people who are here for only a short time and know what they want but who need help finding it.

Antiques

Antiques Magazine (2043 Magazine St., ☎ 504/522–2043) is the place to go for all things Victorian, from chandeliers to pens. You'll find lots of silver.

As You Like It (3025 Magazine St., ☎ 504/897–6915 or 800/828–2311) has a wide selection of discontinued and hard-to-find sterling silver flatware, including Victorian, Art Deco, and Art Nouveau.

Aurat Antiques (3009 Magazine St., ☎ 504/897–3210 or 800/676–8640) carries antiques from India, including dhurries, carpets, furnishings, and decorative pieces.

Bep's Antiques (2051 Magazine St., ☎ 504/525–7726) is a great browsing place for antique glass bottles, porcelain, crockery, and bric-a-brac.

Bush Antiques (2109 Magazine St., ☎ 504/581–3518) has French, English, and American furniture, fine china, and glass.

Charbonnet & Charbonnet (2929 Magazine St., ☎ 504/891–9948) specializes in large mid-19th century cupboards and chests made from Irish and English pine. It also carries brackets, cornices, and stained glass.

Didier, Inc. (3439 Magazine St., ☎ 504/899–7749) is the only antiques shop in New Orleans that specializes in American furniture. It also has a fine selection of paintings and prints.

Dodge Field Antiques (2033 Magazine St., ☎ 504/581–6930) has a good selection of Victorian and Eastlake furniture and accessories.

Dunn & Sonnier Antiques (2027 Magazine St., ☎ 504/524–3235) stocks 18th-century furnishings, lamps, chandeliers, vases, and religious statuary.

Jacqueline Vance Oriental Rugs (3944 Magazine St., ☎ 504/891–3304) sells a large variety of fine antique and contemporary rugs.

Jean Bragg Antiques (3901 Magazine St., ☎ 504/895–7375) has vintage linens, sewing tools, porcelain, silver, picture frames, and banquet napkins at good prices, as well as Newcombe pottery and George Ohr pottery.

73

Magazine Street Shopping

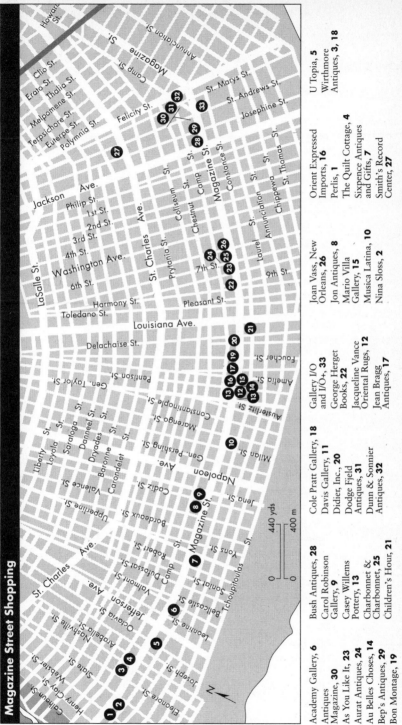

Academy Gallery, **6**
Antiques
Magazine, **30**
As You Like It, **23**
Aurat Antiques, **24**
Au Belles Choses, **14**
Bep's Antiques, **29**
Bon Montage, **19**

Bush Antiques, **28**
Carol Robinson
Gallery, **9**
Casey Willems
Pottery, **13**
Charbonnet &
Charbonnet, **25**
Children's Hour, **21**

Cole Pratt Gallery, **18**
Davis Gallery, **11**
Didier, Inc., **20**
Dodge Field
Antiques, **31**
Dunn & Sonnier
Antiques, **32**

Gallery I/O
and I/O+, **33**
George Herget
Books, **22**
Jacqueline Vance
Oriental Rugs, **12**
Jean Bragg
Antiques, **17**

Joan Vass, New
Orleans, **26**
Jon Antiques, **8**
Mario Villa
Gallery, **15**
Musica Latina, **10**
Nina Sloss, **2**

Orient Expressed
Imports, **16**
Perlis, **1**
The Quilt Cottage, **4**
Sixpence Antiques
and Gifts, **7**
Smith's Record
Center, **27**

U Topia, **5**
Wirthmore
Antiques, **3, 18**

Jon Antiques (4605 Magazine St., ☎ 504/899–4482) offers English furniture, porcelain, mirrors, lamps, tea caddies, and other bric-a-brac.

Nina Sloss (6008 Magazine St., ☎ 504/895–8088) showcases a large assortment of English and Continental pieces from the 18th and 19th centuries. The owner is a nationally known decorator.

Sixpence Antiques and Gifts (4904 Magazine St., ☎ 504/895–1267) imports furniture from France and England. It also carries bric-a-brac and gift items at good prices.

Wirthmore Antiques (5723 Magazine St., ☎ 504/897–9727; 3900 Magazine St., ☎ 504/899–3811) has carefully selected 18th- and 19th-century country furniture from France.

Art

Academy Gallery (5256 Magazine St., ☎ 504/899–8111), where students of the New Orleans Academy of Fine Arts exhibit and sell their work, offers exciting art discoveries at bargain prices.

Carol Robinson Gallery (4537 Magazine St., ☎ 504/895–6130) concentrates on a wide selection of regional and New Orleans artists.

Casey Willems Pottery (3919 Magazine St., ☎ 504/899–1174) welcomes you to view the "Potter at Work" as he creates his imaginative ceramics.

Cole Pratt Gallery (3800 Magazine St., ☎ 504/891–6789) exhibits the paintings, sculptures, and ceramics crafted by contemporary regional and nationally recognized artists.

Davis Gallery (3964 Magazine St., ☎ 504/897–0780) carries rare African, pre-Columbian, and ethnographic art, and supplies collectors and museums.

Gallery I/O and I/O+ (1812 Magazine St. and 1804 Magazine St., ☎ 504/581–2113) is a showcase for popular local artist Thomas Mann's ultramodern furnishings and jewelry.

Mario Villa Gallery (3908 Magazine St., ☎ 504/895–8731) exhibits the internationally known artist's innovative furniture designs, as well as other Louisiana artists' sculpture, photography, pottery, and paintings.

Books

Children's Hour (3308 Magazine St., ☎ 504/899–2378 or 800/769–7695) is a large, cheerful store with tables and shelves filled with children's books and games.

George Herget Books (3109 Magazine St., ☎ 504/891–5595) is a treasure shop, with thousands of rare books, including many regional titles, along with rare postcards, records, sheet music, and Civil War memorabilia.

Clothes

Joan Vass, New Orleans (1100 Sixth St., corner of Magazine St., ☎ 504/891–4502 and 800/338–4864) features the popular designer's full line of women's ready-to-wear clothing. This is the first and largest exclusively Joan Vass outlet in the United States.

Perlis (6070 Magazine St., ☎ 504/895–8661), a New Orleans institution, is the home of the trademark Louisiana crawfish embroidered on shirts and ties. The shop sells top-quality men's and women's clothing.

U Topia (5422 Magazine St., ☎ 504/899–8488) stocks one-of-a-kind block printed cotton knits, all garment dyed. The owners also make tie-dyed wearables. This is a retail shop for their nationally marketed lines.

Music

Musica Latina (4226 Magazine St., ☎ 504/895–4227) is one of the oldest Latin American businesses in the city, and a must for anyone serious about Latin music and local color.

Smith's Record Center (2019 St. Charles Ave., ☎ 504/522–7969 or 504/522–4843) stocks one of the city's best collections of Dixieland jazz and rhythm-and-blues recordings; it has a good selection of classical music, too. The store accepts special orders and ships anywhere in the world.

Novelties and Gifts

Aux Belles Choses (3912 Magazine St., ☎ 504/891–1009) offers an eclectic collection of dried-flower arrangements, notepaper, pottery, imports from France and England, and other beautiful things.

Bon Montage (3719 Magazine St., ☎ 504/897–6295) specializes in custom-made dollhouses, glassware, children's clothes, lamps, and dolls.

Orient Expressed Imports (3905 Magazine St., ☎ 504/899–3060) has a wide selection of Asian pottery and ceramics, plus children's clothing, jewelry, and more.

The Quilt Cottage (801 Nashville St., off Magazine St., ☎ 504/895–3791) is the place to look for new and antique quilts and handmade gift items. Quilting services are available.

Maple Street/Riverbend

There's an old-fashioned aura in this area, where most of the shops are housed in turn-of-the-century cottages. On Maple Street, the shops run for six blocks, from Carrollton Avenue to Cherokee Street; in Riverbend, they dot the streets surrounding the shopping center on Carrollton Avenue. To reach both areas from Downtown, ride the streetcar until St. Charles Avenue becomes Carrollton Avenue, then get off at the first stop, the corner of Maple Street and Carrollton Avenue.

Antiques

O'Keefe's Gallery Interiors (700 Dublin St., ☎ 504/861–7514) carries a good selection of 18th-century English antiques, including break-fronts, drop-leaf tables, and linen presses that go for up to $3,000. Fabrics, wall coverings, trims, carpeting, and Oriental rugs are also found here, as well as brass, china, porcelain, and silver gift items starting at $15. Shipping is arranged.

Arts and Crafts

Carrollton Flower Market (838 Dublin St., ☎ 504/866–9614) is much more than a florist; it also sells pottery, vases, and plant-related items. You'll appreciate the friendly, personal service.

The Sun Shop (7722 Maple St., ☎ 504/861–8338) sells handwoven rugs, blankets, and wall hangings; pottery; jewelry; and a collection of hand-carved Indian masks. For more than 20 years the proprietor has been traveling from Alaska to Peru on a regular basis to select handcrafted works of native Americans.

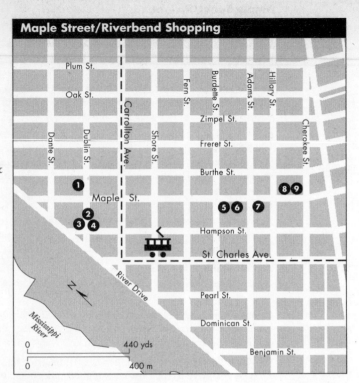

Books

Maple Street Book Shop (7523 Maple St., ☏ 504/866–4916) has outlets around the city; this store is the original. The staff is knowledgeable about the local literary scene past and present. Next door is the **Maple Street Children's Book Shop** (7529 Maple St., ☏ 504/861–2105), the best place in town for children's literature. Bring the kids—there's a reading and activity area for them.

Clothing

Gae-Tana's (7732 Maple St., ☏ 504/865–9625) carries casual, contemporary, and designer-label clothing at 30% to 50% discounts.

Yvonne LaFleur (8131 Hampson St., ☏ 504/866–9666) offers innovative custom-designed fashions, French lingerie, and a full array of shoes and accessories (including a spectacular selection of hats). LaFleur is a New Orleans designer whose boutiques in the Riverwalk and in Esplanade Mall are distinctive in their quality and range.

Food

P. J.'s Coffee & Tea Co. (7624 Maple St., ☏ 504/866–7031) imports coffee beans and exotic teas. Pastries can be purchased in the café and enjoyed at umbrella-covered tables on the patio with cups of freshly brewed coffee or tea.

Jewelry

Mignon Faget Ltd. (710 Dublin St., ☏ 504/865–7361) is the original home of Mignon's internationally acclaimed custom-designed jewelry. Signature pieces include Greek columns, king cakes, and alligators. There's a nice selection of clothing accessories and toiletries, too.

Shopping Centers

These are a few of New Orleans's better shopping centers not previously discussed in this chapter. These centers are open Monday through Saturday 10 AM–9 PM, Sunday 12:30–5:30 PM.

Esplanade Mall (1401 W. Esplanade Ave., Kenner, ☎ 504/468–6116), besides housing impressive department stores such as Macy's and Dillard, features locally owned shops such as Yvonne LaFleur (elegant women's fashions) and a branch of the Café du Monde.

Lakeside Shopping Center (3301 Veterans Memorial Blvd., Metairie, ☎ 504/835–8000) is one of the oldest malls in the country. Here you will find JC Penney, B. Dalton Bookseller, Dillard, Bailey Banks & Biddle Jewelers, five cinemas, Ruby Tuesday's restaurant, and Popeye's Famous Fried Chicken, in addition to the more typical mall shops.

The Plaza at Lake Forest (5700 Read Blvd., ☎ 504/246–1500), totally refurbished in 1993, is where you'll find Dillard, Maison Blanche, Gordon's Jewelers, and plenty more to let you shop till you drop.

4 Sports and the Outdoors

Participant Sports and Fitness

Bicycling

Instead of riding the streetcar, bike at your own pace past the mansions of St. Charles Avenue to lush Audubon Park. City Park and the lakefront are other good alternatives. The **Crescent City Cyclists** bike hotline (☎ 504/486–3683) gives information on biking events.

A linear parkway along Lake Pontchartrain is a 7½-mile path for biking and hiking along the south shore of the lake. (*See* Off the Beaten Track *in* Chapter 2, Exploring New Orleans.)

Rentals are available at **Bicycle Michael's.** *618 Frenchman St.,* ☎ *504/945–9505.* ☛ *$3.50 per hr, $12.50 per day.*

Boating

Lake Pontchartrain awaits the boating enthusiast. **Tim Murray Sailboats** has a Pierson 26 that you can rent for the day. *402 Roadway St.,* ☎ *504/283–2507.*

Pedal boats, rowboats, and canoes are available at **City Park.** *Dreyfous Dr.,* ☎ *504/483–9371.* ☛ *Pedal boats $10 per hr; rowboats and canoes $5, plus $5 deposit required.* ☉ *Wed.–Sun. 8–4.*

Bowling

There are bowling lanes throughout metropolitan New Orleans. Two popular suburban lanes are **Don Carter's All Star Lanes** (3640 Williams Blvd., Kenner, ☎ 504/443–5353) and **Fazzio's Rainbow Lanes** (5555 Bullard Ave., Metairie, ☎ 504/241–2695).

Mid City Bowling Lanes and Sports Palace is the rockin'est bowling alley in the South. Every weekend is Rock'n'Bowl, when the whole neighborhood turns out for bowling and dancing to live music. The alley was built in 1946 and has been carefully maintained. A bar and eating area offer good drinks and local food specials at old-time prices. *4133 S. Carrollton Ave.,* ☎ *504/482–3133.* ☛ *$8 per hr, $10 after 8 PM, $1 shoe rental.* ☉ *Daily noon–1 AM.*

Canoeing

City Park rents canoes for exploring the network of semitropical lagoons that wind through the park's 1,500 acres. *Dreyfous Dr.,* ☎ *504/483–9371.* ☛ *$5 per hr.* ☉ *Daily 8–4.*

Bayou Sauvage National Wildlife Refuge, within the eastern limits of New Orleans, is a 22,000-acre marshland preserve administered by the U.S. Fish and Wildlife Service. Free guided canoe trips are available at the refuge; these include canoes and gear. Individuals with their own canoes are welcome to use the preserve as well, except for mid-November to mid-January when migrating birds are passing through. Call ahead for details. *17158 Chef Menteur Hwy.,* ☎ *504/254–4490.* ☉ *Weekdays 7:30–4.*

Jean Lafitte National Historical Park Barataria Unit has several bayous available to canoers. A local canoe rental shop delivers canoes to the park. The park service hosts a free guided canoe tour Sunday 8:30–11:30 (reservations are advisable). *About a ½ hr's drive from New Orleans near Lafitte,* ☎ *504/689–2002 or 504/589–2330.* ☉ *Daily 9–5.*

Fishing and Hunting

Nonresident visitors intending to fish or hunt in the New Orleans area must purchase the necessary licenses. Seven-day licenses are issued separately for saltwater (which includes Lake Pontchartrain) and freshwater fishing; these are required whether fishing from shore or from a boat. For hunting there is a three-day license. Certain types of crabbing and shrimping also require a license; crawfishing does not. For licenses or information about fishing and hunting regulations, season dates, and archery and trapping information, contact the **Louisiana Wildlife and Fisheries Department** in the French Quarter (400 Royal St., ☎ 504/568–5636).

For $2 per day ($1 children under 16), **City Park** issues one-day permits (sunup to sundown) that allow fishing from the shore in the stocked streams of the park. A state license ($5.50) is also required and can be purchased at the same time. *1 Dreyfous Dr., ☎ 504/483–9371. ☺ Wed.–Sun. 8–3.*

Bayou Sauvage National Wildlife Refuge, a 22,000 preserve, offers some of the best fishing of local brackish and freshwater species. The refuge is open year-round, with the best fishing season from winter to early spring. There is no charge, but a state fishing license from the state Wildlife and Fisheries Department (*see above*) is required. *17158 Chef Menteur Hwy., ☎ 504/254–4490.*

Golf
The public can golf at the following courses in the New Orleans area (greens fees are subject to change).

Audubon Park, 18-hole course. *473 Walnut, ☎ 504/865–8260. ☛ $8 weekdays, $10 weekends.*

Brechtel, 18-hole municipal course. *3700 Behrman Pl., Westbank, ☎ 504/362–4761. ☛ $6.75 weekdays, $8 weekends.*

City Park, four 18-hole courses. *1040 Filmore, ☎ 504/483–9396. ☛ $9 and $12 weekdays, $11 and $15 weekends.*

Joe Bartholomew Golf Course, Pontchartrain Park, 18-hole course. *6514 Congress Dr., ☎ 504/288–0928. ☛ $7.75 weekdays, $10 weekends.*

Plantation Golf Course, 18-hole, par 69 course. *1001 Behrman Hwy., Westbank, ☎ 504/392–3363. ☛ $5.50 weekdays, $7.50 weekends.*

Hiking
The Bartaria Unit of **Jean Lafitte National Historical Park** has several trails that explore Louisiana's delta wetlands and important archaeological sites. A park ranger gives a guided tour daily at 1:15. *About an hr's drive from New Orleans near Lafitte, ☎ 504/689–2002 or 504/589–2330. ☺ Daily 9–5.*

A linear parkway that runs along the south shore of Lake Pontchartrain is a popular 7½-mile route for hiking and biking (*see* Bicycling, *above*).

Louisiana Nature and Science Center also plans hiking and backpacking excursions into areas around New Orleans. *11000 Lake Forest Blvd., New Orleans East, ☎ 504/246–9381.*

Horseback Riding
Cascade Stables in Audubon Park rents horses for riding within the boundaries of the park. Located east of the zoo, off a one-way side road that runs into Magazine Street, the stables are hard to find the first time, but most people in the area will be happy to give directions. *6500 Magazine St., ☎ 504/891–2246. ☛ $20 for an hr ride with guide.*

Jogging

Audubon Park, between St. Charles Avenue and Magazine Street, has a 2-mile jogging path that passes several scenic lagoons as it encircles the golf course. Exercise stations parallel the trail. The **Mississippi River levee** and **City Park** are also popular jogging places. Several organized running events held in New Orleans are open to the public (*see* Spectator Sports, *below*).

Tennis

Audubon Park has 10 courts at the back of the park, off Tchoupitoulas Street. ☎ *504/895–1042.* ☞ *$6.* ☉ *Daily 8–dark.*

City Park has 39 lighted courts. *Dreyfous Dr.,* ☎ *504/483–9383.* ☞ *$5–$6.50.* ☉ *Weekdays 7 AM–10 PM, weekends 7 AM–6 PM.*

Volleyball

Coconut Beach Volleyball Complex, near Lake Pontchartrain, is an open-air sandlot where locals meet for co-ed games. Unless leagues or tournaments are scheduled, playing is open to anyone for a small fee. Visitors welcome. *7360 W. Roadway, West End,* ☎ *504/286–0333.*

Spectator Sports

Baseball

The **New Orleans Zephyrs,** a AAA national baseball team, moved to the city from Denver in 1993. At press time, games were held at the University of New Orleans's Privateer Park; a new Zephyrs stadium in Kenner, across from the Saints training camp, is scheduled to open for the 1996 season. *Zephyrs office,* ☎ *504/282–6777.* ☞ *Tickets: $7 and $5 adults, $2 children, also available from TicketMaster (☎ 504/522–5555).*

Tulane University, the **University of New Orleans** and **Delgado Community College** also field top-flight collegiate teams in the spring.

Basketball

The **Sugar Bowl Basketball Tournament** is held at the Superdome the week preceding the annual football classic. The University of New Orleans plays NCAA Division I Competition; other schools, including Delgado Community College, Dillard, Xavier, and Southern University, also have teams that play home games at gyms and field houses on their respective campuses.

Bowling

The **Professional Bowler's Tour** periodically schedules competition during the last week of January at Fazzio's Rainbow Lanes (*5555 Bullard Ave.,* ☎ *504/241–2695*).

Boxing

The Superdome hosts boxing events from time to time.

Football

The Louisiana Superdome is the place for football. On Sunday the **New Orleans Saints** of the National Football League play their home games; on Saturday afternoons you can usually catch **Tulane University's** home games. The famed LSU–Tulane game is played at the Superdome in odd-numbered years. Grambling and Southern universities renew their annual rivalry in the **Bayou Classic** each November. On New Year's Day the Superdome hosts the **Sugar Bowl.** Every four years the big one comes to town; the next **Super Bowl** at the Superdome is scheduled for 1997. *Saints tickets* ☎ *504/522–2600; Tulane tickets* ☎ *504/861–3661.*

Golf

In April the nation's top professional golfers come to New Orleans to compete in the **Freeport-McMoRan Golf Classic** at English Turn, the Jack Nicklaus golf course. *Hwy. 406, East Canal, Westbank,* ☎ *504/831–4653.*

Horse Racing

At the **Fair Grounds,** the third-oldest racetrack in the nation, the season opens Thanksgiving Day and runs through mid-April. In December 1993, a fire ripped through the Fair Grounds buildings. Facilities were up and running—albeit under tents—within three weeks of the fire; permanent buildings, however, are expected to take several years to complete. Big races include the New Orleans Handicap for older horses and the Louisiana Derby for three-year-olds, a major prep for the Kentucky Derby. Both are run in March. *1751 Gentilly Blvd.,* ☎ *504/944–5515.* ⊙ *Post time 1 PM, Fri. 3 PM. Closed Mon. and Tues., mid-Apr.–Thanksgiving.*

Running

The newly remodeled **Tad Gormley Stadium/Alerion Field** in City Park (☎ 504/483–9359) is a state-of-the-art track facility for local and national events.

Many organized runs take place in New Orleans every year. These include the **Mardi Gras Marathon** in January, the **Crescent City Classic** in April, **Witches Moonlight Run** the night before Halloween, and the **Corporate Run** in December. For further information on these and other running events, contact the Greater New Orleans Runners Association (☎ 504/899–3333 or 504/891–9999).

5 Dining

By Gene
Bourg

CLASSIFYING SOUTH Louisiana cooking can be frustrating. Its two major divisions—the urbane Creole and the more rustic Acadian (or "Cajun")—often merge in a single dish. Mainstream South Louisiana cuisine is fraught with a network of subcuisines drawn from a polyglot of cultures.

Today menus in New Orleans restaurants reflect 270 years of ethnic overlap. The major influences have come from France (both before and after the Revolution of 1789), Africa, Spain, the region's Native Americans, the Caribbean, and, more recently, southern Italy, Germany, and Yugoslavia. In the 1980s, Oriental chefs joined the culinary melting pot with brand-new treatments of seafoods drawn from Louisiana's bountiful coastal wetlands and the Gulf of Mexico.

Despite the increasingly blurred lines separating all these styles, there are some distinguishing characteristics in Creole and Cajun, the two mother cuisines. Creole cooking carries an urban gloss, whether it's a proletarian dish of semiliquid red beans atop steaming white rice or a supremely elegant sauce of wine and cream on delicate-flesh fish.

Cajun food, on the other hand, is decidedly more rough-hewn and rural. The first waves of Acadian settlers found their way to the Louisiana bayous and marshes in the middle of the 18th century. Most had already been farmers and fishermen in Canada and France. Lard was the tie that bound much of the Cajuns' early cooking. For the more sophisticated Creole cooks, it was butter and cream.

To present-day New Orleanians, much of the so-called Cajun food popularized in the 1980s is as exotic as it is to New Yorkers or San Franciscans. One reason is that traditional Cajun gastronomy does not rely heavily on jalapeño peppers, cream sauces, and pasta. Another is that the rest of America discovered chef Paul Prudhomme's blackened fish before Louisiana did. The result is that the number of highly visible New Orleans restaurants serving food that even approaches the lusty spirit of Acadian cooking does not exceed five.

Except in the most luxuriously appointed dining rooms, the best of New Orleans's restaurant food remains a bargain compared to the price levels in other U.S. cities, assuming you restrict your drinking (cocktails will run up the bill considerably). Even the more expensive restaurants are now offering fixed-price menus of three or four courses for substantially less than what an à la carte meal would cost, and coffee or tea is usually included. As a rule, serving sizes are more than generous—some would say unmanageable for the average eater—so many locals order two appetizers rather than a starter and a main course, which can make ordering dessert more practical.

Glossary
The following terms appear frequently in this section:

Andouille (ahn-*dooey*). A mildly spiced Acadian sausage of lean pork, it often flavors gumbos, red beans and rice, and jambalayas.

Barbecue shrimp. The shrimp are not barbecued, but baked in their shells in a blend of either olive oil, butter, or margarine, and usually seasoned with bay leaf, garlic, and other herbs and spices.

Béarnaise (bay-ar-*nayz*). A rich sauce of egg yolk and butter flavored with tarragon and used on meats and fish.

Beignet (ben-*yay*). Originally a rectangular puff of fried dough sprinkled with powdered sugar. In more recent usage, "beignet" can also refer to fritters or crullers containing fish or seafood.

Bisque. A thick, heartily seasoned soup most often made with crawfish, crab, or shrimp. Cream appears in the French versions.

Bouillabaisse (*booey-yah-base*). A Creole bouillabaisse is a stew of various fish and shellfish in a broth seasoned with saffron and often more assertive spices.

Bread pudding. In the traditional version, stale French bread is soaked in a custard mix, combined with raisins and baked, then served with a hot, sugary sauce flavored with whiskey or rum.

Café au lait. A blend, often half and half, of strong coffee and scalded milk.

Café brûlot (broo-*loh*). Cinnamon, lemon, clove, orange, and sugar are steeped with strong coffee, then flambéeed with brandy and served in special pedestaled cups.

Chicory coffee. The ground and roasted root of a European variety of chicory is added to ground coffee in varying proportions. Originally used for reasons of economy, coffee with chicory is now favored by many New Orleanians. It lends an added bitterness to the taste.

Crème brûlée (broo-*lay*). Literally, "burned cream." A cream custard with a crust of oven-browned sugar.

Dirty rice. A cousin of jambalaya. Bits of meat, such as giblets or sausage, and seasonings are added to white rice before cooking.

Etouffée (ay-too-*fay*). Literally, "smothered." The term is used most often for a thick stew of crawfish tails cooked in a roux-based liquid with crawfish fat, garlic, and green seasonings.

Gumbo. From the African word for "okra," it can refer to any number of stewlike soups made with seafood or meat and flavored with okra or ground sassafras ("filé" powder) and myriad other seasonings. Frequent main ingredients are combinations of shrimp, oysters, crab, chicken, andouille, duck, and turkey. A definitive gumbo is served over white rice.

Jambalaya (jam-buh-*lie*-uh). Rice is the indispensible ingredient in this relative of Spain's paella. The rice is cooked with a mix of diced meat and seafood in tomato and other seasonings. Shrimp and ham make frequent appearances in it, as do sausage, green pepper, and celery.

Meunière (muhn-*yehr*). A method of preparing fish or soft-shell crab by dusting it with seasoned flour, sautéing it in brown butter, and using the butter with lemon juice as a sauce. Some restaurants add a dash of Worcestershire sauce.

Mirliton (*merl*-i-*tawn*). A pale green member of the squash family usually identified as vegetable pear. The standard preparation is to scrape the pulp from halved mirlitons, fill them with shrimp and seasoned bread crumbs, and bake them.

Oysters Bienville (byen-*veel*). Oysters lightly baked in their shells under a cream sauce flavored with bits of shrimp, mushroom, and green seasonings. Some chefs also use garlic or mustard.

Oysters en brochette (awn-bro-*shet*). Whole oysters and bits of bacon are dusted with seasoned flour, skewered, and deep-fried. Traditionally, they're served on toast with lemon and burnt butter.

Oysters Rockefeller. Baked oysters on the half shell in a sauce of pureed aromatic greens laced with anise liqueur. The definitive version is served at Antoine's, where the dish was created with a recipe that's still a secret. Most other restaurants make do with spinach.

Panéed veal (pan-*aid*). Breaded veal cutlets sautéed in butter.

Po'boy. A hefty sandwich made with the local French bread and any number of fillings: Roast beef, fried shrimp, oysters, ham, meatballs in tomato sauce and cheese are common. A po'boy "dressed" contains lettuce, tomato, and mayonnaise or mustard. When shellfish are used and the bread is buttered and heated, it becomes a "loaf."

Ravigote (rah-vee-*gote*). In Creole usage, a piquant mayonnaise, usually with capers, used to moisten cold lumps of blue crabmeat.

Rémoulade (ray-moo-*lahd*). The classic rémoulade is a brick-red whipped mixture of olive oil with mustard, scallions, cayenne, lemon, paprika, and parsley. It's served on cold peeled shrimp or lumps of backfin crabmeat.

Soufflé potatoes. Thin, hollow puffs of deep-fried potato. Two fryings at different temperatures produce the puffs.

Tasso (*tah*-so). Acadian cooks developed the recipe for this lean, intensely seasoned ham. It's used sparingly to flavor sauces and gumbos.

Serving Hours

Lunch is normally taken between 11 AM and 2 PM, dinner between 7 PM and 10 PM. Upscale restaurants on the tourist track often serve very reasonable, fixed-price brunch menus, many of them buffet style. A jazz group often supplies live music. Sunday, from late morning to early afternoon, is the prime time for brunch, although a few restaurants offer brunch on other days, too.

Tipping

Tipping practices conform to those in the rest of the United States—about 15% in the inexpensive–moderate ($–$$) restaurants, and 20% in luxury establishments or when a server has performed exceedingly well.

Reservations

Most restaurants accept reservations, and many of the very popular places quickly become booked, especially on Friday and Saturday nights. The best strategy is to reserve as soon as you decide where and when you'd like to go. If you must cancel, let the reservations desk know immediately.

What to Wear

If you're eating in a luxury restaurant, or one of the old-line, conservative Creole places, dress appropriately. If you don't know if jackets are required or if jeans are frowned upon, telephoning to find out is a simple matter. You'll probably be more comfortable, and so will the restaurant's other customers. Also, you may avoid being turned away at the door. Unless otherwise noted, restaurants in this chapter allow casual dress.

Cuisine Categories

Those New Orleans restaurants that specialize in local cuisines have been grouped into the following five categories:

Traditional Creole. These restaurants specialize in rather complex dishes that have been familiar to generations of New Orleans restaurant goers. Shrimp rémoulade, gumbo, trout meunière, and bread pudding are some examples.

Contemporary Creole. The food usually includes some traditional Creole dishes, but there's a heavier focus on creativity. Local ingredients are used in novel ways, but the basic flavors adhere to the Creole standards of richness and deep flavors. Trout with pecans and bread pudding soufflé are typical.

Cajun-Inspired. Kitchens in these restaurants show direct and recognizable influences from the hearty and rustic cuisine of the Southwest Louisiana Acadians. Seasonings are often more intense than in Creole cooking, and pork and game are prominent ingredients.

Creole with Soul. This food reflects both the robust style of Southern black cooks and the spicier aspects of early New Orleans cuisine.

Avant-Garde. The innovative cooking is sometimes lighter than true Creole or Cajun, although many of the dishes still have ties to South Louisiana.

CATEGORY	COST*
$$$$	over $35
$$$	$25–$35
$$	$15–$25
$	under $15

*per person for a three-course meal, excluding drinks, service, and 9% sales tax

Traditional Creole

$$$$ **Antoine's.** What began 150 years ago as a modest French Quarter boardinghouse has evolved into a stronghold of 19th-century classicism. The mystique of New Orleans's oldest restaurant—still operated by descendants of founder Antoine Alciatore—is preserved in a two-story maze of rooms festooned with every kind of memorabilia. The front dining room, enveloped in flouncy, translucent curtains and decorated with stunning crystal lighting, is the most handsome. Antoine's extensive menu, written in French, could serve as a minor encyclopedia of the more aristocratic brand of New Orleans–French cuisine that developed over the decades. This was the birthplace of oysters Rockefeller in the 1880s, and the secret recipe for the green sauce is still followed. Other rich, thick sauces—marchand de vin, bordelaise, hollandaise—hold as much sway today as they did 100 years ago. The oysters are a must-order appetizer, although ramekins of *crawfish cardinal* (a cream sauce with sprightly seasonings) have their fans, too. Souffléed potatoes are natural companions to the beef tournedos, served as is or with the sauce of your choice. The service, by veteran, tuxedoed waiters, can be impersonal. ✕ *713 St. Louis St., French Quarter,* ☎ *504/581–4422. Reservations required. Jacket required. AE, D, DC, MC, V.*

$$$$ **Arnaud's.** This is one of the grandes dames of classic Creole restaurants, and it still sparkles, thanks to a major face-lift made a decade ago. The main dining room's outside wall of ornate etched glass reflects light from the charming old chandeliers, while the late founder, Arnaud Cazenave, gazes from an oil portrait near the extra-high ceiling. When the main room fills up, the overflow spills over into a

French Quarter Dining

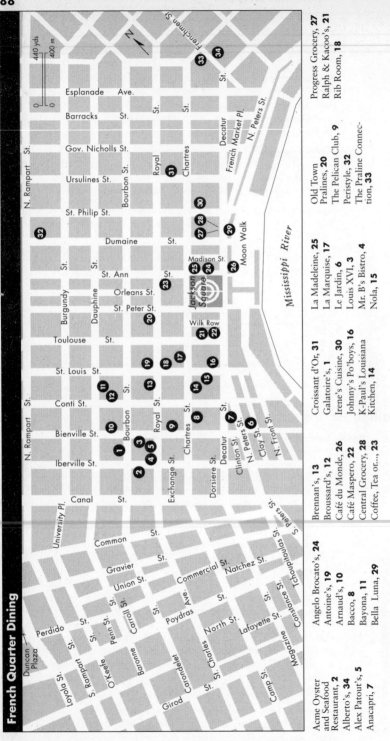

Esplanade Ave.

Barracks St.

Gov. Nicholls St.

Ursulines St.

St. Philip St.

Dumaine St.

St. Ann St.

Orleans St.

St. Peter St.

Toulouse St.

St. Louis St.

Conti St.

Bienville St.

Iberville St.

Canal St.

N. Rampart St.

Burgundy St.

Dauphine St.

Bourbon St.

Royal St.

Chartres St.

Decatur St.

Frenchmen St.

Decatur St.

French Market Pl.

N. Peters St.

Madison St.

Moon Walk

Jackson Square

Wilk Row

Clinton St.

N. Peter's St.

Clay St.

N. Front St.

Exchange St.

Dorsiere St.

Mississippi River

440 yds
400 m

University Pl.

Duncan Plaza

Perdido St.

Common St.

Gravier St.

Union St.

Poydras St.

Girod St.

Loyola St.

S. Rampart St.

O'Keefe St.

Penn St.

Baronne St.

Carroll St.

St. Charles Ave.

Carondelet St.

Camp St.

Magazine St.

Constance St.

Tchoupitoulas St.

S. Peters St.

Commercial St.

Natchez St.

North St.

Lafayette St.

Acme Oyster
and Seafood
Restaurant, **2**
Alberto's, **34**
Alex Patout's, **5**
Anacapri, **7**

Angelo Brocato's, **24**
Antoine's, **19**
Arnaud's, **10**
Bacco, **8**
Bayona, **11**
Bella Luna, **29**

Brennan's, **13**
Broussard's, **12**
Café du Monde, **26**
Café Maspero, **22**
Central Grocery, **28**
Coffee, Tea or..., **23**

Croissant d'Or, **31**
Galatoire's, **1**
Irene's Cuisine, **30**
Johnny's Po'boys, **16**
K-Paul's Louisiana
Kitchen, **14**

La Madeleine, **25**
La Marquise, **17**
Le Jardin, **6**
Louis XVI, **3**
Mr. B's Bistro, **4**
Nola, **15**

Old Town
Pralines, **20**
The Pelican Club, **9**
Peristyle, **32**
The Praline Connec-
tion, **33**

Progress Grocery, **27**
Ralph & Kacoo's, **21**
Rib Room, **18**

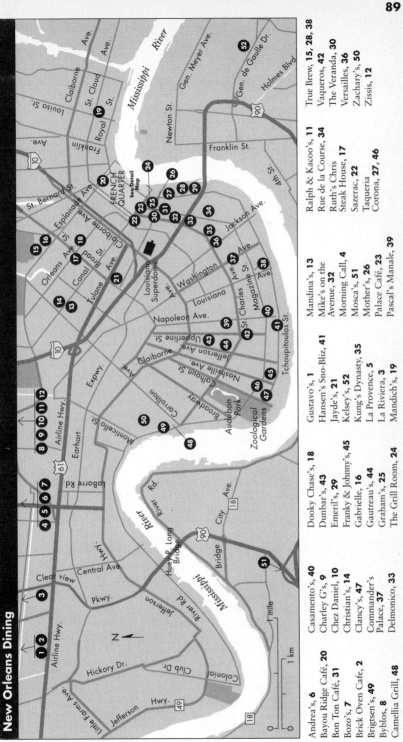

New Orleans Dining

True Brew, **15, 28, 38**
Vaqueros, **42**
The Veranda, **30**
Versailles, **36**
Zachary's, **50**
Zissis, **12**

Ralph & Kacoo's, **11**
Rue de la Course, **34**
Ruth's Chris
Steak House, **17**
Sazerac, **22**
Taqueria
Corona, **27, 46**

Mandina's, **13**
Mike's on the
Avenue, **32**
Morning Call, **4**
Mosca's, **51**
Mother's, **26**
Palace Café, **23**
Pascal's Manale, **39**

Gustavo's, **1**
Hansen's Sno-Bliz, **41**
Jayde's, **21**
Kelsey's, **52**
Kung's Dynasty, **35**
La Provence, **5**
La Riviera, **3**
Mandich's, **19**

Dooky Chase's, **18**
Dunbar's, **43**
Emeril's, **29**
Franky & Johnny's, **45**
Gabrielle, **16**
Gautreau's, **44**
Commander's
Palace, **37**
Graham's, **25**
The Grill Room, **24**

Casamento's, **40**
Charley G's, **9**
Chez Daniel, **10**
Christian's, **14**
Clancy's, **47**
Commander's
Delmonico, **33**

Andrea's, **6**
Bayou Ridge Café, **20**
Bon Ton Café, **31**
Bozo's, **7**
Brick Oven Cafe, **2**
Brigtsen's, **49**
Byblos, **8**
Camellia Grill, **48**

labyrinth of plush banquet rooms and bars. The big, ambitious menu includes classic dishes that have been around for decades, as well as some new creations in a more contemporary style. Always reliable are the cold shrimp Arnaud, in a superb rémoulade, the creamy oyster stew, and rich shrimp bisque, as well as the fish in crawfish sauce, the beef Wellington, and the fine crème brûlée. Expect hurried service on especially crowded nights, but rely on the reservations desk to perform efficiently. ✗ *813 Bienville St., French Quarter,* ☏ *504/523–5433. Reservations required. Jacket required. AE, D, DC, MC, V.*

$$$$ Brennan's. Lavish breakfasts of elaborate poached egg dishes are what first put Brennan's on the map almost 40 years ago. They're still a big draw, although the two floors of luxuriously appointed dining rooms, in a gorgeous 19th-century French Quarter building, often fill up just as quickly at dinner. The best seats include views of the lush, tropical courtyard and fountain, which are illuminated at night. Eye-opening cocktails flow every morning, followed by the tasty poached eggs sandwiched between such things as hollandaise, creamed spinach, artichoke bottoms, Canadian bacon, and fried fish. Headliners at lunch or dinner include blue-ribbon, textbook versions of oysters Rockefeller and seafood gumbo, marvelous sautéed fish blanketed in crabmeat, good veal and beef dishes, and bananas Foster, a legendary dessert that was created here. The dining companion who will enjoy the meal most is the one who's not paying the bill. ✗ *417 Royal St., French Quarter,* ☏ *504/525–9711. Reservations strongly advised. AE, D, DC, MC, V.*

$$$$ Broussard's. No French Quarter restaurant surpasses Broussard's for
★ old-fashioned spectacle. A complete overhaul in the 1970s turned a dowdy Creole bistro into a soft-edged, glittery mix of elaborate wall coverings, chandeliers, porcelain, and polished woods, with a manicured courtyard to boot. If the menu blazes no trails, it contains respectable renditions of the fancier Creole standbys further upgraded with Continental touches. The savory cheesecake of crab and shrimp with dill and roasted sweet peppers is a star among the appetizers, along with lumps of backfin crab in a spicy sauce. Other luxurious sauces crown fillets of fresh pompano, braised quail, and a rack of lamb. Desserts are especially fancy; for example, layers of ice cream and sorbet wrapped in meringue. ✗ *819 Conti St., French Quarter,* ☏ *504/581–3866. Reservations advised. AE, D, DC, MC, V. Lunch Fri. only.*

$$$$ Christian's. A small church in a residential neighborhood has been turned into a front-rank purveyor of Creole cuisine with numerous French flourishes. On crowded banquettes under stained-glass windows, a small army of regulars devour excellent, crunchy smoked soft-shell crab laced with butter, a Creole bouillabaisse of local fish and shellfish in a beautifully seasoned broth, and gulf fish sautéed with fresh oysters and drenched in brown wine sauce. The superb recipe for skewered fried oysters with bacon comes from Galatoire's, and the two restaurants, operated by members of the same family, share other dishes as well. A reservation doesn't guarantee immediate seating, and the bar is tiny. Customers who don't demand a reasonably paced meal may find themselves in and out in 45 minutes or less. The food's the thing in this busy and rather cramped dining room. ✗ *3835 Iberville St., Mid-City,* ☏ *504/482–4924. Reservations required. AE, D, MC, V. Closed Sun. No lunch Sat. and Mon.–Wed.*

$$ **Delmonico.** This is the closest many visitors get to dinner in a handsomely decorated home in the Garden District. Elegance and warmth characterize the atmosphere in Delmonico, which is decorated with traditional wallpapers in relaxing colors, botanical prints, period furniture, and other domestic touches. It's the perfect place for vegetable soup or delicately seasoned okra gumbo, both of which Delmonico does well. The rest of the menu has its weaknesses, but look for the competently done beef fillet in burgundy sauce, a toothsome broiled red snapper, spicy broiled and stuffed shrimp, and home-style chocolate and coconut cream pies. Don't expect frills in the table service. ✘ *1300 St. Charles Ave., Lower Garden District,* ☎ *504/525–4937. Weekend reservations advised. AE, D, DC, MC, V.*

$$ **Galatoire's.** A 90-year-old restaurant that seems as fresh as it was at
★ 20, Galatoire's epitomizes the old-style French-Creole bistro. Few customers tire of the lengthy menu, filled with sauces that can be humdrum in lesser restaurants but somehow escape staleness in this one. The answer may lie in the staff's high standards for ingredients and recipes, which have been fine-tuned over decades. Fried oysters and bacon en brochette court excess but are worth every calorie. The brick-red rémoulade sauce is the touchstone to measure all others against. Lumps of crabmeat, served either cold in a seasoned mayonnaise or warm atop buttery broiled pompano, never tasted better. Others on the long list of time-tested winners include a Creole bouillabaisse, meaty veal or spring lamb chops in béarnaise sauce, seafood-stuffed eggplant, and earthy lyonnaise potatoes. The setting is close to perfect—a single, narrow dining room lit with glistening brass chandeliers, swathed in white-framed mirror panels, and bordered with polished brass coat hooks. The bentwood chairs at the white-clothed tables add to the timeless atmosphere. The quality of service varies from waiter to waiter; the best strategy is to ask for recommendations and then be assertive. Long waits in line outside sometimes can be avoided by eating early. ✘ *209 Bourbon St., French Quarter,* ☎ *504/525–2021. No reservations. Jacket required at dinner. MC, V. Closed Mon.*

$$ **Mandich's.** This many-faceted favorite of locals resists categorizing. It occupies a neat but unremarkable building in a blue-collar neighborhood. The decor—a mix of bright yellow paint, captain's chairs, and wood veneer—won't win prizes. The food ranges from straightforward, home-style dishes to ambitious trout and shellfish dishes. Fried oysters are swathed in a finely balanced butter sauce with garlic and parsley. Shrimp and andouille sausages trade flavors on the grill. The breaded trout Mandich has become a classic of the genre, and more garlic boosts slices of buttery roasted potatoes. Prices are rather steep for a restaurant that invests little in decoration, accepts no reservations, and opens for dinner only two nights a week. ✘ *3200 St. Claude Ave., Ninth Ward,* ☎ *504/947–9553. MC, V. Lunch Tues.–Fri., dinner Fri. and Sat. Closed Sun. and Mon.*

Contemporary Creole

$$$$ **Commander's Palace.** No restaurant captures New Orleans's gastro-
★ nomic heritage and celebratory spirit as well as this one in a stately Garden District mansion. The dishes are consistently creative, but they also deliver the deep flavors and imaginative combinations that have distinguished Creole cooking from the beginning. The upstairs Garden Room's glass walls afford marvelous views of the giant oak trees on the patio below, and the other rooms promote conviviality with their bright pastels or delicate wall paintings. The kitchen's clas-

sics include poached oysters in a seasoned cream sauce with Oregon caviar; a sauté of shrimp and mushrooms in a deceptively simple butter sauce with wine and garlic; a spicy and meaty turtle soup; terrific crab cakes in an oyster sauce; and a wonderful sautéed trout coated with crunchy pecans. Among the addictive desserts are the bread pudding soufflé and chocolate Sheba, a wonderful Bavarian cream. Several hundred people might dine at Commander's on a given day, but its size rarely interferes with the quality of the food or service. The special weekend brunch menus are less ambitious, but also less costly. Lunch specials, with several fixed-price courses at well under $15, are a bargain. Reserve as far in advance as possible. ✕ *1403 Washington Ave., Garden District,* ☏ *504/899–8221. Reservations required. Jacket required. AE, D, DC, MC, V.*

$$$$ **Rib Room.** One focus of this long-popular hotel restaurant is an open grill that dispenses excellent roast prime rib, competently cooked gulf fish in novel sauces, and a good rack of lamb. The manageable menu usually contains distinctive pastas and salads: Fettuccine in cream enriched with wild mushrooms and a watercress salad with pecans are typical. A favorite dish at lunchtime is veal Tanet, a moist and tender cutlet breaded and served atop salad greens dampened with vinaigrette. The wine list is more than serviceable, and table service is correct without being overbearing. The dining room's pleasing combination of warmth and elegance is enhanced by the brick surfaces, cushy furniture, and unusual old metal lanterns, as well as the large windows overlooking Royal Street in the French Quarter's heart. ✕ *Omni Royal Orleans Hotel, 621 St. Louis St., French Quarter,* ☏ *504/529–7045. Reservations advised for dinner. AE, D, DC, MC, V.*

$$$ **Brigtsen's.** Chef Frank Brigtsen's fusion of Creole refinement and ★ Acadian earthiness reflects his years as a protégé of Paul Prudhomme. The owner-chef's ever-changing menus add up to some of the best South Louisiana cooking you'll find anywhere. Everything is fresh and filled with the deep and complex tastes that characterize Creole-Cajun food. The cream of oysters Rockefeller soup is a revelation. Rabbit and chicken dishes, usually presented in rich sauces and gravies, are full of robust flavor. The roux-based gumbos are thick and intense, and the fresh banana ice cream is worth every calorie. Fans of blackened food couldn't do better than with this prime rib, in a spicy charred coating that is perfect with the meat flavors. Fish dishes are likewise elaborate, often showing up as crawfish, shrimp, or oysters in buttery, seasoned sauces. The simple surroundings remain as they were when this was a long, narrow-frame cottage at the turn of the century. Lucky are the customers who can get one of the two tables on an enclosed sunroom out front. ✕ *723 Dante St., Uptown,* ☏ *504/861–7610. Reservations required (call a wk or more in advance). AE, MC, V. Closed Sun. and Mon.*

$$$ **Charley G's.** One of the few restaurants in the New Orleans suburbs that does justice to contemporary South Louisiana cooking, Charley G's has been a runaway success since its opening in mid-1992. One reason is the smart, uncluttered look of the split-level dining spaces, simultaneously elegant and festive. Another is the menu, which contains some of the best Creole-Cajun food around. The crab cakes and chicken-and-sausage gumbo would impress the pickiest bayou gastronome. Game dishes, especially duck and quail, are superb, as are the grilled fish and belt-busting desserts. The mostly California wine list is both impressive in range and beautifully organized. ✕ *Second*

*level, Heritage Plaza building, 111 Veterans Blvd., Metairie, ☎ 504/
837–6408. Reservations advised. AE, D, DC, MC, V. No lunch Sat.*

$$$ **Clancy's.** The easy, sophisticated charm and consistently classy menu
have made this minimally decorated bistro a favorite with profes-
sional and business types from nearby uptown neighborhoods. Most
of the dishes are imaginative treatments of New Orleans favorites.
Some specialties, like the fresh sautéed fish in cream sauce flavored
with crawfish stock and herbs, are exceptional. Other signs of an
inventive chef are the sweetbreads in cream, mustard, and basil; the
expertly fried oysters matched with warm Brie; the grilled chicken
breast in lime butter; and a marvelous peppermint ice-cream pie. Sim-
pler dishes like fettuccine Alfredo and filet mignon in Madeira sauce
benefit from careful and knowledgeable preparation. The decor is
neutral, with grey walls and a few ceiling fans above bentwood chairs
and white linen cloths. The small bar separating the two rooms is
usually filled with regulars who know each other. ✗ *6100 Annuncia-
tion St., Uptown, ☎ 504/895–1111. Reservations advised. AE, MC,
V. Closed Sun. No lunch Mon. and Tues.*

$$$ **Emeril's.** For many seasoned restaurant goers in New Orleans,
★ Emeril's is the pacesetter for Creole cuisine in the 1990s. Proprietor-
chef Emeril Lagasse, former executive chef at Commander's Palace,
opened this large, noisy, and decidedly contemporary restaurant in
early 1990 with an ambitious menu that gives equal emphasis to Creole and modern American cooking. On the plate, this translates as a
fresh corn crepe topped with Louisiana caviar, grilled andouille
sausage in the chef's own Worcestershire sauce, a sauté of crawfish
over jambalaya cakes, fresh-fruit cobblers, and a cornucopia of other
creative dishes. Singles and couples can grab a stool at a food bar and
get close-up views of the chef at work while they eat. The looks of the
place are appropriately avant-garde—brick and glass walls, gleaming
wood floors, burnished-aluminum lamps, and a huge abstract-
expressionist oil painting. ✗ *800 Tchoupitoulas St., Warehouse District, ☎ 504/528–9393. Reservations strongly advised, at least
several days in advance. AE, DC, MC, V. Closed Sun. No lunch Sat.*

$$$ **Gabrielle.** This bright and energetic newcomer, about five minutes by
★ taxi from the French Quarter, was an immediate hit with locals, thanks
to chef Greg Sonnier's marvelous interpretations of earthy and spicy
South Louisiana dishes. Spaces are tight in the single dining room, its
pale walls hung with pleasant pastel still lifes. Regulars come for the
spicy rabbit and veal sausages, buttery oysters gratinéed with artichoke
and Parmesan, a slew of excellent gumbos and etouffées, and Mary
Sonnier's fresh-fruit cobblers and shortcakes. Servings are generous
and sauces are rich, so you may want to skip lunch before dining here.
✗ *3201 Esplanade Ave., Mid-City, ☎ 504/948–6233. Reservations
advised. AE, DC, MC, V. Closed Sun. and Mon. Lunch Fri. only.*

$$$ **Kelsey's.** Randy Barlow, the owner-chef at this modest but very attrac-
★ tive restaurant across the Mississippi from the city center, spent years
working under the celebrated Paul Prudhomme. While the mentor's
influences are obvious in the deep, South Louisiana flavors of Barlow's
food, he has forged a style of his own. His spicy jambalaya of chicken,
sausage, Cajun ham, and rabbit is one of the best versions anywhere. A
home-style gumbo with seafood, chicken, and sausage has just the right
balance of spicy and mellow flavors. Shrimp etouffée, in a moderately
peppery sauce, is loaded with shrimp flavor. Try the orange-poppyseed
cheesecake. The L-shaped dining room, on the second floor of a small

office building, is wrapped in large glass panes, and interesting water-colors and oils add considerable color to the otherwise subdued sur-roundings. ✕ *3920 Gen. DeGaulle Dr., Algiers,* ☎ *504/366–6722. Weekend reservations advised. AE, MC, V. Closed Sun. and Mon.*

$$$ **Mr. B's Bistro.** The energy never seems to subside in this attractive,
★ smart French Quarter restaurant, with waiters darting between the wood and glass screens that reduce the vastness of the dining room. On the green vinyl banquettes, diners choose from a dependable contem-porary-Creole menu centering on meats and seafood from a grill fueled with hickory and other aromatic woods. The barbecue shrimp is one of the best versions in town. Pasta dishes, especially the pasta jambalaya with andouille sausage and shrimp, are fresh and imaginative. The tra-ditional-style bread pudding with Irish whiskey sauce is excellent, too. Lunchtime finds most of the tables taken up by locals, who like the cor-rectly composed club sandwich, pasta carbonara, and other main attractions from the fixed-price menu. ✕ *201 Royal St., French Quar-ter,* ☎ *504/523–2078. Reservations advised. AE, D, DC, MC, V.*

$$$ **Nola.** Fans of chef Emeril Lagasse's who can't get a table at Emeril's
★ in the Warehouse District now have this sassy and vibrant French Quarter restaurant as an alternative. Lagasse has not lowered his sights with Nola's menu, as lusty and rich as any in town. He stews boudin sausage with beer, onions, cane syrup, and Creole mustard before ladling it all onto a sweet-potato crouton. Trout is swathed in a horseradish-citrus crust before it's plank-roasted in a wood oven. Pasta comes laden with sautéed eggplant and a sauce of smoked tomatoes and Parmesan. The combinations seem endless. At dessert time, go for the coconut cream or apple-buttermilk pie with cinna-mon ice cream. ✕ *534 St. Louis St., French Quarter,* ☎ *504/522–6652. AE, D, DC, MC, V. No lunch Sun.*

$$$ **Palace Café.** Members of the Commander's Palace branch of the Brennan family operate this big and colorful new restaurant on Canal Street just a few blocks from the Mississippi riverfront. Crafted from a multistory building that was the city's oldest music store, the Palace is a convivial spot to try some of the more imaginative contemporary Creole dishes. The crab chops, rabbit ravioli in piquante sauce, grilled shrimp with fettuccine, and seafood Napoleon represent the best in both traditional and modern New Orleans cookery. Desserts, espe-cially the white-chocolate bread pudding and Mississippi mud pie, are luscious. An easy elegance pervades the restaurant's two levels. Drugstore-tile floors, stained-cherry booths, and soothing beige walls set the mood. A handsome curved staircase at the center of the lower floor leads to the wraparound mezzanine lined with a large, brightly colored wall painting populated by famous musicians from the city's past and present. Out front, the sidewalk tables are an excellent van-tage point for people-watching along bustling Canal Street. ✕ *605 Canal St., Central Business District,* ☎ *504/523–1661. Weekend reservations advised. AE, DC, MC, V.*

Cajun-Inspired

$$$ **Alex Patout's.** Prints of birds and bayou landscapes contrast with the cushy furnishings and urbane decor of this friendly and reasonably priced restaurant. The owner-chef's Southwest Louisiana roots show up in lusty seasonings and rich sauces. The meaty crawfish cakes have lots of zip, as does the Louisiana court bouillon. Reliable soup choices include the murky and deep-flavored gumbo and the thick and hearty white bean with tasso. Among the good fish dishes is the baked red

snapper stuffed with eggplant and shrimp, and the duck with oyster dressing bursts with complex flavors. ✗ *221 Royal St., French Quarter,* ☎ *504/525–7788. Reservations advised. AE, D, DC, MC, V. No lunch.*

$$$ Bon Ton Café. The Bon Ton's opening in 1953 marked the first appearance of a significant Cajun restaurant in New Orleans. Its crawfish dishes, gumbo, jambalaya, and oyster omelet have retained their strong following in the decades since. The bustle in the excellently maintained dining room reaches a peak at lunchtime on weekdays, when businesspeople from nearby offices come in droves for the baked eggplant with shrimp, the fried catfish, the turtle soup, and a warm and sugary bread pudding. The veteran waitresses are knowledgeable and fleet-footed. ✗ *401 Magazine St., Central Business District,* ☎ *504/524–3386. Reservations advised. AE, MC, V. Closed weekends.*

$$$ K-Paul's Louisiana Kitchen. Chef Paul Prudhomme started the blackening craze and added "Cajun" to America's culinary vocabulary in this rustic French Quarter café. Almost a decade later, thousands still consider a visit to New Orleans partly wasted without a long wait outside for his inventive gumbos, fried crawfish tails, blackened tuna, roast duck with rice dressing, and sweet potato-pecan pie. Although servings are generous, the prices are steep at dinner but moderate at lunch. Some diners may be put off by the community seating downstairs, and the custom of putting a gold paper star on your cheek if you clean your plate. The jalapeño-laced martinis are served in canning jars, and the guru himself makes an occasional appearance. ✗ *416 Chartres St., French Quarter,* ☎ *504/524–7394. Reservations accepted for dinner upstairs. AE. Closed Sun. and Mon.*

Creole with Soul

$$ Dooky Chase's. ★ The roots of many of the home-style dishes at Dooky Chase's go back more than a century. The food, prepared with a technique handed down by generations of local cooks, is served in a warm and elegantly proportioned dining room hung with artworks by local black artists. Crab soup and Creole gumbo are dependable starters. Good meat entrées include the buttery panéed veal and the pork chops sautéed with onions. The sausage jambalaya, stewed okra, and sweet potatoes are as delicious as they are definitive. Homey desserts include bread pudding and a decent apple pie. Late lunch or early dinner at Dooky's on Sunday afternoon has become a tradition for neighborhood families, and the weekday luncheon buffets are a bountiful bargain. ✗ *2301 Orleans Ave., Treme,* ☎ *504/821–2294. Reservations advised. AE, MC, V.*

$ Dunbar's. Red tufted booths and homey, brightly colored paintings perk up the atmosphere at this diamond-in-the-rough, where homestyle Creole cooking is king. Owner-chef Tina Dunbar's fried chicken takes a back seat to none other, and her stuffed sweet peppers, red beans, fried-seafood po'boys, and mustard greens are state-of-the-art as well. Prices are the next best thing to free, and students who produce ID cards get free iced tea. You're not likely to spend more than $5 or $6 for a very filling dinner here, and substantial breakfasts can be had for about $2, all-inclusive. ✗ *4927 Freret St., Uptown,* ☎ *504/899–0734. Reservations for large groups only. MC, V.*

$ Jayde's. In this smartly renovated frame cottage in New Orleans's commercial district, you'll find home-style Creole cooking that's often far above average in both its sophistication and flavor. Bright coral walls are decorated with poster portraits of jazz musicians. The agreeable staff serves a fine, fluffy cornbread, a frothy sweet-potato pie, and good versions of New Orleans–style barbecue shrimp, fried seafoods, cooked-down greens, and candied yams. The restaurant is smoke-free. ✕ *2523 Perdido St., Mid-City,* ☎ *504/822–6814. MC, V.*

$ The Praline Connection. Down-home cooking in the Southern-Creole
★ style is the forte of this laid-back and likeable restaurant a couple of blocks from the French Quarter, with a branch in the Warehouse District as well. The food is the no-nonsense kind that has fueled generations of Southern families, urban and rural, rich and poor. The fried or stewed chicken, smothered pork chops, barbecued ribs, and collard greens are definitively done. And the soulful filé gumbo, crowder beans, bread pudding, and sweet-potato pie are among the best in town. Add to all this some of the lowest prices anywhere, a congenial service staff, and a neat-as-a-pin dining room and the sum is a fine place to spend an hour or two. The adjacent sweet shop holds such home-style delights as sweet-potato cookies, several types of Creole pralines, and all sorts of pies and confections. ✕ *542 Frenchmen St., Faubourg Marigny,* ☎ *504/943–3934; 901 S. Peters St., Warehouse District,* ☎ *504/523–3973. No reservations. AE, D, DC, MC, V.*

$ Zachary's. Inside a brightly colored raised cottage in the Carrollton section, Zachary's offers similarly homey food with strong New Orleans accents. Families often populate the two simple but cheery dining rooms, with crisp, pink tablecloths on the tables, and a few paintings and prints on the walls. You'll find assertively seasoned fried catfish topped with shrimp and crab in a light cream sauce, meaty veal chops drenched in a garlicky bordelaise, first-rate fried chicken, and an old-fashioned Creole bread pudding. Good lunch choices are the beef-brisket po'boy, lavished with brown gravy, and the definitively done red beans and rice, with a rich flavoring of ham. For a true taste of the earthy New Orleans style try the scooped-out French bread filled with a spicy oyster dressing. ✕ *8400 Oak St., Carrollton,* ☎ *504/865–1559. MC, V. Closed Sun. No lunch Sat.*

Avant-Garde

$$$$ The Grill Room. The British furnishings and paintings span several
★ centuries in these dazzling dining spaces. The grandeur and formality are scaled down somewhat by an ingenious arrangement of everything, from the body-hugging chairs and banquettes to the large academic canvases depicting aspects of upper-class England in the early 20th century. The breakfast, lunch, and dinner menus change daily and are filled with appropriately exotic and sumptuous ingredients, often flown in from Europe and the Orient. The day's pasta might be carrot linguine tossed with feta cheese, prosciutto, spinach, and baby artichoke; the fish, fresh sardines from Brittany in a Creole sauce of tomato, peppers, and onions; the meat course, a match of rabbit tenderloin and sweetbreads in Thermidor sauce; and the soup, an ethereal shrimp bisque. Breakfast, with its blend of the familiar (several treatments of poached eggs with meat or seafood in rich sauces) and the unusual (kippers, European cereals, and tropical juices), is an event. The wine cellar and its sterling collection of vintage Bordeaux reds is awesome. Service usually matches the food and atmosphere. ✕ *2nd Level, Windsor Court Hotel, 300 Gravier St., Central Business District,* ☎ *504/522–1992. Reservations strongly advised. Jacket required at dinner. AE, D, DC, MC, V.*

$$$ **Bayona.** "New World" is the label chef Susan Spicer applies to her
★ cooking style—such dishes as turnovers filled with spicy crawfish tails;
a bisque of corn, leeks, and chicken; or fresh salmon fillet in white-
wine sauce with sauerkraut. Her grilled duck breast with pepper-jelly
glaze and shrimp with coriander sauce are among the creations that
originally made Spicer's reputation at her previous post, the Bistro at
Maison de Ville. These and myriad other imaginative dishes are served
in an early 19th-century Creole cottage on a quiet French Quarter
street. The chef herself supervised the renovation of the handsome
building, now fairly glowing with oversized flower arrangements, ele-
gant photographs, and, in one small dining room, trompe l'oeil murals
suggesting Mediterranean landscapes. In good weather drinks and
meals are served in a rear patio overflowing with tropical greenery. ✗
430 Dauphine St., French Quarter, ☎ *504/525–4455. Reservations
strongly advised. AE, DC, MC, V. Closed Sun.*

$$$ **Bella Luna.** If luxurious surroundings, imaginative food, and a knock-
out view of the Mississippi River are high on your list of priorities,
this elegantly turned out restaurant in the French Market complex
should fill the bill. Handsome French-style windows line one wall in
the plush main dining room, offering overhead views of the riverbank
and the ships and excursion boats gliding by. The second dining space
is enclosed on three sides by even more glass, exposing the river on
one side, the city skyline straight on, and French Quarter rooftops on
the other side. The kitchen takes an eclectic approach, although the
strongest accent is Italian. Good bets are the pastas, especially penne
with roasted eggplant, gorgonzola, peppers, and fried herbs in
Fontina sauce. The robust osso buco is a straightforward delight, as
is the coconut meringue pie. Fancier fare includes a delicious group-
ing of quesadillas filled with smoked shrimp and spicy goat cheese. ✗
*French Market complex near the corner of Decatur and Dumaine
Sts., French Quarter,* ☎ *504/529–1583. Reservations advised. AE,
DC, MC, V. No lunch.*

$$$ **Gautreau's.** Modest in size but ambitious in its cooking, this haven of
★ sophistication is half-hidden in a quiet, leafy residential neighbor-
hood. Don't look for a sign outside; there is none. The ever-changing
menu usually includes fine crab cakes with an herbal tartar sauce,
expertly roasted chicken with garlicky mashed potatoes, and a sauté
of wild mushrooms, filet mignon in robust sauces, and a superb
crème brûlée. Those are mere starting points. The 40-seat downstairs
dining room, once a neighborhood drugstore, is encased in lustrous
oxblood enamel. Along one wall extends the old pharmacy's original
polished wood cabinets, now filled with liquors and glassware. A
noise problem has been largely corrected with the opening of a qui-
eter, second-floor dining room. ✗ *1728 Soniat St., Uptown,* ☎ *504/
899–7397. Reservations strongly advised. AE, D, DC, MC, V. Closed
Sun. No lunch.*

$$$ **Graham's.** Not so much as a swatch of fabric hangs on the 10 tall
★ arched windows in the dining room at Graham's, and little else
intrudes on the flat whiteness of the walls. Although the kitchen puts
a premium on simply prepared dishes, the food supplies most of the
color at this establishment, with its bare tabletops of dark-green granite. From the Windsor Court Hotel, his previous post, English-born
proprietor-chef Kevin Graham has brought over a few of his most celebrated dishes, most notably the duck "lacquered" with chicory coffee
and oranges. A luxurious cream sauce covers his roasted monkfish and
horseradish-glazed oysters. Seared yellowfin tuna is glossed with a

marmalade of star anise and lemon, and one of the soups is a match-up of aromatic vegetable bisques, mushroom, and tomato in a single bowl. Desserts can be uncomplicated, as in a crumbly almond tart with amaretto, or very innovative, as in the warm, sweetened polenta flavored with vanilla and topped with mascarpone. The modest wine list takes a back seat to the food. And all the hard surfaces make for a high noise level. ✗ *200 Magazine St., in the Pelham Hotel, Central Business District,* ☎ *504/524–9678. Reservations advised. AE, DC, MC, V. No lunch Sat.*

$$$ **Mike's on the Avenue.** While this newcomer owes more to San Fran-
★ cisco or Santa Fe for the chic spareness of its decor and menu, there is enough of New Orleans here to make it attractive for both locals and out-of-towners. Michael Fennelly is not only the chef and co-owner; his color-splashed abstract-expressionist paintings hang on the white-washed walls. He also oversaw the design of the two big dining rooms, which flank the small lobby of the newly restored Lafayette Hotel. For his cooking, Fennelly draws inspiration from Thai, Japanese, Chinese, Southwestern American, and even some Creole sensibilities. The result is gorgeously presented food bursting with surprising flavors. Orleani-ans have taken quickly to his oysters, grilled on the half-shell with a zippy Korean-style barbecue sauce; his crab-and-sea-scallop cakes with three sauces; and smoky-tasting breast of chicken in a Creole sauce with baked beans. Those enthralled by the Orient will find excellent Chinese dumplings filled with shrimp, ginger, and scallions, as well as crunchy spring rolls filled with crawfish and shredded veg-etables. Desserts, especially a crème brûlée with a hint of ginger to it, are spectacularly good. ✗ *628 St. Charles Ave., in the Lafayette Hotel, Central Business District,* ☎ *504/523–1709. Reservations advised. AE, D, DC, MC, V. No weekend lunch.*

$$$ **The Pelican Club.** Sassy New York flourishes are found throughout
★ the menu of this smartly decorated but eminently comfortable place in the heart of the French Quarter. Still, evidence of chef Richard Hughes' South Louisiana origins also keeps popping up. Hughes spent seven years in Manhattan as the top chef of the acclaimed Memphis. In three handsome dining rooms inside a balconied old town house, he turns out a stew of shellfish that's a clever improvisa-tion on both San Francisco's cioppino and Louisiana's bouillabaisse. A touch of saffron in his jambalaya of chicken, sausage, and shellfish makes it a cousin of Spain's paella. Closer to home are red snapper stuffed with crabmeat; a bisque of bourbon, crab, and corn; and a crème brûlée in the grandest French-Creole tradition. Each of the din-ing rooms, hung with consignment art from local galleries, has its own ambience. ✗ *615 Bienville St., French Quarter,* ☎ *504/523–1504. Reservations advised. AE, D, DC, MC, V. No lunch.*

$$ **Bayou Ridge Café.** While regional seafoods are commonplace on the Bayou Ridge menu, you'll also find lots of dishes with a light, almost Asian sensibility. Freshness is everywhere. Grilled shrimp arrive with herbed rice and a salad of mixed beans. Grilled salmon is brushed with a delicate ginger-plum sauce. Chicken breast crusted with feta and walnuts rests on a bed of fresh greens. And salads, omelets, and pastas are always done with flair and imagination. Decor is minimal in the large, angular dining room, hung with a few large scenic pho-tographs and, occasionally, groups of drawings. In pleasant weather, the large, lush garden is a spectacular place for lunch. ✗ *437 Esplanade Ave., Faubourg Marigny,* ☎ *504/949–9912. Reservations advised. AE, D, DC, MC, V. Closed Mon., Tues.*

$$ **Peristyle.** Some of the most creative cooking in New Orleans emanates
★ from the kitchen of this smartly turned out yet very approachable lit-
tle restaurant on the French Quarter's edge. Chef John Neal takes a
thoroughly modern and personal approach to continental cooking on
a small, ever-changing menu. In either the intimate bar, lined with
tables, or the dining room proper, regulars dig into Neal's superb cas-
soulet-like gratin of white beans with quail breast, shrimp and crab
soup in Creole broth, silky lamb loin in a rich brown sauce, open-
faced ravioli with shrimp, and filet mignon stuffed with garlic cheese.
The look of the place is intimate and simple, which makes concentrat-
ing on the great food even easier. The wine list is small but nicely
matched to the dishes. ✕ *1041 Dumaine St., French Quarter,* ☎ *504/
593–9535. Reservations strongly advised. MC, V. Closed Sun., Mon.
Lunch Fri. only.*

Continental

$$$$ **Le Jardin.** The sweeping 11th-floor views of the Mississippi River are
breathtaking in this luxurious hotel dining room, which is as soft-
edged and comfortable as any in town. The body-hugging chairs,
huge vases and paintings, and other classy appointments make it one
of the city's showplaces. It's a good spot to feast on a wide array of
shellfish, meats, and game in all kinds of rich, herbal sauces. The
kitchen's style is French Provençal, which on the dinner menu trans-
lates as lots of tomato, sweet pepper, and flavors underlined by olive
oil. The Sunday jazz brunch buffet is the bargain of the week. ✕ *Atop
the Westin-Canal Place Hotel, 100 Bienville St., Central Business
District,* ☎ *504/566–7006. Reservations accepted. AE, D, DC, MC,
V. Breakfast, lunch, and dinner daily.*

$$$$ **Sazerac.** From this jewel box of a dining room comes a cornucopia of
dishes, lavish in their composition but overpriced at this fair-to-
middling level of quality. There is little the Sazerac's kitchen cannot
produce on request. Many of the menu choices, like the sautéed red
snapper topped with lump crabmeat in butter sauce, have solid Creole
roots. Others owe more to French classicism. Among the latter are the
lobster bisque, flavored with cognac and enriched with a swirl of
cream, and whole Dover sole meunière, boned tableside after being
brushed with lemon, butter, and parsley. An oyster dressing fills the
roasted chicken, accompanied by garlic mashed potatoes, and the
chateaubriand for two, sauced with both béarnaise and bordelaise, is
done with style. Desserts are traditional: cherries jubilee, and rather
floury soufflés with either chocolate or Grand Marnier liqueur. The
decor is from a fairy tale. The stately dining room is replete with lace
and gilt and gleaming brass chandeliers that reflect from mirrors. Along
the pale-gray striped wall coverings hang full-length oil portraits of his-
torical figures from Louisiana's past. ✕ *Fairmont Hotel, University Pl.,
Central Business District,* ☎ *504/529–4733. Reservations advised.
Jacket required at dinner. AE, D, DC, MC, V. No weekend lunch.*

$$$$ **The Veranda.** The elegant Old South meets modern-day luxury in this
vast complex of rooms on the Hotel Inter-Continental's lobby level.
The most spectacular space is a lofty, glass-enclosed room filled with
tropical plants and lacy garden furniture. The other rooms are done
in a formal, antebellum style. The dinner menu diverts from the
familiar fare of luxury hotels with numerous creations of chef Willy
Coln, a local favorite. The result is smoked Nova Scotia salmon
cheek-by-jowl with shrimp réemoulade, and sautéeed red snapper
with lump crabmeat. The better choices include the crab cakes, mari-

nated shrimp, Wiener schnitzel, and beefsteak in pepper sauce. The extensive pastry buffet is always beckoning. ✕ *Hotel Inter-Continental, 444 St. Charles Ave., Central Business District,* ☎ *504/ 525–5566. Reservations advised. AE, D, DC, MC, V. Breakfast, lunch, and dinner daily.*

$$$$ **Versailles.** Continental sumptuosity and Creole heartiness never kept
★   better company than they do in this plush restaurant, done in Old World–style elegance. The moods in the several elaborate dining rooms vary from cheery to rather somber. The softly lit main room affords leafy views of St. Charles Avenue, while the brighter rooms behind are sheathed in pale wallpapers and pastel-hued flowers. Crab dishes shine, especially the cold marinated crabmeat à la grecque, pre-pared in a scallop shell with spinach mousse and a mustard-dill sauce. Soups range from the subtle clarity of the artichoke Monte Cristo to the richness of shrimp and mirliton in cream. The supreme duckling andalouse and medallions of beef Madagascar are two of the many excellent meat dishes. The appropriately elaborate desserts include a marvelous bittersweet chocolate mousse in a raspberry sauce and a Bavarian cream in a custard sauce tinged with orange liqueur. ✕ *2100 St. Charles Ave., Uptown,* ☎ *504/524–2535. Reservations strongly advised. Jacket required. AE, DC, MC, V. Closed Sun. Lunch Thurs. and Fri. only.*

International

Chinese

$ **Kung's Dynasty.** The Kung family members are among the city's more inventive Chinese restaurateurs, and their restaurant, housed in a bright and airy Garden District cottage, offers reliably good food. The traditional Chinese decorative elements and jade-colored draperies show up especially well against the lofty, off-white walls. The kitchen's strengths are distinctive, well-balanced sauces with occasionally novel ingredients. Examples are tender and spicy eggplant in garlic sauce, wonton with crabmeat, and stir-fried oysters in a Szechuan sauce. The menu amounts to a small catalogue of the familiar regional cuisines of China. Mu-shu pork, shrimp toast, and five-flavor shrimp are among the standouts. There are also good crispy duck and a fine double-cooked pork. ✕ *1912 St. Charles Ave., Lower Garden District,* ☎ *504/525–6669. Reservations advised. AE, D, DC, MC, V.*

French

$$$$ **Louis XVI.** Classic French cream sauces dominate the menu in this plush, handsome restaurant with views of one of the prettiest court-yards in the French Quarter. A Creole flourish occasionally appears on the menu, but the standouts are Gallic creations such as sweet-breads in puff pastry with a Madeira-tinged cream sauce; subtle, deli-cious oysters; beef drenched in red wine and aromatic vegetables; and a chicken breast glazed with its own juices mixed with cream, rose-mary, and thyme. Desserts are appropriately baroque, and the pre-dominantly French wine list is above average. The two dining rooms, plus a bar with a few tables, are soft-edged and colorful, with roomy armchairs and noise-muffling carpets. Owner Antoine Camenzuli, an alumnus of top European hotels, has a firm grip on his service staff. ✕ *St. Louis Hotel, 730 Bienville St., French Quarter,* ☎ *504/581–7000. Weekend reservations strongly advised. Jacket required. AE, D, DC, MC, V. No lunch.*

$$$$ **La Provence.** It's almost an hour's drive from New Orleans, but the
★ glorious provincial-French food and relaxing atmosphere of this
exceptional restaurant are well worth the trip. Owner-chef Chris Ker-
ageorgiu's elegant yet earthy cooking is consistently satisfying. Giant
New Zealand mussels, still in their shells under a garlicky butter sauce,
arrive on angel-hair pasta; tenderloin of rabbit is swathed in a light
gravy redolent of lavender; roasted duck with garlic warms the soul;
and a thick and hearty quail gumbo with rice and andouille sausage is
a revelation. Lamb, fish, and seafood dishes are similarly imaginative
and delicious. Separating the two dining rooms, hung with pleasant
Provençal landscape paintings, is a hearth that welcomes you on damp
winter days. In warmer seasons, the tree-shaded deck is almost as
pleasant. The wine list is more than serviceable, and table service, by
congenial waitresses in provincial-style dresses, is very good. ✕ *Across
Lake Pontchartrain on U.S. 190, Lacombe, LA (about 35 mi from
central New Orleans),* ☎ *504/626–7662. Reservations strongly
advised. AE, MC, V. Closed Mon. and Tues. Lunch Sun. only.*

$$ **Chez Daniel.** The food and atmosphere are a bit recherchée at this sub-
urban French bistro. A huge mural inspired by Belle Epoque Paris
forms one wall, while the rest of the decor is catch-as-catch-can. The
regulars from the nearby upper-middle-class neighborhood seem to
revel in the ambience, as well as in chef Daniel Bonnot's interpretation
of classical French cooking. One signature appetizer is sautéed oysters
in a brunoise sauce (or salsa, if you will) of minced onion, tomato, and
cilantro. The Belgian endive salad is always crisp and bracing. Main
courses, especially meats, are deftly prepared, as in the steak au poivre,
lamb chops in herbed bread crumbs, and veal with lemon sauce. The
place fills up quickly with regulars, but the congenial service staff does
a nice job of making everyone feel quite at home. ✕ *2037 Metairie
Rd., Metairie,* ☎ *504/837–6900. Reservations required. MC, V.
Closed Sun., Mon.*

Greek

$$ **Zissis.** Traditional Greek dishes acquire a fresh, contemporary
sparkle in this vibrant and friendly place, with folksy murals and
paintings imparting the feeling of a village in the Aegean islands. It's
as pleasant a spot as you're likely to find in a suburban strip shopping
center. The appetizer list includes super-thin, crackly phyllo puffs
filled with spinach and cheeses, excellent fried calamari, and an
assortment of traditional spreads and dips. The lamb and fish dishes
feature first-rate ingredients done in imaginative ways. Among the
novelties is angel-hair pasta, which appears almost as often as the
Greek-style orzo pasta. Table service is long on congeniality, but
rather short on efficiency. ✕ *2051 Metairie Rd., Metairie,* ☎ *504/
837–7890. MC, V. Closed Sun. No lunch Sat.*

Italian

$$$ **Anacapri.** A yearning for the richly aromatic cooking of the Mediter-
ranean can be satisfied in this very pleasant restaurant on the ground
floor of a French Quarter hotel. The owner-chef is Andrea Apuzzo of
Andrea's in Metairie (*see below*). Murals and oils of Apuzzo's native
Capri lend their soft colors to the several dining rooms, which over-
look a cool and leafy courtyard. On the lunch and dinner menus is
such up-to-date Italian fare as salmon marinated in olive oil, balsamic
vinegar, and herbs; shrimp and calamari with white beans on radicchio
and arugula; and in tribute to the Italian-Creole tradition, an Italian-
style gumbo. The large menu includes several Louisiana-style dishes as

well. ✗ *In the Bienville House Hotel, 320 Decatur St., French Quarter,* ☎ *504/522–9056. Reservations advised. AE, D, DC, MC, V.*

$$$ **Andrea's.** Regional Italian dishes usually get the Continental treatment in this sprawling, very popular restaurant with a suburban brand of elegance. The chef, a native of Capri, embellishes local seafood with rich and herbal cream sauces or delicately seasoned broths. Pasta dishes are imaginative and satisfying. Some original creations are sautéed shrimp alla Caprese, in a delicious blend of herbed olive oil, white wine, and lemon juice; green and white fettuccine in a cream sauce with bits of beef tenderloin; rolled, sliced chicken breast stuffed with prosciutto ham, spinach, and cheese with mushroom sauce; and red snapper in a lemony sauce with sweet peppers, onions, and oregano. Andrea's has several large dining rooms, some with informal brick walls, others hung with subtly colored wallpapers, still lifes, and lighting fixtures that sparkle with gilt and crystal. Locals are enamored of the Sunday brunch, a never-ending feast with a very attractive price tag. Service is well organized, but the strain shows on weekend nights when the hordes descend. ✗ *3100 19th St., Metairie,* ☎ *504/834–8583. Reservations strongly advised. AE, D, DC, MC, V. No lunch Sat.*

$$$ **Bacco.** Opened in late 1990, this is the most ambitious Italian restau-
★   rant in New Orleans, not only for the diversity of the Italian dishes from the contemporary mainstream, but also for the dazzle of its decor. The brainchild of siblings Ralph and Cindy Brennan of Mr. B's Bistro, Bacco (the Italian name of the wine god Bacchus) courts pasta lovers with a half-dozen freshly made varieties, from a tortellini stuffed with gorgonzola cheese to fettuccine with sausage in a mushroom sauce. You'll also find excellent versions of carpaccio, a hearty Tuscan-style bean soup, several tempting pizzas, and Italian-style treatments of roast pork loin, veal scaloppine, and fish. The decor of the four dining rooms and bar, all swathed in creamy white, beautifully fuses Italian art and architectural styles from the Gothic to the contemporary. ✗ *310 Chartres St., in the Hotel de la Poste, French Quarter,* ☎ *504/522–2426. Reservations advised. AE, DC, MC, V.*

$$$ **Irene's Cuisine.** Its walls are festooned with enough snapshots, olive jars, garlic braids, and crockery for at least two more restaurants. But this just adds to the charm of this cozy, 10-table Italian-Creole eatery on an obscure corner in the French Quarter. From Irene DiPietro's kitchen come garlicky Italian sausage steeped in roasted peppers; succulent roasted chicken brushed with olive oil, rosemary, and garlic; tubes of manicotti bulging with ground veal and mozzarella; and big, fresh shrimp, aggressively seasoned and grilled before joining linguine glistening with herbed olive oil. End it with an Italian-style baked Alaska, covered with a blue flame of ignited grappa liqueur. If you come at peak dinner hours, you may have to wait for a table in the makeshift lounge. ✗ *539 St. Philip St., French Quarter,* ☎ *504/ 529–8811. No reservations. AE, MC, V. Closed Sun. No lunch.*

$$$ **Pascal's Manale.** Few restaurants are as closely identified with one dish as this one is with barbecue shrimp. The original version, introduced a half century ago, remains, with jumbo shrimp, still in the shell, cooked in a buttery pool zapped with just the right amount of spice and pepper. The rest of the menu, mostly seafood and Italian-style creations, is uneven, but often done with respect for local traditions. The turtle soup, fried eggplant, and baked or raw oysters in various sauces are good ways to start. Sautéed veal with shrimp, chicken bordelaise, and seafood with pasta are other reliable choices. The restaurant's popularity with out-of-towners usually means a wait for a table, even if it's reserved, and the bar's party atmosphere makes it comfortable only for the gregarious. Hardly an inch of wall space remains in the bar, filled as it is with memorabilia from the long history of this New Orleans institution. Space is at a premium in the two dining rooms, too, and the clientele is usually in a partying mood. ✕ *1828 Napoleon Ave., Uptown,* ☎ *504/895–4877. Dinner reservations strongly advised. AE, MC, V. No lunch weekends.*

$$$ **La Riviera.** This lively and dependable suburban fixture has a limited regional Italian menu, but overall quality is unusually high for a restaurant that can seat a couple of hundred. Lots of rich tomato and cream sauces and unusually good pastas keep things interesting. The crabmeat-stuffed ravioli deserves its large following, although the shrimp sautéed in wine and herbs with paprika is hard to beat. The red snapper, though somewhat overwhelmed by its butter sauce and a bounty of crab lumps, is also a good choice. Top-quality white veal is another favorite, and the buttery piccata and marsala sauces should impress the pickiest veal lover. Space is at a premium in the two dining rooms, which are hung with large oils depicting Italian Riviera seascapes. Table service, by tuxedoed waiters with prodigious memories, is often speedier than some diners prefer. ✕ *4506 Shores Dr., Metairie,* ☎ *504/888–6238. Reservations advised, especially on weekends. AE, D, DC, MC, V. Closed Sat. No lunch Sun.*

$$ **Brick Oven Cafe.** A few minutes from the airport is this always-crowded, very laid-back restaurant that offers what may be the best home-style Italian cooking in the area. Putting meat in minestrone may be flouting tradition, but this minestrone is fabulous. So are the succulent roasted chicken, spaghetti carbonara, veal piccata, and traditional desserts. If freshness and full flavor are the yardsticks, the Brick Oven measures up to any Italian restaurant and town. You may have to wait a half hour or more for a table at peak dinner hours, and elbow room is at a premium. But the inconveniences are worth it for food as good as this. The three dining rooms are festooned with all sorts of foodstuffs, tins, jars, and culinary artifacts. The booths are the most desirable seats. ✕ *2805 Williams Blvd., Kenner,* ☎ *504/466–2097. Reservations accepted for 6 or more. AE, D, DC, MC, V.*

$$ **Mosca's.** Depending on your point of view, the decor at Mosca's is either charmingly unpretentious or bordering on the primitive, with its sentimental art, bare-wood floors, and practical window treatments. The food, Southern Louisiana ingredients and southern Italian ingenuity, can be good enough to lure city folk to this isolated, super-simple restaurant in a near-swamp about a half hour from the city. Baked oysters with artichoke, bread crumbs, olive oil, garlic, and herbs approach the summit of Italian-Creole cuisine. The Italian shrimp, a close relative of barbecue shrimp, are cooked in an herbed mix of olive oil and spices. The roast chicken with rosemary and Italian sausages are full of homey flavors, and the spaghetti bordelaise is a marvelous accompaniment. Getting a table usually means a wait in the bar, even with reservations. The restaurant is difficult to spot along the highway, so call for directions. ✕ *4137 U.S. 90, Waggaman,* ☎ *504/436–9942. Reservations strongly advised. No credit cards. Closed Sun., Mon. No lunch.*

$ **Alberto's.** Small and bohemian, this casual upstairs eatery serves pasta and seafood dishes in cheery, colorful surroundings at unusually low prices. An herbal tomato-and-cream sauce flavors the canneloni, which is filled with ricotta, crawfish, or shrimp. Freshly made fettuccine comes with shrimp in a sauce tinged with anisette liqueur. The fish, always a dependable option, is sautéed in olive oil. Meat entrées center on chicken breast and veal. Alberto's is extremely popular, so go early. ✗ *609 Frenchmen St., Faubourg Marigny,* ☎ *504/949–5952. No reservations. No credit cards. Closed Sun. No lunch.*

Lebanese

$$ Byblos. Good Middle Eastern cooking is a rarity in New Orleans. So Byblos, just outside the city limits, has the market pretty much to itself, thanks to the freshness of the kitchen's ingredients, used in authentic combinations and admirably spiced and herbed. The walls of the single lofty dining room are painted to depict soothing country scenes, and the welcome at the door is always warm. You'll find such familiar Lebanese fare as hummus (a lemony chickpea dip), *baba ghanouj* (pureed eggplant with lemon and garlic), moussaka, and stuffed grape leaves. Skewered-meat main courses, especially the chicken and beef, are moist and flavorful. Pleasantly seasoned rice accompanies most entrées, and the custardy desserts are very good. To reach Byblos, drive northward (toward Lake Pontchatrain) on Canal Street to Metairie Road. Turn left at Metairie Road and continue about 2 miles to the restaurant. ✗ *1501 Metairie Rd., Metairie,* ☎ *504/834–9773. Reservations accepted for 6 or more. AE, D, DC, MC, V.*

Mexican and Spanish

$$ Vaqueros. Stretched-leather chairs, a little tortilla-cooking station, and folksy decoration are the first visible clues that Vaqueros looks to Mexico and the American Southwest, especially Texas, for its inspirations. Yet the dishes are rarely conventional. Salsas often convey both peppery and mellow sensations. Chili con carne appears with black beans and venison. Grilled fish might show up in a zesty sauce flavored with both chiles and tropical fruit. Yet there is no scarcity of tacos, fajitas, enchiladas, and the like in the two spacious dining rooms, which usually buzz with activity. One of the offbeat desserts is the galleta taco, a thin, folded cookie enveloping fresh diced fruits with pastry cream. The Southwestern-style Sunday brunch buffet, served on the covered patio, is a special treat. ✗ *4938 Prytania St., Uptown,* ☎ *504/891–6441. No reservations. AE, D, DC, MC, V. Closed Mon. No lunch Sat.*

$ Gustavo's. The neat, simple surroundings here are typical of the low-priced Mexican-American restaurants dotting the landscape. What separates it from the crowd is the taste of proprietor-chef Gustavo Gutierrez's food. The true flavors of Mexico come through in a succession of heartily spiced dishes, especially the *tacos al pastor,* filled with lean and moist cubes of roasted pork and beef; a velvety and zestily seasoned guacamole; the chicken in colorado, mole, or adobado sauce; and soul-warming black beans and rice. A few Cuban-style specialties—roast pork with yuca in garlic sauce, for example—augment the Mexican-style bill of fare. Gustavo's is a short drive from New Orleans International Airport, near the intersection of Williams Boulevard and West Esplanade Avenue. ✗ *3515 Williams Blvd., Kenner,* ☎ *504/443–2260. No reservations. MC, V.*

$ Taqueria Corona. You won't find unusual ingredients or fancy plates in this homey Mexican-style grill with two locations, Uptown and in the Warehouse District. The range of entrées is narrow—nachos, tacos, burritos, and flautas. But everything served here is authentic, from the crisp tortilla chips and bracing pico de gallo sauce to the satisfying tacos, made with soft tortillas shipped from Houston and filled with marinated meats and shrimp. Two unusual dishes are the "taco pizza," layers of tortilla, puréed beans, cheese, and beef or chicken, and the "tacocado salad," a mixture of guacamole, lettuce, meat, olives, and cheese inside a fried tortilla. The guacamole and flan wouldn't embarrass a much more expensive restaurant, and the sangria is sweetened with restraint. You can sit at the counter and watch the chicken, beef, and pork sizzle on the grill, or take your chances with table service in one of the dining rooms. The atmosphere is as laid-back as you'll find anywhere. ✕ *5932 Magazine St., Uptown,* ☎ *504/897–3974; 857 Fulton St., Warehouse District, no* ☎. *No reservations. No credit cards.*

Seafood Houses

$$ Ralph & Kacoo's. Getting past the door to the vast dining spaces usually means first taking a ticket and waiting your turn in a crowded bar decorated in a bayou theme (the bar in the French Quarter restaurant is dominated by a fishing-boat hull). The theme continues inside with a variety of nostalgic clutter and swamp prints. The extensive menu mixes and matches a wide range of local fish and shellfish, intensely seasoned and cooked the usual ways. Freshness and consistency are trademarks of Ralph & Kacoo's. You'll find them in the boiled shrimp, raw oysters, shrimp rémoulade, trout meunière, fried seafood platter, and the crawfish dishes, which are served only when they're in season. ✕ *519 Toulouse St., French Quarter,* ☎ *504/522– 5226; 601 Veterans Blvd., Metairie,* ☎ *504/831–3177. No reservations. AE, D, MC, V.*

$ Acme Oyster and Seafood Restaurant. A rough-edged classic in every way, this no-nonsense eatery at the entrance to the French Quarter is a prime source of cool and salty raw oysters on the half shell; great shrimp, oyster, and roast-beef po'boys; and state-of-the-art red beans and rice. Table service is offered in the front dining room. If the tables are all taken, expect rather lengthy queues at the marble-topped oyster bar and cafeteria-style sandwich counter during peak lunch hours. Crowds are sparser in the late afternoon. And don't expect coddling. ✕ *724 Iberville St., French Quarter,* ☎ *504/522–5973. No reservations. AE, DC, MC, V. Closes at 10 PM Fri. and Sat., earlier on other nights.*

$ Bozo's. The menu in this no-nonsense suburban seafood house could hardly be more basic—fresh catfish and shellfish, simply cooked and served with potatoes and bread. Have a few of the top-quality raw oysters at the bar while waiting for a bare-top table in one of the wood-paneled dining rooms. The boiled and fried seafoods are fresh and properly seasoned. Some of the starters—notably the gumbo and stoutly seasoned shrimp Italian—are excellent. Order somehow triumphs over chaos on Friday nights, the only night when reservations aren't taken. ✕ *3117 21st St., Metairie,* ☎ *504/831–8666. Reservations advised. Closed Sun. No lunch Mon.*

$ Casamento's. Encased in gleaming white ceramic tiles, Casamento's has been a haven for Uptown seafood lovers since 1918. Family members still man the long, marble, raw-oyster bar up front and the immaculate kitchen out back. Between them is a small dining room with a similarly diminutive menu. The specialties are oysters lightly poached in seasoned milk, and fried shrimp, trout, and oysters, impeccably fresh and greaseless. They're served with fried potatoes and a good selection of domestic beers. Even the houseplants have a just-polished look. ✕ *4330 Magazine St., Uptown,* ☎ *504/895–9761. No reservations. No credit cards. Closed Mon. and early June–late-Aug.*

$ Franky & Johnny's. Seekers of the quintessential New Orleans neighborhood restaurant need look no further. Team pennants, posters, and football jerseys vie for space on the panelled walls of the low-ceilinged bar and dining room while a jukebox blares beneath them. From the kitchen's steaming cauldrons come freshly boiled shrimp, crabs, and crawfish, piled high and ready to be washed down with ice-cold beer. On the day's po'boy roster might be fried crawfish tails or oysters, meatballs in tomato sauce, or roast beef with gravy. Table service is rudimentary. ✗ *321 Arabella St., Uptown,* ☎ *504/899–9146. No reservations. D, MC, V.*

$ Mandina's. The interior of this white clapboard corner building is a study in 1940s nostalgia, with its functional bar facing a roomful of laminated tables set with sugar shakers, hot sauce, and salt and pepper. Regulars—a cross section of the population—endure a ¼-hour wait for a table under a 30-year-old newspaper clipping or the latest artwork from a St. Louis brewery. Butter, hearty seasonings, and tomato sauce are the staples. The shrimp rémoulade and old-fashioned gumbo are the logical appetizers. Broiled trout and shrimp, wading in seasoned butter, are tasty, as are the fried oysters and shrimp, the seafood or Italian sausage po'boys, and the super-sweet bread pudding. Service amounts to little more than taking and delivering orders. ✗ *3800 Canal St., Mid-City,* ☎ *504/482–9179. No reservations. No credit cards.*

Steaks

$$$ Ruth's Chris Steak House. Ruth's Chris is sacred to New Orleans
★ steak lovers. The all-American menu fairly drips with butter, and the main draw is aged U.S. prime beef in he-man portions, charbroiled and served atop a sizzling seasoned butter sauce. Carefree locals often order a side of bordelaise sauce to add to the excess. The hefty filet mignon is often taller than it is wide, the New York strip is usually packed with flavor, and a monstrous porterhouse serves several. If the salads lack sparkle, the copious potato dishes are consistently first-rate, especially the julienne, shoestring, and lyonnaise. Lighter entrées (chicken breast, veal, seafoods) were added recently to mollify the health-conscious. The large, plush, but unfussy, dining rooms of the flagship Mid-City restaurant are lined in pale-wood paneling and understated landscape paintings. Politicians, both actual and aspiring, are everywhere. The drinks are generous, and the energetic waitresses rarely falter. ✗ *711 N. Broad St., Mid-City,* ☎ *504/486–0810; 3633 Veterans Blvd., Metairie,* ☎ *504/888–3600. Reservations strongly advised, especially on weekends. AE, D, DC, MC, V.*

Dessert

Angelo Brocato's. Traditional Sicilian fruit sherbets, ice creams, pastries, and candies are the attractions of this quaint little sweetshop that harkens back to the time when the French Quarter was peopled mostly by Italian immigrants. The cannoli (cylinders of crunchy pastry filled with sweetened ricotta) and the lemon and strawberry ices are the local favorites. ✗ *On Jackson Square, 537 St. Ann St., French Quarter,* ☎ *504/525–9676; 214 N. Carrollton Ave., Mid-City,* ☎ *504/488–1465. No credit cards.* ☉ *Daily 9:30 AM–10 PM.*

★ Croissant d'Or. Locals compete with tourists for a table in this colorful and pristine pastry shop that serves excellent and authentic French croissants, pies, tarts, and custards, as well as an imaginative selection of soups, salads, and sandwiches. Wash them down with real French breakfast coffee, cappuccino, or espresso. In good weather, the cheerful courtyard, with its quietly gurgling fountain, is the place to sit. A filling lunch can be had for less than $10. ✕ *617 Ursulines St., French Quarter,* ☎ *504/524–4663. No credit cards.* ☽ *Daily 7 AM–5 PM.*

Hansen's Sno-Bliz. Among the outgrowths of New Orleans's six-month summers is the "snowball," a concoction of shaved ice doused with flavored syrups. Makeshift snowball stands dot the city's neighborhoods, but the undisputed champ is Hansen's. For decades, the Hansen family has made its own variety of syrups for the definitive snowballs sold in sizes ranging from pint-size cups to party-size garbage cans. Expect long lines on sultry days. ✕ *4801 Tchoupitoulas St., Uptown,* ☎ *504/891–9788. No credit cards.* ☽ *Sun. and Tues.–Fri. 3–9 PM.*

La Madeleine. The lines are ever present in this bakery-café, which is part of a French chain. The huge selection of pastries includes napoleons, cheesecakes, and éclairs, as well as a variety of superb brioches and breads from the wood-burning oven. Salads, soups, sandwiches, and light entrées are also available. ✕ *On Jackson Square, 547 St. Ann St., French Quarter,* ☎ *504/568–9950; 601 S. Carrollton Ave., Uptown,* ☎ *504/861–8661. No credit cards.* ☽ *Daily 7 AM–9 PM.*

La Marquise. This tiny little coffee shop just off Jackson Square is a satellite of the Croissant d'Or and offers the same good coffees, croissants, and pastries. It's a bit cramped, but practical and cozy. ✕ *625 Chartres St., French Quarter,* ☎ *504/524–0420. No credit cards.* ☽ *Daily 7 AM–5:30 PM.*

Old Town Pralines. Among the great delicacies left us by the 19th-century Creoles are pralines—thin, hardened-sugar-and-pecan patties that are wonderful for capping off a fine dinner or for a quick munch. The most authentic ones are sold by the ladies who operate the Old Town Antique Shop on Royal Street. The pralines are cooked so the pecan flavor permeates the candy, and the firm texture is just right. They're sold individually in wax-paper packets or in boxes holding one to three dozen. The shop will ship them for you, too. ✕ *627 Royal St., French Quarter,* ☎ *504/525–1413. No credit cards.* ☽ *Mon.–Sat. 10 AM–5:30 PM.*

Cafés and Coffeehouses

★ **Café du Monde.** For most visitors, no trip to New Orleans would be complete without a cup of chicory-laced café au lait and a few sugar-dusted beignets in this venerable Creole institution. The dozens of tables, inside or out in the open air, are jammed at almost any hour with locals and tourists feasting on the views of Jackson Square and the hubbub on Decatur Street. The magical time to go is just before dawn, when the bustle subsides and you can almost hear the birds in the crepe myrtles across the way. ✕ *In the French Market, Decatur and St. Ann Sts., French Quarter,* ☎ *504/525–4544. No credit cards.* ☽ *Daily 24 hrs.*

Coffee, Tea or . . . This is the place to ease into the day or while away the afternoon in a quiet, tiny Spanish courtyard with a good book and a cup of your favorite coffee or tea. Several varieties of each are brought over each day from the spice shop next door, and they're served with home-style cookies, cakes, warm croissants, and pastries. If shelter's needed, there are two cozy rooms that shut out the French Quarter's frenetic activity. ✕ *630 St. Ann St., French Quarter,* ☎ *504/522–0830. No credit cards.* ☽ *Daily 8 AM–6 PM.*

Morning Call. Once a beloved fixture of the old New Orleans French Market, Morning Call moved to the suburbs in the 1970s. The chicory coffee and beignets are still unbeatable, and the quirky old counters and stools are still in place. But they're now squeezed into a space between glitzy boutiques in a drab shopping center, which robs the café of whatever nostalgic charm it might have. ✕ *3325 Severn Ave., Metairie,* ☎ *504/885–4068. No credit cards.* ☉ *Daily 24 hrs.*

Rue de la Course. The charm of this little coffeehouse on a quiet corner of Magazine Street lies as much in its lived-in look as in its *caffè latte* (espresso with steamed milk), sturdy espresso, and other coffees flavored with vanilla, hazelnuts, or chocolate-almond. No gimmickry intrudes on the atmosphere, which combines the calm of a library with the spontanaeity of an old-fashioned general store (one wall is lined with bins of coffee beans). A few tables are scattered outside, perfect for lolling on a balmy day while sipping an Italian cream soda, topped with whipped cream. ✕ *1500 Magazine St., Lower Garden District,* ☎ *504/529–1455. No credit cards.* ☉ *Weekdays 7 AM–11 PM, weekends 8 AM–11 PM.*

True Brew. A successful newcomer, True Brew's three cafés offer a wide selection of teas and unflavored or flavored coffees (rum rhapsody, chocolate-raspberry truffle, and Irish creme supreme are popular). Given equal billing in the Julia Street location are the poetry readings, intimate musical performances, and art exhibitions that take place almost every night. A boutique sells gift baskets, jewelry, and crafts. ✕ *3133 Ponce de Leon St., Mid-City,* ☎ *504/947–3948; 200 Julia St., Warehouse District,* ☎ *504/524–8441; 3242 Magazine St., Uptown,* ☎ *504/899–9453. AE, MC, V accepted at Magazine St. shop.* ☉ *All locations open daily at 7 AM; closing hrs vary at each location from 7 to 11 PM.*

Po'boys and Other Sandwiches

Café Maspero. A half-hour wait in line—usually outside the door—is the norm for a sample of Café Maspero's two-fisted hot and cold sandwiches. The pastrami and corned beef are on the greasy side, and the half-pound hamburger (with cheese or chili or both) is long on bulk and short on taste. But low prices and big portions keep 'em coming. Arched doors and windows give the vast brick dining room a little character. Service is perfunctory. ✕ *601 Decatur St., French Quarter,* ☎ *504/523–6250. No credit cards.* ☉ *Daily 11–11.*

★ **Camellia Grill.** Every diner should be as classy as Camellia Grill, a one-of-a-kind eatery that deserves its following. Locals vie until the early morning hours for one of the 29 stools at the gleaming counter, each place supplied with a large, fresh linen napkin. The hamburger—four ounces of excellent beef on a fresh bun with any number of embellishments—is unexcelled in the city. Other blue-ribbon dishes are the chili, the fruit and meringue pies, the garnished omelets, and the "cannibal special"—uncooked hamburger and egg with chopped onion on rye. To wash it down, try an orange or coffee freeze with ice cream. Everything's made on the premises and served by bow-tied, white-waistcoated waiters with the fleetest feet in the business. ✕ *626 S. Carrollton Ave., Uptown,* ☎ *504/866–9573. No credit cards. Breakfast, lunch, and dinner daily.*

Johnny's Po'boys. Strangely enough, good po'boys are hard to find in the French Quarter. Johnny's compensates for the scarcity with a cornucopia of them, put together in the time-honored New Orleans manner. Inside the soft-crusted French bread come the classic fillings—lean boiled ham, well-done roast beef in a garlicky gravy, crisply fried oysters or shrimp, and a wide variety of others. The chili may not cut it in San Antonio, but the red beans and rice are respectable. The surroundings are rudimentary. ✕ *511 St. Louis St., French Quarter,* ☏ *504/523–9071. No credit cards. Breakfast, lunch, and dinner Mon.–Sat. No dinner Sun.*

Mother's. Thousands of tourists leave New Orleans believing that Mother's, an island of blue-collar sincerity amid glittery hotels and office buildings, is the city's ultimate in down-home eats. However, many locals find the place has declined in the several years since the new owners expanded operating hours and enlarged the menu. Still, Mother's keeps dispensing its delicious baked ham and roast-beef po'boys, home-style biscuits and jambalaya, and a very good chicken gumbo in a couple of dining rooms that are always full. Breakfast eggs and coffee are sometimes cold, and cleanliness is not an obsession, but that doesn't seem to repel the hordes fighting for seats at peak mealtimes. Service is cafeteria style, with a counter or two augmenting the tables. ✕ *401 Poydras St., Central Business District,* ☏ *504/523–9656. No credit cards. Breakfast, lunch, and dinner daily.*

★ **Progress Grocery and Central Grocery.** These two old-fashioned Italian grocery stores in the French Quarter produce authentic muffulettas, one of the greatest gastronomic gifts of the city's Italian immigrants. They're good enough to challenge the po'boy as the local sandwich champ, and are made by filling soft round loaves of seeded bread with ham, salami, mozzarella, and a salad of marinated chopped green olives. Each sandwich, about 10 inches in diameter, is sold in quarters and halves. Central is better known, but Progress comes up with a sandwich that many neighborhood folks prefer because it's cheaper, more generous, and available in several varieties. You can eat your muffuletta at a counter in either place, but some prefer to take them out to a bench on Jackson Square or the Moon Walk along the Mississippi Riverfront, both just a few blocks away. ✕ *Progress: 915 Decatur St., French Quarter,* ☏ *504/525–6627.* ◷ *Mon.–Sat. 8 AM–5:30 PM. Central: 923 Decatur St.,* ☏ *504/523–1620.* ◷ *Daily 8 AM–5:30 PM.*

6 Lodging

VISITORS TO New Orleans have a wide variety of accommodations to choose from: posh high-rise hotels, antique-filled antebellum homes, Creole cottages, old slave quarters, or the more familiar hotel chains.

By Nancy Ries

Updated by
Honey Naylor

When planning a stay in New Orleans, try to reserve well in advance—especially during Mardi Gras, the Jazz Festival, and the Super Bowl, which will be played here in 1997, when rates are at least double those listed here; most places require anywhere from a three- to a five-night minimum stay, and some ask for full payment up front. At other times (especially during the summer), hotels frequently offer special packages at reduced rates. Mardi Gras is a very hectic time and anything can happen; don't expect smooth service during this week.

To reserve a room in any property in this chapter, you can contact Fodor's new toll-free lodging reservations hot line (☎ 1–800–FODORS–1 or 1–800–363–6771; 0800–89–1030 in Great Britain; 0014/800–12–8271 in Australia; 1800–55–9101 in Ireland.

Orleans Parish (county) hotels include in the bill an 11% tax, plus an additional charge of $1 to $3 per night per room, depending upon the hotel size. Our ratings are flexible and subject to change. Dollar amounts overlap slightly because of the range of accommodations available in given hotels.

All of the large hotels offer no-smoking rooms and are in compliance with the Americans with Disabilities Act. New Orleans has a number of guest houses in 19th-century structures that, as a rule, do not yet have accommodations for persons with disabilities. If you need assistance in choosing a place to stay, contact the Housing Bureau (☎ 504/566–5021) or the New Orleans Tourist and Convention Commission (☎ 504/566–5011).

The selections provided here are varied in price and have been chosen on the basis of good value and service for your money.

CATEGORY	COST*
$$$$	over $120
$$$	$90–$120
$$	$50–$90
$	under $50

*All prices are for a standard double room, excluding 11% tax.

Hotels

Central Business District

Staying in the Central Business District (CBD) will appeal to visitors who prefer accommodations in luxurious high-rise hotels. All the hotels listed are located within walking distance of the French Quarter, but shuttles, taxis, buses, and the streetcar are readily available. Walking in this area is not recommended after dark.

$$$$
★ **Fairmont Hotel.** The Fairmont, which celebrated its centennial in 1993, is one of the oldest grand hotels in America. The marble floor and Victorian splendor of the massive lobby evokes a more elegant and gracious era. The hotel is composed of three connected historic buildings. Special touches in every room include four down pillows, electric shoe-buffers, and a bathroom scale; suites have fax machines. Impressive murals depicting life in the South enliven the walls of the famed Sazerac Bar; the Sazerac Restaurant offers a romantic elegance with nightly din-

French Quarter and Central Business District Lodging

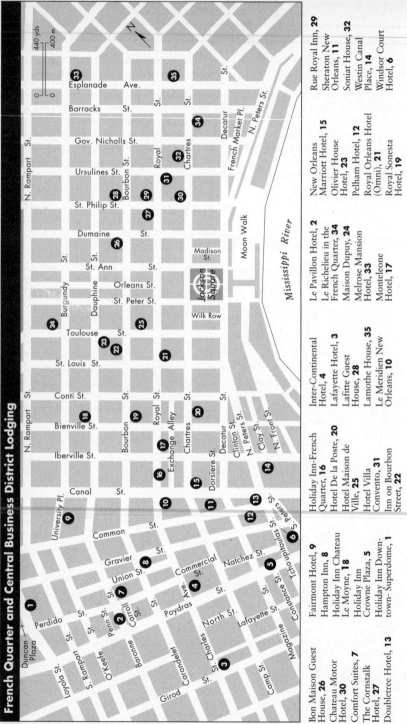

Esplanade Ave.

Barracks St.

Gov. Nicholls St.

Ursulines St.

St. Philip St.

Dumaine St.

St. Ann St.

Orleans St.

St. Peter St.

Toulouse St.

St. Louis St.

Conti St.

Bienville St.

Iberville St.

Canal St.

Common St.

Gravier St.

Union St.

Commercial Ave.

Poydras St.

Natchez St.

North St.

Lafayette St.

Perdido St.

Girod St.

N. Rampart St.

Burgundy St.

Dauphine St.

Bourbon St.

Royal St.

Chartres St.

Decatur St.

N. Peters St.

French Market Pl.

Moon Walk

Madison St.

Jackson Square

Wilk Row

Mississippi River

Exchange Alley

Dorsiere St.

Clinton St.

N. Peters St.

Clay St.

N. Front St.

University Pl.

Loyola St.

S. Rampart St.

O'Keefe St.

Baronne St.

Carondelet St.

St. Charles Ave.

Camp St.

Magazine St.

Constance St.

Tchoupitoulas St.

S. Peters St.

Duncan Plaza

440 yds
400 m

Bon Maison Guest House, **26**
Chateau Motor Hotel, **30**
Comfort Suites, **7**
The Cornstalk Hotel, **27**
Doubletree Hotel, **13**

Fairmont Hotel, **9**
Hampton Inn, **8**
Holiday Inn Chateau Le Moyne, **18**
Holiday Inn Crowne Plaza, **5**
Holiday Inn Downtown- Superdome, **1**

Holiday Inn-French Quarter, **16**
Hotel De la Poste, **20**
Hotel Maison de Ville, **25**
Hotel Villa Convento, **31**
Inn on Bourbon Street, **22**

Inter-Continental Hotel, **4**
Lafayette Hotel, **3**
Lafitte Guest House, **28**
Lamothe House, **35**
Le Meridien New Orleans, **10**

Le Pavillon Hotel, **2**
Le Richelieu in the French Quarter, **34**
Maison Dupuy, **24**
Melrose Mansion Hotel, **33**
Monteleone Hotel, **17**

New Orleans Marriott Hotel, **15**
Olivier House Hotel, **23**
Pelham Hotel, **12**
Royal Orleans Hotel (Omni), **21**
Royal Sonesta Hotel, **19**

Rue Royal Inn, **29**
Sheraton New Orleans, **11**
Soniat House, **32**
Westin Canal Place, **14**
Windsor Court Hotel, **6**

New Orleans Lodging

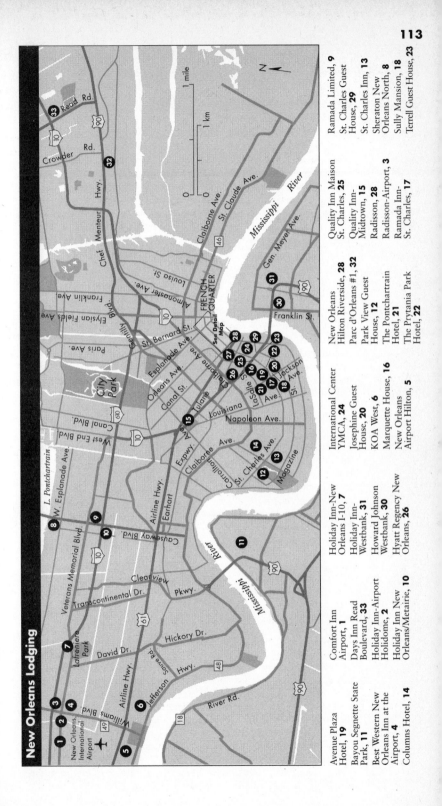

Ramada Limited, **9**
St. Charles Guest House, **29**
St. Charles Inn, **13**
Sheraton New Orleans North, **8**
Sully Mansion, **18**
Terrell Guest House, **23**

Quality Inn Maison St. Charles, **25**
Quality Inn-Midtown, **15**
Radisson, **28**
Radisson-Airport, **3**
Ramada Inn-St. Charles, **17**

New Orleans Hilton Riverside, **28**
Parc d'Orleans #1, **32**
Park View Guest House, **12**
The Pontchartrain Hotel, **21**
The Prytania Park Hotel, **22**

International Center YMCA, **24**
Josephine Guest House, **20**
KOA West, **6**
Marquette House, **16**
New Orleans Airport Hilton, **5**

Holiday Inn-New Orleans I-10, **7**
Holiday Inn-Westbank, **31**
Howard Johnson Westbank, **30**
Hyatt Regency New Orleans, **26**

Comfort Inn Airport, **1**
Days Inn Read Boulevard, **33**
Holiday Inn-Airport Holidome, **2**
Holiday Inn New Orleans/Metairie, **10**

Avenue Plaza Hotel, **19**
Bayou Segnette State Park, **11**
Best Western New Orleans Inn at the Airport, **4**
Columns Hotel, **14**

ner dancing and a Sunday brunch. ⌖ *University Pl., 70140, ☎ 504/529–7111 or 800/527–4727, FAX 504/529–4775. 685 rooms, 50 suites. 4 restaurants, bars, room service, pool, beauty salon, exercise room, 2 tennis courts, valet parking. AE, D, DC, MC, V.*

$$$$ **Hyatt Regency New Orleans.** The lobby area is quite streamlined, with plenty of light, fountains, Oriental rugs, well-spaced conversation areas, and a slew of glittering chandeliers only slightly smaller than your average football field. Go for a corner room where two walls of windows give a sense of space and sometimes a good view. Most rooms in the Lanai Building face the pool and each one has a private patio or balcony. Special rooms for women travelers are larger, close to the elevators, and come with hair dryers and makeup mirrors. The revolving Top of the Dome restaurant offers a great view of the city. A glass atrium connects the hotel with the New Orleans Centre shopping mall and the Superdome. ⌖ *500 Poydras Plaza, 70140, ☎ 504/561–1234 or 800/233–1234, FAX 504/587–4141. 1,184 rooms, 100 suites. 3 restaurants, deli, 2 bars, pool, beauty salon, laundry service, parking. AE, D, MC, V.*

$$$$ **Inter-Continental Hotel.** One of the major convention hotels, the Inter-Continental is a modern rose-granite structure overlooking St. Charles Avenue and Lafayette Square. Rooms in the front of the building afford a splendid view of Gallier Hall, on whose steps the mayor toasts Rex, King of Carnival, during Mardi Gras. (The hotel's main ballroom is the scene of the glittering meeting of the courts of Rex and Comus, the final Mardi Gras event). Stairs and escalators lead from the ground level to a spacious second floor lobby with indirect lighting, potted palms, and displays of modern art. On the fifth floor, you'll find a peaceful sculpture garden. Rooms are large and well lit, with good quality quilted spreads and matching draperies, minibars, and baths with mini-TVs and hair dryers. Forty rooms are equipped for travelers with disabilities. Amenities on the VIP levels include two-line phones, TV teleconferencing, terry-cloth robes, and a lounge with board games, complimentary Continental breakfast, and afternoon cocktails served by a butler. There is a well-equipped fitness center (with Stairmaster, rowing machine, and treadmill), and an outdoor heated pool. The main dining room is the Veranda, bastion of popular chef Willy Coln (*see* Chapter 5, Dining). ⌖ *444 St. Charles Ave., 70130, ☎ 504/525–5566 or 800/445–6563, FAX 504/585–4387. 481 rooms, 30 suites. 3 restaurants, lounge, pool, exercise room, dry cleaning, laundry service, valet parking. AE, D, DC, MC, V.*

$$$$ **Lafayette Hotel.** This small brick building has housed a Lafayette Hotel
★ ever since it was built in 1916. After declining and closing for a time it was renovated and reopened in late 1991 to rave reviews. Special features are the handsome millwork, brass fittings, and marble baths throughout. The lobby is tiny but chic; the rooms are spacious and sunny. Some rooms have four-poster beds; all have cushy easy chairs and ottomans and closets with full-length mirrors. There are books in the bookshelves. Special rooms on the second floor have floor-length windows opening onto a balcony. There are no-smoking rooms and rooms equipped for people with disabilities. ⌖ *600 St. Charles Ave., 70130, ☎ 504/524–4441 or 800/733–4754, FAX 504/523–7327. 24 rooms with bath, 20 suites. Restaurant, dry cleaning, laundry service, concierge, meeting rooms, valet parking. AE, D, DC, MC, V.*

$$$$ ★ Le Meridien New Orleans. Marble, gleaming brass, beveled mirrors, and stunning displays of fresh flowers create contemporary elegance at this French luxury hotel. The hotel faces Canal Street across from the French Quarter; the motor entrance is at 609 Common Street. Le Meridien houses a complete state-of-the-art Nautilus health club, including a personal trainer and a masseuse, and a business center with multilingual service. There are seven no-smoking floors, 26 rooms accessible to people with disabilities, and 32 rooms with computer modem accessibility. Dixieland bands play weekends in the atrium lobby. 🏨 *614 Canal St., 70130,* ☎ *504/525–6500 or 800/ 543–4300,* FAX *504/586–1543. 494 rooms, 7 suites. Restaurant, no-smoking floors, pool, beauty salon, sauna, aerobics, health club, nightclub, laundry service, business services, valet parking. AE, D, DC, MC, V.*

$$$$ New Orleans Hilton Riverside. Two glass-enclosed passageways connect the hotel's 1977 high-rise building with its newer four-story Riverside section. Sprawling multilevel public areas tend to be confusing, but you can register for both hotel sections at the main desk. Try to book into the Riverside—the rooms are larger, the decor more appealing, and the views of the Mississippi unmatched. This is the home of Pete Fountain's nightclub and an official stop of the Riverfront streetcar; moreover, the Flamingo riverboat casino boards at the Riverside. The hotel's extensive fitness facilities include a golf clinic. 🏨 *Poydras St. at the Mississippi River, 70140,* ☎ *504/561–0500 or 800/445–8667,* FAX *504/568–1721. 1,602 rooms, 89 suites. 3 restaurants, 6 lounges, no-smoking floors, 2 pools, beauty salon, outdoor hot tubs, massage, sauna, 11 tennis courts, aerobics, exercise room, health-club, jogging, raquetball, squash, business services, parking. AE, D, DC, MC, V.*

$$$$ Pelham Hotel. A restored four-story office building now houses the chic Pelham, which opened in late 1994. This is the ideal place for those who want to be in the center of the CBD—near Riverwalk, the Convention Center, and Harrah's casino—but who also seek a quiet alternative to the bustling convention hotels. The entire property exudes a sedate, yet inviting, ambience. The small lobby, with green marble floor and fresh flowers, adjoins the restaurant, Graham's, whose chef/owner is the estimable Kevin Graham. Rooms are rather small, and each is individually decorated; some have four-poster beds. All have marble baths with hair dryers, terry-cloth robes, and English soaps. Twice-daily maid service and newspapers delivered to your door are among the amenities. Note that the inside rooms, though attractively furnished, have no windows. There is no VIP level nor sumptuous suites, but a concierge is on duty in the lobby. Guests have use of the fitness center and pool at the nearby Sheraton. 🏨 *444 Common St., 70130,* ☎ *504/522–4444 or 800/659–5621,* FAX *504/539– 9010. 60 rooms. Restaurant, laundry service, dry cleaning, concierge. AE, D, DC, MC, V.*

$$$$ Westin Canal Place. The Westin was definitely designed with views in mind. The huge rose Carrara marble lobby, with its European antiques, jardinières, and grand piano, is on the 11th floor of the Canal Place shopping mall. Its two-story arched windows overlook the great bend in the Mississippi and the French Quarter; the outdoor pool, on the 30th floor, affords a panoramic view. Rooms and suites are decorated in hues of green, rose, or soft peach; each has a marble foyer and marble bath. All have phones with call-waiting, stocked minibars, and TVs with sports and movie channels. The perks on the two executive floors include a VIP lounge, complimentary Continental breakfast, and afternoon hors d'oeuvres. Twenty-four-hour room service is provided by the elegant Le Jardin, which also does a Sunday brunch with live jazz. Tea with scones is served each afternoon in the lobby lounge. The Aquarium, the Canal Street ferry, Riverwalk, and Harrah's casino are a stone's throw away. ⌂ *100 Iberville St., 70130,* ☏ *504/566–7006 or 800/228–3000,* FAX *504/553–5133. Restaurant, 2 lounges, room service, pool, valet parking. AE, D, DC, MC, V.*

$$$$ Windsor Court Hotel. Exquisite, gracious, elegant, eminently civi-
   ★   lized—these words are frequently used to describe Windsor Court, but all fail to capture the wonderful quality of this hotel. From Le Salon's scrumptious afternoon tea, served daily in the lobby, to the unbelievably large rooms, this is one of *the* places to stay in New Orleans. Plush carpeting, canopy and four-poster beds, stocked wet bars, marble vanities, oversize mirrors, dressing areas—all contribute to the elegance and luxury of the Windsor Court. It is across from the site of Harrah's casino and four blocks from the French Quarter. The Windsor's Grill Room is one of the city's finest restaurants (*see* Chapter 5, Dining). ⌂ *300 Gravier St., 70130,* ☏ *504/523–6000 or 800/262–2662,* FAX *504/596–4513. 58 rooms, 264 suites, 2 penthouses. 2 restaurants, lounge, pool, hot tub, sauna, steam room, health club, laundry service, parking. AE, D, DC, MC, V.*

$$$ Doubletree Hotel. The small, comfortable lobby is adorned with flower arrangements and decorative bowls of potpourri, along with the hotel's trademark jar of chocolate chip cookies. Decor is country French and rooms have an open, airy feeling with matching pastel draperies and spreads and light-colored furniture. Rooms ending in 05 are larger and the eighth floor is no-smoking. The hotel is close to the river and Harrah's casino, and a short walk from the French Quarter. The staff is exceptionally helpful. ⌂ *300 Canal St., 70130,* ☏ *504/581–1300 or 800/222–8733,* FAX *504/522–4100. 363 rooms, 15 suites. Restaurant, bar, deli, lounge, pool, health club, laundry service, valet parking. AE, D, DC, MC, V.*

$$$ Holiday Inn Crowne Plaza. Built for the 1984 World's Fair, this Holi-
   ★   day Inn has 23 stories of stunning glass architecture, with concierge perks on the top floor. The hotel is on a Mardi Gras parade route and is close to Harrah's casino. ⌂ *333 Poydras St., 70130,* ☏ *504/ 525–9444 or 800/522–6963,* FAX *504/581–7179. 439 rooms. Restaurant, lounge, pool, exercise room, meeting rooms, parking. AE, D, DC, MC, V.*

$$$ Le Pavillon Hotel. Magnificent chandeliers adorn the European-style
   ★   lobby of this historic hotel (built in 1905), and a handsome display of artwork lines the corridors. Another pièce de résistance is the marble railing in the *Gallery Lounge*, originally from the Grand Hotel in Paris. Good-size rooms have high ceilings and are done in identical traditional decor; suites are particularly elegant. All guests are provided terry robes and nightly turn-down service. Additions in 1995 included rooftop cabanas around the pool, a fitness center, and a whirlpool spa. ⌂ *833 Poydras St., 70140,* ☏ *504/581–3111 or 800/535–9095,* FAX *504/522–5543. 220 rooms, 7 suites. Restaurant, lounge, no-smoking floors, pool, spa, exercise room, laundry service, free parking. AE, D, DC, MC, V.*

$$$ New Orleans Marriott Hotel. In addition to affording a fabulous view of the French Quarter, the CBD, and the river, the Marriott is within walking distance of the French Quarter, Riverwalk, Harrah's casino, and the Convention Center. The rooms are comfortable, the service is friendly, and there's nightly jazz in the lobby. ☎ *555 Canal St., 70140,* ☎ *504/581–1000 or 800/228–9290,* FAX *504/523–6755. 1,236 rooms, 54 suites. 3 restaurants, 2 lounges, pool, sauna, health club, meeting rooms, valet parking. AE, D, DC, MC, V.*

$$$ Radisson. Formerly the Clarion, this hotel has an unusually large lobby, with conversation areas grouped both here and on the mezzanine. Rooms are not exceptional in size or style, but the rates are good for the CBD. Easy access off I–10 and about a 10-minute walk to the French Quarter. ☎ *1500 Canal St., 70112,* ☎ *504/522–4500 or 800/627–4500,* FAX *504/525–2644. 759 rooms, 23 suites. 2 restaurants, deli, lounge, pool, hot tub, exercise room, coin laundry, valet parking. AE, D, DC, MC, V.*

$$$ Sheraton New Orleans. On Canal Street, across from the French Quar-
★ ter, this hotel has a lobby that's large and bright, and usually bustling with conventioneers. A tropical atmosphere permeates the Gazebo Lounge, which features jazz nightly. Café Promenade encircles the second level. Executive rooms on the top floors come with many special amenities. Expect top-quality service. ☎ *500 Canal St., 70130,* ☎ *504/525–2500 or 800/325–3535,* FAX *504/592–5615. 1,100 rooms, 72 suites. 3 restaurants, 2 lounges, no-smoking rooms, pool, health club, parking. AE, D, DC, MC, V.*

$$ Comfort Suites. A boon for budget travelers, this late 1994 entry onto the CBD scene has an uninspiring lobby but large, well-equipped suites: each has a minifridge, microwave, coffeemaker, hair dryer, and safe. Some are equipped for travelers with disabilities; safety features include key cards and an audio fire alarm system. The sauna and whirlpool are a pleasant surprise. Luxury suites feature whirlpool baths. A complimentary Continental breakfast is available, and local calls are free. At the flick of a credit card, your phone will rent a car, make airline reservations, and perform other neat tricks. The hotel is four blocks from the French Quarter. ☎ *346 Baronne St., 70112,* ☎ *504/524–1140 or 800/228–5150,* FAX *504/523–4444. 100 suites. Sauna, spa, exercise room, coin laundry, business services, valet parking. AE, D, DC, MC, V.*

$$ Hampton Inn. Opened in late 1994, this budget hotel is yet another converted office building. Its spartan lobby is shared by the UNO Downtown Center, which occupies the first three levels. Safety features include key-access elevators; local calls are free; and all baths have hair dryers. Two blocks from Bourbon Street, the hotel is a bit closer to attractions than the Comfort Suites. ☎ *226 Carondelet St., 70130,* ☎ *504/529–9990 or 800/426–7866,* FAX *504/529–9996. 186 rooms. Exercise room, concierge, valet parking. AE, D, DC, MC, V.*

$$ Holiday Inn Downtown—Superdome. Its location near the Superdome makes this a favorite hotel for Saints fans, and it fills up quickly for the Sugar Bowl. ☎ *330 Loyola Ave., 70112,* ☎ *504/581–1600 or 800/535–7830,* FAX *504/586–0833. 297 rooms, 4 minisuites, 3 suites. Restaurant, lounge, pool, parking. AE, D, DC, MC, V.*

$$ Quality Inn—Midtown. The Mid-City location makes this a popular place to stay during Jazz Fest and City Park golf tournaments. Children's Hospital and LSU and Tulane medical schools are also nearby. A free shuttle to the French Quarter, the CBD, and the St. Charles streetcar runs throughout the day. ☎ *3900 Tulane Ave., 70119,* ☎ *504/486–5541 or 800/228–5151,* FAX *504/488–7440. 104 rooms.*

Restaurant, lounge, no-smoking rooms, pool, hot tub, free parking. AE, D, DC, MC, V.

French Quarter

Because most people who visit New Orleans stay in the Quarter, the 96-square-block area abounds with every type of guest accommodation. The selections that follow are all high-quality establishments chosen to provide variety in location, atmosphere, and price. Reservations are usually a must.

$$$–$$$$ **Monteleone Hotel.** The grande dame of French Quarter hotels, with its
★ ornate baroque facade, liveried doormen, and shimmering lobby chandeliers, was built in 1886. It's the Quarter's oldest hotel and is operated by the fourth generation of the Monteleone family. Rooms here are extra large and luxurious, and each is decorated differently. Fabrics are rich, and there is a mix of four-poster beds, brass beds, and beds with traditional headboards. Junior suites are a spacious combination bedroom and living room. Extra pampering is provided in the sumptuous VIP suites. The pool and exercise room are on the roof; the slowly revolving Carousel Bar in the lobby is a landmark. ☎ *214 Royal St., 70140,* ☎ *504/523–3341 or 800/535–9595,* FAX *504/ 528–1019. 600 rooms, 35 suites. 3 restaurants, 2 bars, beauty salon, pool, exercise room, concierge, business services, meeting rooms. AE, D, DC, MC, V.*

$$$–$$$$ **Royal Orleans Hotel (Omni).** This elegant, white-marble hotel, built in
★ 1960 in the heart of the Vieux Carré, is said to be an exact replica of the grand St. Louis Hotel of the 1800s. Sconce-enhanced columns, gilt mirrors, fan windows, and three magnificent chandeliers brought from France all blend to re-create an aura that reigned in New Orleans more than a century ago. Rooms, though not exceptionally large, are well appointed with marble baths (telephone in each) and more marble on dressers and tabletops. Balcony rooms cost the most. The well-known Rib Room Restaurant makes its home on the lobby level. The old New Orleans map that covers one wall of the lounge will fascinate anyone interested in history. ☎ *621 St. Louis St., 70140,* ☎ *504/529–5333 or 800/THE–OMNI,* FAX *504/529–7089. 350 rooms, 16 suites. Restaurant, 3 lounges, pool, barbershop, beauty salon, exercise room, business services, meeting rooms, parking. AE, D, DC, MC, V.*

$$$–$$$$ **Royal Sonesta Hotel.** Guests step directly from the revelry of Bourbon Street into the chandeliered, marble elegance of this renowned hotel's lobby, where a cool, serene atmosphere is embellished with a lush array of live plants. Most of the guest rooms are average size and furnished with light-color antique reproductions. Many have French doors that open onto balconies or patios. All have minibars and high-tech phones. Rooms with balconies facing Bourbon Street are noisy; the quietest are those facing the pool or courtyard, and the small top-floor dormer rooms. Live entertainment is featured in both the Mystic Den cocktail lounge and the Can-Can Café & Jazz Club. ☎ *300 Bourbon St., 70140,* ☎ *504/586–0300 or 800/766–3782,* FAX *504/ 586–0335. 500 rooms, 32 suites. 2 restaurants, 3 lounges, pool, exercise room, concierge floor, business services, parking. AE, D, DC, MC, V.*

$$$ **Hotel de la Poste.** Guests here can enjoy room service from a Brennan's restaurant: The hotel's dining room is Bacco, an elegant Italian eatery operated by Ralph and Cindy Brennan. Most rooms are in the main building, and many have balconies that overlook either the

courtyard or Chartres Street; some have French doors that open directly onto the spacious courtyard. The four carriage house suites share a cheery sundeck. The hotel is close to Jackson Square, Bourbon Street, and Canal Street. ☎ *316 Chartres St., 70130,* ☎ *504/581–1200 or 800/448–4927,* FAX *504/523–2910. 87 rooms, 13 suites. Restaurant, lounge, pool, meeting room, valet parking. AE, D, DC, MC, V.*

$$$ Maison Dupuy. Owned by the Delta Queen Steamboat Company, this property attracts steamboat passengers just off the river. Seven restored 19th-century town houses surround one of the Quarter's prettiest courtyards and its spectacular fountain. Le Bon Creole is a reasonably priced restaurant, with the adjacent Toulouse Cabaret for late-night revelers. The hotel is only two blocks from Bourbon Street and the heart of the Quarter; it is also the closest hotel to Harrah's temporary casino, which is scheduled to open in the renovated Municipal Auditorium in April 1995. As a result, Rampart Street and Armstrong Park will benefit from a face-lift and beefed-up security. ☎ *1001 Toulouse St., 70112,* ☎ *504/586–8000 or 800/535–9177,* FAX *504/566–7450. 198 rooms, 10 suites (3 VIP). Restaurant, pool, health club, meeting rooms, valet parking. AE, D, DC, MC, V.*

$$–$$$ Holiday Inn Chateau Le Moyne. Old-world atmosphere and decor can
★ be found just one block off Bourbon Street. Eight suites are in Creole cottages off a tropical courtyard, and all rooms are furnished with antiques and reproductions. ☎ *301 Dauphine St., 70112,* ☎ *504/581–1303 or 800/465–4329,* FAX *504/523–5709. 160 rooms, 11 suites. Restaurant, lounge, pool, valet parking. AE, D, DC, MC, V.*

$$–$$$ Holiday Inn—French Quarter. Close to Canal Street, this is a good home base for walking into the heart of the French Quarter or the CBD, or for boarding the St. Charles streetcar line. A $12-million renovation in 1995 added 26 rooms and a TGI Friday restaurant. ☎ *124 Royal St., 70130,* ☎ *504/529–7211 or 800/465–4329,* FAX *504/566–1127. 276 rooms, 56 suites. Restaurant, indoor pool, coin laundry, parking. AE, D, DC, MC, V.*

$$ Chateau Motor Hotel. Simple, friendly, and filled with historic charm, this moderately priced hotel (only a few blocks from Jackson Square) is a real find. The original carriageway leads to the guest rooms, which vary in size and decor. Some rooms are furnished with antiques, but most rooms are traditional or contemporary; many have balconies and a few open directly onto the courtyard that houses the only silo in the Vieux Carré. (The silo encloses a spiral stairway to the penthouse suites.) A patio suite and a small restaurant are housed in the old slave quarters. Continental breakfast and morning newspaper are complimentary. The only negative note is that the bathtubs aren't full-size. ☎ *1001 Chartres St., 70116,* ☎ *504/524–9636,* FAX *504/525–2989. 45 rooms. Pool, free parking. AE, DC, MC, V.*

$$ Inn on Bourbon Street. This is a Best Western hotel, with courtyard and balcony rooms. Rooms facing the courtyard are quieter, but the 32 rooms with Bourbon Street balconies are coveted during Mardi Gras. ☎ *541 Bourbon St., 70130,* ☎ *504/524–7611 or 800/535–7891,* FAX *504/568–9427. 186 rooms, 2 suites. Cafeteria, piano bar, pool, valet parking. AE, DC, MC, V.*

$$ Le Richelieu in the French Quarter. Tucked in a corner of the French
★ Quarter, close to the old Ursuline Convent and the French Market, Le Richelieu combines the friendly, personal atmosphere of a small hotel with luxe touches (upscale toiletry packages, hairdryers)—all at a

moderate rate. Some rooms have mirrored walls as well as large walk-in closets, many have refrigerators, and all are adorned with brass ceiling fans. To be sure you don't get caught looking rumpled, each room also has a full-size ironing board. Balcony rooms are available at the same rates. There is an intimate bar and café off the courtyard with tables on the terrace by the pool. ☎ *1234 Chartres St., 70116,* ☎ *504/529–2492 or 800/535–9653;* FAX *504/524–8179. 69 rooms, 17 suites. Restaurant, lounge, pool, free parking. AE, D, DC, MC, V.*

Garden District/Uptown

Visitors to New Orleans who prefer accommodations away from Downtown will find the historic Garden District and Uptown area ideal. All the following are on or close to fashionable, mansion-lined St. Charles Avenue, where the St. Charles Avenue streetcar runs (24 hours), making the CBD and the French Quarter a mere 15–20 minutes away. Walking in this area after dark is not recommended.

$$$$ The Pontchartrain Hotel. Maintaining the grand tradition is the hall-
★   mark of this quiet, elegant European-style hotel that has reigned on St. Charles Avenue since it was built as an upscale residential hotel in 1927. Individually appointed accommodations range from lavish sun-filled suites to small pension rooms with shower baths. The romantic Pontchartrain has been the honeymoon hotel for such couples as Prince Aly Kahn and Rita Hayworth; suite names will tell you who else has stayed here. The internationally known Caribbean Room provides memorable dining. ☎ *2031 St. Charles Ave., 70140,* ☎ *504/524–0581 or 800/777–6193,* FAX *504/529–1165. 60 rooms, 42 suites. 2 restaurants, piano bar, concierge, parking. AE, D, DC, MC, V.*

$$$ Columns Hotel. This impressive, white-columned 1883 Victorian-style hotel was the setting for the film *Pretty Baby.* The wide veranda, set with cloth-covered tables for outdoor dining or cocktails, is very inviting, as are the two period-furnished parlors. The dark, intimate lounge with two wood-burning fireplaces is a favorite with locals and features excellent live progressive jazz on Thursday. One of the most impressive staircases you will ever climb leads to large, somewhat sparsely furnished rooms that have phones but no TVs. For budget travelers, there are cheaper rooms with shared bath. Rates include Continental breakfast, served either in the dining room or on the veranda. ☎ *3811 St. Charles Ave., 70115,* ☎ *504/899–9308 or 800/445–9308,* FAX *504/899–8170. 10 rooms with private bath, 9 rooms with shared bath. Lounge, ballroom. AE, MC, V.*

$$–$$$ Avenue Plaza Hotel. The spartan lobby of this St. Charles Avenue accommodation belies the amenities found here. Public rooms include a romantic lounge with dark wood panels from a French chalet and a small, intimate restaurant. The spacious rooms have generous dressing areas and kitchenettes with full-size refrigerators. Rooms are decorated in either traditional or artdeco styles, both equally appealing. Guests may use the Mackie Shilstone Pro Spa, which offers a Turkish steam bath, Swiss showers, and a Scandinavian sauna, for a fee of $7 per day, $30 per week. The pool is in a pleasant courtyard setting; a sundeck and hot tub are on the roof. ☎ *2111 St. Charles Ave., 70130,* ☎ *504/566–1212 or 800/535–9575,* FAX *504/525–6899, ext. 7601. 160 rooms, 80 suites. Restaurant, lounge, pool, spa, parking. AE, D, DC, MC, V.*

$$ **The Prytania Park Hotel.** This small hotel complex, in the Lower Garden District half a block from St. Charles Avenue and the streetcar, has been built to surround an 1834 town house that faces Prytania Street. (The lobby entrance and parking lot are around the corner on Terpsichore Street.) Exposed brick walls and replica period furnishings hand-carved from English pine lend a charm to the 13 rooms in the 1834 house. Rooms in the new buildings are contemporary, and some have loft areas that are great for families traveling with children. Suites have balconies overlooking Prytania, and all rooms, except those in the 1834 house, come with refrigerators and microwaves. The complimentary Continental breakfast can be enjoyed on the cozy patio. ☎ *1525 Prytania St., 70130,* ☎ *504/524–0427 or 800/862–1984,* FAX *504/522–2977. 56 rooms, 6 suites. Free parking. AE, DC, MC, V.*

$$ **Quality Inn Maison St. Charles.** This is a lovely property in six historic
★ buildings that cluster around intimate courtyards. The tunnel entrance features an attractive mural display. A complimentary shuttle to the Convention Center and 24-hour security are among the amenities. ☎ *1319 St. Charles Ave., 70130,* ☎ *504/522–0187 or 800/831–1783,* FAX *504/525–2218. 112 rooms, 20 suites. Lounge, no-smoking rooms, pool, hot tub, valet parking. AE, D, DC, MC, V.*

$$ **Ramada Inn—St. Charles.** This hotel has good-size rooms and an attractive lobby, and is a streetcar-ride away from the French Quarter. It was completely renovated following a 1994 fire. ☎ *2203 St. Charles Ave., 70140,* ☎ *504/566–1200 or 800/443–4675,* FAX *504/581–1352. 132 rooms, 8 suites. Restaurant, lounge, parking. AE, D, DC, MC, V.*

$$ **St. Charles Inn.** This small Uptown hotel features good-size modern rooms, each with a dressing area. Rooms in the front with a St. Charles Avenue view are best unless streetcar noise bothers you. Complimentary Continental breakfast and a newspaper are brought to your room each morning. The staff is friendly and accommodating. The hotel is adjacent to Que Sera Restaurant, a sidewalk café and lounge with an extremely popular Wednesday night drink special. ☎ *3636 St. Charles Ave., 70115,* ☎ *504/899–8888 or 800/489–9908,* FAX *504/899–8892. 40 rooms. AE, D, DC, MC, V.*

Kenner/Airport

$$$–$$$$ **New Orleans Airport Hilton.** Directly across from the New Orleans
★ International Airport is this $32-million hotel, offering unexpected elegance in this area of the city. The decor throughout is superb, with muted pastel colors that coordinate well with the soft pink Caribbean-style exterior. Sculpted area rugs, handwoven in England, highlight the scheme. ☎ *901 Airline Hwy., Kenner, 70062,* ☎ *504/469–5000 or 800/445–8667,* FAX *504/466–5473. 317 rooms, 2 suites. Restaurant, lounge, pool, putting green, tennis court, exercise room, business services, airport shuttle, car rental, free parking. AE, D, DC, MC, V.*

$$$ **Radisson–Airport.** Converted from a Sheraton in 1993, renovations include the addition of 11,000 square feet of banquet and meeting space. There's easy access to I-10, and the large Esplanade shopping mall and the Pontchartrain Convention Center are nearby. ☎ *2150 Veterans Blvd., Kenner, 70062,* ☎ *504/467–3111 or 800/333–3333,* FAX *504/469–4634. 244 rooms, 3 suites. Restaurant, oyster bar, pool, airport shuttle, free parking. AE, D, DC, MC, V.*

$$ **Best Western New Orleans Inn at the Airport.** This entire property was renovated in 1993, and shopping is available on nearby Williams Boulevard and at the Esplanade Mall. The Treasure Chest riverboat casino is nearby. There's no restaurant, but Denny's restaurant is next door. ☎ *1021 Airline Hwy., Kenner, 70062,* ☎ *504/464–1644 or 800/333–8278,* FAX *504/469–1193. 166 rooms. Pool, airport shuttle, free parking. AE, D, DC, MC, V.*

$$ Comfort Inn Airport. Three miles from the airport, this chain motel sports a handsome courtyard, and one room has a Jacuzzi and a working fireplace. Fax and other business services are available for guests. The hotel is a mile and a half from the Treasure Chest casino. ☎ *1700 I–10 Service Rd., Kenner, 70065,* ☎ *504/467–1300 or 800/777–7036,* FAX *504/468–1714. 289 rooms. Restaurant, lounge, room service, pool, meeting rooms, airport shuttle. AE, D, DC, MC, V.*

$$ Holiday Inn—Airport Holidome. Many of the rooms here face the dome-covered pool area, which is popular with families with children. It's convenient to I–10 and close to Rivertown, U.S.A. and the Treasure Chest Casino. ☎ *2929 Williams Blvd., Kenner, 70062,* ☎ *504/467–5611 or 800/465–4329,* FAX *504/469–4915. 303 rooms, 1 suite. Restaurant, lounge, indoor pool, hot tub, sauna, exercise room, meeting rooms, airport shuttle, free parking. AE, D, DC, MC, V.*

Metairie

$$$$ Sheraton New Orleans North. Formerly called Sheraton Inn-on-the-Lake, this property is part of a glass office complex that towers beside Lake Pontchartrain. The art-deco-style lobby is decorated with marble mirrors and brass. Request a room overlooking the lake. ☎ *3838 N. Causeway Blvd., Metairie, 70002,* ☎ *504/836–5253 or 800/936–5253,* FAX *504/836–5262. 210 rooms. Restaurant, lounge, no-smoking rooms, beauty salon, tennis courts, health club, meeting rooms, airport shuttle. AE, D, DC, MC, V.*

$$ Holiday Inn New Orleans/Metairie. There's easy access to I–10 and a free shuttle to the nearby Lakeside Shopping Mall. ☎ *3400 I–10 Service Rd., Metairie, 70001,* ☎ *504/833–8201 or 800/522–6963,* FAX *504/838–6829. 194 rooms. Restaurant, lounge, pool, free parking. AE, D, DC, MC, V.*

$$ Holiday Inn–New Orleans I–10. As the name suggests, this hotel is convenient to I–10; it's also across the street from the large Lafreniere Park, complete with barbecue areas, a walking track, sports fields, duck-filled lagoons, and several fairs and music festivals throughout the year. ☎ *6401 Veterans Blvd., Metairie, 70003,* ☎ *504/885–5700 or 800/465–4329,* FAX *504/454–8294. 217 rooms. Restaurant, lounge, pool, hot tub, airport shuttle, free parking. AE, D, DC, MC, V.*

$$ Ramada Limited. Several excellent restaurants are very close, including Ruth's Chris Steak House (*see* Chapter 5, Dining). Free shuttles will take you to the French Quarter and Lakeside Shopping Mall, except during Mardi Gras and other special events. A Continental breakfast is included with all rooms. The hotel is near I–10. ☎ *2713 N. Causeway Blvd., 70002,* ☎ *504/835–4141 or 800/874–1280,* FAX *504/833–6942. 138 rooms. Lounge, pool, airport shuttle, free parking. AE, D, DC, MC, V.*

New Orleans East

$$ Days Inn Read Boulevard. All rooms in this newly renovated high-rise have a separate vanity area and private balconies. It's across from Lake Forest Shopping Mall and three blocks from the Louisiana Nature Center, making this a good spot for families with children. ☎ *5801 Read Blvd., 70127,* ☎ *504/241–2500 or 800/331–6935,* FAX

504/245–8340. 143 rooms. Restaurant, pool, playground, free parking. AE, D, DC, MC, V.

Westbank

$$ Holiday Inn—Westbank. Don't get confused—the address here is exactly the same as the Howard Johnson Westbank, but this hotel is a few blocks farther along the expressway, on the opposite side of the expressway when coming off the Crescent City Connection Bridge. Golfers stay here during tournaments at the nearby English Turn Golf and Country Club. It's also close to the country-western club Mudbugs, which is billed as "the world's largest honky-tonk." ☎ *100 Westbank Expwy., Gretna, 70053,* ☎ *504/366–2361 or 800/465–4329,* FAX *504/362–5814. 309 rooms. Restaurant, lounge, pool, free parking. AE, D, DC, MC, V.*

$ Howard Johnson Westbank. Formerly the Sheraton, this hotel is just across the Crescent City Connection and near the Oakwood Shopping Mall. ☎ *100 Westbank Expwy., Gretna, 70053,* ☎ *504/366–8531 or 800/635–7787,* FAX *504/362–9502. 168 rooms. Restaurant, lounge, pool, free parking. AE, D, DC, MC, V.*

Guest Houses

Guest houses are for those who come to New Orleans with a desire to savor the old-world charm and atmosphere that is so proudly preserved in this city. All have a limited number of rooms, so it is advisable to make reservations well in advance of arrival—a full year is not an unreasonable amount of time.

French Quarter

$$$$ Melrose Mansion Hotel. A stretch limo to whisk guests from and to
★ the airport; down pillows and fine milled soaps; full breakfast served poolside, in a formal dining room, or in your room; and individually decorated rooms filled with 19th-century Louisiana antiques (including four-poster and canopy beds) are among the attractions of this handsome 1884 Victorian mansion, which opened as a hotel in 1990. Rooms and suites are spacious, with high ceilings and polished hardwood floors; guests gather each evening for cocktails in the formal drawing room. Baths are sumptuous affairs; those in suites feature marble whirlpool tubs or Jacuzzis. Suites also boast wet bars and private patios. Smoking is not encouraged here. The hotel is quite grand, but it's inadvisable to venture onto nearby Rampart Street at night. ☎ *937 Esplanade Ave., 70116,* ☎ *504/944–2255,* FAX *504/945–1794. 4 rooms, 4 suites. Air-conditioning, pool. AE, MC, V.*

$$$–$$$$ Hotel Maison de Ville. This small, romantic hotel lies in seclusion
★ amid the hustle and bustle of the French Quarter. Tapestry-covered chairs, a gas fire burning in the sitting room, and antiques-furnished rooms all contribute to a 19th-century atmosphere. Some rooms are in former slave quarters in the courtyard; others are on the upper floors of the main house. Fully stocked minibars and robes are provided for all guests. The complimentary Continental breakfast is served with a rose on a silver tray, and port and sherry are served in the afternoon. Other meals can be enjoyed at a small adjacent restaurant called the Bistro. Visitors who seek a special hideaway will love the hotel's Audubon Cottages—off the street in a private, enclosed area, each with kitchen and individual patio—two blocks from the hotel. ☎ *727 Toulouse St., 70130,* ☎ *504/561–5858 or 800/634–1600,* FAX *504/528–9939. 14 rooms, 2 suites, 7 cottages. Restaurant,*

pool at cottage location, parking. No children under 12. AE, D, DC, MC, V.

$$$–$$$$ **Soniat House.** This property in 1995 was further expanded to include
★ the former French Quarter Maisonettes directly across the street. This
addition was renovated and converted into seven luxury Jacuzzi
suites. Proprietors Rodney and Frances Smith's hotel includes those
suites, plus rooms and suites in their restored 1830 town houses and
the six apartments of Girod House on nearby Esplanade Avenue. All
accommodations are elegantly appointed with fine European and
American antiques; amenities include Crabtree & Evelyn soaps,
down pillows, and pure cotton percale sheets from Egypt. Breakfast
(at an extra charge) is homemade biscuits and strawberry jam, served
with juice and café au lait. ☎ *1133 Chartres St., 70116,* ☎ *504/
522–0570 or 800/544–8808,* FAX *504/522–7208. 18 rooms, 13 suites,
6 apts. Concierge, business services, valet parking. AE, MC, V.*

$$–$$$ **The Cornstalk Hotel.** The historic cast-iron Cornstalk Fence surrounds
this 1816 Victorian-style Vieux Carré landmark. Antique mirrors
reflect the glow of crystal chandeliers in the plush entrance hall. Each
room is unique and has a sitting-room atmosphere of another era. Fur-
nishings include armoires, canopy or four-poster beds, marble-top
tables or nightstands, stained-glass windows, Oriental rugs, and fire-
places. Guests can enjoy a complimentary Continental breakfast either
on the balcony overlooking Royal Street, or outside on the gallery or
patio. Parking is available on the grounds. ☎ *915 Royal St., 70116,* ☎
504/523–1515, FAX *504/522–5558. 14 rooms. AE, MC, V.*

$$–$$$ **Lafitte Guest House.** A four-story 1849 French manor house, the
Lafitte is meticulously restored, with rooms individually decorated in
period furnishings. Room 40 takes up the entire fourth floor and
overlooks French Quarter rooftops. Complimentary Continental
breakfast can be brought to your room, served in the Victorian sitting
room, or enjoyed in the courtyard, and the owner serves wine and
hors d'oeuvres each evening. ☎ *1003 Bourbon St., 70116,* ☎
504/581–2678 or 800/331–7971, FAX *504/581–2678. 13 rooms, 1
suite. Free parking. AE, D, MC, V.*

$$–$$$ **Lamothe House.** This white-columned 1849 town house, which rests
★ on Esplanade Avenue at the edge of the French Quarter, radiates
Southern grace and charm. A wide entrance hall, formerly a carriage-
way, and a sweeping staircase lead to the second-floor reception par-
lor and formal dining room. An array of antiques furnishes each
room, and lace curtains cover every window; baths are small and
modern. Guests can choose the main house, former slave quarters,
carriage house, or a Creole cottage with its own patio. Complimen-
tary Continental breakfast is served in the dining room or courtyard.
Off-street parking is provided free of charge. ☎ *621 Esplanade Ave.,
70116,* ☎ *504/947–1161 or 800/367–5858,* FAX *504/943–6536. 11
rooms, 9 suites. AE, MC, V.*

$$–$$$ **Olivier House Hotel.** Owned and operated by the friendly Danner fam-
ily, this informal, very casual guest house is popular with Europeans
and theatrical troupes that play the Saenger. It was built as a Creole
town house in 1836, and no two rooms are alike: Some are done with
canopy beds and antiques, others have a tropical flavor. Many have
balconies and kitchenettes with microwaves; some are split-level.
Rooms 107 (a two-bedroom, two-bath suite) and 103 open directly
onto the pool area in one of the two plant-filled courtyards. (The col-
orful caged birds in the other courtyard are pretty, but they can be

chattering nuisances.) A refurbishment of all rooms and baths was completed in 1992. ☎ *828 Toulouse St., 70112,* ☎ *504/525–8456,* FAX *504/529–2006. 42 rooms with bath. Pool. AE, DC, MC, V.*

$$–$$$ **Rue Royal Inn.** A pot of hot coffee, a tin of cookies, and three Persian cats greet you in the lobby. Many rooms are pleasantly oversize in this circa-1830 home; four have balconies overlooking Royal Street and a school playground; and one has a Jacuzzi. Each room has a coffeemaker. On Sunday only, the complimentary Continental breakfast comes from nearby Croissant d'Or. Off-street parking is available for a fee. ☎ *1006 Royal St., 70116,* ☎ *504/524–3900 or 800/776–3901,* FAX *504/947–7454. 17 rooms. AE, D, DC, MC, V.*

$–$$ **Hotel Villa Convento.** Lela and Warren Campo and their son Larry provide round-the-clock attention and service to guests in their four-story 1848 Creole town house. The guest house is in a quiet end of the French Quarter, close to the old Ursuline Convent. Each morning guests can enjoy croissants and fresh-brewed coffee on the lush patio. Furnished with reproductions of antiques, rooms with chandeliers or ceiling fans vary from inexpensive to moderate, based on location, size, and amenities. Some have balconies; all have private baths and phones. The elevator is padded with a tapestry, which creates a sensation not to be missed. ☎ *616 Ursulines St., 70116,* ☎ *504/522–1793,* FAX *504/524–1902. 25 rooms. AE, D, DC, MC, V.*

$ **Bon Maison Guest House.** Quaint accommodations lie within the gates of this 1840 town house, situated on the quiet end of Bourbon Street. Rooms off the lush courtyard in the slave quarters are pleasantly furnished and have ceiling fans. Two large suites with fully equipped kitchenettes are located in the main house. There's no elevator—so be prepared for lots of stair climbing to upper floors. All accommodations have air-conditioning, phone, and color TV. Breakfast is not included. ☎ *835 Bourbon St., 70116,* ☎ *504/561–8498. 3 rooms, 2 suites. MC, V.*

Garden District

$$–$$$ **Josephine Guest House.** This Italianate mansion, built in 1870, has ★ been perfectly restored to provide visitors with the pleasures of the graceful lifestyle of an old New Orleans home. European antiques fill the rooms, and Oriental rugs cover gleaming hardwood floors. Four rooms and a parlor are in the main house; there are two smaller but still spacious rooms in the *garçonnier* (where the original owners' sons stayed). The bathrooms are impressive in both size and decor. A complimentary Creole breakfast of fresh-squeezed orange juice, café au lait, and homemade biscuits can be brought to your room (Wedgwood china on a silver tray) or served on the secluded patio. The Josephine had a face-lift in 1994 that included upgrading the plumbing and installing phones in guest rooms. ☎ *1450 Josephine St., 1 block from St. Charles Ave., 70130,* ☎ *504/524–6361 or 800/779–6361,* FAX *504/523–6484. 6 rooms. AE, D, DC, MC, V.*

$$–$$$ **Park View Guest House.** Adjacent to beautiful Audubon Park, this historic Victorian guest house has graced St. Charles Avenue as an Uptown landmark since 1884, when it was built as a hotel for the World Cotton Expo. Rooms on the east side offer great views of the park. The general rule here is that you get either antiques or a view, but brass beds and ceiling fans adorn the "view" rooms. There is a lounge replete with TV and fireplace. Complimentary Continental breakfast is served in a large bay-windowed dining room. ☎ *7004 St.*

Charles Ave., 70118, ☎ 504/861–7564, ℻ 504/861–1225. 23 rooms (7 with shared bath). AE, D, MC, V.

$$–$$$ **Sully Mansion.** More than a century ago, New Orleans architect Thomas Sully built this handsome, rambling Queen Anne–style house; these days it's a bed-and-breakfast. In the foyer, where there is a grand piano, light filters through stunning pastel-colored stained-glass windows, which are original to the house. The public rooms feature high ceilings, oil paintings, fireplaces, tall windows with swagged, floor-length drapes, and Victorian hand-me-downs. All guest rooms have TVs and phones. In a 1994 renovation, new furnishings, including four-poster beds and handsome rugs, were added and baths were enlarged. Common rooms upstairs and down have TVs and shelves full of books, magazines, and board games. A Continental breakfast (cereals, juices, yogurt) is included in the rate. Neighbor to other grand mansions, the house is on a pretty tree-lined street, a block from the streetcar. ☎ *2631 Prytania St., 70130, ☎ and* ℻ *504/891–0457. 5 rooms with bath, 2 suites. AE, MC, V.*

$$–$$$ **Terrell Guest House.** This restored 1858 mansion is located in the lower Garden District, where a renovation project called "Operation Comeback" is in full swing. Some may feel the area is undesirable until they step inside the guest house's double parlors (furnished with period antiques), where guests gather each evening for a hospitality hour. A Waterford chandelier graces the formal dining area, where a Continental breakfast is served each morning. Rooms in the carriage house and slave quarters face a large patio with a fountain. Two rooms and a suite are in the main house. ☎ *1441 Magazine St., 70130, ☎ 504/524–9859 or 800/878–9859. 9 rooms, 1 suite. AE, D, DC, MC, V.*

$ **St. Charles Guest House.** Simple, clean, and comfortable, this European-style pension is an affordable find in four buildings one block from St. Charles Avenue. Rooms in the A and B buildings are larger. The small "backpacker" rooms share a bath and do not have air-conditioning. Guests receive a survival manual from proprietors Joanne and Dennis Hilton, which includes self-guided Garden District and streetcar tours. A pleasant surprise is the large swimming pool and deck. A Continental breakfast is served daily, and on occasion Dennis and Joanne delight their guests with an impromptu crawfish boil or an introduction to New Orleans's red beans and rice. ☎ *1748 Prytania St., 70130, ☎ 504/523–6556. 36 rooms (8 with shared bath). Pool. AE, MC, V.*

Bed-and-Breakfast Reservation Services

Bed-and-breakfast means overnight lodging and breakfast in a private residence. Begin by writing or calling a reservation service and discussing price range, type of residence, location, and length of stay. The service, in turn, will provide you with descriptions of several choices of B&Bs that meet your criteria. From these choices you'll make a decision and send a 20% deposit. You'll receive the address and other pertinent details before you arrive.

$–$$ **Bed & Breakfast, Inc.—Reservations Service.** This service offers a variety of accommodations in all areas of New Orleans. Some homes are 19th-century historic homes. Guest cottages, rooms, and suites are also available. Prices range from $40 to $150. ☎ *Write or call Hazel Boyce, 1021 Moss St., Box 52257, 70152, ☎ 504/488–4640 or 800/729–4640, ℻ 504/488–4639. No credit cards.*

$–$$$$ **New Orleans Bed & Breakfast and Accommodations.** Among 200 properties citywide are private homes, apartments, and condos. Prices range from $45 to $250. ☎ *Contact Sarah-Margaret Brown, Box 8163, 70182, ☎ 504/838–0071 or 838–0072, FAX 504/838–0140. AE, D, MC, V.*

Hostels

$ **International Center YMCA.** Accommodations are for both men and women. Guests can use the weight room, gym, track, and pool. Rooms in the Pratt Building are newer. Here's a hint for Mardi Gras: 20 of these rooms face St. Charles Avenue or Lee Circle and provide excellent parade views. All rooms have color TVs. There are bathrooms and showers on each floor. ☎ *920 St. Charles Ave., 70130, ☎ 504/568–9622, FAX 504/568–9622, ext. 268. 50 rooms, no private baths. Restaurant, indoor pool, exercise room, parking. MC, V.*

$ **Marquette House, New Orleans International Hostel.** A devastating fire in 1993 barely slowed down the activity at the fourth largest youth hostel in the country, run by Steve and Alma Cross. Reconstruction of the 100-year-old main house is expected to be completed by 1995; the interim accommodations are just as pleasant in the six other Marquette properties. The hostel is one block from St. Charles Avenue and the streetcar. There are bunk beds in dorms, private rooms with shared baths, and apartments with bedroom, living room, and kitchen. Separate dorms are available for male and female guests with disabilities. Smoking is allowed outside only. Reservations are essential for Mardi Gras and the Jazz Fest; a four-day package is offered for Mardi Gras. Unlike many other hostels, there are no curfews or lock-outs. ☎ *2253 Carondelet St., 70130, ☎ 504/523–3014, FAX 504/529–5933. 160 dorm beds, 5 rooms with shared bath, 12 apartments. 2 lounges, 2 equipped community kitchens, dining room, picnic area. MC, V.*

Travel Parks and Campgrounds

Good camping facilities close to the city are rare, since open, solid land is a premium in New Orleans. These three lie within 20 minutes of the city, traffic pending. Others can be found farther out or across Lake Pontchartrain.

$ **Bayou Segnette State Park** has 100 sites in a wooded area, with water and electricity, tent pads, picnic tables, and barbecue grills; no reservations. There are also 20 furnished loft cabins that sleep six to eight with screened porches overlooking the bayou; reservations are required for these. The park, which is home to the state's largest wave pool, is off the Westbank Expressway near the Huey P. Long bridge. ☎ *7777 West Bank Expressway, Westwego, 70094, ☎ 504/736–7140. 2 comfort stations, 2 washaterias, dump station, picnic area, pay telephones, boat launch. MC, V.*

$ **KOA West** offers 96 large back-in sites with well-kept grass areas around tree-shaded concrete pads; it also has 10 tent sites. Reservations are required. It's close to Rivertown, U.S.A. in Kenner (take the Williams Blvd. exit off I–10). ☎ *11129 Jefferson Hwy., River Ridge, 70123, ☎ 504/467–1792. Convenience store, pool, picnic area, playground, laundry, shuttle bus to French Quarter. D, MC, V.*

$ **Parc d'Orleans #1** is a brick-enclosed park with 71 back-in concrete pads. There is grass at each site and a tree-shaded area for tents. Reservations are required for Mardi Gras and special events. It's located eight blocks east of the Chef Menteur exit off I–10. ☎ *7676 Chef Menteur Hwy., 70126,* ☏ *504/241–3167 or 800/535–2598. Lobby with TV, pool, laundry, propane delivery. MC, V.*

7 Nightlife and the Arts

NIGHTLIFE

By Jason Berry
and Honey
Naylor

Updated by
Michael
Tisserand

NO OTHER American city places such an exalted premium on good times as New Orleans. From the well-appointed lounges in high-end hotels to the trendy House of Blues and bustling bars of the French Quarter, out into rocking music clubs in far-flung neighborhoods, and the smaller watering holes, a lush spirit permeates the urban topography.

One legacy of the city's Latin temperament is the absence of a curfew law. Many bars stay open all night, so long as a crowd is on hand. During Mardi Gras season or holiday events, such as the Sugar Bowl, human traffic is tight in the French Quarter. On more placid autumn and spring weekends, club-hopping on the old rues can be as charming as tapa-tasting in Madrid. Bourbon Street may be the gaudiest walk in the Deep South—all those T-shirts!—but the Quarter still exudes an elemental European charm. How then to enjoy the town at its best?

A lot of that depends on when you eat. Long meals are a tradition here. With so many good restaurants concentrated between Canal Street and Esplanade, an early dinner reservation allows one to finish in time for the 9 PM set at Quarter jazz spots or in the adjacent Faubourg Marigny. Farther uptown, pop music clubs tend to have later opening sets, anywhere from 10 to 11 PM.

One must toil with Puritan restraint to have a bad time in the Quarter. But where tourists flock, traps will thrive. Strip joints tend to be expensive, with high covers or steep prices on drink minimums.

Many bars advertise the Hurricane—a rum-and-fruity red concoction that is the signature drink at **Pat O'Brien's,** which is the best place to order one. "Go-cups" are ubiquitous here, especially in the Quarter, and since Pat's is next door to **Preservation Hall,** which serves neither food nor drink, you can buy a Hurricane-to-go to enjoy in the Hall.

Perhaps the most famous local drink is the Sazerac, brewed of bourbon and bitters, with a coating of ersatz absinthe. The **Sazerac Bar** in the Fairmont Hotel does a stellar job with its namesake. In a previous incarnation the hotel was called the Roosevelt, and the late Governor Earl K. Long used it as bivouac during his torrid career.

The 500 and 600 blocks of Frenchmen Street—in the neighborhood just outside the Quarter, known as Faubourg Marigny—should not be missed. Here you will find three of the hottest music clubs. **Snug Harbor** is the mecca of modern jazz (maestro Ellis Marsalis plays regularly). **Cafe Istanbul,** a hub of salsa and Latin rhythms, also showcases up-and-coming young brass bands like the Soul Rebels. **Cafe Brasil** on the same block features reggae, Afro-Caribbean, and jazz. It's also a magnet for poets, with readings throughout the year. If you're old enough to remember Greenwich Village in the '60s, Frenchmen Street's little zone of bohemia is an echo of beat culture, suffused with the lazy aura of a semitropical environment. If you're not old enough to remember, don't worry; just enjoy the colorful slice of life.

Dress codes are rare as snow in New Orleans. There are, of course, upscale clubs and bars where people come to see and be seen. On any given night in the French Quarter—but especially during the Carnival season—you'll see anything from tuxedos and ball gowns to T-shirts and torn jeans. Once you head into the neighborhoods, the fashions betray a decidedly casual tilt.

The big draw in New Orleans is music, and the range of venues is broad indeed. If you have never been here before, you should consider the following standouts. **Preservation Hall** is grungy and uncomfortable, with crude wooden benches, cramped standing room—and the best traditional jazz in the world. The Hall isn't for creature comforts; it's for your soul. Next door, the internationally known watering hole **Pat O'Brien's** is very loud and very lively till very late. At the **Palm Court Jazz Café** you can have dinner to superb traditional jazz and, as a bonus, chat with proprietress Nina Buck, who knows all there is to know about New Orleans music. The lineup at **Tipitina's** varies nightly, from rhythm and blues to rock. For great live Cajun and zydeco music, head for **Mulate's, Michaul's, the Maple Leaf** (on Thursday night), **Mid-City Bowling Lanes** (also on Thursday), or **Tipitina's** (on Sunday). Though the only music at the **Napoleon House** is taped classical, the ancient bar is enormously popular and a great place to soak up local atmosphere. All are described in more detail below.

In neighborhood clubs featuring music or just drinks, it's best to bring cash. Some take plastic but many more do not. Unlike government, this is a pay-as-you-go kinda town, perhaps as an antidote to the state's bottomless history of corruption.

Prices range from $3 to $5 a drink in hotel lounges, and get cheaper the farther away from Downtown or the Quarter you go. Some music clubs on Bourbon Street and its environs have a two-drink minimum, and some require that you take both drinks at the same time. Music clubs elsewhere in town generally charge a flat cover of between $5 and $10.

A music calendar is broadcast five times a day on WWOZ, 90.7 FM, the community radio station devoted to New Orleans music. You can also call the station's "Second Line" for a prerecorded calendar (☎ 504/840–4040). For up-to-date listings, consult the Friday "Lagniappe" entertainment supplement of the *Times-Picayune,* or *Gambit,* the alternative weekly, which appears on Monday and is carried free in major newsstands. The *TP*'s daily listing features only the major clubs. The monthly *OffBeat* magazine has in-depth music coverage and is available in many hotels and restaurants. Never be shy about calling clubs to ask what kind of music a given group plays.

Music Venues

For a city of only 500,000, New Orleans offers a vast selection of live music. To list every club and bar would be a massive undertaking. Many hotels, for example, feature piano bars. One of the most elegant, in the Royal Orleans main floor, is **The Esplanade,** a warm, moody lounge serving cocktails, desserts, and postprandial liqueurs. *621 St. Louis St., French Quarter,* ☎ *504/529–5333. AE, D, DC, MC, V. ☉ Nightly Mon.–Sat. to 1 AM, Sun. to 11 PM.*

Other hotels feature musical groups either on a seasonal basis or for weekend jazz brunches. New Orleans also has a good middle range of neighborhood restaurants or taverns that periodically offer music on weekends.

The heaviest concentration of music is in the French Quarter. Most visitors discover the hot spots as they stroll through the old city.

Hence, the descriptive sections on neighborhood clubs—those outside the Quarter and Downtown—in our listing are a bit longer, as these places are off the beaten track for most out-of-towners.

The clubs we have selected feature good bands on a regular basis, usually most nights of the week. This rundown is not a definitive list, only a reliable and reasonably thorough guide to the places best known for keeping the flames lit.

First, a few tips: Showtimes can vary greatly. Quarter clubs featuring Dixieland or traditional jazz get rolling early in the evening, usually by 8 PM; several clubs feature music in the afternoons as well, especially on weekends. The first set at most neighborhood clubs usually begins about 10 PM; unless a club features wee-hours music on a regular basis, the last set usually ends around 2 AM. But it's advisable to call the club to double-check times and ask for directions if you need them.

French Quarter

The Absinthe Bar is a late-night haunt given to hard-driving blues that rocks into the wee hours. Regular guitarist Bryan Lee is the hardest-working musician on Bourbon Street. *400 Bourbon St.,* ☎ *504/525–8108. AE, D, MC, V.* ☉ *Daily, noon–3 AM.*

Al Hirt's Place. The trumpet legend himself holds forth at his club a few times each week—the schedule varies, so call for times. Other popular acts such as the Neville Brothers and Cajun fiddler Doug Kershaw play here. *501 Bourbon St. (upstairs),* ☎ *504/568–0501. AE, D, DC, MC, V.* ☉ *Daily noon–4 AM.*

Cafe Brasil. Actor Julia Roberts and singer Lyle Lovett had their first date here, dancing to local favorites The New Orleans Klezmer All-Stars. It's strictly standing and dancing inside, but tables line the sidewalk and the music pours through the open doors. All kinds of music and people come to this bohemian hot spot, and it's a popular place to show off costumes on Mardi Gras. *2100 Chartres St., Faubourg Marigny,* ☎ *504/947–9386. No credit cards.* ☉ *Nightly; hrs vary.*

Café Istanbul. The mood is Middle Eastern and exotic; the range of entertainment is from brass band to salsa to belly dancing. *534 Frenchmen St., Faubourg Marigny,* ☎ *504/944–4180. AE, MC, V.* ☉ *Live music Wed.–Sun. from 10:30 PM.*

Cajun Cabin. Here's Cajun music and food right on Bourbon Street. One-drink minimum. *501 Bourbon St.,* ☎ *504/529–4256. AE, D, DC, MC, V.* ☉ *Daily, 11 AM until people are ready for the last waltz.*

Cats Meow. Locals and tourists alike flock to this lively karaoke nitery, which also features videos, "hand jive," "hokey pokey," and other diversions. *701 Bourbon St.,* ☎ *504/523–1157. AE, D, DC, MC, V.* ☉ *Weekdays 5 PM–4 AM, weekends 2 PM–5 AM.*

Checkpoint Charlie's. This place draws a young, local crowd that comes here to shoot pool and listen to late-night blues and rock—the louder the better. There's also a paperback library and even a laundromat. The 1993 film *The Pelican Brief* featured several scenes here. *501 Esplanade Ave.,* ☎ *504/947–0979. MC, V.* ☉ *24 hrs.*

Chris Owens Club. Chris, a Quarter icon, is a dancer-singer. Her acts are only slightly risqué, and are always entertaining. *502 Bourbon St.,* ☎ *504/523–6400. AE, D, DC, MC, V.* ☉ *Doors open 9 PM, shows at varying times. Occasionally closed Sun.*

Donna's Bar & Grill. This barbecue joint has become the hottest place in town to hear both new and established brass bands in a neighborhood setting. *800 N. Rampart St.,* ☎ *504/596–6914. No credit cards.* ☉ *Live music Tues.–Sun. from 8:30* PM.

Dragon's Den. This most bohemian of music cafés features pillows on the floor, Thai food, and acts like New Orleans poet John Sinclair and the Blues Scholars. *435 Esplanade Ave.,* ☎ *504/949–1750. AE, D, MC, V.* ☉ *Live music nightly from 10* PM.

Famous Door. Music has been pouring out of this place for more than 30 years; the patio is a fairly recent addition. There's Dixieland 5 PM–9 PM, R&B from 9 till the traffic thins. *339 Bourbon St.,* ☎ *504/522–7626. AE, D, MC, V.* ☉ *Daily till 3 or 4* AM.

544 Club. For more than 15 years, house band Gary Brown and Feelings has been playing pop and R&B standards with energy and style. *544 Bourbon St.,* ☎ *504/566–0529. AE, DC, MC, V.* ☉ *Sun.–Fri. 8 PM–3* AM, *Sat. 3–3.*

Gazebo Cafe and Bar has local ambience in the French Market with outdoor dining, good drinks, and jazz. *1018 Decatur St.,* ☎ *504/522–0862. AE, D, DC, MC, V.* ☉ *Daily 11* AM–6 PM, *with live music 11–5 depending on the weather.*

House of Blues. Part-owner Dan Aykroyd opened this club in 1994 with his Blues Brothers Band. If a $7-million blues joint sounds ironic, just wait until you see this mammoth, high-tech theme bar that combines blues history lessons on CD-ROM, top local and national bands (Bob Dylan and Eric Clapton played here in 1994), and a dazzling collection of Southern folk art. The adjoining restaurant has an eclectic menu, including vegetarian dishes and classic Southern fare. This is the second H.O.B.; the first opened in Cambridge, MA, and others are opening in major cities nationwide. *225 Decatur St.,* ☎ *504/529–BLUE, concert line 504/529–1421. AE, D, MC, V.* ☉ *Mon.–Thurs. and Sun. 5* PM–2 AM, *Fri.–Sat. 8* PM–4 AM; *gospel brunch at 11* AM *Sun.*

Maison Bourbon. Come here for a variety of live jazz nightly, including the Bourbon Brass Band. *641 Bourbon St.,* ☎ *504/522–8818. No credit cards.* ☉ *Nightly till 1:45* AM.

Margaritaville Cafe. Yes, it's named after *that* song. Jimmy Buffett's devoted fans, called "parrotheads," flock to this shrine to the singer-songwriter. Such menu items as "Cheeseburger in Paradise" derive from Buffett songs, and there are several varieties of the salt-rimmed signature drink. Decor consists mainly of Jimmy photos, and the real thing does occasionally come around. Top local funk and R&B acts like George Porter and Walter "Wolfman" Washington play here. *1104 Decatur St.,* ☎ *504/592–2565. AE, D, MC, V.* ☉ *Daily 11* AM–2 AM; *music Wed.–Sun. from 9:30.*

Maxwell's Toulouse Cabaret. Geared toward tourists, this venue in the former Toulouse Street Theatre is a roomy place that features big band and traditional jazz nightly. On rare occasions, Harry Connick, Jr. stops by to sing along with his dad, Harry, Sr., the New Orleans District Attorney-cum-big band vocalist who frequently performs here. *615 Toulouse St.,* ☎ *504/523–4207. AE, D, DC, MC, V.* ☉ *Tues.–Sun. 10* AM–2 AM, *with live music stomping off at 8* PM.

O'Flaherty's Irish Channel. Irish brothers Patrick and Danny O'Flaherty hold court in Gaelic in this Celtic-style pub and cultural center.

Live music nightly—be prepared to sing along. *514 Toulouse St., ☎ 504/529–1317. AE, D, DC, MC, V. ⏲ Daily noon–3 AM.*

Palm Court Jazz Café. Banjo player Danny Barker immortalized this restaurant in his song, "Palm Court Strut." The best of traditional jazz is presented in a classy setting, with tile floors, exposed brick walls, and a handsome mahogany bar. The fine Creole and international kitchen stays open until the music stops, but if you're not hungry you can sit at the bar and rub elbows with local musicians. There's a wide selection of records, tapes, and CDs on sale. *1204 Decatur St., ☎ 504/525–0200. ⏲ 7 PM–11 PM; live music nightly from 8 PM. Closed Mon. and Tues. ☛ $4 cover per person at tables. AE, D, MC, V.*

Preservation Hall is a cultural landmark. The jazz tradition that flowered in the 1920s is devotedly enshrined here by a revolving calendar of distinguished New Orleans musicians, including Percy Humphrey, Harold Dejan and the Olympia Brass Band, and Wendell Brunious, among others. A rustic environment; tight seating on wooden benches and floor cushions. No beverages are served, but you can BYO. *726 St. Peter St., ☎ 504/523–8939. ☛ $3. No credit cards. ⏲ Nightly 8:30–midnight.*

Rhythms. A handsome courtyard and blues (mostly) are features of this addition to the Bourbon Street beat, home to Willie Lockett and the Blues Krewe. *227 Bourbon St., ☎ 504/523–3800. No cover. AE, D, DC, MC, V. ⏲ Mon.–Thurs. 7 PM–1:30 AM, Fri.–Sun. 4 PM–2:30 AM.*

Snug Harbor. This decidedly New Orleans jazz club just outside the Quarter serves as the local home of Charmaine Neville. It is also the home base of Ellis Marsalis, the distinguished pianist, UNO professor, and father of Wynton and Branford Marsalis. The restaurant attached to the music space serves good local dishes but is best known locally for its burgers. You can sit at the bar and listen to the music in the next room without paying the cover. *626 Frenchmen St., ☎ 504/949–0696. AE, MC, V. ⏲ Nightly sets at 9 and 11, closing around 2 AM.*

CBD and Warehouse District

Howlin' Wolf. This local favorite is housed in a former grain and cotton warehouse. Live music offerings include an acoustic open mike on Monday, Sunday's "BBQ Hoedown," and a grab bag of alternative rock and R&B the rest of the week. Visiting musicians often hang out here and occasionally get on stage. *828 S. Peters St., ☎ 504/523–2551. No credit cards. ⏲ Daily 3 PM–3 AM.*

Mermaid Lounge. A strictly low-key, low-cost hangout, Mermaid presents emerging acts such as local rock band Blood 'n' Grits. *1102 Constance St., ☎ 504/524–4747. No credit cards. ⏲ Live music Thurs.–Sat. from 10 PM.*

Michaul's Live Cajun Music Restaurant is a spacious and homey place with a huge dance floor on which patient teachers give free Cajun dance lessons nightly. *840 St. Charles Ave., ☎ 504/522–5517. AE, D, DC, MC, V. ⏲ Dinner Mon.–Thurs. 6–11, Fri.–Sat. 6–midnight. Live Cajun music Mon.–Thurs. 7:30–11, Fri.–Sat. 8 PM–midnight. Closed Sun.*

Mulate's. Just across the street from the Convention Center, this large Cajun restaurant-bar seats 400, and the dance floor is always full of couples twirling to the best Cajun bands. Friday nights are held down by an exceptional group called Steve Riley and the Mamou Playboys.

The first Mulate's opened more than a decade ago in Breaux Bridge to instant fame (see Dining and Lodging in Chapter 8, Excursions). *201 Julia St., ☎ 504/522–1492. AE, D, DC, MC, V. ⊗ Daily 11–11. Live music nightly 7:30–11.*

Pete Fountain's. The Dixieland clarinet maestro plays one show from 10 to 11:15 on Tuesday, Wednesday, Friday, and Saturday in his plush club on the third floor of the Hilton—at least he does when he's at home. He's often on tour, and the schedule varies from month to month. Wear your good duds. *2 Poydras St. at the river, ☎ 504/523–4374 or 504/561–0500. AE.*

Vic's Kangaroo Cafe. The Australia-born owner combines Down-Under food with lowdown blues, with music starting around 10 PM. This is home court to gentleman harmonica player Rockin' Jake. *636 Tchoupitoulas St., ☎ 504/524–GDAY. AE, D, DC, MC, V. ⊗ Daily 11:30 AM–3:30 AM.*

Uptown

Uptown means upriver from the French Quarter, but the area described by this generic term stretches from the Garden District past the university neighborhoods, all the way to the end of the St. Charles streetcar line, which stops at Carrollton and Claiborne avenues. The area runs the gamut from elegant residential blocks to middle- and lower-class neighborhoods. The difficulty is that it's often hard to tell where serene neighborhoods end and rougher ones begin—if you have doubts, it's best to take a taxi.

Carrollton Station. This small club is as cozy as a lake cabin and features acts like blues guitarist John Mooney and the beloved chanteuse L'il Queenie. Sunday acoustic night is popular with locals who refuse to worry about waking up Monday morning. *8140 Willow St., ☎ 504/865–9190. AE, D, MC, V. ⊗ 3:30 PM–2 AM; music from 10 PM.*

Jimmy's Music Club & Piano Bar. Next to Carrollton Station and across the street from the streetcar barn, this club presents rock, rap, reggae, and more. *8200 Willow St., ☎ 504/861–8200. No credit cards.*

Maple Leaf. Down-home and funky, with pressed-tin walls and over-worked ceiling fans, this is the place to hear and dance to good local music. There's a romantic, tropical patio out back to enjoy when the main room overflows, and it's not unusual for dancers to spill onto the front sidewalk, too. The Cajun band File plays its own style of French honky-tonk music on Thursday; other nights the Leaf features a variety of R&B, brass band, and rock artists. Although the club is only a few blocks from the Oak and Carrollton streetcar stop, it's wise to take a cab. *8316 Oak St., ☎ 504/866–9359. No credit cards. ⊗ Sets stop around 2 AM or as late as 5 AM on weekends.*

Mid-City Bowling Lanes & Sports Palace. The saying "Only in New Orleans . . ." applies to this combination bowling alley/music club near Uptown. It's a working alley, but dancers edge into the lanes when a favorite local band, such as The Iguanas, takes the stage. Thursday zydeco night brings the best Creole musicians in from rural Louisiana. Be sure to ask club owner John Blancher for a dance lesson. It doesn't get more fun than this. *4133 S. Carrollton, ☎ 504/482–3133. AE. ⊗ Daily noon–about 2 AM; music 10 PM–about 2 AM, depending on the band.*

Muddy Waters. Muddy's is known for its funky blues and is a favorite of Uptown college students. With the Maple Leaf Bar across Oak

Street from the club, the evening occasionally turns into a block party. *8301 Oak St.,* ☎ *504/866–7174. AE.* ☯ *Nightly 10 PM–2 AM.*

Tipitina's. Tip's was founded in the mid-'70s as the home base for Professor Longhair, the pioneering rhythm-and-blues pianist and singer who died in 1980; the club takes its name from one of his most popular songs. A bust of "Fess" stands prominently between the bar and short-order grill, and a tapestry of his face hangs behind the stage. As the multitude of concert posters on the walls indicates, Tip's features a wide variety of local acts and big names passing through. There's dancing to The Bruce Daigrepont Cajun Band Sunday 5–9, with free red beans and rice. *501 Napoleon Ave.,* ☎ *504/897–3943. AE, MC, V.* ☯ *Sets end between 2 AM and 5 AM.*

Bars and Lounges

French Quarter

Hard Rock Cafe. The Crescent City contribution to the popular chain is a big space with totems of rock culture adorning the walls. Fats Domino's piano top lies above the guitar-shaped bar; Elton John's shoes are on display, and so are Dr. John's cape, top hat, and walking cane. Other icons include the standing bass that the Rolling Stones used to record "Ruby Tuesday," jackets that belonged to Professor Longhair, and a Wild Tchoupitoulas Mardi Gras Indian display. *418 N. Peters St.,* ☎ *504/529–5617. AE, DC, MC, V.* ☯ *Mon.– Thurs. 11:30 AM–midnight, Fri.–Sun. 11:30–1 AM.*

Lafitte's Blacksmith Shop. Very popular with locals, Lafitte's is an atmospheric bar in a rustic 18th-century cottage. Miss Lilly, the pianist-vocalist who had a flock of devoted fans, is no longer at the keys, but there is still piano music nightly from 9 PM. *941 Bourbon St.,* ☎ *504/523–0066. No credit cards.* ☯ *Daily noon–2 AM.*

Napoleon House Bar and Cafe. Directly behind the Royal Orleans, this is a vintage hub, long popular with writers, artists, and locals of varying stripes. Murmuring ceiling fans, paintings, soft lights, and a lovely patio create a European mood. Sandwiches, soups, salads, and cheese boards are also available. The waiters are unstintingly polite and will never rush you. The perfect place for either late-afternoon people watching or an evening nightcap. *500 Chartres St.,* ☎ *504/ 524–9752. AE, D, DC, MC, V.* ☯ *Mon.–Thurs. 11 AM–midnight, Fri.–Sat. 11 AM–1 AM, Sun. 11 AM–7 PM.*

The Old Absinthe House. This popular watering hole draws folks from afternoon to late at night. The decor consists of hundreds of business cards pinned to one wall, money papering another, and absinthe jugs hanging from the ceiling for added character. *240 Bourbon St.,* ☎ *504/523–3181. AE, DC, MC, V.* ☯ *Daily 9:30 AM–2 or 3 AM.*

Pat O'Brien's. One of the biggest tourist spots in town and home of the oversized alcoholic beverage known as the Hurricane (many people like to take their glass home as a souvenir). Actually five bars in one, Pat O's claims to sell more liquor than any other establishment in the world. The bar on the left of the entrance is popular with Quarterites, the patio in the rear draws the young (and young-at-heart) in temperate months, and the piano bar on the right side of the brick corridor packs in raucous celebrants during every season of the year. *718 St. Peter St.,* ☎ *504/525–4823. MC, V.* ☯ *Daily 10 AM–5 AM.*

CBD and Warehouse District

City Lights is a cavernous place in the Warehouse District, and a chic one (jeans, T-shirts, shorts, and tennis shoes must be neat, please), with a lively bar, DJ music, and 6-foot video screens. *310 Howard Ave.,* ☎ *504/568–1700. AE, MC, V.* ☾ *Thurs.–Sat. from 8 PM.*

The Fairmont Hotel. The hotel has three distinctive lounges: **Fairmont Court** has large, lush murals on two sides of the seating area off the lobby. A bustling bar lines the third wall. ☾ *Nightly 11 AM–2 AM.* Down the hall is the smaller, more elegant **Sazerac Bar,** adjoining the famous restaurant of the same name. ☾ *Weekdays 11:30 AM–10 PM, weekends 6 PM–11 PM.* **Bailey's** is a late-night bar and restaurant, a rarity in the CBD. *123 Baronne St.,* ☎ *504/529–7111. AE, D, DC, MC, V.* ☾ *Nightly till 11.*

Riverwalk

LeMoyne's Landing. A seafood restaurant–oyster bar with a grand view of the Mississippi River, LeMoyne's sometimes features music. The open-air café, adjacent to the Spanish Plaza, has a large fountain and circular seating area. Concerts are held here in warm months; check the newspaper for details. *Riverwalk,* ☎ *504/524–4809. AE, D, DC, MC, V.* ☾ *Daily from 11 AM. Live music starts Fri. 5 PM, weekends 1 PM.*

Uptown

F&M Patio Bar. For some people, a night in New Orleans isn't complete until they've danced on top of the pool table at this lively wee-hours college hangout. There's a loud juke box, a popular photo booth, and a late-night kitchen, and the tropical patio can actually be peaceful at times. *4841 Tchoupitoulas St.,* ☎ *504/895–6784. MC, V.* ☾ *Mon.–Thurs. 1 PM–4 AM, Fri.–Sat. 3 PM–6 AM.*

Pontchartrain Hotel. The **Bayou Bar,** a lovely lounge, is just off the lobby as you enter. Popular with businesspeople and Uptown residents, the bar is easy to reach by streetcar. *2031 St. Charles Ave.,* ☎ *504/524–0581. AE, D, DC, MC, V.* ☾ *Sun.–Thurs. till midnight, Fri. and Sat. till 1 AM.*

Que Sera. A lively café-restaurant on the tree-shrouded streetcar line, this popular spot resembles a Parisian bistro with its enclosed terrace (windows are open on warm days). A popular lunch spot for uptown professionals, it features a Wednesday night happy hour that draws a huge singles crowd. Dinner is also served, and Saturday and Sunday brunch. *3636 St. Charles Ave.,* ☎ *504/897–2598. AE, D, DC, MC, V.* ☾ *Sun., Mon., Tues., Thurs. till 11 PM, Wed., Fri., Sat. till 2 AM.*

Victorian Lounge. In the Columns Hotel, the lounge has a lovely ambience and draws professionals of all ages. Top local jazz combos perform Tuesday through Thursday in the French ballroom, adjacent to the lounge. *The Columns Hotel, 3811 St. Charles Ave.,* ☎ *899–9308. AE, MC, V.* ☾ *Weeknights till midnight, weekends till 2 AM.*

Coffeehouses

Kaldi's. This massive stone structure was built as a bank in 1907, and that's what it was used for in the 1993 film, *Undercover Blues.* Otherwise, it's a relaxed, spacious coffeehouse perfect for reading, writing letters, or playing chess. There's music on some weekend nights, usually jazz or gospel. *941 Decatur St., French Quarter,* ☎ *504/586–8989. AE, D, MC, V.* ☾ *Sun.–Thurs. 7 AM–midnight, Fri.–Sat. 7 AM–2 AM.*

Neutral Ground Coffee House. This one-of-a-kind 1960s-style coffee-house and folk music spot operates as a co-op. Overstuffed sofas, chess boards, laid-back counter service, and a bulletin board encourage an intimacy unmatched in most other cafés. Sunday nights feature an open mike when any aspiring musician or performer may take the small stage. Other nights, regulars—some fairly well known in town—treat the audience to every musical genre from bluegrass to rock. The coffees, teas, and homemade baked goods, all with exotic names, are generally well worth the reasonable prices. It's a short cab ride from downtown. *5110 Danneel St.,* ☎ *504/891–3381.* ☉ *Tues.–Thurs., Sun. 8 PM–midnight, Fri. and Sat. till 1 AM.*

True Brew Cafe/True Brew Theater. Enjoy live music and theater in an intimate setting, served up with exotic coffees, teas, and pastries. *200 Julia St., Warehouse District,* ☎ *504/524–8441. MC, V.* ☉ *Mon.–Wed. 7 AM–8 PM, Thurs.–Sun. 7 AM–1 AM.*

Rollin' on the River

Creole Queen Paddlewheeler. Among the various cruises on the Big Muddy is a "Dinner on the River & All That Jazz" outing. Boarding and a Creole buffet begin at 7 PM; cruises are 8–10. The band features the renowned clarinetist Otis Bazoon, who has played with Al Hirt, among others. *Poydras Street Wharf at Riverwalk,* ☎ *504/529–4567 or 800/445–4109. AE, MC, V. Departures nightly.*

Steamboat Natchez. The city's only autentic steamboat stern-wheeler does an evening excursion featuring traditional jazz by the Dukes of Dixieland and a Cajun-Creole buffet. Boarding is at 6 PM; the cruise is from 7 to 9. Day cruises also feature live jazz. *Toulouse St. Wharf (behind the Jax Brewery),* ☎ *504/586–8777 or 800/233–BOAT. AE, D, MC, V. Departures nightly; Fri. and Sat. only from Thanksgiving to Mardi Gras.*

Gay Bars and Nightclubs

New Orleans, and in particular the French Quarter, has a sizable gay community. *This Week Guide,* a brochure published weekly and available in many of the following places, has up-to-date listings of entertainment and resources for lesbians and gay men.

Many of the gay bars are on or near Rampart, St. Ann, and Dumaine streets in the vicinity of Armstrong Park. This area is not safe, so be very careful. You should not go into the park at night unless there is a major event. A housing project lies across Rampart at Bienville, and this area is also unsafe.

Bars

Bourbon Pub. This video bar, with its youngish male clientele, has been around for some two decades now. *801 Bourbon St.,* ☎ *504/529–2107.* ☉ *Happy hr Mon.–Sat. 5–9 PM.*

Café Lafitte in Exile. Gay men have been gathering for ages at this large and lively two-story bar, which has videos and a balcony overlooking Bourbon Street. *901 Bourbon St.,* ☎ *504/522–8397.*

Charlene's. Around since the mid-'70s, Charlene's has juke-box dancing for a predominantly lesbian crowd. *940 Elysian Fields Ave.,* ☎ *504/945–9328.* ☉ *Tues.–Sun. from 5 PM. Happy hr Thurs. 5–8.*

Golden Lantern is a 24-hour gay men's bar near Esplanade Avenue. *1239 Royal St.,* ☏ *504/529–2860.* ◷ *Happy hrs daily 5–9* AM *and 5–9* PM.

The Mint. Just behind the French Market, in a large, 19th-century former government building, the Mint features local comedians and, on Friday night, pop diva Mary Griffin. The bar draws all manner of people, but its clientele is predominantly gay. *504 Esplanade Ave.,* ☏ *504/525–2000.* ◷ *Shows Fri. at 10* PM, *Sun. at 4* PM.

MRB. Another round-the-clock gay men's bar, this one has a pretty patio. *515 St. Philip St.,* ☏ *504/586–0644.* ◷ *Happy hr 4–9* PM.

Rawhide is a boisterous neighborhood leather/Levis bar 2 blocks from the busiest corner of Bourbon Street. *740 Burgundy St.,* ☏ *504/525–8106.*

Sterling Club. An elegant full-service restaurant, Sterling's offers lunch and dinner, bar service till 2 AM daily, and a happy hour weekdays 4–9. The neighborhood crowd includes gay men, lesbians, transvestites, and transsexuals. *700 Burgundy St.,* ☏ *504/522–1962.*

Footloose. This 24-hour neighborhood spot attracts a lesbian, gay, leather/Levis, transvestite/transsexual, and straight clientele. *700 N. Rampart St.,* ☏ *504/524–7654.* ◷ *Happy hr daily 2–8.*

Dance Bars

Oz. Opened in summer 1993, this dance-and-cruise bar has quickly become one of the Quarter's most popular. The crowd is young and equal parts gay and lesbian. *800 Bourbon St.,* ☏ *504/593–9491.* ◷ *24 hrs daily.*

Parade Disco. Women are welcome at this glitzy, high-energy disco, which draws a younger crowd with its lasers and videos. There are tea dances Sunday at 3 PM. *801 Bourbon St., above the Bourbon Pub,* ☏ *504/529–2107.* ◷ *Mon.–Sat. from 9* PM, *Sun. from 3* PM.

Rubyfruit Jungle. Named for a book by lesbian novelist Rita Mae Brown, Rubyfruit is the latest lively addition to the Frenchmen Street scene. Weekend DJ dancing attracts both a gay and straight crowd. *640 Frenchmen St.,* ☏ *504/947–4000.* ◷ *Tues.–Sat. from 8* PM.

Wolfendale's. Popular with gay black men, this club features DJ dancing Wednesday, Friday, Saturday, and Sunday from 8 PM. There's a Rampart Revue Thursday and Sunday at 11. *834 N. Rampart St.,* ☏ *504/524–5749.* ◷ *Daily 5* PM*–4* AM; *happy hr 5–8.*

Gambling

Gambling has been the hottest topic in town for several years. Although at press time plans were not finalized, the state legislature has approved one land-based casino for New Orleans and riverboat gambling on several state waterways, including the Mississippi River and Lake Pontchartrain. The designated developer, Harrah's Jazz Co., has begun the demolition of the Rivergate Exhibition Hall at the foot of Canal Street, the proposed site of the world's largest casino. A temporary casino is slated to open in the Municipal Auditorium in Armstrong Park by summer 1995. The plan is highly controversial, and what the outcome will be is anybody's guess. Construction of the land-based casino could begin in 1995, but it's a crapshoot.

Meanwhile, the announcement of a land-based casino has complicated the operations of the new riverboats. In 1994, the boats began to take advantage of a loophole that allowed them to remain dock-side if conditions did not permit cruising. Not surprisingly, conditions rarely—if ever—were deemed safe. Attempts to prosecute the boats were thwarted in early 1995, but at press time an appeal was pending. In response to the action, some of the riverboats have suggested that they may set sail from New Orleans, in search of friendlier territory. There were two floating casinos in New Orleans at press time; stay tuned.

Flamingo Casino. This 2,400-passenger boat, a joint operation by Hilton and New Orleans Paddlewheels, features bar service and food stands from such local landmarks as Mother's Restaurant and Lucky Dogs. Dixieland bands perform during evening cruises, and on the outside decks you can hear a narrated historical tour. *Poydras St. Wharf adjacent to Hilton Riverside and Riverwalk,* ☎ *504/587–7777 or 800/587–LUCK,* FAX *504/587–1755. 75 gaming tables, 1,333 slots, video poker, and specialty games. Gift shop, arcade room, no-smoking gaming areas.* ☛ *Free.* ⊙ *24 hrs.*

Treasure Chest Casino. Each room on this Lake Pontchartrain boat has a Caribbean theme. The kitchen cooks up Louisiana-Caribbean specialties, and a free shuttle picks you up from the nearby airport. *5050 Williams Blvd.,* ☎ *504/443–8000 or 800/298–0711,* FAX *504/443–1747. 43 gaming tables, 854 slots, video poker. Gift shop; Skylight Room is no-smoking.* ☛ *Free.* ⊙ *24 hrs.*

THE ARTS

Theater

The performing arts are alive and well in New Orleans, where a number of small companies offer an impressive variety of fare. You must keep in mind, however, that the stage in New Orleans—although entertaining, reasonably priced, and generally good—can't and shouldn't be compared to New York. For current productions and performances, consult the daily calendar in the *Times-Picayune* and "Lagniappe," the Friday entertainment section. *OffBeat, Where,* and *Gambit* are free publications (distributed in hotels and other public places) that also have up-to-date entertainment news.

The Contemporary Arts Center (900 Camp St., ☎ 504/523–1216) features two theaters that offer experimental works and plays by local playwrights.

La Maison des Beaux Arts (1140 St. Charles Ave., ☎ 504/524–4278), a complex housed in a 90-year-old restored building, includes a ground-floor café, a second-floor photography studio, and a theater presenting contemporary works.

Le Petit Théâtre (616 St. Peter St., ☎ 504/522–2081) is the oldest continuously running community theater in the United States. Located in a historic building in the French Quarter, it has a children's corner to complement its usual fare of classics, musicals, and dramas. Events for the Tennessee Williams Festival take place here in March.

NORD Theater of the New Orleans Recreation Department (☎ 504/565–7860) presents local playwrights and the Dashiki Players at Gallier Hall.

Movie Pitchers (3941 Bienville Ave., ☎ 504/488–8881) has live comedy improv and plays, as well as a regular movie schedule (*see* Film, *below*).

Rivertown Repertory Theatre (4th and Minor Sts., Kenner, ☎ 504/468–7221) is a community theater that presents contemporary musicals, comedy, and drama year-round.

The Saenger Performing Arts Center (143 N. Rampart St., ☎ 504/524–2490), a splendidly restored theater, presents national and international talent. It is on the national theater circuit for Broadway revivals and road shows.

Southern Repertory Theater (3rd Level, Canal Place, 333 Canal St., ☎ 504/861–8163) has an annual season of regional plays and classics.

Theatre Marigny (616 Frenchmen St., ☎ 504/944–2653) has had more than a decade of success presenting avant-garde plays in an intimate setting just outside the French Quarter.

Concerts

The city has several major concert facilities, including the **Louisiana Superdome**, the **Theatre of the Performing Arts**, the **Municipal Auditorium**, the **Saenger Performing Arts Center**, and the **Kiefer UNO Lakefront Arena** of the University of New Orleans. For a current schedule of concerts in these facilities check the *Times-Picayune*.

Free year-round musical events are held in the city's parks and universities. The **Louisiana Philharmonic Orchestra** (821 Gravier St., ☎ 504/523–6530) performs in the Saenger Performing Arts Center.

Opera

New Orleanians have had a long love affair with opera, but unfortunately the city has not had an opera house since the French Opera House was destroyed by fire in 1919. The **New Orleans Opera Association** (☎ 504/529–2278) now performs a number of operas each season in the Theatre of the Performing Arts. **Xavier University** (☎ 504/486–7411) has an opera school in its music department, and it stages occasional student productions.

Dance

The **New Orleans Ballet Association** (☎ 504/522–0996) is the only major professional ballet company in the city. It performs in the Theatre of the Performing Arts.

Film

The city has many cinemas. Art films and less well-known works are usually screened at the **Prytania** (5339 Prytania St., ☎ 504/895–4513). Loyola University also has a **Film Buffs Institute** (☎ 504/865–2152), which offers an excellent selection of art and foreign films during the school year. Both of these institutions publish schedules of upcoming films, available by request.

Movie Pitchers (3941 Bienville Ave., ☎ 504/488–8881) has art, foreign, and second-run films in a laid-back setting that includes sandwiches and drinks—get here early for the comfy easy chairs. The N.O. Film and Video Society (☎ 504/523–3818) presents the **N.O.**

Film and Video Festival in early October, bringing top international films and visits from directors and scriptwriters.

Galleries

In recent years New Orleans has become a major art center, both in the quantity and quality of artists working here and in galleries and exhibit areas. Julia Street in the stretch between St. Charles Avenue and the river, called the Warehouse District, is now the center of the city's art community because of the many new galleries and the relocation of established ones on and near that street. It is also home to the Visionary Imagists, a home-grown art style. Other areas worth visiting are along Royal Street in the French Quarter and along the burgeoning Magazine Street, following the river uptown. Gallery openings tend to occur 6 PM–9 PM on the first Saturday of each month, but the action slacks off during the summer. The following galleries are generally open Tuesday–Saturday, 11–5—but it's wise to call.

Academy Gallery (5256 Magazine St., ☎ 504/899–8111) is connected with the New Orleans Academy of Fine Arts and exhibits local professional artists.

Arthur Roger Gallery (432 Julia St., ☎ 504/522–1999) is a well-established, state-of-the-art gallery featuring mostly avant-garde local and national painters, sculptors, and site artists. It represents New Orleanians George Dureau, Ida Kohlmyer, Robert Gordy, and Lin Emery.

Carol Robinson Gallery (4537 Magazine St., ☎ 504/895–6130) has a high-quality, diverse collection.

Davis Gallery (3964 Magazine St., ☎ 504/897–0780) has a national reputation for high-quality African art and artifacts.

Galerie Simonne Stern (518 Julia St., ☎ 504/529–1118), one of the oldest and most respected galleries in New Orleans, has an even mix of both ultramodern and contemporary styles.

Gallery I/O (1812 Magazine St., ☎ 504/581–2113; 829 Royal St., ☎ 504/523–5041) is a showcase for Thomas Mann's "techno-romantic" jewelry and sculpture.

Gasperi Gallery (854 S. Peters St., ☎ 504/524–9373) showcases folk art (and handles only the best).

Hall-Barnett Gallery (320 Exchange Alley, ☎ 504/525–5656) shows quality up-and-coming regional artists in group shows. Prices are modest.

Icons Gallery (3324 Magazine St., ☎ 504/899–1127) emphasizes the fun and the funky, with a vintage juke box and emerging young artists who work with photography and multimedia.

Kurt E. Schon Ltd. (510 St. Louis St. and 523 Royal St., ☎ 504/524–5462) is the definitive gallery for 18th- and 19th-century British and French art.

LeMieux Galleries (332 Julia St., ☎ 504/522–5988) handles avant-garde, realism, and expressionism; it often shows new local and national talent.

Marguerite Oestreicher Fine Arts (626 Julia St., ☎ 504/581–9253) represents fine contemporary painting, photography, sculpture, and works on paper.

New Orleans School of Glassworks (727 Magazine St., ☎ 504/529–7277) exhibits works by students and faculty in the front gallery; in back, a 75,000-square-foot workshop is open to the public—Saturday glassblowing classes are held here for children and adults by reservation.

Rhino Gallery (Canal Place, 333 Canal St., ☎ 504/523–7945) is the place for crafts by top regional artisans. The name is an acronym for "Right Here In New Orleans."

Shadyside Pottery (3823 Magazine St., ☎ 504/897–1710) is a showcase for Charlie Bohn's 15th-century-style Japanese raku pottery, including bowls, vases, lamps, and urns.

Still-Zinsel (328 Julia St., ☎ 504/588–9999) has a broad cross section of contemporary fine art.

Sylvia Schmidt Gallery (400A Julia St., ☎ 504/522–2000) reflects the pluralistic interest in contemporary art and shows top local works of new as well as established artists.

Tilden-Foley Gallery (4119 Magazine St., ☎ 504/897–5300) exhibits Louisiana artist Linda Benglis and the late American artist Manniere Dawson, and brokers early 19th-century landscapes and 19th-century Southern artists.

Wyndy Morehead Fine Arts (603 Julia St., ☎ 504/568–9754) exhibits contemporary art, particularly landscapes.

Ya/Ya, Inc. (628 Baronne St., ☎ 504/529–3306) is the home of the nationally popular Ya/Ya (Young Aspirations/Young Artists) Kids, New Orleans inner-city high school students who recycle old furniture by painting whimsical and abstract designs on it.

8 Excursions

THE GREAT RIVER ROAD

By Honey
Naylor

ALTHOUGH NEW ORLEANS has never been a typical Dixie city, the word "Dixieland" was coined here in the early 19th century. And you have but to look away, look away to the west of town to see that old times here are not forgotten. The Old South is in a state of grace along the Great River Road, between New Orleans and Baton Rouge, where elegant antebellum plantation homes have been carefully restored and furnished with period antiques.

Alas, the Great River Road itself is not as scenic as it once was. Along some stretches industrial plants mar the landscape on one side of the road, and on the other side the levee obstructs a view of the Mississippi. However, you can always park your car and climb up on the levee for a look at Ol' Man River. The Great River Road is also called, variously, LA 44 and 75 on the east bank of the river, and LA 18 on the west bank. All of the plantations described are listed in the National Register of Historic Places, and some of them are bed-and-breakfasts.

If you've seen one plantation you've by no means seen them all; each has its own charm. However, if your time is limited, the real knockouts are Houmas House, Madewood, and Nottoway. The grounds of Oak Alley are spectacular. Also of interest is the ongoing restoration of Laura Plantation, which began in 1994.

Exploring

Numbers in the margins correspond to points of interest on the River Road Plantations map.

1 An appropriate place to begin a River Road ramble is **Destrehan Plantation.** The oldest plantation left intact in the lower Mississippi Valley, this simple West Indies-style house, built in 1787, is typical of the homes built by the earliest planters in the region. *13034 River Rd., 5 mi upriver from St. Rose, LA,* ☎ *504/764–9315.* ☛ *$6 adults, $3 children 13–17, $2 children 6–12.* ۩ *Daily 9:30–4. Closed Thanksgiving, Dec. 24–25, Jan. 1, Mardi Gras Day, Easter.*

2 Twenty minutes and a million style miles away is **San Francisco.** Completed in 1856, the elaborate "Steamboat Gothic" house was once called St. Frusquin. The name is derived from a French slang term, *sans fruscins,* which means "without a penny in my pocket"—the condition the owner found himself in after paying exorbitant construction costs. Note the unusual louvered roof, ornate millwork, and colorful painted ceilings. *LA 44 near Reserve, LA, 35 mi from New Orleans,* ☎ *504/535–2341.* ☛ *$7 adults, $4 children 12–17, $2.75 children 6–11.* ۩ *Daily 10–4. Closed Thanksgiving, Dec. 25, Jan. 1, Mardi Gras Day, Easter.*

3 Different from the dressed-up River Road mansions, **Laura Plantation** is a restoration-in-progress of the main house and six slave cabins of a former sugar plantation. It opened for tours in 1994 and is named for the 1805 owner-manager Laura Locoul. The restoration is based on historical documents that include 100 pages of her diary. The story of the plantation is told by costumed docents who portray past residents. The Br'er Rabbit stories are said to have been first told here by Senegalese slaves. The $1.3-million project, scheduled

River Road Plantations

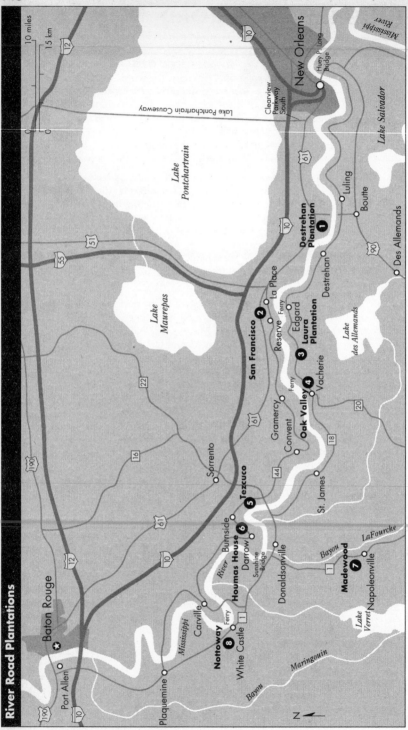

for completion in 2005, will include bed-and-breakfast accommodations. *2247 Hwy. 18, Vacherie,* ☎ *504/265–7690.* ☛ *$5 adults, $3.50 students 13–18, children under 12 free.* ⊙ *Daily 9–5. Closed Thanksgiving, Dec. 25, Jan. 1.*

❹ The 28 gnarled oak trees that give **Oak Alley** its name were planted in the early 1700s; the house dates from 1839. If you're into trees, do take in the view from the upper gallery of the house. This was the setting for the TV remake of *The Long Hot Summer,* which featured Don Johnson and Cybill Shepherd, and for the film *Interview with a Vampire,* shot in 1993. *LA 18, 6 mi upriver of the Gramercy–Vacherie ferry,* ☎ *504/265–2151.* ☛ *$6.50 adults, $3.50 ages 13–18, $2 children 6–12.* ⊙ *Mar.–Oct., daily 9–5:30; Nov.–Feb., 9–5. Closed Thanksgiving, Dec. 25, Jan. 1.*

❺ Built in 1855, **Tezcuco** is a graceful raised cottage with delicate wrought-iron galleries, ornate friezes, an antiques shop, and overnight cottages. *LA 44, about 2 mi above Sunshine Bridge,* ☎ *504/562–3929.* ☛ *$6 adults, $3.25 children 4–12, $5.50 students and senior citizens; $4 to tour grounds only.* ⊙ *Daily 9–5. Closed Thanksgiving, Dec. 25, Jan. 1.*

❻ Docents in antebellum garb guide you through **Houmas House,** an 1840 Greek Revival masterpiece famed for its three-story spiral staircase. *Hush Hush, Sweet Charlotte,* with Bette Davis and Olivia DeHavilland, was filmed here. The rear cottage, connected to the main house by a carriageway, was built in 1790. *LA 942, ½ mi off LA 44 near Burnside,* ☎ *504/473–7841.* ☛ *$7 adults, $5 children 13–17, $3.50 children 6–12.* ⊙ *Feb.–Oct., daily 10–5; Nov.–Jan., daily 10–4. Closed Thanksgiving, Dec. 25, Jan. 1.*

❼ Bayou Lafourche also boasts a movie star in **Madewood.** The galleried, 21-room, Greek Revival mansion with its massive white columns was the setting for *A Woman Called Moses,* which starred Cicely Tyson. Noted 19th-century architect Henry Howard designed the house. *4250 Hwy. 308, 2 mi south of Napoleonville,* ☎ *504/369–7151 or 800/ 749–7151; in LA, 800/375–7151.* ☛ *$5 adults, $3 students and children under 12, 10% discount for senior citizens.* ⊙ *Daily 10–5. Closed Thanksgiving, Dec. 25, Jan. 1.*

❽ The South's largest plantation home, **Nottoway,** should not be missed. With 64 rooms, 53,000 square feet of space, 22 columns, and 200 windows, this white castle (the nearby town of White Castle was named for it) was the pièce de résistance of architect Henry Howard. Completed in 1859, the Greek Revival–Italianate mansion was refurbished and painted in 1993; its white ballroom, famed in these parts for its original crystal chandeliers and hand-carved Corinthian columns, was restored in 1992. There is an excellent restaurant on the premises. *2 mi north of White Castle,* ☎ *504/545–2730.* ☛ *$8 adults, $3 children under 12.* ⊙ *Daily 9–5. Closed Dec. 25.*

Dining and Lodging

For price categories, *see* Dining and Lodging *in* Cajun Country, *below.*

Dining
BURNSIDE
$$$$ **The Cabin.** Yellowed newspapers cover the walls and ancient farm implements dangle here and there in a 150-year-old slave cabin-cum-restaurant. Crawfish etouffée is a specialty, but there are po'boys, burgers, and steaks, too. ✗ *Junction of LA 44 and 22,*

☏ *504/473–3007. Reservations not required. AE, D, MC, V. Closed Thanksgiving, Dec. 25, Jan. 1.*

Lodging

NAPOLEONVILLE

$$$$ Madewood. Expect gracious Southern hospitality, lovely antiques, and a homey atmosphere in either the 21-room Main House or Charlet House, a smaller house on the plantation grounds. The cost includes breakfast and, later in the day, wine and cheese and a Southern meal in a candlelit formal dining room. ☎ *4250 Hwy. 308, 70390 (2 mi south of Napoleonville),* ☏ *800/375–7151. 5 rooms with bath in Main House, 3 suites in Charlet House. AE, D, MC, V. Closed Thanksgiving, Dec. 25, Jan. 1.*

WHITE CASTLE

$$$$ Nottoway. Thirteen antique-filled rooms are let to overnighters. In three of the rooms a chilled bottle of champagne is included in the rate; guests in the other rooms receive a complimentary welcome glass of sherry. Mornings begin with a Continental breakfast in bed, followed by a full breakfast in the dining room. There's a pool and a gift shop on the premises. ☎ *30907 Hwy. 405, 70788,* ☏ *504/545–2730. 13 rooms with bath. AE, D, MC, V. Closed Dec. 25.*

The Great River Road Essentials

Getting Around

BY CAR

Take I–10 west or U.S. 61 to Williams Boulevard. Drive toward the river and turn right on the Great River Road. Driving time to the nearest plantation is about 20 minutes from the airport. Plantation touring can take anywhere from an hour to two days, depending upon how many homes you want to see.

Guided Tours

Tours by Isabelle (☏ 504/367–3963, FAX 504/391–3564) offers two half-day tours, each one taking you through two antebellum homes. **Gray Line** (☏ 504/587–0861 or 800/535–7786, FAX 504/587–0708) offers several plantation tours, ranging from 3½-hour excursions to 7½-hour outings, the latter with lunch (not included in the tour cost) at Nottoway.

SWAMPS AND BAYOUS

Bayou is an Native American word that means creek. The brackish, slow-moving waters of South Louisiana were once the highways and byways of the Choctaw, Chickasaw, and Chitimacha. Jean Lafitte and his freebooters easily hid in murky reaches of swamp, which were covered with thick canopies of subtropical vegetation. Pirate gold is said to be buried in the swamps. Ancient, gnarled cypresses with gray shawls of Spanish moss rise out of still waters. The state has an alligator population of about 500,000, and most of them laze around in the meandering tributaries and secluded sloughs of South Louisiana. Wild boars, snow-white egrets, bald eagles, and all manner of exotic creatures inhabit the swamps and marshlands. There are even rumors of a swamp monster, said to be 7 feet tall and 350 pounds, with long orange locks and wild, wide eyes.

Unless you are a fur trapper, an alligator hunter, or a wild-eyed monster with orange hair in search of a mate, it is not recommended that you strike out into the swamps alone.

Guided Tours

The following tour operators are prepared to trek with you through the murky waters.

Honey Island Swamp Tours (☎ 504/641–1769). Dr. Paul Wagner, a wetland ecologist, guides flora and fauna tours of the 250-square-mile Honey Island Swamp on the Pearl River.

Tours by Isabelle (☎ 504/367–3963). A bilingual Cajun alligator hunter and fur trapper guides you through remote cypress swamps.

CAJUN COUNTRY

The cradle of the Cajun craze rocks merrily away amid the bayous, rice paddies, and canebrakes to the west of New Orleans. Other parts of the country have only recently leapt on the Cajun bandwagon, but Southwestern Louisiana was Cajun long before red-hot Cajun was cool.

In Cajun Country (also called Acadiana), Cajun is not a trend—it's a tradition, dating from about 1604 when French settlers colonized a region they called *l'Acadie* in the present-day Canadian provinces of Nova Scotia and New Brunswick. The British seized control of the region in the early 18th century and the French were expelled. Their exile, called *le grand dérangement,* was described by Henry Wadsworth Longfellow in his poem "Evangeline." Many Acadians eventually settled in 22 parishes of Southwestern Louisiana. Their descendants are called "Cajun," a corruption of "Acadian"; some continue the traditions of the early French settlers of l'Acadie, living off the land by fishing and fur trapping.

Lafayette, the largest city in Acadiana, offers a number of attractions, including art galleries and museums, devoted to the Acadian heritage. It is also a center for the performing arts and sports events, many of them presented with a Cajun flair.

The surrounding countryside is dotted with tiny towns and villages where antique-seekers and explorers can blissfully poke around. Centuries-old live oaks with ragged gray buntings of Spanish moss form canopies over the bottle-green bayous. Country roads follow the contortions of the Teche (pronounced Tesh), the state's largest bayou, and meander through ancient Acadian villages where cypress cabins rise up out of the water on stilts and moored fishing boats and pirogues scarcely bob on the sluggish waters.

Louisiana is not called a sportsman's paradise for nothing. Laced as it is with waterways and wilds, this part of the state is largely responsible for that sobriquet. If fishing or boating is your thing, paradise lies 15 miles to the east of Lafayette in the Atchafalaya Basin, an 800,000-acre wilderness swamp. Saltwater fishing in the Gulf of Mexico is also within easy reach of Lafayette. During winter months, hunters in search of waterfowl head for the coastal marshes to the south.

Food, music, and dancing are the very essence of Cajun life. Almost every hamlet has an annual festival of some sort, usually involving food, when townspeople raise the cypress rafters with foot-stomping music.

Cajun Mardi Gras in Lafayette is second only to its sister celebration in New Orleans. And in Acadia Parish, the *Courir du Mardi Gras,* or Mardi Gras run, is a wild affair with masked and costumed horseback riders following *le Capitain* for a mad dash through the countryside in search of gumbo ingredients.

Cajun French is an oral tradition, a 17th-century French that differs from modern-day French in much the same way that Elizabethan English differs from modern-day English. English is also spoken throughout Cajun Country, but you will hear Gallic accents and see many signs that read, *Ici on parle français*.

You'll also often hear the Cajun phrase, *Laissez les bons temps rouler.* It means, "Let the good times roll." Cajuns are fun-loving and friendly, and they love to show visitors *les bons temps*.

Exploring

Numbers in the margins correspond to points of interest on the Cajun Country map.

❶ **Lafayette,** which calls itself the Capital of French Louisiana, is an appropriate place to get acquainted with Cajun life and lore. We'll take a look at that city first, and then tour the surrounding towns and villages.

The **Acadian Village** is a re-creation of an early 19th-century bayou settlement. The village nestles in 10 wooded acres complete with a meandering bayou crisscrossed by wooden footbridges. Each of the houses—authentic, but built elsewhere in the 1800s and moved to this site—represents a different style of Acadian architecture and is decorated with antique furnishings, utensils, and tools. The rustic general store, blacksmith shop, and chapel are all replicas of 19th-century buildings. *Greenleaf Rd., south of Lafayette,* ☎ *318/981–2364.* ☛ *$5.50 adults, $4.50 senior citizens, $2.50 children 6–14.* ⊙ *Daily 10–5. Closed Thanksgiving, Dec. 24–25, Jan. 1, Mardi Gras Day, Easter.*

In downtown Lafayette, several buildings played a part in Acadian history. A galleried town house, topped by a cupola, houses the **Lafayette Museum.** Built in the early 1800s, it was the *Maison Dimanche*, or Sunday House, of Jean Mouton, the city's founder. Later it served as home to Alexandre Mouton, ninth governor of Louisiana. The museum contains historical memorabilia and Carnival regalia. *1122 Lafayette St.,* ☎ *318/234–2208.* ☛ *$3 adults, $2 senior citizens, $1 students 6–18, children under 5 free.* ⊙ *Tues.–Sat. 9–5, Sun. 3–5. Closed Mon.*

The **First City Hall** (217 Main St.) was home to the Bank of Lafayette and the town's first public library. The deco-style building now contains offices of the Council for the Development of French in Louisiana (CODOFIL). The Lafayette Artists Alliance has a gallery in the former **Lafayette Hardware Store** (121 W. Vermilion St.), which has stood at the corner of Vermilion and Buchanan streets since before 1890. The barn-red shotgun house at East Vermilion and Congress streets, built in 1885, has been a post office, an inn, a tinsmith shop, and a saddle shop. It isn't open now, but for many years it was a well-known bookstore where book parties were held for the likes of Bennett Cerf, Frances Parkinson Keyes, and Irving Stone.

TIME OUT   **Dwyer's Café** is a diner jammed with locals having hot biscuits and grits at 5 AM. It features Cajun plate lunches, burgers, and sandwiches, and has been going strong since 1927. *323 Jefferson St.,* ☎ *318/ 235–9364.* ⊙ *Weekdays 4 AM–4 PM, Sat. 4 AM–2 PM. No credit cards.*

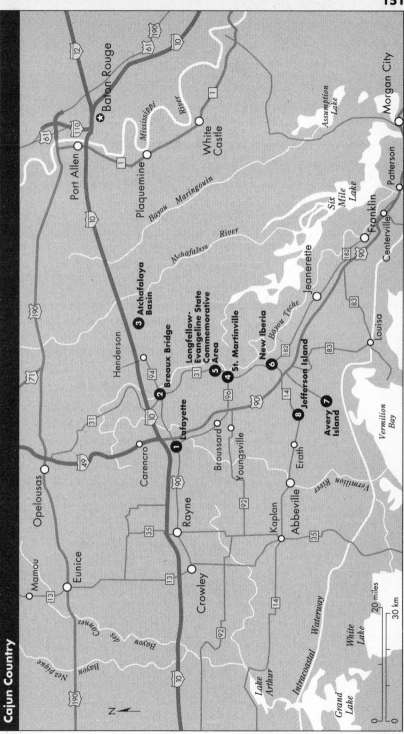

As you stroll around Lafayette Centre, the downtown area, you'll see four colorful outdoor murals. Muralist Robert Dafford painted the Cajun accordion on the side of the Lee Furniture store, the Louisiana swamp scene across from Dwyer's Café, and the splashy cars on the Jefferson Tower Building. The microcosm of Lafayette at the Parc Auto du Centre Ville is the work of local artist Tanya Falgout.

The Louisiana Live Oak Society was founded in Lafayette more than 50 years ago, and a charter member of that silent but leafy set dominates the 900 block of St. John Street. The **St. John Oak** is 500 years old and has a waistline of about 28 feet. Next to the tree is the **Cathedral of St. John the Evangelist** (914 St. John St.), a Romanesque church with Byzantine touches and an old cemetery behind the church. The cathedral began as a small mission of the St. Martin de Tours Church in St. Martinville. The church lawn was a campground for Union soldiers during the Civil War.

Changing exhibits at the **Lafayette Natural History Museum** examine the South Louisiana environment, and programs at the museum's planetarium explore the heavens. Workshops, movies, concerts, and light shows take place regularly at the museum, as does the annual Louisiana Native Crafts Festival in September. *116 Polk St.,* ☎ *318/268–5544.* ☞ *Free.* ⊙ *Mon., Wed.–Fri. 9–5; Tues. 9–9; weekends 1–5.*

The museum's sister facility, **The Acadiana Park Nature Station,** is a three-story cypress pole structure that overlooks a 40-acre park. Naturalists are on hand in the interpretive center, and discovery boxes help children get to know the wildflowers, birds, and other outdoorsy things they'll see on the 3½-mile nature trail. *E. Alexander St.,* ☎ *318/261–8448.* ☞ *Free.* ⊙ *Weekdays 8–5, weekends 11–3.*

Lafayette Art Gallery gives visitors a close look at local arts and crafts. *700 Lee Ave.,* ☎ *318/269–0363.* ☞ *Free.* ⊙ *Tues.–Fri. 10–4.*

The **Acadian Cultural Center,** a unit of the Jean Lafitte National Historical Park and Preserve, traces the history of the area through numerous audiovisual exhibits of food, music, and folklore. Before you begin wandering through the exhibits, be sure to watch the introductory film, which is a dramatization of the Acadian exile. Black-and-white clips from the 1929 movie *The Romance of Evangeline* are incorporated in the film; aficionados of old motion pictures will love it. *501 Fisher Rd.,* ☎ *318/232–0789 or 318/232–0961.* ☞ *Free.* ⊙ *Daily 8–5.*

Vermilionville, directly behind the Acadian Cultural Center, is a living history village where the early life of the region's Creoles and Cajuns is re-created. There are exhibits in 22 Acadian structures, including a music hall in which live Cajun music is played weekdays 1:30–3:30, and weekends 12:30–5. A large, rustic restaurant serves "whatever mama's cooking today," and cooking demonstrations are presented weekdays at 11 and 1:30; weekends, 11:30 and 1:30. This is a good place to practice your French; costumed artisans speak the language throughout the village. Guided tours are conducted weekdays at 10:15, 12:30, and 3, with additional tours on weekends. Or, you can pick up a self-guided walking tour brochure at the entrance. *1600 Surrey St.,* ☎ *318/233–4077 or 800/992–2968.* ☞ *$8 adults, $6.50 senior citizens, $5 students 6–18, children under 5 free.* ⊙ *Daily 10–5.*

The towns described below can be explored in an easy day excursion from Lafayette. If your time in Cajun Country is limited, they may be seen as you return to New Orleans, in which case you can pick up U.S. 90 in New Iberia and continue on to the Crescent City.

❷ **Breaux Bridge** lies 10 miles northeast of Lafayette on LA 94. The tiny town calls itself the Crawfish Capital of the World, and the Crawfish Festival held annually in May draws upward of 100,000 people.

Pontoon boats at McGee's Landing take passengers for tours of the
❸ **Atchafalaya Basin.** You'll find McGee's on the levee road in Henderson, a 25-minute drive from Lafayette on I–10E. *Exit 115 at Henderson. Drive up onto the levee and turn right. McGee's Landing is 2 mi down the levee road on the left.* ☎ *318/228–2384.* ✆ *$8.50 adults, $7.50 senior citizens, $5 children under 12. Daily tours of 1½–2 hrs.*

❹ Following the writhings of Bayou Teche on LA 31 you'll come to **St. Martinville,** 15 miles south of Breaux Bridge, in the heart of Evangeline country.

Longfellow's poem about the star-crossed lovers Evangeline and Gabriel was based on a true story. According to the oft-told tale, the real-life lovers, Emmeline Labiche and Louis Arceneaux, met for the last time under the **Evangeline Oak** (Evangeline Blvd. at Bayou Teche). As in Longfellow's poem, the lovers were separated during the arduous Acadian exodus. Louis arrived in St. Martinville, a major debarkation port for the refugees, but it was many years before Emmeline came. The legend has it that the two saw each other by chance just as she stepped ashore. He turned deadly pale with shock and told her that having despaired of ever seeing her again, he was betrothed to another. *The Romance of Evangeline* was filmed in St. Martinville in 1929. The privately owned movie was never distributed, but clips from it are incorporated in the film presentation at the Jean Lafitte National Historical Park Acadian Cultural Center (*see* Lafayette, *above*). Its star, Dolores Del Rio, posed for the bronze statue of Evangeline that the cast and crew donated to the town.

The statue of Evangeline is in the cemetery behind the church of **St. Martin de Tours** (123 S. Main St.), near the final resting place of Emmeline Labiche. St. Martin de Tours is the Mother Church of the Acadians, and one of the oldest Catholic churches in the country. Inside is a replica of the Lourdes grotto and a baptismal font said to have been a gift from Louis XVI.

St. Martinville was founded in 1761, and became a refuge for royalists who escaped the guillotine during the French Revolution. Known as Petit Paris, the little town was once the scene of lavish balls and operas.

The **Petit Paris Museum** on the church square contains historical records, Carnival costumes, a video history of Mardi Gras and of the Durand wedding of Oak and Pine Alley (*see below*), and a chariot exhibit. *103 S. Main St.,* ☎ *318/394–7334.* ✆ *$1 adults, 75¢ senior citizens, 50¢ children under 13.* ⊗ *Daily 9:30–4:30.*

In 1870, when the two daughters of Gerome Charles Durand decided to marry simultaneously, their father determined to make the double wedding an unforgettable occasion. Several days before the wedding giant spiders were released in the mile-long archway of trees leading to the house. On the wedding day the spiders' webs were sprayed with gold and silver dust to make a shimmering canopy for the wedding party. The Durand plantation is gone with the gold dust, but the Oak and Pine Alley remains, 2 miles out of town on the Catahoula Road.

The chariots displayed in the museum are from an annual one-of-a-kind event, the **Chariot Parade,** a colorful procession of wagons, made by children, that depict anything from a streetcar to a castle. The children and their fanciful chariots circle the church square, beginning at dusk on the third Sunday of August every year.

North of the city limits on Highway 31 and Bayou Teche is the **⑤ Longfellow-Evangeline State Commemorative Area.** The 157-acre park, shaded by giant live oaks draped with Spanish moss, has picnic tables and pavilions, a boat launch, and early Acadian structures.

The Evangeline legend claims that Louis Arceneaux lived in the **Acadian House** on the park's grounds, but there is no evidence that he did. The house was built in the mid-18th century of handmade bricks, wooden pegs, and *bousillage* (an insulating mixture of mud, animal hair, and moss), and it contains Louisiana antique furnishings. ☎ *318/394–3754.* ☛ *$2 adults, children under 13 free.* ☉ *Park: daily 9–5; House: Wed.–Sun. 9–4:30.*

⑥ New Iberia, 14 miles south of St. Martinville, proudly calls itself the Queen City of the Teche and the capital of sugar-cane country. Several of the city's attractions are located relatively close to each other on Main Street.

Shadows-on-the-Teche, one of the South's most famous homes, was built for a wealthy planter more than a quarter of a century before the Civil War. Surrounded by lush gardens and oaks, the two-story rose-hued house has white columns, exterior staircases sheltered in *cabinets* (cabinetlike enclosures), and a pitched roof pierced by dormer windows. The Shadows is a museum property of the National Trust for Historic Preservation. *317 E. Main St.,* ☎ *318/369–6446.* ☛ *$6 adults, $5.50 senior citizens, $3 children 6–11.* ☉ *Daily 9–4:30. Closed Thanksgiving, Dec. 25, Jan. 1.*

The **Gebert Oak** (541 E. Main St.) is a member in good standing of the Live Oak Society. Planted in 1831 and dripping with ferns and moss, the massive tree stretches over almost an entire lawn. At the corner of Weeks and St. Peter streets there is a 7-foot white marble statue of the **Emperor Hadrian** that was sculpted in Rome in AD 130.

The **Conrad Rice Mill** is the country's oldest rice mill, dating from 1912, and it produces a distinctive wild pecan rice. Next to the mill is the **Konriko Company Store,** with Cajun crafts, foods, and a sight-and-sound show. *307 Ann St.,* ☎ *318/367–6163 or 800/551–3245.* ☛ *Mill: $2.75 adults, $2.25 senior citizens, $1.25 children under 12.* ☉ *Mon.–Sat. 9–5 (mill does not operate on Sat.); tours at 10, 11, 1, 2, and 3.*

⑦ ⑧ Avery Island and **Jefferson Island,** to the south and southwest, respectively, of New Iberia, are not islands at all, but salt domes.

Avery Island, 9 miles to the south, is the birthplace of Tabasco sauce, which pleases the Cajun palate and flavors many a Bloody Mary. The sauce was invented by Edmund McIlhenny in the mid-1800s, and the factory is presided over by the fourth generation of the McIlhenny family. Avery Island's other attractions are its 200-acre Jungle Gardens, in which sits a 1,000-year-old Buddha, and Bird City, a bird sanctuary sometimes so thick with egrets that it appears to be blanketed with snow. *LA 329,* ☎ *318/369–6243 (Jungle Gardens) or 318/365–8173 (Factory).* ☛ *Gardens and sanctuary: $5.25 adults, $3.75 children 6–12. Tabasco factory free.* ☉ *Weekdays 9–4, Sat. 9–noon.*

American actor Joseph Jefferson toured the country in the 19th century portraying Rip van Winkle. He became enamored of South Louisiana life and live oaks, and in 1870 he purchased 20 acres on Jefferson Island on which he built a winter home. In 1980, the salt dome beneath the house collapsed, draining Lake Peigneur and causing severe damage to the property, but not to the house or gardens.

Live Oak Gardens has been restored to its former luxuriant 1870 state, with formal gardens and groves of oaks, crêpe myrtle, camellias, and azaleas. Jefferson's home is a three-story Steamboat Gothic house with Moorish flourishes, opulent furnishings, and rocking chairs on the wide veranda. A café in the reception area overlooks Lake Peigneur. An art gallery showcases rotating traveling exhibits, and a collection of antique duck decoys is also displayed. *5505 Rip van Winkle Rd., off LA 14,* ☎ *318/365–3332.* ☛ *$10 adults, $9 senior citizens, $5.50 children 5–16.* ☉ *Daily 9–5.*

What to See and Do with Children

Lafayette Public Library. The Children's Department offers a variety of activities, including crafts workshops, films, and puppet shows. *301 W. Congress St.,* ☎ *318/261–5779.* ☛ *Free.* ☉ *Mon.–Thurs. 9–9, Fri.–Sat. 9–5.*

Other attractions of interest to children, which are described in Cajun Country Exploring, *above,* include:

Acadian Village

Atchafalaya Boat Basin Tours

Avery Island

Jefferson Island

Lafayette Natural History Museum and Nature Trail

Longfellow-Evangeline State Commemorative Area

Off the Beaten Track

"Factory" conjures up images of assembly lines and high-tech equipment, but **D. L. Menard's Chair Factory** (outside Erath) fits no such description, and the chairs made by Mr. Menard are very much in demand in this part of the country. In fact, Mr. Menard himself is very much in demand: Besides turning out chairs, he is a songwriter, a musician and performer (he plays the guitar, and some folks say he's Hank Williams reincarnated), a Cajun raconteur, and a *traiteur,* or healer.

In 1993, a fire destroyed Mr. Menard's original factory, and his friends (including country singer Ricky Scaggs) put on a series of benefit concerts to help replace the structure. At press time, the building had been rebuilt and Mr. Menard was awaiting new equipment. The factory will be back in operation by summer 1995.

Ladderbacks, old-fashioned rockers, stools, and Early American kitchen chairs are made by hand by Mr. Menard. The factory is a family business, with Mr. Menard's son making porch swings and his wife and daughter doing the weaving for the rush-bottom chairs.

Be sure to call before you go (☎ 318/937–5471). Mr. Menard is a very busy man. As he puts it, "Sometimes I'm too busy to work, I guaran*tee.*" He's been touring professionally with his Cajun band since 1973, performing not only in the United States, but also in 32 foreign countries.

You'll have to keep a sharp eye out to spot his shop. *To reach D. L. Menard's from Lafayette, take U.S. 90 south to the junction of LA 89 and turn right. In the tiny town of Erath, make a left turn on LA 331, cross the railroad track, and drive 1½ mi. The shop is on the left next to a small frame house.*

A sign inside reads, "This is not a dance hall. If anyone is injured while dancing we are not responsible." **Fred's Lounge** may not be a "formal" dance hall, but plenty of dancing is done here; it gets pretty lively during Mamou's Mardi Gras and Fourth of July celebrations. And every Saturday morning for more than 40 years live Cajun radio shows have been broadcast from Fred Tate's place. News, weather, sports, and, of course, lots of music emanate from the "studio," which is roped off like a boxing ring in the center of the small room. Cajuns who have chank-a-chanked (danced) late Friday night pack into Fred's on Saturday morning, waltzing around the ropes and keeping the bartender busy. Things get revved up at 8 AM and keep going till 1 PM, and the show is aired on KVPI in Ville Platte. Fred's Lounge is an hour's drive from Lafayette. *420 6th St., Mamou,* ☎ *318/468–5411. Take I–10 west, exit onto LA 13, and drive north through Eunice to Mamou, a town so small you can drive around for 5 min and find Fred's.* ☛ *Free.*

Got a mule you'd like to enter in a race? A pig, maybe? For more than 100 years all kinds of critters have been pounding the turf at **Cajun Downs,** south of Lafayette. The "bush track"—so-called because it's in the bush—is way out yonder next to a cane field. There's nothing fancy here, like grandstands or pari-mutuel windows. Well, there is an official betting window—a cash box under a ramshackle shed. Every Sunday morning, weather permitting, Cajuns back their pickups right up to the dirt track, turn their radios up full-blast, and watch the goings-on from lawn chairs in the back of their trucks. There are as many "pari-mutuel windows" as there are people. The crowd could be described as Cajun Runyonesque, and they're nothing if not colorful and friendly. Watch out around the finish line—there's a lot of hollering, especially if a race is contested. You can get beer, burgers, and such in an extremely rustic "clubhouse." Folks around here call this "Clement's track," after the septuagenarian former owner, Clement Hebert. Clement is usually around, but today the track is operated by his son Doris and Doris's wife Alice. There are usually half a dozen races or more on Sunday. ☎ *318/893–8160 or 318/893–0421 to see if the races are on or to enter an animal of your own. On LA 338 off the LA 14 bypass in Abbeville, about 20 min south of Lafayette.*

Little Pecan Island is so far off the beaten track that you have to take a boat to get there. Just 10 miles inland from the Gulf of Mexico (about 40 miles southeast of Lake Charles), Little Pecan is an 1,800-acre property of the Nature Conservancy replete with alligators, migratory birds, a stunning cypress swamp, and a slew of live oak trees dressed to the nines in Spanish moss. It's a dream of a place for hunters, anglers, birders, nature lovers, and photographers. Group trips are led by the Nature Conservancy; accommodations are in a very simply furnished lodge with seven bedrooms, four baths, a sauna, a large living room with a fireplace, a dining room with family-style seating and picture windows facing the setting sun, and a game room where you can play Ping-Pong or shoot pool. You can prepare your own meals in the huge kitchen, or (at extra cost) have meals provided. The cost of boat transportation to and from the lodge is included in the rate (a two-day, one-night trip costs $175 per person; a three-day, two-night trip $450 per person), as is a guided tour through the preserve. *Trips are generally offered Jan.–May and Oct. For more information, contact the*

Nature Conservancy of Louisiana, Box 4125, Baton Rouge, LA 70821, ☎ 504/338–1040.

In no way is the **Cajun Riviera** to be confused with the French Riviera. Instead of glitzy condos and posh resorts, there are simple cabins, campsites, RV hookups, and motels with kitchenettes. But Cameron Parish also has some 26 miles of unspoiled beaches, smack on the Gulf of Mexico, fine for swimming, crabbing, and shelling. **Holly Beach,** with 10 miles of sand at the end of the Creole Nature Trail (LA 27), is the largest and somewhat more developed, but **Constance Beach, Rutherford Beach,** and **Hackberry Beach** are also quiet, secluded getaways. This area is awash with wildlife refuges, notably the **Rockefeller Wildlife Refuge,** a major alligator research center, and the **Sabine National Wildlife Refuge,** the largest waterfowl refuge on the Gulf Coast. Cameron Parish is a bird-watcher's paradise, lying as it does right in the middle of the trans-Gulf of Mexico migratory flight path. Surf and deep-sea fishing are superb in this area, as is the duck- and goose-hunting. Bring along a camera for shots of lazing 'gators. *For further information, contact the Cameron Parish Chamber of Commerce, Box 590, Cameron, LA 70631, ☎ 318/775–5222.*

Shopping

Gift Ideas
Restaurants all over the country serve their own versions of Cajun food, but you can take some of the real thing home with you. Among the shops that sell Cajun gift packages are the **Cajun Country Store** (401 E. Cypress, Lafayette, ☎ 318/233–7977 or 800/252–9689) and **B. F. Trappey's & Sons** (900 E. Main St., New Iberia, ☎ 318/365–8281). For Cajun and zydeco music recordings and related products, **Floyd's Record Shop** (434 E. Main St., Ville Platte, ☎ 318/363–2138) is well worth the drive.

Flea Markets
Country crafts and collectibles are available at the **Antique Flea Market** (205 E. Louisiana Ave., Rayne, ☎ 318/334–9520. ☉ Weekends).

Antiques
Antiques hunting is a favorite pastime in these parts. You can root around **Ruins & Relics** (802 Jefferson St., Lafayette, ☎ 318/233–9163. ☉ Mon.–Sat. 10–5), **The Crowded Attic** (400 Plantation Rd., Lafayette, ☎ 318/237–5559. ☉ Mon.–Sat. 9–5), **Ole Fashion Things** (402 S.W. Evangeline Thruway, ☎ 318/234–7963. ☉ Tues.–Sat. 10–6), and deal with 10 dealers in the **Travel Treasures Antique Mall** (Hwy. 93 and W. Congress St., Lafayette, ☎ 318/981–9414. ☉ Wed.–Sat. 10–5, Sun. noon–5).

Outdoor Activities

Biking
Summer's high humidity can discourage rigorous exercise, but the flatlands offer easy riding. Bikes can be rented from **Pack and Paddle** (601 E. Pinhook Rd., Lafayette, ☎ 318/232–5854).

Bird-Watching
Don Thornton takes small groups to his camp in the coastal marshes, where 53 different species of birds can be seen (☎ 318/364–2752).

Boating and Fishing

The 800,000-acre Atchafalaya Basin is 15 miles east of Lafayette. Boat rentals, guides, and fishing gear can be rented at **McGee's Landing** (Levee Rd., Henderson, ☎ 318/228–2384).

Camping

There are 6,000 acres with picnic areas, a boat ramp, cabins, hiking trails, and camping facilities at **Lake Fausse Point State Park** (Rte. 5, Box 4658, St. Martinville, 70502, ☎ 318/229–4764).

Golf

Birdies and eagles can be sought in **City Park** (Mudd Ave., Lafayette, ☎ 318/268–5557) and **Vieux Chene Golf Course** (Youngsville Hwy., Broussard, ☎ 318/837–1159).

Spectator Sports

Cajundome

NBA exhibition and collegiate basketball, professional soccer exhibition games, wrestling, and other sports events take place here during the year (444 Cajundome Blvd., Lafayette, ☎ 318/265–2100).

Horse Racing

There's thoroughbred racing April through Labor Day at **Evangeline Downs** (1 mi north of I–10 on I–49, Lafayette, ☎ 318/896–7223), where each race begins with, *Ils sont partis!*

Jousting

The sport of knights was introduced here by early French settlers and revived in 1952. The **Tournoi,** with costumed knights on speedy steeds, takes place in mid-October during the annual Cotton Festival in Ville Platte (☎ 318/363–4521).

Dining and Lodging

Dining

Cajun food is often described as the robust, hot-peppery country kin of Creole cuisine. Ubiquitous sea critters turn up in a wide variety of exotic concoctions, such as étouffées, bisques, and boulettes, and almost every Acadian menu offers jambalaya, gumbo, and some blackened dish. Alligator meat is a great favorite, as are boudin and andouille, which are hot-hot sausages. Cajun food is very rich, and portions tend to be ample. Biscuits and grits are breakfast staples, and many an evening meal ends with bread pudding. You can dress casually at all the restaurants included in this section.

CATEGORY	COST*
$$$$	over $35
$$$	$25–$35
$$	$15–$20
$	under $15

per person, excluding drinks, service, and 7.5% tax

Lodging

The greatest concentration of accommodations is in Lafayette, which has an abundance of chain motels and a few luxury hotels. In nearby towns there are antique-filled antebellum plantation homes that offer overnights complete with old-fashioned plantation breakfasts.

CATEGORY	COST*
$$$$	over $120
$$$	$90–$120
$$	$50–$90
$	under $50

All prices are for a standard double room, excluding 6% tax.

Abbeville

DINING

$ Black's. In a vast, high-ceilinged building opposite the St. Mary Magdalen Church, Black's offers its specialty—fresh topless salty oysters. There's much more here than oysters, but fresh seafood does reign supreme. The only offerings for carnivores are a lone burger and a rib eye. Shrimp and oysters dominate the appetizer list; po'boys include catfish loaf and soft-shell crab loaf, in addition to the oyster and shrimp. Seafood platters, fried blue channel catfish, and stuffed crabs are entrées tucked amid the array of shrimp and oyster dishes. ✗ *319 Père Megret St.,* ☎ *318/893–4266. Reservations suggested. AE, MC, V. Closed Sun. and Mon. No lunch.*

$ Richard's Seafood Patio. Not far from Cajun Downs (*see* Off the Beaten Track, *above*), this family-style place is well known in these parts for superb boiled crawfish, shrimp, and crabs. You can even arrive by boat and dock right in front of the restaurant. ✗ *1516 S. Henry St.,* ☎ *318/893–1693. Reservations not necessary. MC, V. Closed July–late Nov. No lunch.*

LODGING

$$$ **A la Bonne Veillée.** At this secluded little two-story Acadian cottage
★ on a quiet country road between Lafayette and Abbeville, the only noise you're likely to hear is the quack of ducks in the nearby pond. A century ago this house, now perfectly restored, was a "Sunday house," or town house, of a prominent country family. Downstairs are the living room, kitchen, bath, and master bedroom; a steep stair leads to an attic room. The furnishings are American Empire (upstairs has a brass bed, patchwork quilts, and other items "from grandmother's trunk"). There are two fireplaces, plenty of books, and a back porch that overlooks 30 acres of farmland. Cupboards and a fridge are stocked with all the makings for a Continental breakfast, and there's an intercom to the nearby Le Blanc house, where the owners live. ▣ *LeBlanc House, Rte. 2, Box 2270, 70510,* ☎ *318/937–5495. 1 housekeeping cottage. Air-conditioning. No credit cards.*

Breaux Bridge

DINING

$–$$ Mulate's. A roadhouse with flashing yellow lights outside and red-and-white plastic tablecloths inside, Mulate's is a Cajun eatery, a dance hall (live Cajun music every weekday during lunch and daily during dinner), an age-old family gathering place, and a celebrity that has been featured on *The Today Show* and *Good Morning, America,* among other programs. A dressed-down crowd digs into the likes of stuffed crabs and the Super Seafood Platter. ✗ *325 Mills Ave. (Hwy. 94),* ☎ *in LA 800/634–9880; elsewhere in USA 800/42-CAJUN. Reservations not required. AE, MC, V. Closed Thanksgiving, Dec. 25.*

Carencro

DINING

$ Enola Prudhomme's Cajun Cafe. Famous sister of a famous brother
★ (Chef Paul, in New Orleans), Enola Prudhomme has her country Cajun café in a little frame cottage just north of Lafayette, in the town of Carencro. The down-home place serves blackened dishes, pan-fried

rabbit in cream sauce, eggplant pirogue, jalapeño-and-cheese corn-bread, baby back ribs, and all manner of mouth-watering dishes. There is even a special low-calorie menu. If you prefer, you can order "mild" renditions; otherwise, be prepared for "red-hot." ✘ *I–49 near Carencro, 7 mi north of I–10, 3 mi north of Evangeline Downs,* ☎ *318/896–7964. MC, V.*

Lafayette

DINING

$–$$ **Cafe Vermilionville.** A stately, two-story, white-columned house that was an inn in the 19th century, it offers casual elegance, with crisp white napery, old-brick fireplaces, and cocktails in a graceful gazebo. Among the specialties are fried soft-shell crab with crawfish fettuccine, smoked turkey and andouille gumbo, and Kahlua grilled shrimp. ✘ *1304 W. Pinhook Rd.,* ☎ *318/237–0100. Reservations advised. AE, D, DC, MC, V. Closed Labor Day, Mardi Gras, Dec. 25, Jan. 1.*

$ **Don's Seafood and Steakhouse,** a Landry family restaurant, has been a local favorite since 1934. The focus is on fish; the signature dish is a superb stuffed red snapper. The bread pudding is made by celestial beings. ✘ *301 E. Vermilion St.,* ☎ *318/235–3551. Reservations not necessary. AE, D, DC, MC, V. Closed Mardi Gras.*

$ **Prejean's.** This restaurant is set in a small cypress house with a wide
★ front porch and a 50-foot shrimp boat parked outside. Oyster shuckers work in a cozy bar, and locals gather at tables with red-and-white checked cloths to partake of Prejean's seafood platter (gumbo, fried shrimp, oysters, catfish, and seafood-stuffed bell peppers), as well as Cajun rack of elk, American buffalo au poivre, and steak and chicken prepared in various ways. There's live Cajun music every night. ✘ *3480 U.S. 167N, next to Evangeline Downs,* ☎ *318/896–3247. Reservations not necessary. AE, D, DC, MC, V. Closed Thanksgiving, Dec. 25, Jan. 1.*

LODGING

$$–$$$ **Bois Des Chênes Inn.** A 19th-century carriage house at the rear of the Mouton Plantation, which dates from about 1820, contains this bed-and-breakfast inn. Each of the suites offers a different style. The upstairs suite, which can accommodate five adults, is done in Early Acadian antiques. Downstairs, the Louisiana Empire Suite has a queen-size bed and the Victorian Suite has a tester double bed. In 1995, two rooms in the main house, both with cable TV, were being renovated to accommodate guests. Smoking is not permitted. Included in the rate are a welcoming glass of wine and a tour of the plantation house. 🏠 *338 N. Sterling St., 70501,* ☎ *318/233–7816. 3 suites. AE, MC, V.*

$$ **Best Western Hotel Acadiana.** The lobby is replete with cushy sofas, lots of gold leaf, and a huge chandelier. VIPs may opt for the Crown Service concierge floor, but all rooms are large and have thick carpets, marble-top dressers, and wing chairs. Even-numbered rooms face the pool, and most rooms have wet bars and minirefrigerators. 🏠 *1801 W. Pinhook Rd., 70508,* ☎ *318/233–8120, in LA 800/874–4664, elsewhere 800/826–8386;* ᴲ *318/234–9667. 296 rooms with bath. Restaurant, lounge, pool, 2 outdoor hot tubs, exercise room, airport shuttle, free parking. AE, D, DC, MC, V.*

$$ **Holiday Inn Central–Holidome.** A huge complex sprawling over 17 acres, this motel-cum-indoor recreation center is like a streamlined small town designed by a hyperactive Yuppie planning committee. The split-level public areas are spacious, airy, and filled with lush plants. Guest rooms are a cut above the average Holiday Inn. 🏠 *2032 N.E. Evangeline Thruway, 70501,* ☎ *318/233–6815 or*

800/942–4868, FAX *318/235–1954. 242 rooms with bath. Restaurant, lounge, picnic area, indoor pool, hot tub, sauna, 2 tennis courts, jogging, recreation room, playground, airport shuttle. AE, D, DC, MC, V.*

$$ **Lafayette Hilton & Towers.** Mirrored pillars and medieval tapestries fill
★ the ballroom-size lobby, and guest rooms are only slightly smaller. Traditional furnishings outfit the standard rooms; rooms on concierge floors come with Jacuzzis and wet bars. Riverside rooms have a view of the Bayou Vermilion, upon whose bank this high-rise rises. ⊡ *1521 Pinhook Rd., 70508,* ☎ *318/235–6111 or 800/332–2586,* FAX *318/237–6313. 327 rooms with bath. Restaurant, lounge, pool, exercise room, airport shuttle, helipad, free parking. AE, D, DC, MC, V.*

$$ **T'Frere's House.** Built in 1880 of native cypress and handmade bricks, "little brother's house" has been a bed-and-breakfast since 1985. Located 2 miles from the Oil Center (an office and shopping complex), the Acadian-style house with Victorian trim is furnished with French and Louisiana antiques. Guests are greeted with a complimentary mint julep and "Cajun Canapés," an hors d'oeuvre made with boudin, and a plantation breakfast is served in the formal dining room. ⊡ *1905 Verot School Rd., 70508,* ☎ *318/984–9347. 4 rooms with bath. Hot tub, washer/dryer. No pets, smoking only in gallery and gazebo. AE, D, MC, V.*

St. Martinville

DINING

$$ **Old Castillo Hotel/La Place d'Evangeline.** In the late 19th century, the Castillo Hotel, a two-story redbrick building next to the Evangeline Oak and Bayou Teche, was an inn for steamboat passengers and a gathering place for French Royalists. Since June of 1987, diners have feasted in the spacious, high-ceilinged rooms where the Royalists attended balls and operas. Seafood is king here, with the menu listing the likes of crawfish pie, corn and crab bisque, red snapper (broiled, fried, stuffed, and blackened), and frogs' legs. The Evangeline Special is a dinner for two featuring steak and seafood and a complimentary bottle of wine. This is also a B&B, with five rooms let to overnighters. ✕ *220 Evangeline Blvd.,* ☎ *318/394–4010 or 800/621–3017. Reservations not necessary. AE, MC, V.* ☉ *Daily 8 AM–9 PM. Call for weekend closing times. Closed Thanksgiving, Dec. 25, Jan. 1.*

The Arts, Festivals, and Nightlife

Theater

The University of Southwestern Louisiana's Performing Arts Department presents contemporary plays and dance concerts from early fall until late spring, in USL's Burke Hall. *For tickets and information, contact the Performing Arts Department, Box 43850, Lafayette 70504,* ☎ *318/231–6357.*

Lafayette's **Théâtre 'Cadien** (☎ 318/262–5810) performs plays in French at various venues.

Lafayette Community Theatre presents contemporary plays. *529 Jefferson St., Lafayette, 70501,* ☎ *318/235–1532.*

Concerts

Internationally renowned guest artists perform with the **Acadiana Symphony Orchestra** (☎ 318/232–4277) during its September-through-April season.

The **Lafayette Concert Band's** season includes both classical and pop, with appearances by guest artists. *For information, write to Box 53762, Lafayette 70505, ☎ 318/233–7060.*

Major concert attractions are featured at Lafayette's **Cajundome.** *For information and tickets, contact the Dome at 444 Cajundome Blvd., Lafayette 70506, ☎ 318/265–2100.*

Choral music is performed fall through spring by **Chorale Acadienne.** *For information, write to 704 Lee Ave., Lafayette 70501, ☎ 318/233–7060.*

International symphony orchestras and dance companies are presented by **Lafayette Community Concerts.** *Box 2465, Lafayette 70502, ☎ 318/233–7060.*

Festivals

The biggest bash in this neck of the woods is **Cajun Mardi Gras** (Feb. or Mar.), which features colorful parades and King Gabriel and Queen Evangeline. **Mamou's Mardi Gras** is a two-day town blowout with Cajun music in the streets and the taverns. Other notable fêtes involving Cajun food and Cajun music are the **Festivals Acadiens** (Sept.), the **Zydeco Festival** (Sept., in Plaisance, near Opelousas), and the **Crawfish Festival** (May in Breaux Bridge). Contact the Lafayette Visitors & Convention Commission for information on all events.

Lafayette's **Festival International de Louisiane,** which takes place on the third weekend of April, is a free event that fills the streets with entertainers, artisans, and chefs from French-speaking nations and communities. Opening ceremonies for the premier event included a 400-voice chorus and hundreds of musicians and dancers in native costume. *For information, contact Festival International de Louisiane, Box 4008, Lafayette 70502, ☎ 318/232–8086.*

Nightlife

While you're deep in the heart of Cajun Country you'll have a chance to chank-a-chank at a *fais-do-do*. Chank-a-chank? Fais-do-do? The little iron triangles played in Cajun bands make a rhythmic chank-a-chank sound, and dancing to the beat is chank-a-chanking. A fais-do-do (pronounced fay-doh-doh, meaning go to sleep) is a country dance. The term comes from words mothers murmured to put their babies to sleep while the fiddlers tuned up before a dance.

Fais-do-dos are family affairs, with young and old two-stepping and waltzing together to the fiddles, accordions, and chank-a-chanking triangles. They're held either in dance halls or outdoors in the square throughout the region. Attire is very informal, and so is the ambience.

The traditional dance music for southwest Louisiana's Creole population is the bluesy, hard-driving zydeco. While zydeco has been influenced by Cajun music, it has a unique sound and history. The name is said to derive from *"Zydeco sont pas salé"* ("The Snapbeans Are Not Salty"), a song by the late accordionist Clifton Chenier, widely considered "The King of Zydeco." Chenier and his brother, Cleveland, are also credited with inventing the *froittoir,* a metal washboard played with spoons, that helps give zydeco its exciting rhythms. In recent years, zydeco has been featured in such movies as *The Big Easy* and *Passion Fish,* but zydeco clubs still attract a mainly local crowd. Most places have live bands on Saturday; call to "mark" (reserve) a table. Admission is usually $5.

Pick up a copy of the *Times of Acadiana* and check the "On the Town" listings for fais-do-dos and zydeco dances, as well as for other forms of nighttime fun. The newspaper is free and available in hotels, restaurants, and shops.

The places below feature Cajun and/or zydeco music and dancing.

Belizaire's. Alligator meat and two-stepping feet are what you'll find in this Cajun restaurant near I–10. *2307 N. Parkerson Ave., Crowley,* ☎ *318/788–2501.*

El Sido's is a family-run zydeco club in Lafayette. Sid Williams manages the club while his brother's band, Nathan Williams and the Zydeco Cha-Chas, performs frequently. *1523 Martin Luther King, Jr. Dr., Lafayette,* ☎ *318/235–0647.*

Hamilton's. This weather-beaten, country-style zydeco dance hall has been around since the 1920s; the owner occasionally has to move his cattle herd to make extra parking spaces. *1808 Verot School Rd., Lafayette,* ☎ *318/984–5583.*

La Poussière, an age-old Cajun honky-tonk, is where local favorite Walter Mouton plays every Saturday. *1212 Grand Point Rd., Breaux Bridge,* ☎ *318/332–1721.*

Mulate's (*see* Dining, *above*).

Prejean's (*see* Dining, *above*).

Randol's. This Cajun "fern restaurant" has music and dancing nightly. *2320 Kaliste Saloom Rd., Lafayette,* ☎ *318/981–7080 or 800/YO–CAJUN.*

Rendez Vous des Cajuns. In addition to showcasing the best Cajun and zydeco bands, this two-hour variety program presents local comedians and even a "Living Recipe Corner." The show, mostly in French, has been dubbed the Cajun Grand Ole Opry; it's broadcast weekly on local radio and TV from a lovingly restored 1924 movie house. *Liberty Center for the Performing Arts, corner of 2nd St. and Park Ave., Eunice,* ☎ *318/457–6575.* ☛ *$2. Shows Sat. at 6* PM.

Richard's Club. "That's the place that the people love," sings popular zydeco musician Beau Jocque, about this rural, wood-frame zydeco club. *Hwy. 190, Lawtell (west of Opelousas),* ☎ *318/543–6596.*

Slim's Y-Ki-Ki. A rural zydeco club since 1947, this establishment has huge industrial fans to cool down the regular dance crowd. *Hwy. 182 in Opelousas,* ☎ *318/942–9980.*

Cajun Country Essentials

Getting Around

BY CAR
I–10 runs east–west from coast to coast and through New Orleans. Take I–10 west to the Lafayette exit, 128 miles from New Orleans. The interstate route will take about 2 hours. It is recommended that you return to New Orleans via U.S. 90 to take advantage of many scenic stopovers.

BY BUS
Greyhound Lines (☎ 800/231–2222) has numerous daily departures from New Orleans to Lafayette. The trip takes 3 to 3½ hours due to frequent stops along the way.

Amtrak (☎ 800/872–7245) connects New Orleans and Lafayette. Trains make the 3- to 4-hour scenic trip each way three times a week.

Guided Tours

Tours by Isabelle (☎ 504/367–3963) offers customized, multilingual tours from New Orleans to Cajun Country.

Allons à Lafayette (☎ 318/269–9607) provides bilingual guides for escorted, customized tours.

Important Addresses and Numbers

EMERGENCIES
Dial 911 for assistance. Or go to the emergency room, **Medical Center of Southwest Louisiana** (2810 Ambassador Caffery Pkwy., Lafayette, ☎ 318/981–2949).

24-hour pharmacy: Eckerd (3601 Johnston St., Lafayette, ☎ 318/984–5220).

VISITOR INFORMATION
Lafayette Convention and Visitors Commission (1400 N.W. Evangeline Thruway, Box 52066, Lafayette 70505, ☎ 318/232–3808 or 800/346–1958. ⊙ Weekdays 8:30–5; weekends 9–5).

9 Portraits of New Orleans

NEW ORLEANS: A HISTORY

KNOWN TO generations as the
Crescent City and more recently as the "Big Easy,"
New Orleans is a city whose magical
names conjure up images of a Gallic-
Hispanic and Caribbean heritage in a predominantly Anglo-Saxon culture, an
amalgamation that forms a unique city and
people. It was founded by the French on
the banks of the Mississippi River in 1718,
taken over by the Spanish in 1762, regained by Napoleon in 1800, and sold to
the United States in 1803.

During most of its 275 years of history,
New Orleans has survived yellow fever and
cholera epidemics, Indian wars, slave uprisings, economic depressions, revolts,
conspiracies, hurricanes, floods, the American and French revolutions, the Civil War
and Reconstruction, racial riots, and political corruption. Today its jazz, Vieux
Carré (the French Quarter), cuisine, Mardi
Gras, and port are known worldwide.

New Orleans is a city whose mystique has
captured the imaginations of generations of
writers and motion picture and television
producers, a city of tourists, beignets (French
doughnuts), Creoles, aboveground cemetery tombs, William Faulkner's French
Quarter, Tennessee Williams's *A Streetcar
Named Desire*, Walker Percy's *The Moviegoer*, and John Kennedy Toole's *A Confederacy of Dunces*. It stands like a curious
island of Roman Catholicism (of the
Mediterranean variety) in a southern sea of
hard-shell Protestantism that looks upon
New Orleans as "Sin City." Novelist Walker
Percy once wrote that to reach New Orleans
the traveler must penetrate "the depths of
the Bible Belt, running the gauntlet of Klan
territory, the pine barrens of south Mississippi, Bogalusa, and the Florida parishes of
Louisiana. Out over a watery waste and
there it is, a proper enough American city,
and yet within the next few hours, the
tourist is apt to see more nuns and naked
women than he ever saw before."

As San Francisco is often called the most
Asian of occidental cities, New Orleans
could be considered the most northern

Caribbean city. Perhaps journalist A. J.
Liebling best characterized it when he de-
scribed New Orleans as a cross between
Port-au-Prince, Haiti, and Paterson, New
Jersey, with a culture not unlike that of
Genoa, Marseilles, Beirut, or Egyptian
Alexandria. Colonial New Orleans was
very much a part of the economic, political, and social milieu of the French and
Spanish Caribbean; its earliest population
consisted of lesser French and Spanish gentry, tradesmen, merchants, prostitutes, crim-
inals, clergy, farmers from the fields of
France and Germany, Acadians from
Canada, Canary Islanders, Indians,
Africans, Englishmen, Irishmen, and En-
glish-Americans. Later came the Italins,
Greeks, Cubans, Vietnamese, and others
from the Earth's four corners, who have
made New Orleans one of the nation's
most cosmopolitan cities.

Because of the large Irish, German, and
Yankee immigration into this river-port
city in the middle of the last century, visitors are likely to hear a Brooklyn-style
accent spoken in one section of the city,
while hearing an interesting blend of New
England and southern accents in another
part of town. Tune your ear for the familiar "choich" for church and "zink" for
sink, and particularly for the "downtown" greeting, "Where y'at!" New Orleans's southern accent has a lot less
magnolia and mint julep than a Mississippi or Georgia accent.

It all began on Mardi Gras day in 1699
when a small French-Canadian expedi-
tion dropped anchor near the mouth of the
Mississippi to explore and colonize "La
Louisiane." For the next few years the ex-
pedition built a series of posts and fortifi-
cations along the river and the Gulf Coast,
including what is today Mobile, Alabama,
and Biloxi, Mississippi. By 1718, a permanent settlement was deemed necessary
to hold France's claim to the Mississippi;
the British and Spanish had their eyes on
the vast Mississippi Valley. When French-
Canadian Jean Baptiste, Sieur de Bienville,
established that settlement, it must have
seemed only natural (and politically wise)

to name it after Philippe, Duc d'Orléans, who was ruling France as regent for young Louis XV. Local legend has it that Bienville gave the settlement the feminine form of the adjective "new" and called it "Nouvelle Orléans" because the duke, who was a little effeminate, preferred to wear women's clothes.

New Orleans has had its glories and problems over the years, with two major standouts—hurricanes and politics. Contrary to orders from France, Bienville insisted upon building his settlement where New Orleans still stands today. He claimed the site was high and dry and protected from hurricanes, but during its first four years, the little village was wiped out four times by hurricanes. Politics have been an equally stormy art form here since the city's beginning; even the naming of the first city streets was a stroke of diplomatic genius. As historian John Chase notes in his delightful book on the origins of New Orleans street names, *Frenchmen Desire Good Children* (each name in the title is a street name), Bourbon, Orleans, Burgundy, and Royal streets were so named in honor of the royal families of France. Also honored were the Conti, Chartres, and Conde families, cousins to the Bourbons and Orleanses. (Conde Street was once a section of Chartres Street from Jackson Square to Esplanade Avenue before the name was dropped in 1865; Chartres now extends from Canal Street to Esplanade.) St. Peter Street was named for an ancestor of the Bourbon family; Louis IX, the Saint-King, was honored with St. Louis Street; Louis XIII's widowed Queen Ann got St. Ann Street; and Toulouse and Dumaine streets were named for Louis XIV's politically powerful royal bastard children.

The best place to get a real feel for the city's unique history is Jackson Square, the heart of the French Quarter, where you are surrounded by the river, St. Louis Cathedral, the colonial Cabildo and Presbytere, and the Pontalba Apartments. Called the Place d'Armes by the French and Plaza de Armas by the Spanish, this was the town square where the militia drilled and townsfolk met. It also was where public hangings, beheadings, "breakings at the wheel," and brandings were carried out. Of the countless stories of public executions and floggings, perhaps the most bizarre case concerned the 1754 mutiny of several

Swiss soldiers stationed on Cat Island (just off today's Mississippi Gulf Coast), who killed their oppressive and sadistic commander. The soldiers were captured and executed in the Place d'Armes; two were broken at the wheel with sledgehammers, and a third, a Swiss soldier, was nailed alive in a coffin and then sawed in half.

The Place d'Armes, site in 1803 of the Louisiana Purchase ceremony, was renamed Jackson Square in the 1850s in honor of Andrew Jackson, the hero of the Battle of New Orleans in the War of 1812 and later president of the United States. In the center of the square is an equestrian statue of Jackson erected in 1856, one of three cast: A second stands in Lafayette Park in front of the White House in Washington, D.C., and a third, in Nashville, Tennessee, Jackson's hometown. Today Jackson Square springs to life each day with artists, street musicians, jugglers, and a host of wandering minstrels who follow the sun and tourist trade.

THE OLD CITY, fanning out from the square, is filled with the legends and romances of an ever-changing people. Although the French Quarter is a living city and not a re-created fantasy world, history and time hang over the Vieux Carré like the thick, damp fogs that roll in from the river. You see the past everywhere—through the wrought-iron gates and down the ancient alleys, in the steamy courtyards tucked out of sight, in the graceful colonial dwellings that hang over narrow streets. You find it in museums and the old stories about Madame Lalaurie's tortured slaves, the romantic drama surrounding the Baroness Pontalba, Père Antoine, pirate Jean Lafitte, voodoo and its queen, Marie Laveau, revolutions, the Civil War, and yellow fever.

The history of New Orleans is inseparable from the port of New Orleans. The port is why the city was founded and why it survived. France wanted to colonize Louisiana, and built New Orleans to reap imagined riches from the vast interior of North America. Despite the expectations of the first explorers and the French crown, gold and silver did not come pouring out of the North American wilderness; different treasures waited. Quantities of tobacco, lumber, indigo, animal hides, and other indigenous products were floated downriver on flatboats to the new city, where ships from France, Spanish Florida, the West Indies, and the British colonies waited to trade for them with spices, cloth, cutlery, wine, utensils, foods, and other such goods. New Orleans became a commercial center, connecting Europe and the West Indies with the back country and upper regions of the Mississippi.

Trade was not without its difficulties. Storms, poorly built ships, privateers, colonial wars, and financially shaky entrepreneurs all added risks to commerce. There were other troubles as well; by the mid-18th century, serious international problems were brewing.

In 1754 the long-running dispute between France and England over who owned what in America erupted into war. Dubbed the "Seven Years' War" in Europe and the "French and Indian War" in the British colonies along the Atlantic seaboard (a war begun by British militiaman George Washington), it ultimately eliminated France as a colonial power in America. Despite an alliance with Spain (organized in the war's last years) France was defeated, and in 1763 it ceded to England all French territory east of the Mississippi River, keeping for itself just two small islands in the St. Lawrence Seaway.

NOT INCLUDED in the package, however, was New Orleans. Along with all the Louisiana territory west of the Mississippi River, the port had been signed over to Louis XV's cousin, King Carlos III of Spain, in the secret Treaty of Fontainebleau in 1762. (Perhaps that's where the long tradition of backroom deals got its start in Louisiana.) Louis gladly turned Louisiana over to his Spanish cousin. The colony was costing him his royal shirt, and the merchant class in France wanted nothing more to do with it. Carlos III, for his part, accepted the unprofitable holding as a buffer to keep the British away from nearby Mexico.

Louisiana Frenchmen, however, generally opposed the change to Spanish rule. When the first Spanish governor, Don Antonio de Ulloa, arrived, he did little to court their favor. After a few breaches in local etiquette and several commercial edicts that hurt the colony's already sagging economy, the settlers drove Ulloa out in a bloodless coup in October 1768. (Local historians, trying to upstage the British colonies along the Atlantic, claim this was the first revolution on American soil against a foreign monarch.)

Retaliation from the mother country was quick and complete. In July 1769 the Spanish fleet dropped anchor at the mouth of the Mississippi, with 2,600 Spanish soldiers under the command of General Alexander O'Reilly, an Irishman in Spanish service. O'Reilly quashed the short-lived rebellion, set up a new government in the colony, and executed the ringleaders of the rebellion.

The American Revolution afforded two of O'Reilly's successors, Unzaga and Galvez, the opportunity to attack their British colonial rival. Through the Louisiana colony, the Spanish sent supplies and munitions to the American rebels and allowed American raiding parties to launch forays into British West Florida. Galvez attacked and captured the British forts at Pensacola, Mobile, and Baton Rouge; and while the British were kept busy with the rebellious colonies, the Spanish took the opportunity to regain West Florida, which they had lost to the British during the French and Indian War.

The Spanish governors of Louisiana opened New Orleans's gates to a great variety of peoples by establishing an open-minded immigration policy that welcomed British-Americans escaping the Revolution as well as Acadians (whose descendants are Louisiana's famous Cajuns) fleeing the British in Canada. (The Cajuns later moved on to south-central and southwest Louisiana.) Canary Islanders came and settled just below New Orleans, where their descendants still live and speak their ancient language today.

Spanish New Orleans weathered several storms during the last decades of the 18th century, including the French Revolution. Mobs roamed the streets calling New Orleans Governor Carondelet a *cochon de lait* (suckling pig) and shouting "Liberty, Equality, and Fraternity." Carondelet brought in troops and outlawed publications concerning the Revolution in France.

Diplomatically, he also gave refuge to French aristocrats fleeing the carnage, which won him back some favor with the Louisiana French.

Carondelet also had problems upriver with the westward-expanding Americans (usually Kentuckians, called "Kaintocks"). During the American Revolution, the rebels had assured the Spanish that they had no designs on Louisiana. But by the 1790s their assurances began to carry less weight; Americans' use of the river had grown, and so, too, had American desire for free navigation along its length.

AS TIME PASSED, the situation worsened. Spanish officials in New Orleans occasionally seized American flatboats; the Americans responded by rattling sabers, urged on by the "Kaintocks," who called for an invasion of the Louisiana colony. War between the United States and Spain over Louisiana was narrowly averted in 1795 upon the signing of the Pinckney Treaty.

By the end of the 18th century, New Orleans had become a major North American port handling cargo from all over the world, with a population close to 10,000 and a well-earned reputation as a gay and colorful city. Mardi Gras was celebrated regularly (though it wasn't yet the extravagant carnival of parades seen today), and Creole food—that unique combination of French, Spanish, West Indian, and African cuisines for which New Orleans is so famous—had found its place on local palates. Unfortunately, much of the old colonial city was destroyed by fire in 1788 and 1794, but each time it was quickly rebuilt; most of the French Quarter of today was constructed during the Spanish colonial days and after the Louisiana Purchase in 1803. The oldest building in the French Quarter, and the only one remaining from French colonial years, is the former Ursuline Convent on Chartres Street, constructed in the 1730s.

For all the changes of the 18th century, the opening of the 19th was to bring even more. In France, Napoleon had reestablished the country as a formidable military force on the Continent. In 1800 he forced Spain to retrocede Louisiana to the French; New Orleans was back in the hands of its first colonial parent, though Spanish officials continued to run the colony for the next three years.

This news sat poorly with U.S. President Thomas Jefferson, who feared that war with France had become inevitable. The issue that concerned him was free navigation along the Mississippi River. To solve the problem, he resolved to buy New Orleans and a portion of West Florida bordering the Mississippi, including Baton Rouge. Napoleon, anxious for money to finance his imminent war against England (and reasonably sure that he would lose the land to England or the United States when war came), went Jefferson one better; he offered to sell the entire Louisiana colony.

On April 29, 1803, American emissaries agreed to pay $11,250,000 for Louisiana and, at the same time, to write off $3,750,000 in French debts, setting the territory's cost at $15 million. Short on cash, the United States borrowed the money to buy the territory from banking houses in London and Amsterdam. After the sale, Napoleon commented: "This accession of territory affirms forever the power of the United States, and I have just given England a maritime rival that sooner or later will lay low her pride."

The Americanization of New Orleans moved quickly during the first decade of the 19th century. The city's first suburb, Faubourg St. Mary (today's Central Business District), sprang up and bustled with construction and commerce; this was the American Section. Mississippi flatboatmen made their way downriver from the Missouri and Ohio rivers to sell their cargoes in New Orleans, then made their way home overland along the Natchez Trace.

The year 1812 brought statehood to Louisiana, and, almost equally important, the arrival of the first steamboat, the *New Orleans,* captained by Nicholas Roosevelt, ancestral kinsman of the two presidents; 1812 also brought war against Britain. Though its first effects on New Orleans were slight, the War of 1812 eventually came hard to the city. In 1815 Andrew Jackson with a ragged army of Louisianans and helped by Jean Lafitte, Lafitte's Baratarian pirates, and Tennessee and Kentucky volunteers, fought the British and stopped them in a bloody battle at Chalmette Plantation, a few miles downriver from the city. Although casualty estimates for the Battle of New Orleans conflict somewhat, reports placed American losses at 13 killed and 39 wounded, and British losses at 858 killed and 2,468 wounded. Ironically, the battle took place two weeks after the United States and Britain signed a treaty ending the war. Every January 8 local historical groups reenact the victory at Chalmette Battlefield, which is now a national park.

The years between the Battle of New Orleans and the Civil War were the city's golden era. By 1820 the population had reached 25,000; during the next 10 years it doubled. By 1840 it had doubled again, with a census count of 102,000 people within New Orleans; about half were black, both free and slave. The burgeoning port was choked with seagoing ships and riverboats laden with sugar, molasses, cotton, raw materials from upriver, and refined goods from Europe and the Northeast.

The golden age also gave birth to one of New Orleans's most famous pastimes: the Mardi Gras parade. Mardi Gras had been celebrated on the European continent, one way or another, for centuries. The parades, however, originated in Mobile, Alabama, but later moved to New Orleans, where the custom flourished. Begun in the 1820s when bands of maskers marched through the streets throwing confetti and flour (and sometimes lye) in the faces of onlookers, the parades were first staged by Americans in the American Section, and not by the French or Spanish populace, who preferred their gala balls. Vehicles were first used in 1839, and the first carnival organization, the Mistick Krewe of Comus, was formed in 1857.

Through the years of prosperity and celebration, disease continued to stalk the city. The almost yearly visits of yellow fever, cholera, and typhus—encouraged by widespread poverty—took thousands of lives; 8,000 fell to yellow fever in 1853, and another 2,700 in 1856. In that same year cholera claimed the lives of more than 1,000 people, and tuberculosis killed 650. New Orleans was known as one of the unhealthiest cities in the northern hemisphere.

If the 18th century can be seen as New Orleans's childhood, then the antebellum period was its adolescence and young adulthood; by its end, the city had reached full maturity. Prosperous and growing, it possessed an international personality that distinguished it from every other city on the North American continent.

But the Civil War was to change that. On January 26, 1861, Louisiana seceded from the Union. It was a difficult choice for New Orleanians, many of whom had strong commercial and family ties with the Northeast and Midwest. Less than three months after secession, the war began when Southern troops, under the command of New Orleans's own General Pierre Gustave Toutant Beauregard, opened fire on Fort Sumter in Charleston harbor. A month later a Union fleet blockaded the mouth of the Mississippi River, causing severe economic hardship in the city.

The Confederate flag waved barely a year over New Orleans before it fell to Union forces under "damn the torpedoes" Admiral David Glasgow Farragut in April 1862. When the Union fleet arrived and trained its guns on a panicked city, the mayor refused to surrender; Farragut threatened to bombard the city, but backed down. After a brief standoff, a naval squad went ashore and lowered the Confederate flag. New Orleans, the Confederacy's largest city, had fallen, and Reconstruction had begun.

NEW ORLEANS HAD the dubious distinction of being under Reconstruction longer than any other place in the Confederacy—from May 1862 to April 1877. The city's port and nearby fertile plantations were sources of immense profits for corrupt politicians under Reconstruction; the social and political upheaval it brought on was often violent, with bloody street battles between New Orleans natives and factions of the military-backed Reconstruction government. Withdrawal of federal troops in April 1877 brought an end to 15 years of Reconstruction; it also ended a flicker of hope that blacks in New Orleans would enjoy the same constitutional rights and protections as whites. With the end of Reconstruction came home rule and New Orleans's Gilded Age.

The last two decades of the century saw an era of conscious boosterism, economic booms and busts, corruption and reform, labor unrest and racial retrenchment. With a population of more than 216,000, New Orleans was still the largest city in the South. Large and elaborate Victorian homes, decorated with mass-produced gingerbread frills, sprang up along major avenues and thoroughfares.

New Orleans entered the 20th century with an air of optimism. North and South put aside their differences to defeat the Spanish in the Spanish-American War in 1898. Uptown continued to grow with new mansions along St. Charles Avenue, and skyscrapers in the Central Business District hovered over the early 19th-century buildings of the old American Section. The New Orleans World Cotton Exposition of 1884 clearly forecast a century of new promises.

THE PROSPERITY continued until the Great Depression of the 1930s, as skyscrapers towered even higher above the old city. World War II, however, was a turning point. Although the city prospered during the war years, its population began to fall behind that of other American and Southern cities. By 1950 it was no longer the South's largest city, falling to second place behind Houston. By 1970 the Crescent City had dropped to fifth place in the South, and the 1980 and 1990 censuses showed it slipping even further behind.

Census returns those years also showed a decline in the urban population, while surrounding suburbs grew dramatically. Since the early 1960s, tens of thousands of middle-class white and black families have moved to the sprawling suburban communities surrounding the city; thousands of acres of soupy marshlands have given way to tract housing and shopping centers. Unfortunately, the flight to suburbia has destroyed most of New Orleans's old neighborhoods.

Many New Orleanians, however, especially young and affluent couples, have refused to abandon the city, preferring to stay behind to buy and renovate old homes in the declining Victorian neighborhoods. Their work, courage, and good taste have revitalized entire sections of the city. The restoration craze has even spread to the Central Business District, which is experiencing its biggest construction boom since the 1850s. During the 1960s and 1970s, developers thought everything old had to be razed to make way for the new; scores of buildings dating from the 1850s and earlier gave way to the wrecker's ball. In more recent years, however, developers have found it profitable to adapt pre–Civil War buildings and warehouses to modern use, with magnificent results, especially in what has become known as the Warehouse District.

The construction of the Louisiana Superdome in the early 1970s and the 1984 New Orleans World's Fair also had considerable impact on the Central Business District. One glance at the city's skyline quickly reveals that the Central Business District is taking on all the trappings of a Sun Belt city. During the last decade the district has experienced phenomenal growth, despite the downturn in the region's oil and gas industries, with more than a dozen new skyscrapers rising above New Orleans's early 19th-century suburb. Major oil companies have built regional corporate offices here, and big-name hotel chains, including Hyatt-Regency, Hilton, Marriott, Westin, Meridien, and Sheraton, have constructed luxurious high-rise hotels in the district.

More than 270 years have passed since Bienville's engineers and work crews built the first palmetto huts at the crescent in the Mississippi River. Today New Orleans, the Crescent City, the Big Easy, is scarred and somewhat decayed, but it can be the most beautiful and charming of hostesses. Its people, history, cuisine, and its alluring 19th-century mystique and Caribbean-like culture make it resemble no other city in the nation.

— *John R. Kemp*

A columnist for New Orleans Magazine, *John R. Kemp has written several books about the city, including* New Orleans: An Illustrated History.

VOODOO AND THE LIFE OF SPIRITS IN NEW ORLEANS

IMAGINE New Orleans in the colonial era. Rain-sodden, prone to yellow fever epidemics, it is a remote port whose plantation economy turns on the toil of African slaves. Indian communities dot swampy woodlands that are well removed from the great estates where Creole aristocrats, their society welded to interests of the Church, eat sumptuously and party well.

Voodoo charges the territory with powerful impulses, bewildering planter and priest. Away from the plantation house, in the secluded woods near river and bayou, booming drums summon slaves to torchlit ceremonies in the night. Men and women gyrate to the percussive rhythms as a cult priest chants. Slap goes his knife, slicing through a chicken's neck—up gushes the blood, covering his hands. Around and around the worshipers dance, shouting in response to the priest's African chants.

Voices pulsate to the beat of hands and sticks on drums, pulsating on and on until the spirit hits and a woman is possessed by a current of psychic energy. Her shoulders shake, her body twists, her tongue speaks words no white man understands. The cultists gather round, calming her till the possession passes and she is released from her spell. Now the drumbeats become more insistent and the ceremony resumes.

In the nearby mansion, a Creole planter does not like what he hears; he tells himself he treats his slaves well. But what do those cries mean? A foreboding seeps into his night.

In the 18th century, voodoo was the most dramatic symbol of division between master and slave, and it loomed as a sinister threat to the ruling class. In 1782 the governor of Louisiana, fearing rebellious uprisings of the cults, put a clamp on voodoo-worshiping slaves imported from the Caribbean island of Martinique. But by then it was too late—voodoo had taken root.

Voodoo was a religion that had journeyed to the New World in the hearts and minds of African slaves uprooted from the animist culture of their homeland. Its origins lay in West Africa, particularly in the ancient kingdom of Dahomey (today the People's Republic of Benin) and in neighboring Yorubaland (what is now Nigeria).

In the 1720s, millions of Africans were captured by West African kings and sold as slaves to foreign merchants. Chained and hungry, the hostages were shipped in the holds of large ships that crossed the ocean. The Africans, as beheld by Caribbean and Southern planters, were people without religion, redeemed from the savage world they had left behind.

In reality, they came from large, extended families. Their African culture revolved around communal ceremonies that honored the spirits of departed ancestors. Music and dance rituals recognized the dead as existential presences; devotees wore masks to embody ancestral figures, deities, animals, and forces of nature.

The Yoruba believed that existence consists of three interconnected zones: the living, the dead, and the unborn. In rituals (still performed today) masked figures danced to percussive rhythms that evoked the ancients, or *orisas*.

The tone of the "talking drums" communicated the tribal vocabulary. The drum voice and dancer's mask formed a continuum—one gave language through music, and the other an image of the spirit. Voodoo was the faith, the center of gravity for the tribe, and it, along with its followers, crossed the Atlantic Ocean in the overloaded slaveholds. However, the masks would now lie buried in the savannas of the mind: Communications with the orisas in the white man's land would be dangerous and difficult.

The deepest implanting of voodoo occurred on the island of Saint Domingue, as Haiti was known before 1804. The Fon, natives of Dahomey, cast a large influence over the island's slave communities. Just as the Yoruba evoked their orisas, the Fon summoned their spirits, called *loa*. To the Fon, "vodun" meant "god" or "protective spirit."

Indoctrinated as Catholics, slaves on Haiti used the Mass in melding African spirits with visages of Christian saints. The Mass provided a New World ritual for voodoo's elastic reach; cultists could forsake the knife from chicken or goat and transform their worship in a less bloody rite while maintaining its inner core complete with sacrificial gods and drumbeats.

ON THE NIGHT of August 22, 1791, while a storm raged through Saint Domingue, a cult priest named Boukman led a voodoo incantation, drank blood from a pig, and, as reported by historian C. L. R. James, told his followers: "The gods of the white man inspire him with crime. . . . Our god who is good to us orders us to revenge our wrongs." Boukman was killed, but his revolt was one in a succession of slave rebellions culminating with the overthrow of French forces in 1804 and the founding of the Republic of Haiti.

Over the next decade, waves of planters, free Creoles of color, and slaves reached New Orleans, many via Cuba, scattering seeds that sprouted new voodoo cults. By then nearly a century had passed since the first slaves had arrived in Louisiana; the vocabulary of African drum voices had been effectively erased, but the religious sensibility had found a new cultural passageway.

In the early 1800s, land along the ramparts of New Orleans (what is now Louis Armstrong Park) became known as Place Congo, or Congo Square. On Sundays, slaves gravitated there for massive drum-and-dance convocations. They were not actual voodoo ceremonies, though the underlying impulse was similar, and white planters and their wives gawked at these spectacles performed in the open sunlight. Congo Square was outlawed about 1835; however, the sustained impact of tribal drums and dancing created for the slaves a link to their African past.

New Orleans was fast becoming a culture métissage—a mixture of bloodlines. Segregation was the law, but social intercourse was fluid among the peoples, especially between Creole planters and mistresses they found among the mulatto women. As the antebellum era wore on, the voodoo sensibility—adaptive to the culture in which it found itself—worked its way into the thoughts and culture of aristocratic white society.

In the 1820s, voodoo queen Marie Laveau (believed to have been of Negro, Indian, and white blood) worked as a hairdresser in white homes, where she gathered secrets of the Creole elite by utilizing domestic servants to spy on whites, many of whom sought her advice as a spiritual counselor. A practicing Catholic, she nevertheless frequently prescribed the sticking of a pin into a voodoo doll to provoke trouble for someone's nemesis or magical gris-gris dust (spell-casting powder) as a curative or protective hex. Her influence with blacks was greater by virtue of her sway over whites.

Marie made quite a living as a spiritual guide, selling her hexes and charms; she also made regular visits to the local prison. She groomed her daughter Marie to carry on the voodoo tradition; it was the second Marie whose exotic ceremonies of the night became legendary. Sex orgies reportedly occurred during voodoo rites of the late 19th century.

Dr. John, another important voodoo legend, was a towering black man (reputed to be a Senegalese prince in his former life) who owned slaves and was apparently a polygamist. He cultivated his own network of informants among slaves and servants who worked for whites. Aristocrats are said to have sought his advice, making him a legendary figure to blacks, but an outright cult priest he apparently was not.

In New Orleans today, voodoo is a bare whisper of its former self, a shadow along the margins of a different spirit world, grounded in the folkways of black Christian churches. As voodoo waned with early 20th-century urbanization, spiritualistic religions took root in New Orleans's churches. In these mostly small chapels, blacks honored the presence of

St. Michael the Archangel, Black Hawk the Indian, Leith Anderson, Mother Catherine, and other benevolent figures. While the base religion was Christianity, Haitian voodoo had turned African deities into images of Catholic saints; the spiritualistic churches transformed the faces once again, finding North American spirits to fit the visages of the new pantheon. Spirits may change as culture goes through upheavals, but the coil of memory springs the imagination, triggering messages in music and dance, myth and symbol.

American Indian tribes shared this imaginative process. Black Hawk was a powerful Sauk chief in Illinois who died in 1838. As Yoruba and Fon spirits resurfaced in Haiti, so the spirit of Black Hawk coursed through the mental chambers of a people with native American heritage. In 1919 the consciousness of Black Hawk reached New Orleans's spiritualistic churches through Leith Anderson, a woman of black and Indian ancestry who had come from Chicago.

In a WPA interview conducted during the Depression, Mother Dora, another spiritualistic leader, recalled Leith Anderson: "She wanted us to pray to Black Hawk because he was a great saint for spiritualism only . . . Ah think he came to her one time and said dat he was de first one to start spiritualism in dis country way before de white men come heah."

A Black Hawk cult flourishes in spiritualist churches today. Mother Leith Anderson—also called Leafy—is memorialized as well.

The trancelike possessions are powerful testimony to the belief system—a benevolent Christian vision of spirits-as-seed-carriers of culture across space and time.

In 1967, a crusty rock-and-roller named Mac Rebenneck adopted the stage name and persona of Dr. John. He sported bone and teeth necklaces, face paint, and a turban with billowing colored feathers. Confronting this bizarre persona, Mac's mother, a good Catholic lady, fretted. "I didn't want him for his soul's sake to be doing this. But actually, I could see the creativeness of what he was doing."

In "Gris-Gris Gumbo Ya-Ya," Mac sang as Dr. John: "Got a satchel of gris-gris in my hand/Got many clients that come from miles around."

Perhaps the most visible emblem of voodoo's hold on the popular imagination today is the number of visitors who flock to the tomb of Marie Laveau in St. Louis Cemetery No. 1 and to the Voodoo Museum in the French Quarter. Both are tributes to a time in Louisiana's history when mask and drum voice moved to an African beat. Their shadowy appeal is a reminder of the world of blood sacrifice and orisas still living within us all.

— *Jason Berry*

Author of Amazing Grace: With Charles Evers in Mississippi *and co-author of* Up From the Cradle of Jazz: New Orleans Music Since World War II, *Jason Berry has written, most recently,* Lead Us Not Into Temptation: Catholic Priests and the Sexual Abuse of Children.

CARNIVAL

WHAT COULD convince a prominent New Orleans businessman to wear a pageboy wig, gold crown, jeweled tunic, and white tights in public—and consider it the honor of a lifetime? Or cause people to ask with interest, "Who found the baby in the king cake?" Or prompt little old ladies to jostle strangers and shout that phrase New Orleanians learn at mama's knee—"Throw me something, Mister!"

Come to New Orleans during Carnival and find out.

Carnival is a mad game in which New Orleanians beg masked men on passing floats to toss them handfuls of plastic beads, go-cups, or aluminum doubloons (known generically as "throws") that eventually are pitched into the trash or mailed to family members who have married Yankees and moved away.

Don't be smug; if you visit, you'll catch the fervor. After a few moments of astonished gaping, you'll yell for throws, too, draping layers of beads around your neck, sipping from a plastic cup as you prance along the street, bebopping with the marching bands, and having a grand old time—assuming you like crowds.

Get one thing straight right away: There is a difference between Mardi Gras and Carnival—always with a capital C to differentiate it from carnivals that set up portable Ferris wheels and dart booths in vacant lots.

Carnival refers to an entire season that begins January 6 with an elegant debutante ball called Twelfth Night (as in "twelfth night after Christmas") and a separate, less aristocratic ball held on a streetcar by a group of Carnival devotees calling themselves Phunny Phorty Phellows.

Lasting for one to two months, Carnival explodes in its final days into a party that envelops the entire city and suburbs, with balls in every hall and hotel room on the final two weekends, and parades day and night, all of them organized and paid for by members of private clubs called "krewes." Since the parades are free (although the balls are strictly by invitation), New Orleanians refer to Carnival as "the greatest free show on earth."

During Carnival just about everybody overdoses on king cake, a sweet-dough coffee cake shaped like a wreath and topped with icing or sugar sprinkles in the Carnival colors of green, gold, and purple. Baked inside is the mysterious "baby," a fingernail-long pink plastic baby doll. Whoever bites into the baby is supposed to give the next king cake party or bring the next king cake to the office. Some New Orleanians prefer swallowing the baby to having to buy yet another king cake.

Mardi Gras (French for Fat Tuesday) is the final day of Carnival, the only day that it is legal to wear costumes, face paint, and masks in the streets. It's the final bash-of-a-celebration before Ash Wednesday, the beginning of Lent—that period of fasting for 40 days (and six Sundays that don't count) that leads up to Easter. Mardi Gras is an official city holiday, with just about everyone but the police taking the day off.

It's also the day that a middle-aged man in a pageboy wig reigns over the parade of Rex—the most important of the 50 or more parades—and 100 or so Carnival balls (all with their own maids and queens accompanying their own draped and bewigged kings).

But there is only one Rex (the king of this krewe is also known as Rex, Latin for king), and he is always an outstanding citizen who has done some high-profile volunteer work and who is a member of the men's group sponsoring the parade. Unlike kings of some of the less socially prominent balls, who sometimes pay hundreds or even thousands of dollars to their organizations for the honor (and for their costumes), Rex pays nothing to be king, and his club owns his outfit.

The queen of Rex is a young debutante chosen by the group's leaders on the basis of her father's prominence. Rex and his queen are considered the monarchs of the entire Carnival celebration. Their identities are kept secret until the day before Mardi Gras, when they are announced publicly.

The queen of Rex watches the parade from a grandstand in front of a hotel (the Inter-Continental in 1995); though she wears a traditional white suit, she waves her arms for throws like everyone else. That night the king and queen of Carnival wear jeweled clothes as they promenade around the white-cloth-covered floor at a ball in the Fairmont Hotel. At the end of the evening, they leave the Rex ball and cross to the other side of the auditorium to join the ball of the Mistick Krewe of Comus, the oldest and most exclusive of all Carnival balls in New Orleans. (The identity of Comus is never publicly revealed—a tradition that all the aristocratic krewes except Rex follow.)

The kings swap queens and all sit together on a throne, then leave the floor grandly, one at a time, in a regal ceremony that used to be televised but is now open only to invited guests. And that is the end of Mardi Gras; at midnight, police cars cruise through the French Quarter, loudspeakers blaring "Mardi Gras is over."

THE NEXT MORNING, Ash Wednesday, the more than half the New Orleanians who are Roman Catholic go to church to receive the sign of the cross on their foreheads in ashes. And Lent begins.

The city's residents are of two minds about Carnival. Most think it's the grandest thing since the invention of beer; the rest leave town. So many locals seek exile skiing in Colorado that they call themselves the Krewe of Aspen.

There are complications to Mardi Gras. First there's the matter of the date, which changes yearly because it is based on the movable feast of Easter. Mardi Gras can occur from early February to early March, and, whenever it is, New Orleanians invariably say "Mardi Gras is early this year" or "Mardi Gras is late this year." Mardi Gras falls on February 20 in 1996

(February 11, February 24, and February 16 in 1997, 1998, and 1999).

How it all started, no one is absolutely sure. Some say the Carnival celebration is an offshoot of pagan holidays. Others point to the Middle Ages. The faithful abstained from meat, eggs, and milk during Lent, and partied at vast feasts before the fasting began. There were rowdy celebrations in Rome during the Renaissance; in fact, festivities were held in most Christian countries, including France. So when French-Canadian explorer Pierre Le Moyne, Sieur d'Iberville, landed on a plot of ground near the mouth of the Mississippi River on Mardi Gras, March 3, 1699, he named it Pointe du Mardi Gras.

There's not much in history books about early Louisiana Carnival celebrations until the 1800s, when private balls were held by the Creole descendants of French and Spanish settlers, the city's aristocracy in those days. And there were "quadroon" balls where wealthy white men mingled with beautiful "free women of color" who were one-quarter black.

There also were street processions of the raucous sort. Young men from the so-called good families (as well as the not-so-good) wore masks and costumes and sometimes dumped flour on passersby, more intent on getting drunk than anything else. Occasionally the parades were splendid, but more often they were coarse. Then, on February 24, 1857, Mardi Gras changed.

At 9 PM, 60 or so men dressed like demons paraded in the streets with two floats in a torchlit cavalcade. The group called itself the Mistick Krewe of Comus, after the god of revelry. Arthur Burton LaCour wrote in his classic 1952 book *New Orleans Masquerade* that the men were Creoles from the French Quarter and Saxons (as LaCour referred to the nouveau riche Americans) from the other side of Canal Street across the so-called "neutral ground" (a name still used in New Orleans to refer to the median of a wide street).

Comus, LaCour wrote, was started by 13 New Orleanians and six men from Mobile, Alabama, where Mardi Gras parades had begun a few years earlier. Wanting to observe the holiday more fully, they formed a secret men's society, went to Mobile for costumes, and sent 3,000 invitations to a ball held at New Orleans's Gaiety Theater. They had begun a tradition.

As time passed (with lapses for the Civil War), invitations to the Comus ball became so coveted that one year the krewe captain advertised a $2,000 reward for two missing invitations. Comus crowned Robert E. Lee's daughter, Mildred Lee, as its first queen in 1884.

Through the years, other groups of men organized Carnival krewes. Then, in 1872, 40 businessmen founded Rex and sponsored a daytime parade for the Mardi Gras visit of His Imperial Highness, the Grand Duke Alexis of Russia. They chose as Carnival colors green for faith, gold for power, and purple for justice. Today's standard Carnival song, "If Ever I Cease to Love," was in a play called *Bluebeard*, which featured an actress who infatuated the grand duke, and bands of the day played it ceaselessly. The first Rex parade was thrown together quickly with borrowed costumes, but there was no ball. The first reception was not until the next year, when a queen was chosen on the spot at a public ball. Eventually invitations and formal dress became required.

AS MORE AND MORE carnival organizations were founded, young white girls who made debuts at afternoon teas held by their grandmothers were invited to be queens and maids. Traditionally, debutantes wear subdued white dresses, giving the 18 or so socially elite balls the nickname "white gown balls." The queens and maids of less socially prominent balls may be teen-agers, young single women of debutante age (typically college juniors), or married women; they tend to wear lavish costumes depicting some aspect of the ball's theme. As with the kings, debutantes of the social balls pay only for their dresses, while the mock royalty in less prestigious balls may also pay several hundred dollars for their right to reign.

Balls were strictly segregated; even Jews and Italians were banned from guest lists of the exclusive older balls (known as the "old-line krewes"). Some balls still keep up the practice—even now, among the ultrasocial krewes, only Rex invites black

guests. So other segments of society started clubs of their own.

A black butler and dance instructor from Chicago started the Illinois Club in 1895, copying the format of the old-line balls. Though this club split into two krewes— the Original Illinois Club and the Young Men Illinois Club—the African-American debutantes, usually high-school seniors or college freshmen, still perform the founder's dance, the Chicago Glide, in parallel black galas. The Illinois clubs don't sponsor parades, but the Zulu Social and Pleasure Club, organized in 1909 by working-class black men, does. The Zulu king (Louis Armstrong reigned in 1949) and his entourage toss glitter-covered coconuts to the crowds. In days gone by the Zulu parade would wander wherever the drivers chose, stopping at various bars along the way; these days, it's more organized. Doctors and bishops mingle with blue-collar members at a splashy, racially integrated party, and the parade follows a route published in city newspapers. The Krewe of Ashanti, another predominantly black Carnival club, paraded for the first time in 1993, taking as its regular date the second Friday before Mardi Gras.

After the Depression and World War II, Carnival clubs started popping up everywhere. Some were for doctors, others for businessmen, some for residents of certain neighborhoods, for military men, or for gays. There are only a few organizations for women, none in the socially elite category; so a few years ago, former old-line debutantes started joining a women's krewe, Iris, so they, too, could parade. The gay balls are splendid extravaganzas, but invitations for straights are scarce. Even mothers of debutantes have been known to beg invitations from their gay hairdressers for these lavish productions, featuring court members in drag and with headdresses so heavy that some krewe members have trouble standing up straight. (The number of gay krewes dropped from eleven to four in the past decade, partly because of AIDS, partly because of the recession, and partly—and less bleakly— because of other social activities.)

Membership fees in krewes can range from $150 to $600, but joining parading krewes costs much more, because members must buy the trinkets they throw.

Though new krewes proliferated after the Depression, their members, revering the traditions of the older groups, never dreamed of competing for status with them. Then, in 1969, an upstart group of businessmen looking to entertain tourists the Sunday before Mardi Gras founded Bacchus, named after the god of wine. The sassy group stunned the city by setting new rules and strutting out with a show as stupendous as the Rex gala. The Bacchus floats (designed by Blaine Kern, who also creates the Rex parade) were bigger than any seen before, and the king was Danny Kaye, not a homegrown humanitarian but a famous entertainer. The party was in the Rivergate Convention Center, not at Municipal Auditorium or a hotel ballroom. There was no queen, no court, and the party was called a rendezvous, not a ball. All guests could dance, not just members and their wives, as was the custom in old-line balls, where nonmembers merely watched the proceedings. The floats rode right into the Rivergate, and you didn't have to be socially prominent to join—or even white.

The crowds have loved Bacchus from day one, and guessing which celebrities will follow the likes of Danny Kaye, Bob Hope, and Jackie Gleason has become almost as popular as wondering about the identity of Rex. The 1995 Bacchus was actor (and New Orleans native) John Larroquette.

In 1974, another "krewe" of businessmen, Endymion, borrowed some of Bacchus's ideas and took over an abandoned slot in the Saturday night parade lineup. Nationally known celebrities are invited to be grand marshal and to entertain at a party for 10,000 called the Extravaganza, now held in the Louisiana Superdome. Endymion has super floats, a local king (drawn in a members' raffle at $25 a chance), and a court consisting of daughters of members. It can cost a queen's father $15,000 in expenses that include an elaborate dress and party. By the time members of Bacchus and Endymion buy throws and pay dues, they've dished out $2,000 to $3,000 each.

The last weekend before Mardi Gras is a whirlwind of parades and parties. Some krewes stage Carnival balls for convention groups willing to pay to see a simulated version of the real thing. Occasionally, lucky out-of-towners can buy extra tickets to the Bacchus or Endymion parties. Or they may be able to obtain invitations (always invitations, never tickets) to Rex, the most accessible of the old-line balls, if they happen to know a prominent New Orleanian with connections. The best parades tend to be near the end of Carnival. A favored (and crowded!) spot to watch the floats and marching bands is downtown on Canal Street, where the parades end around 8 to 9 PM. Families tend to prefer watching Uptown, particularly on St. Charles Avenue between Napoleon and Jackson avenues, although a proliferation of new parades in the suburbs of Metairie, Kenner, Gretna, St. Bernard Parish, and Covington now keeps many families in their own neighborhoods even on Mardi Gras itself. Argus, for example, which parades in Metairie on Mardi Gras, always has a local or national celebrity rider—in 1995 it was Steven Seagal.

THE PARADES BEGIN in earnest two weekends before Mardi Gras, and the public part of the celebration really goes into gear the Thursday before Mardi Gras with the procession of the Knights of Babylon, the so-called doctors' krewe, whose path is lighted by flambeaux (torches) carried by young black men who dance as they collect change thrown by onlookers. Though some think it demeaning, the tradition flourishes.

The ordinance was directed at the socially elite old-line organizations, particularly Comus, Momus, Proteus, and Rex—all limited to white men. Rex complied, reportedly inviting three black civic leaders to join the organization, which puts on the main parade of the season on Mardi Gras. Two black men joined—or so members say, since membership in all of the organizations is supposedly secret. But Comus and Momus both decided not to parade in 1992 (they said they feared for their safety), and Proteus joined them in 1993. These old-line krewes rebelled at the notion of being forced to accept members, when they could tell stories of sons and brothers of members (even of officers) who had been blackballed when they tried to join.

In 1992 the city was split over the issue. While few cotton to the idea of discrimination, 55 percent of the city's black residents told one pollster that they objected to the ordinance. People here accept Mardi Gras with all its limitations, many said, because everybody enjoys the parades.

In 1993 the principal mutterings of discontent came from the white social elite and from a few historians who hated to see the oldest traditional krewes cease parading. In a letter to *New Orleans Magazine,* Comus, Momus and Proteus (which still held their private Carnival balls) stated, "Be certain, our Societies will endure. . . . Adieu, Fair City, until the coming of some happy day when the Furies are done and the Fates call us to ride again to greet you." Whether they will ever actually parade again is anyone's guess. Other krewes have taken over Momus's and Proteus's traditional parade dates, though Comus's Mardi Gras night slot is still vacant.

The issue barely came up in 1995. For its part, the city partied as usual. A new celebration, Lundi Gras, has turned the formerly dull Monday before Mardi Gras into a day of music, food, and activities centered around welcoming the kings of Rex (actually, you're never supposed to say "king of Rex," since literally it's saying "King of King") and of Zulu, which parades before Rex on Mardi Gras. A new celebrity-studded krewe called Orpheus was organized by locals including District Attorney Harry Connick Sr., whose superstar son headlined their inaugural Mardi Gras eve parade in 1994. Orpheus continued to grow in stature in 1995, featuring celebrity riders such as Delta Burke, Gerald McRaney, Salt 'n Pepa, and headliner David Copperfield.

Tuesday is Mardi Gras. Zulu and Rex are followed by parades of trucks decorated by anyone who wants to organize a group of friends. Walking clubs (they march instead of riding on floats), including the Jefferson City Buzzards and Pete Fountain's Half Fast Marching Club, zigzag all over town, stopping in bars and swapping kisses for paper flowers and beads.

The Mardi Gras Indians also roam the city, particularly near Orleans and Claiborne avenues. The Indians are neighborhood groups of black men who stitch and glue their own stupendous Indian headdresses and costumes. Hometowners and visitors alike enjoy wandering through the French Quarter, where those with the flashiest costumes tend to gather. Though the Quarter can be wild and drunken, it's worth seeing the mind-boggling costumes that frequently are the result of a year's work. If a woman is in a particularly stunning costume, look twice—she may be a he.

— *Millie Ball*

Travel editor of the New Orleans Times-Picayune, *Millie Ball won a Lowell Thomas Award from the Society of American Travel Writers for the best newspaper story about foreign travel.*

Updated by Michael Tisserand

THE CRADLE OF JAZZ

MUSIC IS THE SOUL of New Orleans. Since the 1890s her melodies, rhythms, and musicians have enriched America's artistic heritage, and today, the city's musical texture is an interweaving of jazz, rhythm and blues, gospel, rock and roll, Latin beat, and then some.

The sound of New Orleans extends from the classic jazz of the early 1920s through the sterling sound of Louis Armstrong and his mates; from the mid-century dance-hall beat of Fats Domino, Professor Longhair, and a legion of rhythm-and-bluesmen to the polished modern improvisations of Wynton Marsalis and the young jazz lions of the 1980s.

As a distinctive sound, New Orleans's music is marked by a parade-time backbeat on drums, rocking, vocally suggestive horns, and a percussive piano style with liberal shadings of the blues.

The root of this sound is called the "second line"—the waves of marching dancers who engulf the brass bands with a dazzling body language of gyrating steps, following the musicians as they parade through the streets. Above all, it's music to make you clap your hands and move your feet.

The power of New Orleans's music has always come from the neighborhoods. Like Brazilian samba and the Beatles' Liverpool rock, jazz polyrhythms rose like a vox populi from working-class environs of this port city. Louis Armstrong in his memoir, *Satchmo*, recalled with a measure of tenderness the Back-o'-Town streets where he was raised. "The toughest characters in town used to live there," he wrote, "—as did churchpeople, gamblers, hustlers, cheap pimps, thieves, prostitutes, and lots of children."

But the seedbed of jazz music and its later offshoots lay in distant reaches of the past, at Congo Square, the early 19th century grassy plain (on what is now Louis Armstrong Park) where each Sunday slaves gathered for drum-and-dance celebrations that drew crowds of varied onlookers, including landed gentry.

Congo Square was the cultural transshipment point where African percussions and tribal dance steps, akin to those developing across the Caribbean map, began the long, slow march into European instrumentation and melody that would culminate a century later in the birth of jazz.

By the 1930s, Armstrong had given the music a grand voice, with lovely lyrical flourishes and gritty blues-like voicings. Since then, New Orleans has produced a continuing line of distinguished musicians. On October 22, 1990, the cover of *Time* magazine featured trumpeter Wynton Marsalis, a virtuoso superstar and eloquent advocate of jazz, as a metaphor of democracy. As Armstrong had done two generations earlier, the 29-year-old Marsalis became the spokesman of America's indigenous art form.

The seeds of New Orleans jazz first took root in the 1890s. New Orleans was then legally segregated, but was a town where rare degrees of social intercourse prevailed. It was a society of many layers—Creole descendants of European settlers, Italians, Irish, Germans, blacks, Native Americans, and Creoles of color (or *gens de couleur*).

Music held a common currency among these peoples. Outdoor festivals and indoor dances followed the calendar of Catholic feasts, the biggest of which was Mardi Gras, "Fat Tuesday," ushering in 40 days of Lent. The society orchestras and smaller ensembles that performed for parties and other events were playing syncopated rags; French quadrilles and polkas were popular, too.

A more potent influence, at least for the impetus of jazz, was the brass bands—groups that marched in uniforms, playing parade music with new rhythmic flavorings that reflected an African percussive tradition.

The musicianship of black Creoles was a primary factor in the emergence of jazz. They were a distinct caste, descendants of

African mothers and fathers of French or Spanish ancestry; many first arrived from Haiti in the early 1800s, settling in the Treme neighborhood (behind what is now Louis Armstrong Park) and, in later years, the Seventh Ward, which lies downtown, well beyond the French Quarter. The lines of racial intermixture were perpetuated by New Orleans aristocrats who kept mulatto mistresses and often supported second, "shadow" families.

SOME CREOLES amassed great wealth before the Civil War, and even owned slaves. They were generally better educated than the blacks who lived in uptown wards, upriver from the French Quarter. By the end of Reconstruction and with the tightening of racial laws, the sturdy familial lines and artisan skills of the downtown Creoles had produced a burgeoning tradition of families who taught music and performed professionally.

One such professor, James Brown Humphrey, played a variety of instruments and was a catalyst for jazz. In 1887 he began regular trips to outlying plantation communities to teach poor blacks, a number of whom moved to town to join brass bands. In 1987 two of his grandsons, Willie and Percy Humphrey, were regular performers in Preservation Hall.

A more legendary figure—universally deemed the first great jazzman—was Buddy Bolden, who played cornet (a smaller version of the trumpet) with strong, bluesy currents. Though his music was popular, Bolden suffered a mental breakdown in 1907 and never recorded.

In time, the musical division between blacks, who learned to play by ear—listening to songs, replicating what they heard—and Creoles, who read sheet music, began to blur. Meanwhile, a red-light district called Storyville gave piano professors like Jelly Roll Morton quite a venue until its closure in 1917.

Nineteen seventeen was a milestone year for another reason: In New York, a group of white New Orleans musicians led by Nick LaRocca, the Original Dixieland Jazz Band, recorded the first jazz disk. Jazz was an idiom rooted in the African improvisational genius; many white practitioners, whose style became known as Dixieland, began to flourish in New Orleans as well.

The first generation of New Orleans jazzmen produced three brilliant artists—Louis Armstrong, Jelly Roll Morton, and Sidney Bechet—each of whom left the city to establish his reputation. Morton, a Creole with great talent as a composer-pianist, was a peripatetic figure who died in 1941, down on his luck. Bechet, also a Creole, was a virtuoso clarinetist who left behind a string of memorable recordings. He settled near Paris, where he became a celebrity, and died in 1959.

Armstrong's life was a rags-to-riches odyssey. Records show that Armstrong was born August 4, 1901—however he preferred the more romantic, fabricated birthday of July 4, 1900. He grew up in the Back-o'-Town ghetto, and after a stint in the Colored Waifs Home, found an early mentor in Papa Joe Oliver, the popular cornetist and bandleader also known as King Oliver. In 1918 Armstrong began traveling the Mississippi, playing on riverboats, refining his technique. In 1922 he left New Orleans to join Oliver's band in Chicago, and for the next half-century he traveled the globe, elevating jazz to an international art form.

The music stylizations and recordings of Armstrong, Morton, and Bechet had an enormous influence; yet to all but aficionados of jazz, the historical sensibility they shared is frequently overlooked. Each man worked hard on a biography; their books are solid works of literature, as well as classics of jazz history—Armstrong's *Satchmo: My Life in New Orleans*, Bechet's *Treat It Gentle*, and Morton's *Mister Jelly Roll* (written by Alan Lomax, but based on long interviews with Morton).

The sounds of jazz continued to flow in New Orleans through the 1930s and '40s. The tidal shift toward a new idiom came after World War II: rhythm and blues.

A blues sensibility ran deep in New Orleans, and the many lyrics about love lost, love found were fashioned into a style, enhanced by gospel techniques, the soaring choirs and drums of the churches, and saxophones and trumpets that blasted like preachers and moaned like bluesmen.

Fats Domino put R&B on the map. In 1949 "The Fat Man," with his rocking piano style and rolling, mellifluous voice, triggered a line of golden records that made teenagers put on their dancing shoes.

Domino had the advantage of a highly skilled producer, trumpeter-bandleader Dave Bartholomew, who molded Fats's sound for the Imperial label. His biggest hit, "Blueberry Hill," was a country boy's song that wedded Fats's appeal to an audience of blue-collar workers and rural folk.

The other influential early rhythm and bluesman was Henry Roeland Byrd, who took the stage name Professor Longhair in 1949, and who played in Domino's shadow most of his life. Fess, as he was fondly known among locals, was quite a ticket. A tap dancer in his youth, he made the rounds of Rampart Street honky-tonks in the Depression, studying the blues piano of Champion Jack Dupree and Sonny Boy Williamson.

Professor Longhair called his own style "a mixture of mambo, rumba, and calypso." He infused the dance steps of his youth into an intricate, percussive keyboard style and he sang with the deep heart of a bluesman. He simulated the street pace of Carnival in "Mardi Gras in New Orleans" and "Go to the Mardi Gras," which became local anthems. "Big Chief" was his homage to the Mardi Gras Indians, groups of blacks who create grand Native American costumes and still parade in neighborhood tribes through New Orleans's back streets.

In a sense, Professor Longhair's death in 1980 marked the end of the postwar R&B era. His unique style never caught on as a national chart buster, but he had enormous influence on younger musicians. Even before his death, younger jazzmen in the brass bands he had begun performing his Carnival tunes.

Domino and Longhair divided New Orleans R&B into two stylistic camps—one a building block of rock and roll, the other a more improvisational, Afro-Caribbean beat. Between these styles was a generation of exceptional musicians.

Allen Toussaint harnessed the talents of a stable of singers in the 1960s. A skilled pianist with a seasoned lyrical touch, Toussaint composed songs for Irma Thomas ("Queen of the Blues"); Aaron Neville, a brawny balladeer with a falsetto reach that chills the spine; Ernie K-Doe, an extravagant stage performer and blues shouter who scored a hit with "Mother-in-Law"; and Benny Spellman, a hefty ex-football player for whom Toussaint penned the memorable "Fortune Teller."

The music of the 1950s fit a new urban groove. White teenagers were the big market; of the many New Orleans artists who reached the kids, Huey "Piano" Smith did it with a colorful entourage known as the Clowns. Drawing on nursery rhymes, Huey wrote uncomplicated, if offbeat lyrics—"I got the rockin' pneumonia and the boogie-woogie flu"—and the dancers loved it.

WHEN THE BEATLES and Rolling Stones swept America in the 1960s, the New Orleans R&B scene fell into decline. In the early 1970s, the annual Jazz and Heritage Festival ignited a revival.

One of the most talented 1950s session artists, Mac Rebenneck, played piano, guitar, and penned dozens of compositions before hitting pop stardom in 1968 as Dr. John. James Booker, who dubbed himself the Piano Prince, also had commanding talent; he could jump from classical chords into R&B bounces with sizzling heat and witty lyrics. Booker, Dr. John, and Art Neville were prime exponents of a piano idiom that roamed the bridge between the Longhair-Domino styles. Booker's death in 1983 was greatly felt in New Orleans's jazz community.

In 1977, Art joined his brothers to form the Neville Brothers band, today the city's preeminent pop group. Charles plays saxophone; Cyril sings and plays congas; Aaron, whose 1966 hit "Tell It Like It Is" is still a showstopper, sings and plays hand percussions. The Nevilles' four-part harmonies, set against Afro-Caribbean lines, gave R&B a warm new shading. At the same time, the Nevilles wrote a new chapter in popular music through their association with the Wild Tchoupitoulas, a

Mardi Gras Indian tribe led by their uncle, George Landry.

The Nevilles hit their stride in 1990, winning a Grammy for "Yellow Moon." The following year, Aaron Neville took another Grammy for his vocal duet with Linda Ronstadt, and in 1992 won his first gold record, "Warm Your Heart," which sold 500,000 copies. His odyssey from stevedore work on the river docks of the Mississippi to musical celebrity is one of the most poignant artistic careers in New Orleans.

There are approximately 25 black neighborhood groups that masquerade as Indians each Mardi Gras; the folk tradition dates to Reconstruction. As Big Chief Jolley, Landry founded the Wild Tchoupitoulas in the uptown neighborhood where he and his nephews lived. A 1976 LP, *The Wild Tchoupitoulas*, combined the instrumental prowess of the Nevilles and the Meters bands with Jolley's hearty vocals, based on the old a capella tribal chants, to become a classic. By the time Landry passed away in 1980, Mardi Gras Indian music was emblematic of the Neville sound.

In the 1980s, New Orleans experienced a jazz renaissance led by the brilliant trumpet work of a young Wynton Marsalis, the product of yet another musical family. As high-school students, Wynton and his brothers studied at the New Orleans Center for the Creative Arts, where Ellis Marsalis, their father, directed the jazz program. With brother Branford on saxophone, Wynton emerged as a national star by the time he was 20, and in 1984 won two Grammy awards. Branford has also worked with rock star Sting for several years and contributed to the score of *Do the Right Thing,* the controversial Spike Lee film.

A gifted composer-pianist in his own right, Ellis Marsalis molded three other young talents who have since achieved national recognition: trumpeter Terence Blanchard and saxophonist Donald Harrison, who perform together, and pianist Harry Connick, Jr., who in 1987 released his debut album at age 19 and recorded the score for the 1989 film *When Harry Met Sally.* The Marsalis brothers, Blanchard, and Harrison all got their professional start in New York with Art Blakey's Jazz Messengers. Yet another Marsalis brother, Delfayo, produced the Blanchard-Harrison

1988 LP *Crystal Stair.* After a short hiatus, Ellis has returned to New Orleans to continue his laudable work at the New Orleans Center for the Creative Arts.

Harry Connick, Jr., meanwhile, began dazzling audiences with a polished blend of jazz piano and a golden mellifluous singing voice that drew comparisons with Frank Sinatra. He also became a heartthrob in the youth market, a rare feat for a jazz artist. Connick has now emerged as a superstar vocalist, touring with a big band known for its lush arrangements. He shows promise as an actor, with a minor role in the film *Memphis Belle* and a supporting role in *Little Man Tate,* directed by Jodie Foster.

THE YOUNG LIONS of the 1980s are products of a teaching tradition and a society rooted in musical families. Their myriad innovations draw from a large canvas of sounds. The Dirty Dozen and Rebirth bands have led the brass band resurgence, a fourth generation of young musicians improvising with blues, bebop, R&B, and jazz.

Yet a new line of young jazz talents emerged in 1991—trumpeter Nicholas Payton, son of esteemed bassist Walter Payton; drummer Brian Blade, who learned music in a Shreveport gospel church; and bassist Chris Thomas, a University of New Orleans (UNO) jazz student, among others. The impact of the UNO program under Ellis Marsalis is the most important musical development in the city in years. Molding professional artists, Marsalis and Harold Battiste, a pioneer of the post–World War II heritage jazz, are laying the groundwork for a much more sophisticated approach to the business of music.

Although a full-blown recording industry has yet to emerge, New Orleans is making dramatic strides as a music city. New Orleans in no way rivals Nashville as a production and song-publishing center. Yet tourists flock here by the millions each year, especially for the annual Jazz and Heritage Festival in late April to early May. Despite the 1991 recession, the heightened activity in local studios and a sturdy club circuit signaled growth in the entertainment economy. The main obstacle to building a bonafide music industry is capturing a record distribution base.

Artists who make it big often head for New York, such as Armstrong, Dr. John, Wynton Marsalis, and Harry Connick, Jr. Yet for all those who moved, many more choose to live here—including some of the city's best talent, such as Fats Domino, the Nevilles, and younger groups like the Dirty Dozen and Rebirth brass bands—while playing long stretches on concert tours each year.

Despite its drawbacks, a distinctive cultural sensibility—more Latin and African than Anglo-American—has endowed New Orleans with a unique musical society. As saxophonist Harold Battiste, a pioneer of 1950s heritage jazz that came out of small clubs around the Magnolia housing project, once put it: "Musicians come and go, and their creations always seem directed at the city. Because after all is said and done, *New Orleans* is the star."

— Jason Berry

SOME LIKE IT HOT: NEW ORLEANS'S SULTRY BILL OF FARE

ALTHOUGH a child of France, New Orleans has always been a melting pot of ethnic culinary styles. Africans, Spaniards, Frenchmen, Choctaw Indians, and Acadians all contributed to what is now known as New Orleans–style cooking.

Traditional New Orleans cuisine is usually called "Creole," a word that originally referred to the descendants of the city's French and Spanish colonists. The word has since evolved to describe a culinary style, blending European, Caribbean, and African influences.

Closely related to Creole is the brand of cooking found in Acadiana, a region of coastal prairie, bayous, and marshlands in southwestern Louisiana. This is the land of the Acadians (or "Cajuns"), whose ancestors had settled the French colony of Acadie in eastern Canada during the 17th century but later resettled in Louisiana after being expelled from the territory when it came under British control.

Creole and Cajun cooks share a large number of common ingredients and dishes. *Roux* (flour browned in oil or lard) is a frequent thickener for stews and gumbos in both styles. Jambalaya also can be either Creole or Cajun. But the two cuisines also have significant differences. The Cajun diet traditionally has centered mostly on pork, poultry, fish, shellfish, and game. New Orleans cuisine contains those, too, but it always has had a more urban character, influenced by whatever cultures found their way up the Mississippi River to the city's port. In the 19th century, these influences included elegant cream or butter sauces brought over by immigrants from France. In the early 20th century, Italians, Germans, and even Yugoslavs contributed to the city's culinary melting pot.

Slaves, the foundation of the 18th-century colonial economy, brought with them from their native lands *gombo* (an African word for okra) and couscous (a North African dish they transformed into a warm breakfast cereal made of cornmeal).

New Orleans was ceded by France to Spain in 1762, but reclaimed in 1800 by Napoleon. Three years later, it was sold to Thomas Jefferson as part of the Louisiana Purchase. The Spanish legacy included a new style of cooking and a love of tomatoes and peppers, which were later utilized in jambalaya, a variation on Spanish paella.

The Choctaw Indians, who traded with the French, introduced them to sassafras, which is used to thicken certain non-okra-based gumbos, and to corn, which resulted in grits and *macquechoux,* an Acadian dish of corn, bell peppers, and onions.

From this blending of cultures have come the innovations in Creole cooking that continue today, creating a regional style that today has many facets.

The emergence of chef Paul Prudhomme in the early 1980s gave Creole-Cajun cooking an international reputation. Other South Louisiana chefs, such as Emeril Lagasse of Emeril's in New Orleans and John Folse of Lafitte's Landing in Donaldsonville, north of the city, have expanded on Prudhomme's innovations. Prudhomme's most recognized dish, blackened redfish, became so popular that a commercial fishing ban was levied on redfish in early 1988. The Cajun cooking craze, with staying power at the national level, has resulted in an explosion of the crawfish industry.

Cajuns, however, would never have dreamed of creating either Prudhomme's blackened redfish or his oyster and brie soup. Etouffées and stuffed mirlitons (a vegetable pear), which Prudhomme also serves at K-Paul's, are closer to the heart of Cajun cookery. Generally, the food served at Prudhomme's restaurant, as well as at a handful of other Cajun establishments in the city, is far removed from what is consumed daily in the bayou parishes.

An Acadian's pantry is never without rice, filé, red pepper, Tabasco sauce, a hen, and the "Holy Trinity"—onion, bell pepper, and celery. Other necessities are wild game and fresh shellfish. It's said that a Cajun will cook and eat anything that won't eat him first.

While the Cajun-Creole cooking is taking an international spotlight, Creole cuisine is undergoing some important transformations—with a twist in nomenclature—into Nouvelle Creole. Establishments devoted to this style are currently the rage. Pasta is now more popular than rice in many Louisiana restaurants, and the growing presence of Vietnamese staff in some of the finest New Orleans kitchens has introduced diners to eastern herbs and spices.

The French Market gave birth to many dining traditions that have remained in New Orleans. As a result of colonial trading, eating styles evolved around the marketplace.

Brunch is a mainstay in New Orleans. Originally devised to accommodate the butchers and French Market merchants who breakfasted late in the day, it was introduced to the public by the chef-restaurateur Madame Begue in the mid-1800s. Tujague's Restaurant (823 Decatur St.) preserves her memory at the original site of her restaurant with a Madame Begue room, replete with photographs and memorabilia. Today, Brennan's Restaurant (417 Royal St.), the most popular brunch spot in town, carries on the brunch tradition and boasts of serving over 1,000 brunches each Saturday and Sunday.

Brunch is merely the beginning of what eating in New Orleans is about. Traditions abound here, and the best way to begin an exploration of them is with a cup of café au lait and a beignet. The famed Creole coffee, or café au lait, is sold everywhere, but the best version of this rich chicory blend laced with steaming hot milk or cream can be savored at Café du Monde (open 24 hours a day), across from Jackson Square. The accompaniment to this rich coffee is a Café du Monde beignet—a deep-fried pastry doused with powdered sugar.

The legacy of the New Orleans po'boy is rich. Available today at almost every lunch counter, restaurant, and grocery store, this oversized sandwich came into being during a late 1920s streetcar strike. The sandwich was originally made from a loaf of French bread sliced lengthwise and filled with a generous portion of potatoes, meat, or whatever the chef's whim of the day

was; the cost was five cents. Today, po'boys are more expensive, but they're still as a rule as long as a person's forearm. The sandwiches today are stuffed with everything from roast beef to meatballs, Italian sausage, fried oysters, and soft-shell crabs. Among the best po'boys in the city are those at Mother's on Poydras Street.

Another great New Orleans sandwich is the Italian *muffuletta*, which is made with a dense, round bread dressed with olive salad and stuffed with layers of meats and cheeses. Central Grocery (923 Decatur St.) makes one of the best muffulettas in town. Napoleon House (500 Chartres St.) serves its own variation of the muffuletta, hot from the oven. Muffulettas are so large that most people halve and quarter them; one makes a meal for two adults.

WHEN YOU ORDER barbecue shrimp in a New Orleans restaurant, you may be surprised at what arrives on the table: It's not barbecue at all, but jumbo shrimp baked in their shells in a spicy herbal sauce. Some restaurants, like Ruth's Chris Steak House, peel them; Pascale's Manale offers bibs. You can find barbecue shrimp everywhere from casual eateries to the best restaurants.

Oysters on the half shell are offered everywhere in town. The Acme Oyster Bar in the French Quarter has some of the best. Wherever they are consumed, the important thing to remember is that you shouldn't ever sit down to eat them. Tradition has it that cold oysters are eaten standing up, then washed down with a bottle of Dixie beer.

Oysters Rockefeller are served at many fine restaurants in the city, but none are as fine as those consumed at their place of birth, Antoine's (713 St. Louis St.)—founded in 1840 by Antoine Alciatore—the oldest dining establishment in New Orleans. Traditional oysters Rockefeller are served in a sauce of puréed greens tinged with Pernod. The dish is so rich that it was named for the richest man in the world at the time of its creation. Brennan's, unlike most restaurants, has an outstanding version that uses no spinach. Two other baked-oyster dishes that have become famous are Bienville and

Lafayette; some better restaurants offer an appetizer of 2-2-2, which means two of each type on a platter.

Jambalaya and red beans and rice are sold almost everywhere, and some of the tastiest are found at lunch counters. Jambalaya, like gumbo, can be made with any variety of ingredients, from sausage to shellfish, and in some cases both. The common denominators are rice, tomatoes, onions, and plenty of pepper.

Steaming platters of red beans and rice, often with a huge link of spicy sausage, are a New Orleans mainstay. There are numerous places that do this dish justice, including Popeye's Famous Fried Chicken, a fast-food chain with 40 outlets in New Orleans, which sells a delicious liquidy, spicy version without meat. Most casual restaurants serve this dish on Mondays, a tradition that originated long ago when women served it after doing Monday's wash—the beans simmering all day while the women completed their chores.

Gumbo is considered a staple in most places, yet it is rare to find a great gumbo in New Orleans. It typically lacks a dark brown, slow-cooked roux, and it is often overladen with pepper, watered down or overly thick, and short on meat or fish. Seafood gumbo is served most frequently. Even gumbos made by the so-called specialists like the Gumbo Shop fall short when compared to what is lovingly prepared in Acadiana at such places as Don's Seafood Hut in Lafayette. Gumbo is an event. Most Cajuns make gumbos either with chicken, sausage, and oyster, or with duck and oyster. Unfortunately, very few restaurants in the city do justice to this dish.

Boiled seafood is quite popular, and the freshest seasonal shrimp, crabs, and crawfish can be had at numerous seafood restaurants around town. Orleanians eat boiled crawfish served cold, and in relatively small portions compared to Cajuns, who generally figure three pounds per person. Crawfish shacks like Richard's in Abbeville (a charming town of 12,000 near Lafayette) serve up enormous tubs of spicy crawfish, steaming hot and accompanied by boiled onions, potatoes, and corn. Patrons eat with their hands (yours will need a good scrubbing with hot water and lemon after this!). Nothing could be tastier than this small crustacean, which is far better served hot than cold.

Bananas Foster, the world-famous dessert, originated at Brennan's and is now a mainstay in most fine Creole kitchens, although none does it as well. Other flaming desserts associated with New Orleans are cherries jubilee (great at Galatoire's), and crêpes suzette (best at Arnaud's).

The thing to remember about dining in New Orleans is the pace: No one ever rushes through a meal here. In fact, dining out constitutes an event. Friends often talk about where they ate yesterday, as well as where they will eat tomorrow. The only other subject that interests Orleanians as much as food is politics—a topic almost as sizzling as their cuisine.

— Lisa LeBlanc-Berry

Lisa LeBlanc-Berry is currently a contributing editor for Where Magazine *in New Orleans.*

MORE PORTRAITS

Further Reading

For a good mixture of romance and adventure with an eccentric cast of characters, pick up *Bandits* by Elmore Leonard. Frances Parkinson Keyes's *Dinner at Antoine's* is a charming murder mystery set in a famous New Orleans restaurant. In Susan Shankman's *Now Let's Talk of Graves,* a journalist/detective travels to New Orleans for a Mardi Gras holiday and investigates a possible murder.

A Feast of All Saints, by Anne Rice, describes the lives of the "free people of color" (a localism for blacks who were not enslaved prior to Emancipation) in pre–Civil War New Orleans. Rice's *Vampire Chronicles* trilogy also has a New Orleans background.

Other novels set in the city include: *Lives of the Saints,* by Nancy Lemann, a fun novel about a wacky New Orleans family; Kate Chopin's *The Awakening,* about the life of one New Orleans woman in the mid-1800s; *The Moviegoer,* by Walker Percy, full of details about the city as it follows a charming, neurotic native of New Orleans; and *A Confederacy of Dunces,* by John Kennedy Toole, a Pulitzer Prize–winning novel set in New Orleans.

For an interesting history of the city—through an explanation of New Orleans street names—read *Frenchmen Desire Good Children,* by John Chase. Al Rose's *Storyville* gives a good account of the origins of jazz and New Orleans's once infamous red-light district, Storyville. The pocket-size history *The Free People of Color of New Orleans,* by Mary Gehman, explains the origins and contributions of that unique group, today often referred to as Creoles.

Fodor's The South's Best Bed and Breakfasts (2nd edition) has a chapter devoted to Louisiana with reviews of B&Bs in Greater New Orleans, Plantation Country, Cajun Country, and North Central Louisiana. For those planning to visit places in Louisiana beyond New Orleans, *Fodor's The South '96* covers South Louisiana, Baton Rouge, Natchitoches, and North Central Louisiana.

For anyone serious about planning for Carnival, Arthur Hardy's annual *Mardi Gras Guide* is a must. It costs $5.50 (including shipping) and can be ordered from Box 19500, New Orleans, LA 70179, ☏ 504/838–6111.

The New Orleans daily *The Times-Picayune* publishes an annual Carnival guide a few weeks before Mardi Gras each year. Write the Special Sections Department, *Times-Picayune,* 3800 Howard Ave., 70140, ☏ 504/826–3464.

Gambit, a weekly newspaper, also publishes parade guides in the weeks before Mardi Gras. Write *Gambit,* 4141 Bienville St., 70119, ☏ 504/486–5900.

Videos

The Big Easy (1987) features Lake Pontchartrain, the Piazza d'Italia, and a catchy zydeco music soundtrack as it unfolds its tale of a wise-guy police lieutenant (Dennis Quaid) who uncovers corruption in the New Orleans police force and falls in love with a district attorney (Ellen Barkin).

Interview with the Vampire (1994), based on the two novels by Anne Rice, has vampires Tom Cruise and Brad Pitt appearing in various locations around the French Quarter, in Lafayette Cemetery in the Garden District, and at Oak Alley plantation on the Great River Road.

In *JFK* (1991), directed by Oliver Stone, New Orleans district attorney Jim Garrison (Kevin Costner) tries to prosecute a city businessman (Tommy Lee Jones) for conspiracy in the assassination of President John F. Kennedy. Scenes were photographed at the Louisiana Supreme Court Building (the former New Orleans Court Building) and Napoleon House on Chartres Street.

In *The Pelican Brief* (1993), based on the John Grisham best-seller, Julia Roberts plays a law student who discovers through research that two supreme court justices have been murdered. During the film, she is chased by bad guys through Bourbon

Street in the French Quarter; she also appears on the Tulane University campus, near Lafayette Square in the Central Business District (when a car explodes), and at Checkpoint Charlie's, a French Quarter blues-and-rock club.

Pretty Baby (1978), directed by Louis Malle, focuses on the lives of residents (Brooke Shields and Susan Sarandon) in the turn-of-the-century Storyville red-light district of New Orleans, as well as on photographer E.J. Bellocq (Keith Carradine) who takes pictures of them. The film was shot inside the Columns Hotel on St. Charles Avenue and around the Garden District.

Tune in Tomorrow (1990), based on Mario Vargas Llosa's novel *Aunt Julia and the Scriptwriter*, tells the story of a young man (Keanu Reeves) who becomes involved with his aunt (Barbara Hershey) and assists a writer of a radio serial, *Kings of the Garden District*. Audubon Park, St. Charles Avenue and the Garden District, and parts of the French Quarter serve as backgrounds for the characters.

Other films photographed in New Orleans include *Angel Heart* (1987), *Blaze* (1989), *Cat People* (1982), *Hard Target* (1994), *The Kingfish* (1995), *Panic in the Streets* (1950), *Miller's Crossing* (1990), *Sex, Lies, and Videotapes* (1989), and *Tightrope* (1984). For a glimpse of Cajun country, take a look at *Belizaire the Cajun* (1986) and *Passion Fish* (1992).

NOTES

NOTES

NOTES

NOTES

NOTES

Fodor's Travel Publications

Available at bookstores everywhere, or call 1–800–533–6478, 24 hours a day.

Gold Guides

U.S.

Alaska	Florida	New Orleans	Santa Fe, Taos, Albuquerque
Arizona	Hawaii	New York City	
Boston	Las Vegas, Reno, Tahoe	Pacific North Coast	Seattle & Vancouver
California		Philadelphia & the Pennsylvania Dutch Country	The South
Cape Cod, Martha's Vineyard, Nantucket	Los Angeles		U.S. & British Virgin Islands
	Maine, Vermont, New Hampshire	The Rockies	USA
The Carolinas & the Georgia Coast	Maui	San Diego	Virginia & Maryland
Chicago	Miami & the Keys	San Francisco	Waikiki
Colorado	New England		Washington, D.C.

Foreign

Australia & New Zealand	Egypt	London	Provence & the Riviera
Austria	Europe	Madrid & Barcelona	Scandinavia
The Bahamas	Florence, Tuscany & Umbria	Mexico	Scotland
Bermuda	France	Montréal & Québec City	Singapore
Budapest	Germany	Moscow, St. Petersburg, Kiev	South America
Canada	Great Britain		South Pacific
Cancún, Cozumel, Yucatán Peninsula	Greece	The Netherlands, Belgium & Luxembourg	Southeast Asia
Caribbean	Hong Kong		Spain
China	India	New Zealand	Sweden
Costa Rica, Belize, Guatemala	Ireland	Norway	Switzerland
	Israel	Nova Scotia, New Brunswick, Prince Edward Island	Thailand
Cuba	Italy		Tokyo
The Czech Republic & Slovakia	Japan	Paris	Toronto
	Kenya & Tanzania	Portugal	Turkey
Eastern Europe	Korea		Vienna & the Danube

Fodor's Special-Interest Guides

Branson	Fodor's London Companion	Kodak Guide to Shooting Great Travel Pictures	Walt Disney World for Adults
Caribbean Ports of Call	France by Train		Where Should We Take the Kids? California
The Complete Guide to America's National Parks	Halliday's New England Food Explorer	Shadow Traffic's New York Shortcuts and Traffic Tips	
		Sunday in New York	Where Should We Take the Kids? Northeast
Condé Nast Traveler Caribbean Resort and Cruise Ship Finder	Healthy Escapes	Sunday in San Francisco	
	Italy by Train		
Cruises and Ports of Call		Walt Disney World, Universal Studios and Orlando	

Special Series

Affordables
Caribbean
Europe
Florida
France
Germany
Great Britain
Italy
London
Paris

Fodor's Bed & Breakfasts and Country Inns
America's Best B&Bs
California's Best B&Bs
Canada's Great Country Inns
Cottages, B&Bs and Country Inns of England and Wales
The Mid-Atlantic's Best B&Bs
New England's Best B&Bs
The Pacific Northwest's Best B&Bs
The South's Best B&Bs
The Southwest's Best B&Bs
The Upper Great Lakes' Best B&Bs

The Berkeley Guides
California
Central America
Eastern Europe
Europe
France
Germany & Austria
Great Britain & Ireland
Italy
London
Mexico

Pacific Northwest & Alaska
Paris
San Francisco

Compass American Guides
Arizona
Canada
Chicago
Colorado
Hawaii
Hollywood
Las Vegas
Maine
Manhattan
Montana
New Mexico
New Orleans
Oregon
San Francisco
South Carolina
South Dakota
Texas
Utah
Virginia
Washington
Wine Country
Wisconsin
Wyoming

Fodor's Español
California
Caribe Occidental
Caribe Oriental
Gran Bretaña
Londres
Mexico
Nueva York
Paris

Fodor's Exploring Guides
Australia
Boston & New England

Britain
California
Caribbean
China
Florence & Tuscany
Florida
France
Germany
Ireland
Italy
London
Mexico
Moscow & St. Petersburg
New York City
Paris
Prague
Provence
Rome
San Francisco
Scotland
Singapore & Malaysia
Spain
Thailand
Turkey
Venice

Fodor's Flashmaps
Boston
New York
San Francisco
Washington, D.C.

Fodor's Pocket Guides
Acapulco
Atlanta
Barbados
Jamaica
London
New York City
Paris
Prague
Puerto Rico

Rome
San Francisco
Washington, D.C.

Rivages Guides
Bed and Breakfasts of Character and Charm in France
Hotels and Country Inns of Character and Charm in France
Hotels and Country Inns of Character and Charm in Italy

Short Escapes
Country Getaways in Britain
Country Getaways in France
Country Getaways Near New York City

Fodor's Sports
Golf Digest's Best Places to Play
Skiing USA
USA Today The Complete Four Sport Stadium Guide

Fodor's Vacation Planners
Great American Learning Vacations
Great American Sports & Adventure Vacations
Great American Vacations
National Parks and Seashores of the East
National Parks of the West

Before Catching Your Flight, Catch Up With Your World.

Fueled by the global resources of CNN and available in major airports across America, CNN Airport Network provides a live source  of current domestic and international news,  sports, business, weather and lifestyle pro- gramming. Plus two daily Fodor's features for the facts you need: "Travel Fact," a useful and creative mix of travel trivia; and "What's Happening," a comprehensive round-up  of upcoming events in major cities around the world.

With CNN Airport Network, you'll never be out of the loop.

HERE'S YOUR OWN PERSONAL VIEW OF THE WORLD.

Here's the easiest way to get up-to-the-minute, objective, personalized information about what's going on in the city you'll be visiting—before you leave on your trip! Unique information you could get only if you knew someone personally in each of 160 destinations around the world. Everything from special places to dine to local events only a local would know about.

It's all yours—in your Travel Update from Worldview, the leading provider of time-sensitive destination information.

Review the following order form and fill it out by indicating your destination(s)

and travel dates and by checking off up to eight interest categories. Then mail or fax your order form to us, or call your order in. (We're here to help you 24 hours a day.)

Within 48 hours of receiving your order, we'll mail your convenient, pocket-sized custom guide to you, packed with information to make your travel more fun and interesting. And if you're in a hurry, we can even fax it.

Have a great trip with your Fodor's Worldview Travel Update!

Customized to your interests and dates of travel

Time-sensitive

Insider perspective

DESTINATIONS

Worldview covers more than 160 destinations worldwide. Choose the destination(s) that match your itinerary from the list below:

Europe
Amsterdam
Athens
Barcelona
Berlin
Brussels
Budapest
Copenhagen
Dublin
Edinburgh
Florence
Frankfurt
French Riviera
Geneva
Glasgow
Lausanne
Lisbon
London
Madrid
Milan
Moscow
Munich
Oslo
Paris
Prague
Provence
Rome
Salzburg
Seville
St. Petersburg
Stockholm
Venice
Vienna
Zurich

**United States
(Mainland)**
Albuquerque
Atlanta
Atlantic City
Baltimore
Boston
Branson, MO
Charleston, SC
Chicago
Cincinnati
Cleveland
Dallas/Ft. Worth
Denver
Detroit
Houston
Indianapolis
Kansas City
Las Vegas
Los Angeles
Memphis
Miami
Milwaukee
Minneapolis/St. Paul
Nashville
New Orleans
New York City
Orlando
Palm Springs
Philadelphia
Phoenix
Pittsburgh

Portland
Reno/Lake Tahoe
St. Louis
Salt Lake City
San Antonio
San Diego
San Francisco
Santa Fe
Seattle
Tampa
Washington, DC

Alaska
Alaskan Destinations

Hawaii
Honolulu
Island of Hawaii
Kauai
Maui

Canada
Quebec City
Montreal
Ottawa
Toronto
Vancouver

Bahamas
Abaco
Eleuthera/
 Harbour Island
Exuma
Freeport
Nassau &
 Paradise Island

Bermuda
Bermuda Countryside
Hamilton

**British Leeward
Islands**
Anguilla
Antigua & Barbuda
St. Kitts & Nevis

British Virgin Islands
Tortola & Virgin
 Gorda

**British Windward
Islands**
Barbados
Dominica
Grenada
St. Lucia
St. Vincent
Trinidad & Tobago

Cayman Islands
The Caymans

Dominican Republic
Santo Domingo

Dutch Leeward Islands
Aruba
Bonaire
Curacao

**Dutch Windward
Island**
St. Maarten/St. Martin

French West Indies
Guadeloupe
Martinique
St. Barthelemy

Jamaica
Kingston
Montego Bay
Negril
Ocho Rios

Puerto Rico
Ponce
San Juan

Turks & Caicos
Grand Turk/
 Providenciales

U.S. Virgin Islands
St. Croix
St. John
St. Thomas

Mexico
Acapulco
Cancun & Isla Mujeres
Cozumel
Guadalajara
Ixtapa & Zihuatanejo
Los Cabos
Mazatlan
Mexico City
Monterrey
Oaxaca
Puerto Vallarta

South/Central America
Buenos Aires
Caracas
Rio de Janeiro
San Jose, Costa Rica
Sao Paulo

Middle East
Istanbul
Jerusalem

**Australia & New
Zealand**
Auckland
Melbourne
South Island
Sydney

China
Beijing
Guangzhou
Shanghai

Japan
Kyoto
Nagoya
Osaka
Tokyo
Yokohama

Pacific Rim/Other
Bali
Bangkok
Hong Kong & Macau
Manila
Seoul
Singapore
Taipei

INTERESTS

For your personalized Travel Update, choose the eight (8) categories you're most interested in from the following list:

1.	Business Services	Fax & Overnight Mail, Computer Rentals, Protocol, Secretarial, Messenger, Translation Services
	Dining	
2.	**All-Day Dining**	Breakfast & Brunch, Cafes & Tea Rooms, Late-Night Dining
3.	Local Cuisine	Every Price Range — from Budget Restaurants to the Special Splurge
4.	European Cuisine	Continental, French, Italian
5.	Asian Cuisine	Chinese, Far Eastern, Japanese, Other
6.	Americas Cuisine	American, Mexican & Latin
7.	Nightlife	Bars, Dance Clubs, Casinos, Comedy Clubs, Ethnic, Pubs & Beer Halls
8.	Entertainment	Theater – Comedy, Drama, Musicals, Dance, Ticket Agencies
9.	Music	Classical, Opera, Traditional & Ethnic, Jazz & Blues, Pop, Rock
10.	Children's Activites	Events, Attractions
11.	Tours	Local Tours, Day Trips, Overnight Excursions
12.	Exhibitions, Festivals & Shows	Antiques & Flower, History & Cultural, Art Exhibitions, Fairs & Craft Shows, Music & Art Festivals
13.	Shopping	Districts & Malls, Markets, Regional Specialties
14.	Fitness	Bicycling, Health Clubs, Hiking, Jogging
15.	Recreational Sports	Boating/Sailing, Fishing, Golf, Skiing, Snorkeling/Scuba, Tennis/Racket
16.	Spectator Sports	Auto Racing, Baseball, Basketball, Golf, Football, Horse Racing, Ice Hockey, Soccer
17.	Event Highlights	The best of what's happening during the dates of your trip.
18.	Sightseeing	Sights, Buildings, Monuments
19.	Museums	Art, Cultural
20.	Transportation	Taxis, Car Rentals, Airports, Public Transportation
21.	General Info	Overview, Holidays, Currency, Tourist Info

Please note that content will vary by season, destination, and length of stay.

Name

Address

City   State   Country   ZIP

Tel # (   )   -   Fax # (   )   -

Title of this Fodor's guide:

Store and location where guide was purchased:

INDICATE YOUR DESTINATIONS/DATES: You can order up to three (3) destinations from the previous page. Fill in your arrival and departure dates for each destination. **Your Travel Update itinerary (all destinations selected) cannot exceed 30 days from beginning to end.**

		Month	Day	Month	Day
(Sample) **LONDON**	From:	**6** /	**21**	To: **6** /	**30**
1	From:	/		To:	/
2	From:	/		To:	/
3	From:	/		To:	/

CHOOSE YOUR INTERESTS: Select up to eight (8) categories from the list of interest categories shown on the previous page and circle the numbers below:

1 2 3 4 5 6 7 8 9 10 11 12 13 14 15 16 17 18 19 20 21

CHOOSE WHEN YOU WANT YOUR TRAVEL UPDATE DELIVERED (Check one):
❑ Please send my Travel Update immediately.
❑ Please hold my order until a few weeks before my trip to include the most up-to-date information.
Completed orders will be sent within 48 hours. Allow 7–10 days for U.S. mail delivery.

ADD UP YOUR ORDER HERE. SPECIAL OFFER FOR FODOR'S PURCHASERS ONLY!

	Suggested Retail Price	Your Price	This Order
First destination ordered	$ 9.95	$ 7.95	$ 7.95
Second destination (if applicable)	$ 6.95	$ 4.95	+
Third destination (if applicable)	$ 6.95	$ 4.95	+

DELIVERY CHARGE (Check one and enter amount below)

	Within U.S. & Canada	Outside U.S. & Canada
First Class Mail	❑ $2.50	❑ $5.00
FAX	❑ $5.00	❑ $10.00
Priority Delivery	❑ $15.00	❑ $27.00

ENTER DELIVERY CHARGE FROM ABOVE: +

TOTAL: $

METHOD OF PAYMENT IN U.S. FUNDS ONLY (Check one):
❑ AmEx   ❑ MC   ❑ Visa   ❑ Discover   ❑ Personal Check (U. S. & Canada only)
❑ Money Order/International Money Order

Make check or money order payable to: Fodor's Worldview Travel Update

Credit Card __/__/__/__/__/__/__/__/__/__/__/__/__/__/__/__/ **Expiration Date:__/__**

Authorized Signature

SEND THIS COMPLETED FORM WITH PAYMENT TO:
Fodor's Worldview Travel Update, 114 Sansome Street, Suite 700,
San Francisco, CA 94104

OR CALL OR FAX US 24-HOURS A DAY
Telephone **1-800-799-9609** • Fax **1-800-799-9619** (From within the U.S. & Canada)
(Outside the U.S. & Canada: Telephone 415-616-9988 • Fax 415-616-9989)

(Please have this guide in front of you when you call so we can verify purchase.)
Code: FTG   Offer valid until 12/31/97